And The Music Lives On

Manek Premchand

notionpress.com

INDIA • SINGAPORE • MALAYSIA

Copyright © Manek Premchand 2024
All Rights Reserved.

ISBN
Hardcase 979-8-89588-690-8
Paperback 979-8-89588-290-0

This book has been published with all efforts taken to make the material error-free after the consent of the author. However, the author and the publisher do not assume and hereby disclaim any liability to any party for any loss, damage, or disruption caused by errors or omissions, whether such errors or omissions result from negligence, accident, or any other cause.

While every effort has been made to avoid any mistake or omission, this publication is being sold on the condition and understanding that neither the author nor the publishers or printers would be liable in any manner to any person by reason of any mistake or omission in this publication or for any action taken or omitted to be taken or advice rendered or accepted on the basis of this work. For any defect in printing or binding the publishers will be liable only to replace the defective copy by another copy of this work then available.

For my Friend, Guru, and Philosopher
Chandu Bardanwala

Contents

And The Music Lives On

This book is a compendium of articles that have to do with the Hindi film music of yesteryear. Besides the several fresh essays that you will find on these pages, *And The Music Lives On* has articles that have been published earlier in many journals. The platforms and dates of such appearances have been mentioned, and all those articles have been updated and enhanced. This book joins my earlier compilations, i.e., *Hitting the Right Notes*, *The Hindi Music Jukebox*, and *Windows to the Soul*, with *And The Music Lives On* being the last in the series of four. I hope you find some merit in them.

In the second half of 2023, I received an opportunity to edit a book on an actor called Shyam, who had passed away way back in 1951. That beautiful book, chronicling Shyam's exciting story and populated with arresting photos, was released in Delhi later, in February 2024. The actor was just 31 when during a shoot, he fell off a horse and was dragged a considerable distance because his foot was caught in the stirrup. They rushed the bleeding young man to Bombay Hospital twenty miles away, but he was dead on arrival. His death stunned the film community as well as his fans, who were in the millions. After all, the debonair actor was around just yesterday. He was young and healthy, riding horses, singing songs, romancing many heroines, and clearly in control of life. But he was gone today. Just like that. Whoosh!

His tragic death got me thinking about the many people from our films who too had died young. Sushant Singh Rajput is a recent case, but there was Divya Bharati, and much before her, there were others like Guru Dutt, Geeta Dutt, Meena Kumari, Madhubala, Madan Mohan, Sanjeev Kumar, and even before them, KL Saigal. Some of these had abused their bodies with an overdose of drugs or alcohol, but others hadn't done any such thing.

One recalls music and film celebrities from the West too. The actress Marilyn Monroe died when she was only 36, the "God of Guitar" Jimi Hendrix passed away when he was 27, the ex-Beatle John Lennon was just 40 when someone shot him dead, and Rock n Roll's greatest name, Elvis Priestly died when he was 42.

Among Indian singers, the gifted Mukesh was just 53 when he passed away. A few years after he left us, the legendary Mohammad Rafi went away when he was 56, which isn't old either. When Rafi died, his close associate, composer Naushad (who was also a good poet) wrote this quatrain:

Goonjte hain tere naghmon se ameeron ke mahal
Jhopdon mein bhi ghareebon ke teri awaaz hai
Apni mausiqi par sab ko fakhr hota hai magar
Aaj mausiqi ko tujh par naaz hai

(Your songs resonate in the palaces of the rich
But they are also enjoyed in the shanties of the poor
Everyone takes pride in their music
But today music itself is proud of you)

Naushad's imagery offered a role reversal here because he brought to life an inanimate idea—music—to offer an ode to a dead man.

It was such concerns about some of our music people leaving us early, combined with Naushad's quote that gave life to music, which triggered in me thoughts about the lifespan of our music itself. Technically speaking, Hindi film music was born in 1931, when films with sound arrived in India. *Alam Ara* was India's first "talking film" and it featured seven songs too, the first of them being *De de khuda ke naam pe, taaqat hai gar dene ki,* rendered directly on the screen by singing actor Wazeer Mohammad Khan. In the same technical way, music still comes out of our films, so it's still living, never mind that it has no resemblance to its ancestors.

So technically film music is living, fine. But is the current music alive?

We must explore this idea because millions of people feel that today's music has very little to praise it for. This is a famous couplet:

Zindagi zinda dili ka naam hai
Murda dil kya khaak jeeya karte hain?

(Roughly: Life is about people who are not just living, but alive.
Just living is a humdrum existence)

So let us move away from the technical picture and find the real one, meaning the years our film music had its high *zinda dili*. This can take time and effort, but it's not difficult. For this, we can try to reflect and go back in time to pick the first specific year whose songs we love *in good numbers*. The years before that will not have too many good tracks for us. Once we find that year, it becomes, for us, the point our music starts shining its gold. After that, we can advance in time and decide the last year that, for us, had *a great number* of enjoyable songs. In other words, after that year, we see a drop in *the quantity of good songs*. That is a good way to arrive at the year our music stopped entertaining us so relentlessly.

Consider for a moment an example from physiology. We all have some blood pressure, which is the force of our blood pushing against the walls of our arteries. But for ascertaining our exact BP parameters, a doctor takes two readings, an upper and a lower one. That gives him an accurate picture. Our two readings in music can similarly give us an accurate picture of the beautiful run of our music. Sandwiched somewhere between these two readings lies the glorious youth of our music.

That glorious youth—the golden era—was characterised by great composers who gave us thousands of fascinating and inventive tunes. It was a time when singers had original voices and sang beautifully with all the challenges they faced in the technology of their time. Most of all, this was an age when there were gifted lyric writers who wrote incredible poetry that was not just relevant to specific situations in films, but whose emotions continue to resonate in our hearts even today, bringing out our *wah wah* and *kya baat hai* so often.

That's fine, but wait, there is some debate among music buffs about when the golden era began and when it ended. More importantly, what are the reasons the golden age started and ended? That becomes a question difficult to answer.

Art is subjective

Give people a question: "According to you, which 20-year period had the best Hindi film music?" Most Indians born in the 1970s do not value the 1940s or 1950s as a great film-music age. They name the 1960s and the 1970s as the best. But people born in the 1950s generally mention the '50s and '60s as the very best, and so on. Fair enough, to each his own. But when you stretch the 20 years to 30, you get greater consensus, with most people saying it was the mid-1940s to the mid-1970s period. That's the result some of us friends have found in repeated informal meets.

Coming specifically to me, my real music started in 1943 (meaning it was the first year with a high number of enjoyable songs), and it ended in 1973 (the last year with many beautiful songs). Perhaps I can offer some thoughts on why these years.

I believe that till 1942, while we had *some* good music, the tidal wave of melody hadn't started. There was no Rafi, Lata, Talat, Hemant, Asha, Manna, Geeta, or Kishore. In the early years, there was no playback singing; one had to be both an actor and singer and very few people handled both jobs excellently, so one of the two areas was compromised. There were no likes of Naushad, SD Burman, and Nayyar, nor had our music opened up to Western instruments in a significant way. That happened after many Parsi and Christian musicians joined our films when their British employers were leaving the country during Independence. There was no Sahir, Majrooh, or Shailendra yet. Such people began coming when films started offering gainful opportunities to them, i.e., in the late '40s. The film medium was still new, and the recording techniques were still basic. Plus the singing sensation Noor Jahan had just arrived in Bombay. Moreover, there were no great directors of the kind that would come later, such as Mehboob Khan, Bimal Roy, Guru Dutt, Raj Kapoor, AR Kardar, and BR Chopra. But 1943 brought with it the first critical mass of great songs. Consider just a few:

- *Prabhuji, Prabhuji tum raakho laaj hamaari* (Kanan Devi/ *Hospital*)
- *Door hato aye duniya waalo Hindustan hamaara hai* (Amirbai, chorus/ *Kismet*)
- *Aaye bhi wo gaye bhi wo* (Parul Ghosh/ *Namaste*)
- *Beena madhur madhur kachhu bol* (Saraswati Rane/ *Ram Rajya*)
- *Jeevan ki nao na dole* (Jaishree/ *Shakuntala*)
- *More baalapan ke saathi chhaila bhool jaiyo na* (Saigal, Khursheed/ *Tansen*)
- *O jaane waale aaja tadpaane waale aaja* (Shamshad, Motilal/ *Taqdeer*)

More baalapan ke saathi chhaila

This is not to say that the music before 1943 was not nice. Nothing could be further from the truth. There were gifted singers like Saigal and KC Dey, competent composers like Ghulam Haider and Gyan

Dutt, and great lyricists such as DN Madhok and PL Santoshi. Their cinema did give us wonderful songs, but not in a relentless, tidal wave kind of way. This is also not to suggest that 1943 was a fantastic year for music. It's just that, for some of us, it was a *great start year*, with many beautiful songs. The coming years would attract great musicians of all hues, and we would get knee-deep into the golden era.

But, as the saying goes, all good things come to an end. For people like me, the curtain came down in 1973. Think of these songs from that year:

> *Hasne ki chaah ne itna mujhe rulaaya hai* (Manna/ *Aavishkaar*)
> *Piya bina* (Lata/ *Abhimaan*)
> *Beshak mandir masjid todo* (Narendra Chanchal/ *Bobby*)
> *Mere dil mein aaj kya hai* (Kishore/ *Daag*)
> *Tum jo mil gaye ho* (Rafi/ *Hanste Zakhm*)
> *Diye jalte hain* (Kishore/ *Namak Haram*)
> *Sandhya jo aayi* (Lata/ *Phagun*)
> *Chain se humko kabhi* (Asha/ *Pran Jaye Par Vachan Na Jaye*)

There were many more wonderful songs coming out of our films in 1973, but we have just listed a few. Also, many enjoyable songs showed up after that year, and they continue to show up even today. Think of these films with good music: *Kora Kaagaz, Prem Nagar,* and *Roti Kapda Aur Makaan* (all 1974), *Aandhi, Amanush,* and *Ek Mahal Ho Sapnon Ka* (all 1975), and so on, through the following decades. We have a bit of beautiful music even today. As I see it, though, while great music mothered some good songs, a few rogue children were born too. These last have multiplied faster over the decades.

But sandwiched between those 30 remarkable years were thousands of unforgettable songs in hundreds of Hindi films. Our composers used concepts like Scherzando and Doo-wop, which many current musicians may not have any idea about. Such concepts are identified and explained in these pages, with many examples. You will find songs sung on bullock carts, a decent chapter on qawwalis, and how the actor Balraj Sahni would shoot during the day and spend his nights in prison.

During this era, everyone wanted to leave their footprint of excellence. This book attempts to record some of that excellence.

Somewhere in the '70s, that excellence evaporated. Hence, millions of us enthusiasts became heavily disappointed. Since then, we have found it difficult to identify with most of what has been coming out of our recording studios. To us, the music being made these days is an imposter. I want to lyricize my thoughts with a famous Urdu couplet:

Pehle badi raghbat thi tere naam se mujhko
Ab sun ke tera naam main kuchh soch raha hoon

(Earlier, I would be excited to hear your name,
Nowadays your name makes me wonder)

But thank God we have the wonderful music of our glorious past to entertain and educate us. Such music is a moral compass when we want one, a beacon when we need hope, and an entertainer when we are celebrating. Thank God there were hundreds of music artists who wanted to give us joy forever and leave a footprint of excellence for future generations. They created songs that were not just lip-synched by huge stars like the ones on this book's cover, but also by smaller names. In fact, *And The Music Lives On* also has a chapter on people who made just one entry in a specific area, like acting, singing, or filmmaking, and then withdrew at once. For instance, prolific songwriter Anand Bakshi dressed up as a faqir and faced the camera just once. The film was *Picnic* (1966), and the song was *Bijli giri kahaan se* (Rafi). Biswajit was known for his acting and singing in Bengali films, but he also sang a Hindi song, *Aye dil meri jaan teri manzil hai kahaan* in *Do Shikari* (1979). Southern belle KR Vijaya couldn't manage her Hindustani well, so all she got by way of a role in Hindi films was in *Oonche Log* (1965). She performed to *Aa ja re mere pyaar ke raahi* (Lata, Mahendra) with Feroz Khan acting opposite her.

Recently, my music-loving friend, Yogesh Kamdar, a Director at Bharatiya Vidya Bhavan, asked me an interesting question: "Can you, in the next 24 hours, recall 30 songs created in the past 30 years?"

I couldn't. Nor could two of my friends, born in the mid-1970s. I announced my inability to Yogesh the next day. To which he observed: "From the Golden Era, you can probably name 30 songs made *each year*". So absolutely true!

That era can be found in this book, along with the time before and since. There's a pirate's ransom of wealth in these pages. Let's go discover it!

Manek Premchand

Email: manekpremchand@gmail.com

25th October 2024

♪♫♩♪

2

Welcomed with Arrows

In the Bay of Bengal, two and a quarter hours flying time from Kolkata or Chennai, and about 1300 kilometres away from them lies Port Blair, the capital of Andaman and Nicobar Islands, which are a part of India. These islands were recently in the news for two reasons. One was about Prime Minister Narendra Modi's visit there, on 30th December 2018. He renamed three islands, i.e., Ross Island, Neil Island and Havelock Island to Subhash Chandra Bose Dweep, Shaheed Dweep, and Swaraj Dweep respectively. But by far the bigger news from the region was of the death of a young American missionary named John Chau in a place called North Sentinel Island, a place considered too dangerous to approach.

The North Sentinel Island is part of the Andaman Islands and is the habitat of the Sentinelese aborigine people, who remain a bunch of uncontacted and uncontactable people, even in today's interconnected world. For thousands of years, these tribes have been living there with a pathological resentment of civilization, and so they want to be left alone, thank you. No one has any idea what language they speak. Anthropologists know that these tribes have been in utter isolation forever, and since even other islanders have failed to get close enough to hear them, the Sentinelese people's language may not have any contemporary relatives. We do know just a bit about their other lifestyle from the observations of a handful of people who have made quick and stealthy entries and exits over the decades.

These xenophobic people live in hutments, make and use bows and arrows, and thrive on fish and berries. They know how to light and douse fires for cooking. Since 1956, the Indian government has declared the island an exclusion zone, because the outside world is dangerous to these people, and the natives in turn are dangerous to any outsider who wants entry. As such, India's Protection of Aboriginal Tribes regulation makes it unlawful to attempt contact or come within 5 kilometres of the island's coastline. It is extremely hard to access this place anyway, not just because of the coral reefs that form a natural defence of the island, but also because of the antagonistic belief systems of its natives. To sustain this belief system, they invest a lot of time and resources in making bows and arrows. An economist would perhaps note that the islanders spend the highest amount of their GDP on defence! But since they have never been immunized against many diseases that exist in the civilized world, the Sentinelese are highly vulnerable to them. Even flu or chicken pox could manage to wipe off their entire, tiny population in weeks. Although no one knows how many of them are there on that island, estimates vary between 150 and 350 people.

If you try to get into their territory, they'll immediately welcome you with arrows. You'll be lucky if you can dodge these missiles. Many intrepid adventurers did manage to escape them in the 1970s, 1980s, and later. But the American John Chau persisted. He went near the island on 15th November, got hurt, withdrew, refreshed his resolve, and neared the colony again the next day. He was to learn a fatal lesson on 16th November 2018, when tribal archers eliminated him with arrows.

To avenge the death of its citizen, the Americans could have responded of course. They could have bombed the place in a matter of hours. But it's not a good time to be an American, in geopolitical popularity. Besides, such a response would be seen as an attack on Indian soil, and so an act of war with us. Most importantly, in terms of the law, the natives didn't go after John Chau without a reason; he was trespassing on their private space, which was an illegal act. It also gets a bit sticky for America's image that the man was a missionary, going in there to spread the message of the Bible and convert the people to Christianity.

Saluting the Sentinelese

Arrows and bows are called *teer* and *kamaan* respectively in Hindustani. They are also called *baan* and *dhanushya*. Our poets have used *teer* and *baan* as metaphors in poetry, both to ignite love—in the Cupid way— as well as to injure it. Check out these songs from our films, that refer to such ammunition:

- *Nainon ke baan ki reet anokhi* (Shamshad, Ghulam Haider/ *Khazanchi*, 1941)
- *Saajan ke naina jaadu baan* (Amirbai, Mumtaz/ *Najma*, 1943)
- *Nainon ke teer chala gayi ek sheher ki laundiya* (Sunder/ *Shukriya*, 1944)
- *Wo teer kaleje par ik shokh ne maara hai* (Mukesh/ *Anjuman*, 1948)
- *Chubh gaye nainan baan* (Geeta/ *Hip Hip Hurray*, 1948)
- *Ek teer chalaane waale ne* (Mukesh, Sitara Kanpuri/ *Pugree*, 1948)
- *Ek teer chala…haaye mera dil* (Rajkumari/ *Mahal*, 1949)
- *Dil par kisi ka teer-e-nazar kha ke reh gaye* (Talat/ *Raakhi*, 1949)
- *Teer pe teer khaaye ja zulm-o-sitam utthaaye ja* (Rafi/ *Roop Lekha*, 1949)
- *Chhup chhup ke teer chalaaye na koi* (Mukesh, Rajkumari/ *Thes*, 1949)
- *Has ke na teer chala* (Lata, Rafi/ *Beqasoor*, 1950)
- *Maaro na nainwa ke baan* (Shamshad/ *Nirdosh*, 1950)
- *O chale hain teer nazar ke idhar se bhi udhar se bhi* (Asha/ *Daman*, 1951)
- *Teer khaate jaayenge* (Lata/ *Deewana*, 1952)
- *Teer chala teer chala teer chala* (Talat/ *Naghma*, 1953)
- *Ek teer chala ke gori bijli gira ke mohe chhod ke akeli kahaan jaaye re* (Chitragupt, Shamshad/ *Nav Durga*, 1953)
- *Na maaro najariya ke baan* (Lata/ *Pehli Jhalak*, 1954)
- *Dil hai nishaana naino ke teer ka* (Asha/ *Char Paise*, 1955)
- *Tere teer-e-nazar ka balam dil nishaana hua* (Asha, Rafi/ *Bhagam Bhaag*, 1956)

- *Kaise kaise teer chalaaye* (Asha/ *Mr. Lambu*, 1956)
- *Jab teri nazar ke teer chale kuchh idhar gaye kuchh udhar gaye* (Rafi, Shamshad/ *Noor-e-Yaman*, 1956)
- *Teekhe hain nainwa ke baan* (Asha, SD Batish/ *Dushman*, 1957)
- *Nainon ke baan chale* (Sudha/ *Chalta Purza*, 1958)
- *Teer ye chhupke chalaaya kisne* (Asha/ *Phagun*, 1958)
- *Nazron ke teer maare kus kus kus* (Rafi, Asha/ *Do Ustad*, 1959)

Nazron ke teer maare kus kus kus

- *Tere teer ko humne pyaar se dil mein rakh liya* (Lata/ *Qaidi No 911*, 1959)
- *Tera teer o be-peer dil ke aaraam paar hai* (Lata/ *Shararat*, 1959)
- *Humen maaro na nainon ke baan* (Asha/ *Kalpana*, 1960)
- *Chalenge teer jab dil par to armaanon ka kya hoga* (Rafi, Lata/ *Kohinoor*, 1960)
- *Wo teer dil pe chala jo teri kamaan mein hai* (Rafi, Asha/ *Aarti*, 1962)
- *Kya kehne mashallah nazar-e-teer aap ki* (Rafi, Suman/ *Jee Chahta Hai*, 1964)
- *Main tum pe teer chala doon to kya karoge* (Asha/ *Veer Bhimsen*, 1964)
- *In aankhon se nazar ka teer* (Asha/ *Neela Akash*, 1965)
- *Teer aankhon ke jigar ke paar kar do yaar tum* (Mukesh/ *Gunahon Ka Devta*, 1967)

Judging from the merit in the above songs, it is clear that they share a central quality with arrows: reusability. Many arrows and such songs can be recalled for repeated 'use'. Seen in that light, firearms are not so much fun, which also may be why lyrics featuring them are few and far between. For instance, take the songs *Sandook mein bandook hai, bandook mein goli* (Shamshad/ *Hoor-e-Arab*, 1955) and *Goli maar bheje mein* (Mano/ *Satya*, 1998). To many of us, such songs are like spent bullets, i.e., finished after one use.

As for the 26-year-old John Chau, his excursion into North Sentinel Island has sparked a hot debate. Were the Sentinelese justified in killing a harmless intruder? Or did John Chau have no business to go in? Observes the dead man's friend, Daniel Wesley in The Christian Post:

"Was John merely a rogue 'adventurer' harboring an unspoken death wish who foolishly went to a remote Island in the Indian Ocean to kick a soccer ball around with the most isolated tribe on the planet or is it possible he was someone much more?"

Adds he: "His desire was to become one of them, hunting alongside the North Sentinelese, sleeping in their huts, eating the same diet and learning their language. His intention was never to simply drop in and preach to them in English as some have erroneously suggested. In fact, one learns from his updates, his journal entries, and from conversations with his friends that John was fully committed to living there for the rest of his life, something that tragically came to pass far earlier than he hoped".

Wonder what you think.

~~~~

The above was originally featured in DNA Jaipur on 12 January 2019. It has since been updated and enhanced.

~~~~

3

Musically Vending

Vendors on the street
Entertaining us
Selling merchandise
With their song precious
Hoping what we buy
Will make us come for more
But
Are they really vending
Their stuff compelling
Or is it an act—
Musical yelling—
To distract us so
We spend our cash galore!

(Sung to the tune of *Strangers in the Night* by Frank Sinatra)

Busking

Entertaining to expect money on the street, also called busking, is the act of doing a show in a public place, without a formal platform. Whatever people enjoy watching or hearing is brought to the public place: singing, playing instruments, juggling, ventriloquism, comedy, making animals ride bicycles, snake-and-mongoose fights, cock fights, drawing pictures on a pavement, skills with fire, street theatre, miming, becoming a living statue, riding a cycle for days on end, and so on. Busking also includes singing door-to-door carols during Christmas, or folk music during the Lohri festival, the latter an annual occurrence that many residents of Punjab and Delhi are acquainted with.

Vending versus busking

If your act insists on payment, you are not busking. You are vending. Consider these examples. Recall Waheeda Rehman's tightrope walk to the accompaniment of the song *"Jo hain deewaane pyaar ke, sada chalen talwaar pe"* from *Baat Ek Raat Ki* (1962). That's entertaining the crowds with a balancing act, in the hope of raising funds, so it is an example of busking. So is *"Jhumka gira re, Bareilly ke baazaar mein"* from *Mera Saaya* (1966), in which gypsy-girl Sadhana and her musicians busk inside a circle of men enjoying the oomph in her song and dance. In neither of the two instances are the ladies selling anything. But consider Mumtaz who is entertaining us on a Bharat-darshan tour in *"Dekho dekho dekho, biscope dekho"* in *Dushman* (1971). She is vending, not busking, because she also says, *"Paisa phenko, tamaasha dekho"*. She is entertaining us with a trailer; for the real bioscope show, you have to pay her. Again, when the same Mumtaz sells coconut water for a rupee in *"Le ro le lo baabu pee lo nariyal paani"* in *Apna Desh* (1972), she is musically vending. Buskers hope for financial rewards, but vendors insist on payment.

All street performers are not buskers or vendors

Busking is a huge thing abroad, and vending too. But while the definition of vending has no grey areas (straightforward goods or services against money), busking has grey areas. For some reason, when beggars sing or play music, it is not called busking, maybe because they always seek our sympathy for tips. Most of them are just mediocre singers, to begin with, so singing is just a bit of an attention-getter. Perhaps they are musically begging. Also, singing in a public place without any financial expectation or insistence can be called musically entertaining. Examples: you sing out loud in public when you are happy or have just been dumped, or do a *"Govinda aala re"* act on Janmashtmi, or inch forward in a loud music procession during Ganesh Chaturthi. In fact, many cities abroad have quite clear ideas of what *does not* constitute busking. The City of Melbourne for instance treats the following as non-busking activities: Vending—selling of goods or services—of any kind, political rallying, touting for business, religious spruiking, palmistry, tarot card reading, and a few more, like a traffic policeman giving signals comically, something that happens in our cities too, like Bangalore.

Different cities around the world have their own ideas about street performances, but most remain in concord that vending is not an act of busking. In India, we do not generally take street performances seriously, but we have for long had street vendors musically offering their goods and services. The man who comes to our neighbourhood to sharpen our scissors and knives is a vendor, and he may have a musical note in his loud cry. The fish-seller vending Pomfret ("Paaplet!") and the mango vendor selling choice Alphonsos ("Haapus!") can be quasi-musical in their call too. The dense Indian ice cream called kulfi is sometimes sold with a euphonious call that goes Kulfeee! The *raddi-waala kabaadi* announces his presence with a musical call so he can buy our used valuables or newspapers, the *kalai waala* wants to re-line our utensils, and many of us may have seen the man who comes around to refluff the cotton in our quilts, pillows and mattresses, with his harp-like gadget plucked to make a musical twang as he beats out the lumpy cotton. In several parts of India, the mobile idli vendor carries a standard cycle bell horn with a rubber bulb to send us a note pitched high. All these tell us that we have had a long and diverse history of vending goods and services musically.

Selling on the street is in fact universal and goes back centuries, with people traditionally offering us elixirs for youth and magic potions for getting healthier or younger. But plain selling isn't so much fun as selling in a musical way. Think of these film songs, all of which had someone vending goods or services musically. The products are mentioned before the singers and films:

- *Koi le lo le lo…main meettha doodh laayi* (Milk/ Rajkumari/ *Brandy Ki Bottle*, 1939)
- *Chane jor garam baabu main laaya mazedaar* (Spiced black grams/ Arun Kumar/ *Bandhan*, 1940)
- *Koi le lo bhaiya, taaweez hai mera bade kaam ka* (The locket called *taaweez*/ KC Dey/ *Meenakshi*, 1942)
- *Boot karoon main paalish babu* (Shoeshine/ Suraiya/ *Nayi Duniya*, 1942)
- *Tera khilona toota* (Toys/ Rafi/ *Anmol Ghadi*, 1946)
- *Mere phoolon mein chhipi hai jawaani* (Flowers/ Lata/ *Anokha Pyaar*, 1948)
- *Boot paalish karwa le baabu* (Shoeshine/ Meena Kapoor/ *Ghar Ki Izzat*, 1948)
- *Theher zara o jaane waale* (Shoeshine/ Manna Dey, Asha Bhosle, Madhubala Jhaveri/ *Boot Polish*, 1953)
- *Naarangi le lo ji* (Oranges/ Unknown singer/ *Bahut Din Hue*, 1954)
- *Yaad rakhna pyaar ki nishaani gori yaad rakhna* (Bangles/ Hemant, Lata/ *Nagin*, 1954)
- *Aao hamaare hotal mein chai piyo ji garam garam* (Tea and biscuits/ SD Batish, Sudha/ *Kundan*, 1955)
- *Mera naam Abdul Rehman, pista waala main hoon pathaan* (Pistachios and almonds/ Lata, Kishore/ *Bhai Bhai*, 1956)
- *Tarkaari le lo maalan to aayi maalo desh ki* (Vegetables/ Asha/ *Dhola Maru*, 1956)
- *Phoolon ke haar le lo* (Stringed flowers/ Hemant/ *Inspector*, 1956)
- *Lo har cheez le lo* (Shoe polishes, combs, lipsticks, toys, stringed flowers and hairpieces/ Sudha, Asha, Geeta/ *Ab Dilli Door Nahin*, 1957)
- *Saiyaan jhoothon ka bada sartaaj nikla* (Toys/ Lata/ *Do Aankhen Baarah Haath*, 1957)
- *Albela main ik dil waala* (Balloons, dusting cars/ Asha/ *Miss India*, 1957)

- *Sar jo tera chakraaye ya dil dooba jaaye* (Head massages/ Rafi/ *Pyaasa*, 1957)
- *Surma mera niraala aankhon mein jisne daala* (Kohl/ Kishore/ *Kabhi Andhera Kabhi Ujala*, 1958)
- *Main riksha waala* (Hand-pulled rickshaw rides/ Rafi/ *Chhoti Behen*, 1959)
- *Dilbar pe ho na qaabu* (Instant photographs/ Rafi/ *Pehli Raat*, 1959)
- *Laila ki ungliyaan bechoon* (Cucumbers/ Rafi/ *Ghar Ki Laaj*, 1960)
- *Baabu insurance kara lo* (Insurance/ Rafi/ *Kaala Aadmi*, 1960)
- *Ek aana boot polish do aana tel maalish* (Shoeshine and head massages/ Mukesh/ *Tel Malish Boot Polish*, 1961)
- *Aaj ki taaza khabar* (Newspapers/ Shanti Mathur/ *Son Of India*, 1962)
- *Ber le o ber le o* (Berries/ Asha/ *Paisa Ya Pyaar*, 1969)
- *Aaya re khilone waala* (Toys and masks/ Rafi/ *Bachpan*, 1970)
- *Ari muniya re muniya tu bata main kaun hoon* (Toys and masks/ Kishore/ *Bachpan*, 1970)
- *Le lo choodiyaan* (Bangles/ Kishore, Lata/ *Saas Bhi Kabhi Bahu Thi*, 1970)
- *Aahen na bhar thandi-thandi…garam-garam chai pee le* (Tea/ Lata/ *Banphool*, 1972)
- *Le lo champa chameli gulaab le lo* (Flowers/ Asha/ *Sone Ke Haath*, 1973)
- *Chakku chhuriyaan tez kara lo* (Knives and scissors honing/ Asha/ *Zanjeer*, 1973)
- *Aaya re aaya khilone waala aaya* (Balloons and masks/ Rafi/ *Sone Ka Dil Lohe Ke Haath*, 1978)
- *Logon ka dil agar haan jeetna tumko hai to* (Teeth-cleaning twig called *datoon*/ Rafi, Tina Munim/ *Manpasand*, 1980)

Logon ka dil agar haan

The following songs were also the musically vending kind, but in a faux way, because they happened only on a stage in the film:

- *Choodi main laaya anmol re* (Bangles/ Mumtaz Ali, Sunita Devi/ *Achhut Kanya*, 1936)
- *Pune se laayi paan re* (Paan/ Sitara Devi, Nazir Ahmed/ *Aabroo*, 1943)
- *Laayi re lo gajre le lo* (Strung flowers/ Manju, Durrani/ *Nayi Kahani*, 1943)
- *Le lo le lo malaniya se haar* (Garlands/ Rajkumari/ *Panna*, 1944)
- *Le lo le lo do phooldaani le lo* (Flower bouquets/ Shamshad, Zohra, Rafi/ *Jaadu*, 1951)
- *Chana jor garam baabu main laaya mazedaar* (Spiced black grams/ Kishore, Shamshad/ *Naya Andaz*, 1956)

The last song above, *Chana jor garam* had an ancestor, the grammatically-correct *Chane jor garam* (*Bandhan*, 1940), which we found in the earlier list. We discovered one more from the family, *Chana jor garam*, rendered by Lata, Rafi, Kishore, and Nitin Mukesh in *Kranti* (1981).

In a case of oversell, in one song, *Babu aana, sunte jaana* (Kishore, Asha/ *Jhumroo*, 1961) Kishore Kumar and Chanchal were selling so many things in a village fair. She was musically vending Kohl, a dagger, and a "German masala" to fix your broken utensils. He couldn't be outsmarted, so he went about offering eyewear, a whip, and a "jungle ki booti" to fix your health issues. They competed so creatively.

The Indian economy has crossed the cusp of a crucial phase with the new General Sales Tax coming into force. According to Government of India figures, there are about 10 million street vendors in India, many of them children. They are in what is called the Informal Sector. Let's hope they will not be affected because come on folks, these guys really entertain us. Plus they are the poorer lot. Let them fly under the radar.

~ ~ ~

The above was originally published in DNA Jaipur on 2 July 2017. It has since been updated and enhanced.

Maan Gaye, Munshiji!

*Peepra ke patawa sareekhe dole manwa, ke jiyara mein utthata hilor,
Purawa ke jhonkawa se aayo re sandesawa ke chal aaj desawa ki ore* (Rafi/
Anjaan/ Pt. Ravi Shankar)

Last month, on 24 December (Mohammad Rafi's birthday), as I was on my way to suburban Mumbai to witness the renaming of a street after the singer, the radio was airing many Rafi songs, including the above-mentioned happy Bhojpuri one from *Godaan* (1963), a story about the gift of a cow written by Munshi Premchand.

The mind started thinking of the special connection between Munshi Premchand and Mohammad Rafi. That the singer had sung songs in films based on Premchand's stories was known to many of us, but they also had a cosmic connection. The singer passed away on 31st July 1980, exactly 100 hundred years to the day when the prolific writer was born, ie, 31st July 1880. While listening to the Bhojpuri song on the air, the mind also wandered to the sad state of Bhojpuri cinema today. For, it was in 1962 that the first Bhojpuri film, *Ganga Maiya Tohe Piyari Chadhaibo* was screened in cinema halls. After that came *Bidesia* (1963), *Laagi Naahin Chhoote Raam* (1963), and *Kab Hoihen Gavanwa Hamaar* (1964), followed by many good films. It had started so meaningfully, so what had gone so wrong today? Why weren't good Bhojpuri or Poorbi films being made now, and also why were we not hearing good songs in these languages?

Instinctively I called my friend Sadhana Singh, who played the lead in many films like *Nadiya Ke Paar* (1982), with its UP touches. In fact, it was her father-in-law Bishwanath Prasad Shahbadi who had produced *Ganga Maiya Tohe Piyari Chadhaibo*, mentioned above. Moreover, she had acted in the lead role (as AK Hangal's daughter-in-law) in the Indian People Theatre Association's *Hori*, based on Munshi Premchand's *Godaan*. Later on, she also went on to act in the Bhojpuri film *Ganga Jaisan Paawan Piritiya Hamaar* (2004).

Munshi Premchand

Sadhana Singh too felt that Bhojpuri cinema had nosed down so badly, it was utterly rudderless now. We will examine more of Bhojpuri cinema and its amazing music in a separate story, but right now let's engage with the other thought I was thinking while listening to the radio on that pleasant afternoon last December.

That would be the understated story of Munshi Premchand, whose real name was Dhanpat Rai Srivastav (he took the pseudonym Nawab Rai later, and Munshi Premchand even later). Here was a person who suffered so much as a boy and young man, and yet, this is what he said: "My life is a level plain. There are pits here and there, but no cliffs, mountains, jungles, deep ravines, or ruins. Gentlemen who have a taste for mountaineering will be disappointed here".

No ravines? That cannot be true. He suffered so much privation. When he was 8, he lost his mother. His father remarried, but the lady was quite an unkind woman who arrived with two unfriendly children. Young Dhanpat became lonely and in much turmoil. To put an emotional Band-Aid on Dhanpat, his father had him married off when he was just 15. But he himself passed away a year later. Meantime the young couple was entirely ill-matched. So that now, after his father died, the 16-year-old lad had to take care of his unfriendly wife, difficult stepmother, and the latter's two intractable children. The lad got a job selling books at a wholesaler's but here he also took to reading all manner of books. Then he began writing. He read and wrote to stay sane in a world beset by hunger and impoverishment. Many have wondered how the young lad faced all these obstacles and went on to become one of the greatest short story writers of this country. You wonder too about this boy who had no idea of Hindi till he was 13—he could read only Urdu and Persian till then since his early schooling was in a madrasa in Varanasi. Hindi happened later.

On the work front, Premchand attempted many other things but kept failing much of the time. He had a government job as a school teacher for several years, but apart from that, consider: he opened a Khadi centre and flopped, he tried getting an editor's assignment in Gorakhpur but failed. He did become an editor of a journal in Banaras but didn't click. Then he taught briefly in two more schools, without much success. He forayed into a printing press business but that didn't work. After that, he started publishing a magazine called Hans, from Banaras. His is a story of many professional obstacles, as well as much emotional pain. Lots of valleys. And yet he left us with so much value.

For, consider. Premchand went on to write some 250 short stories in Urdu and Hindi and translated many foreign stories for Indian readers. In time he came to be called "Upanyas Samrat" meaning Emperor of the Novel. The few films that were inspired by his stories include *Mazdoor* (1945), *Heera Moti* (1959), *Godaan* (1963), *Gaban* (1966), *Shatranj Ke Khiladi* (1977), and *Sadgati* (1981). But his romance with cinema was not a happy one. This is what he wrote: "The people who control the destiny of films unfortunately think of it as an industry. What has industry got to do with taste or reforming it? Industry only knows how to exploit and here it is exploiting the most sacred sentiments of man".

Literary outpourings of a lasting kind have also been left behind by dozens of other Indians like the poet Hasrat Jaipuri. In my meetings with the latter, there was one thing he was so sure about: that to be effective as a poet, you need, in your formative years, to have experienced pain of some kind. His own emotional pain was in being spurned by a girl named Radha. This is not the philosophy of many other writers, especially of the contemporary kind. But failure, rejection, isolation and financial deprivation are often known to be strong triggers that propel people to go on a lifelong mission of sorts. Perhaps such people find it hard to forget their downbeat days, the memories helping them breeze purposefully through life's vicissitudes.

Some of the examples of such great writers who experienced pain are William Shakespeare, Albert Camus, Dale Carnegie, and our own Mirza Ghalib and Sahir Ludhianvi. Munshi Premchand also belongs to the list of people who suffered privations, only to leave us with a rich treasure of his writings.

But back to 24 December 2016. I am sure no radio station's day-long tribute to Rafi would have been complete without a certain Hasrat Jaipuri song. As mentioned earlier, Radha was the young girl Hasrat Saab was besotted with in his salad days. Years later, he wrote a song in *Sangam* (1964): *Ye mera prempatra padh kar, ke tum naaraaz na hona.* This was Rajendra Kumar singing to Vyjayanthimala, whose name in the movie was Radha. "A penny for your thoughts while writing this, Sir", I would have asked the lyricist were he alive now.

~ ~ ~ ~

The above was published under the heading No Pain, No Gain in DNA Jaipur on 29 January 2017. It has since been updated and enhanced.

5

Messenger of Love and Peace

The day before yesterday, 7th September, was the 40th death anniversary of a remarkable lyricist and filmmaker named PL Santoshi. Not many under the age of 40 have heard his name, and that's understandable since life is so fast and there's so much information to process these days. PL Santoshi does belong to the past, and who remembers death anniversaries nowadays, at least in public? When we are with others, it is time only for the display of happiness. But we could use this man's work in today's fragile atmosphere of distrust and divisiveness. His corpus was remarkable and has stood the test of time. Consequently, I request your indulgence.

Pyarelal Shrivastava (his real name) was born on 16th August 1916 and in his salad days, showed a lot of interest in reading. One of his favorite reads was Rudyard Kipling's Jungle Book, stories of animals that lived in a forest in Seoni, not too far from Jabalpur where Pyarelal was born. After some years, the young lad started writing, short poems mainly. One day, a film was being shot in his town and they were looking for a dialogue writer's assistant. He applied, got the job and was later appreciated for his work. Soon, he became known for his feelings of human inclusivity and respect for life, even from the animal kingdom. It is in the fitness of things then, that in the mid-'40s, when India was sizzling with a clamour for independence, Prabhat Films Poona decided to make a theme on national unity and invite the charged-up man to write its songs. Not just that, they even asked him to direct the feature, which appropriately was called *Hum Ek Hain*. It worked beautifully for PL Santoshi. Here the young director came in contact with Rehana, the film's leading lady. His future would have a lot to do with this lady as also with poetry engaging with respect for everything that breathes.

Pyarelal worked in many films—as a songwriter, director, or both—in which Rehana was the star. After *Hum Ek Hain* (1946), these were *Shehnai* (1947), *Khidki* (1948), *Roshni* (1949), *Sargam* (1950), *Saudagar* (1951), *Chham Chhama Chham* (1952), and *Shin Shinaki Bubla Boo* (1952). He wrote before and after Rehana as well, and he also directed films with other heroines, like *Barsaat Ki Raat* (1960), *Dil Hi To Hai* (1962. Credits shared with CL Rawal), and *Qawwali Ki Raat* (1964. Credits shared with Durgesh Kumar). But the one he fell in love with was Rehana, and for many years they were on Cloud 9. At least he was, till she left him for Pakistan and his cloud came crashing down to earth. The jungle telegraph says he used to earn a lot of money, and she was high maintenance. By the time she left, he was in deep financial trouble. Somehow though, he managed to survive, in his art too. But her departure forever changed him for the worse.

His son, the successful filmmaker Rajkumar Santoshi, recalls, "My father turned producer and suffered losses; that brought him down. We had to move to Thane (a suburb of Bombay) and rent a small home. My dad died penniless out of kidney failure in 1978"[1].

In *Hum Ek Hain* the theme was about a Hindu, a Muslim and a Christian living together. For that film, Santoshi wrote a few songs, like the title song, *Hum ek hain, ek hai naiyya*. Later, his poem on the different linguistic groups living with mutual respect on our land was articulated in *Hum Panchhi Ek Daal Ke* (1957). It began with *'Aika ho aika* (Marathi)…*Hoon chhu Gujarati* (Gujarati)'…and so on it proceeded, taking in *'Punjabi, Bihari, Bengali, Madrasi…sab hain Bhaaratwaasi'*, it went on to say. The song became transnational when it said *Hum bachche hain Cheen ke, Japan ke, Iran ke, Roos ke,* and it named many more countries. After that came *'Sab ko apna mulk hai pyaara, sab ka apna apna naara, par hum sab hain bhai bhai bhai bhai. Bachche hain jahaan ke'.* Then it turned religious, *'Mohammad se seekha, Isa se seekha, Gautam se seekha, Gandhi se seekha'.*

Before this, Santoshi had written a national integration song for V Shantaram's *Teen Batti Char Rasta* (1953): *Teen deep aur chaar dishaayen juda juda raston se aayen*, as also the Hindi lyrics in the multilingual *O re o puran bondu re*.

Fables are genres that use animals and often have a moral. Santoshi's ballad *Suno suno re kahaani ik bahut puraani jise kehti thi naani ho*, is a wonderful story of how different animals, scared to death of the hungry King of the Jungle, the Lion, finally get together to face the beast. In Unity Lies Strength, that's the song's central message, but how they get the lion to eat out of their hands in a win-win way forms the substance of that extraordinary poem, easily without equal in our films. Santoshi ended up doing a beautiful lyrical job here, a la Jungle Book.

Santoshi used high imagination in his lyrics, and his work has stood the test of time. He made us visit the heavens in his sad thoughts in *Mehfil mein jal utthi shama parwaane ke liye* (*Nirala*, 1950) with its *Ulfat dekho aag bani hai milne se majboor rahe, Yehi saza hai duniya mein deewaane ke liye*. Not to forget *Tum kya jaano tumhaari yaad mein hum kitna roye* (*Shin Shinaki Bubla Boo*, 1952) (*Kitne baadal ghire gagan mein, ghir ke phir na barse, Pyaas bujha kar dil hi dil mein kitna tadpe tarse, Dard hamaara dil jaane ya naina khoye-khoye*). He also wrote funny songs with the charming use of English words, as in *Aana meri jaan Sunday ke Sunday...I love you!* (*Shehnai*, 1947). Also *Mere gore gore gaal...that's all!* (*Dulhan*, 1958). And *Dekh babu dekh, dukaan se main laayi hoon cake, marzi ho to take* (*Mr. Superman Ki Waapasi*, 1960).

Santoshi also penned an imaginative masterpiece for Talat to sing in *Teen Batti Chaar Rasta* (1953). But first about the situation that warranted such imagination in the film. In the narrative, the hero Karan Dewan is a writer and has just fallen in love with girl-next-door, Sandhya. He wants to impress her with his art through a love letter, but that has to be worded just right. Now Santoshi was a writer himself and he knew how this breed worked. Most good writers make drafts and then keep changing the words and syntax till the result reads fine for them. Thus in the song we hear the hero sing as he writes. *Ishq …preet…pyaar…haan! Pyaar! Tumse hai pyaar mujhe tumse hai pyaar…Hum jaante hain pyaar mein hota naheen vishwaas… vishwaas? Hn hn…yaqeen…naheen…aitbaar…haan! Hum jaante hain pyaar mein hota naheen aitbaar.* Voila, he's got the rhyme right! Hear this song and marvel at how creative Santoshi's mind and art could get.

Here are just a few more of his wonderful songs, with the films and singers mentioned:

> ➤ *Maar kataari mar jaana* (*Shehnai*, 1947/ Amirbai)
> ➤ *Jo mujhe bhula ke chale gaye* (*Sangeeta*, 1950/ Lata)
> ➤ *Jab dil ko sataave gham, tu chhed sakhi sargam* (*Sargam*, 1950/ Lata, Saraswati Rane)
> ➤ *Wo humse chup hain, hum unse chup hain* (*Sargam*, 1950/ Lata, Chitalkar)

Wo humse chup hain

> ➤ *Aa teri tasweer bana loon* (*Naadaan*, 1951/ Talat)
> ➤ *Aisa kya qasoor kiya dil jo choor choor kiya* (*Naadaan*, 1951/ Lata, Rafi)
> ➤ *Hanste hanste rona pada* (*Najariya*, 1952/ Lata)
> ➤ *Kitna meettha hota hai* (*Teen Batti Chaar Raasta*, 1953/ Lata)
> ➤ *Teriya teriya teriya* (*Chalees Baba Ek Chor*, 1954/ Lata, Chitalkar)
> ➤ *Tum mere Swami antaryaami* (*Chhote Babu*, 1957/ Manna Dey)

- *Bichhde hue milenge phir* (*Post Box No. 999*, 1958/ Rafi, Asha)
- *Jogi aaya le ke sandesha Bhagwan ka* (*Post Box No. 999*, 1958/ Manna Dey)
- *Mere dil mein hai ik baat* (*Post Box No. 999*, 1958/ Manna Dey, Lata)
- *O neend na mujhko aaye* (*Post Box No. 999*, 1958/ Hemant, Lata)
- *Tirchhi nazar ka piya waar hai* (*Madari*, 1959/ Lata)

It is said that PL Santoshi spent his last days listening to sad songs, including his own *Umeed unse kya thi aur kar wo kya rahe hain* (*Basant*, 1942/ Parul Ghosh). But he had composed many for Lata, where she sounded her sacrificial lamb best. Some of us cannot have enough of such songs too either. Here are a few of those: *Jo dil ko jalaaye sataaye dukhaaye* (*Nirala*, 1950), *Koi kisi ka deewaana na bane* (Lata/ *Sargam*, 1950), and *Koi aa jaaye…bigdi taqdeer bana jaaye* (*Post Box No. 999*, 1959)

~~~~

The above was originally published in DNA Jaipur on 9 September 2018. It has since been updated and enhanced.

♪♫♩♪
~~~~

Triangles of a Different Kind

Could you look for a few moments at the six types of triangles we have? These triangles are called Obtuse, Acute, Right, Equilateral, Isosceles, and Scalene. Trigonometry is the branch of mathematics that deals with the sides and angles of triangles. But Trigonometry is not just for textbooks. It's a big help in the real world. It can help us design a roof for our home. Doctors use trigonometry to understand X-rays and ultraviolet waves. The science has many other uses, like in aviation, satellite systems, space explorations, and even in studies of music theory. The world, in general, noticed its early high-profile use a long time ago when it ascertained that Mount Everest, at 29028 feet, was the highest mountain in the world. Directly or otherwise, the idea of triangulation has spared no one. Not even scriptwriters.

Good writers have lots of imagination, so they have used the idea of triangles to term relationships between three lovers (two men in love with a woman, or two women in love with a man) as love triangles. In such stories, there usually is some kind of conflict resolution, with two sides finally getting together, after which the losing third person is referred to as the unfortunate third angle of the story.

For recall, here is a small list of Hindi films that had love triangle stories, with the three stakeholders. The name in brackets eventually became the third angle.

- *Baazi* (1951). Kalpana Kartik and Dev Anand. (Geeta Bali)
- *Badal* (1951). Madhubala and Premnath. (Purnima)
- *Deedar* (1951). Ashok Kumar and Nargis. (Dilip Kumar)
- *Aan* (1952). Nadira and Dilip Kumar. (Nimmi)

- *Aah* (1953). Raj Kapoor and Nargis. (Vijaylaxmi)
- *Aar Paar* (1954). Shyama and Guru Dutt. (Shakila)
- *Amar* (1954). Nimmi and Dilip. (Madhubala)
- *Taxi Driver* (1954). (Kalpana Kartik and Dev Anand (Sheila Ramani)
- *Devdas* (1955). Suchitra Sen and Dilip Kumar (even if she couldn't end up with him. Dilip and Suchitra were the twosome here). (Vyjayanthimala)
- *Bhai Bhai* (1956). Nirupa Roy and Ashok Kumar. (Shyama)
- *Nau Do Gyarah* (1957). Kalpana Kartik and Dev Anand. (Shashikala)
- *Amar Deep* (1958). Vyjayanthimala and Dev Anand. (Padmini)
- *Dhool Ka Phool* (1959). Nanda and Rajendra Kumar. (Mala Sinha)
- *Chaudhvin Ka Chand* (1960). Guru Dutt and Waheeda Rehman. (Rehman)
- *Kohinoor* (1960). Meena Kumari and Dilip Kumar. (Kum Kum)
- *Dil Ek Mandir* (1963). Raaj Kumar and Meena Kumari. (Rajendra Kumar)
- *Mere Mehboob* (1963). Rajendra Kumar and Sadhana. (Ameeta)
- *Shagun* (1964). Waheeda Rehman and Kanwaljit (Libi Rana)
- *Devar* (1966). Deven Verma and Sharmila Tagore. (Dharmendra)
- *Palki* (1967). Rajendra Kumar and Waheeda Rehman. (Rehman)
- *Saathi* (1968). Vyjayanthimala and Rajendra Kumar. (Simi)
- *Kabhi Kabhie* (1976). Rakhee and Shashi Kapoor. (Amitabh Bachchan)
- *Silsila* (1981). Jaya and Amitabh Bachchan. (Rekha)

Just as not all triangles are of one kind, not all love triangles end up in the way suggested above. Some stories give it a different spin. Let's take one kind. In this, there are two lovers, but the man marries another woman. However, after this marriage, his wife passes away, so he reunites with his sweetheart. Examples:

- In *Dil-e-Nadaan* (1953), Talat Mahmood loves Peace Kanwal but ends up marrying Shyama. When the latter dies, he teams up with Peace Kanwal again.

- ➢ In *Vachan* (1955), Geeta Bali and Balraj (a newcomer, not the famous Balraj Sahni) are lovers, but he has to marry someone else. When the wife dies, Balraj connects romantically with Geeta Bali again.
- ➢ *Dil Apna Aur Preet Parayi* (1960) tells us that Meena Kumari and Raaj Kumar are sweethearts. His circumstances compel him to marry Nadira instead. But when Nadira dies, Raaj Kumar returns to Meena Kumari.
- ➢ *Bandini* (1963) features Nutan and Ashok Kumar in a romantic situation. He marries another woman, who passes away. Nutan and Ashok Kumar get together once more.

In the following cases, there's a romantic couple, but for some reason, the lady has to forget her sweetheart and marry someone else. Not all these are examples of love triangles, but they are triangles anyway. After the marriage, the husband comes to realise his wife had a relationship with someone before she married him. Interestingly, the script allows the rejected man to die at the end, simultaneously for the husband to realise his wife was only in a platonic relationship. Instances:

- ➢ In *Andaz* (1949). Dilip Kumar and Nargis are together. But she has to marry Raj Kapoor, who begins to smell a rat. But Dilip Kumar dies, synchronously clearing her name.

A still from Andaz

➤ In *Usne Kaha Tha* (1961), we find Sunil Dutt and Nanda romancing. Then he goes to the Army, and upon his return finds her married to his boss in the Army. Events make Sunil Dutt save his boss's life and also clear her reputation. She is exonerated, and Dutt dies.

➤ *Dil Ek Mandir* (1963) shows us love blossoming between Rajendra Kumar and Meena Kumari. Then she marries Raaj Kumar who has good reasons to believe his wife was in a relationship with Rajendra. Like in *Usne Kaha Tha* above, here too the rejected lover (Rajendra Kumar) saves the husband's (Raaj Kumar's) life, but he himself dies soon after. Everything gets clear for Raaj now, who realises his wife was as pure as Sita, her name in the story. Incidentally, Raaj Kumar's name in the films was Ram. Very appropriate, wouldn't you say?

➤ In *Sangam* (1964), Rajendra Kumar and Vyjayanthimala are happily in love, but Rajendra's buddy Raj Kapoor is nuts about her too. Rajendra steps back, but things turn sour when Raj suspects that his wife and best friend have been doing a number behind his back. But Rajendra is made to die, and that's when it dawns upon Raj that his suspicions were without any foundation.

➤ In *Mohabbat Isko Kehte Hain* (1965), Shashi Kapoor and Nanda sing happy love songs. But her universe is shattered when she has to marry Ramesh Deo. Shashi Kapoor dies at the end, and the truth of innocent love is laid bare for the suspecting husband.

➤ The same thing happens in *Prem Kahani* (1975). Lovers Rajesh Khanna and Mumtaz part ways for Shashi Kapoor to become the lucky husband. Rajesh Khanna passes away at the end, and their platonic relationship is made clear to all.

In the following cases, we see a romantic couple, happy in love, singing, laughing together, and making plans for a golden tomorrow. But she is made to marry someone else. On the wedding night, she commits suicide. What a twist that is! The instances are:

- ➤ *Goonj Uthi Shehnai* (1959). Rajendra Kumar and Ameeta are strongly committed lovers. But she ties the knot with someone else. Amita commits suicide immediately after the wedding.
- ➤ *Bazaar* (1982) Farooq Sheikh and Supriya Pathak are blissfully in love. The family elders get her married to someone else. She commits suicide right after the marriage.

Unusual endings involving a much older man

The following love stories are interrupted by a third angle. Here, an old man gets married to a young girl in love with someone else. And then there is a twist.

In *Rattan* (1944), Swaranlata and Karan Dewan are together. But her marriage is arranged to the much-older widower Wasti. Soon after, Karan Dewan dies as a result of eating a poisoned paan, and Swaranlata passes away, possibly as a result of shock.

In *Sharda* (1958), Raj Kapoor and Meena Kumari are seeing each other. The interruption comes from an old man, who is none other than Raj Kapoor's recently widowed father. So Meena is married off to the old man, while Raj marries Shyama. After a while, Meena passes away, but not before telling them that she will be born again. Shyama has a baby with Raj, a daughter who in manners is just like Meena when she was small. She can even recite the shlokas effortlessly, exactly as Meena could.

7

A Gutsy Award Wapasi?

Last month, while a few of us were waiting in a government office, a friend of mine introduced me to a lady named Radhika Gupta. She was happy to know we lived a few hundred meters from each other. I was introduced to her as a film historian, upon which the lady seemed happier. It soon emerged that she was the only child of parents who had to do with films: costume designer Bhanu Athaiya and her husband, occasional songwriter Satyendra Athaiya. It was my turn to be enthusiastic. Of course, a union of such artists sounds wonderful.

Bhanu was the first Indian to get an Oscar (for Costume Design in Attenborough's *Gandhi*, 1982), and Satyendra was the lyricist who adapted a Meera bhajan so beautifully: *Aeri main to prem deewaani*, went Lata Mangeshkar in Roshan's *Naubahar* (1952), her vocals ushered in and supported divinely by Pandit Pannalal Ghosh's flute.

Ms. Gupta, settled in Kolkata, was currently staying with her sick mother in Mumbai. She informed me that her mother hailed from Kolhapur in Maharashtra, while her father was from Uttar Pradesh, and he had passed away many moons ago. She added many more tidbits while we waited for the bureaucrat to arrive. I asked her if I could meet Mrs. Athaiya to learn about the dozens of actors who had worn clothes and accessories designed by her. Perhaps she could tell us if Vyjayanthimala had felt all right wearing those sizzling, sleeveless and strapless blouses in *Amrapali*. Of course anyone who imitated Vyjayanthimala after that film was said to wear an Amrapali blouse, famously designed by Bhanu Athaiya. Such tops are most visible during the annual 9-day Navratri holidays when they dance the *dandiya raas*.

Bhanu Athaiya must know so much about Hindi Cinema, I thought, even about the songs that were filmed when actors wore her outfits and accessories. The daughter's enthusiasm waned immediately, as she informed me tersely, "My mother doesn't recall too much these days". That was sad.

Later, while examining the spectacle of many Indian winners returning their various national awards (*Award Wapasi*, as the movement came to be called), I stumbled upon an interesting fact: not only was Bhanu Athaiya the first Indian to have received an Oscar (even till today there are just a handful who have got it), she was the only Indian to have returned it. This was in 2012. And the reason for the return? She was unsure of the people around her. This is what she told the Press: "It was a burden. I wanted the trophy to be safe in future and in the right hands".

Everyone who receives the Oscars has to pass on. The same thing holds for every award across the globe. The family keeps the statue, medal, and citation, whatever. When you return an award and offer such a comment as Mrs. Athaiya did, rumour mills get to work. They are not always without foundation.

Many Indians have returned important awards before, and some have even refused to accept one; in both acts a deeply felt statement is showcased. The rejection probably began happening after Bimal Roy's *Devdas* (1955), for which the Filmfare Best Supporting Actress was announced for Vyjayanthimala. She turned it down, saying she was not the film's supporting actress. She was the lead female. Why, her name appeared just after Dilip Kumar in the credits, before the names of Motilal and Suchitra Sen. Here are a few other people who refused one: Sonu Nigam for Best Singer (Filmfare, 1997), Kathak exponent Sitara Devi (Padma Bhushan, 2002), and screenplay and story writer Salim Khan (Padma Shri, 2015). On the world stage, these gents refused an award: French philosopher and writer Jean-Paul Sartre (Nobel Prize in Literature, 1964), Vietnamese politician Le Doc Tho (Nobel Peace Prize, 1973), and Marlon Brando (Oscar for Best Actor, 1975).

In 1915, the British Government knighted India's greatest poet, the multi-talented Dr. Rabindranath Tagore. Four years later, he returned this knighthood. Sardar Khushwant Singh, prolific writer, was awarded the Padma Bhushan in 1974; he returned it in 1984. Later, in 2007, he went on to accept the higher Padma Vibhushan.

But back to Bhanu (nee Rajopadhye) Athaiya who in her autobiography, The Art of Costume Design, shows us how she entered films in 1953, and went on to design costumes, alone or with shared credits, for about one hundred and thirty films. Many of these were landmark features, with costumes that stood out as lighthouses of visual excellence. She also made dozens of actors sing or dance in the outfits she thought were right for them.

She first received acclaim for dressing up Nadira gorgeously in the song *Mud mud ke na dekh mud mud ke* (*Shree 420*, 1955), the vamp wearing a beautifully shimmering, sleeveless, ankle-high gown, her hair tied up behind, her forehead covered with a curled pixie-cut hair-do, all that accessorized with a magnificent choker around her neck.

Bhanu's fame was boosted big-time for helping give Guru Dutt the look of a defeated old film-maker, as he reminisces about his past, the song *Dekhi zamaane ki yaari* running in his thoughts in *Kaagaz Ke Phool* (1959).

It was also hard to ignore the upper-class Indian elegance of Sadhana as she sang *Kaun aaya ke nigaahon mein chamak jaag utthi* in *Waqt* (1965), with her famous fringe on the forehead, and a long thick plait coming down her left side. And what was she made to wear? An off-white cut-in blouse, matching sari with brocade on it, and once again an elegant chocker, this time made of six rings of pearls.

It was in *Guide* (1965) that Ms. Athaiya showcased Dev Anand as a swami, so credibly too. As he wore a cream full-sleeved kurta with a Chinese collar, a saffron shawl around his shoulder, and tears dropping down from his cheeks, the village folks prayed in song. *He Ram hamaare Ramchandra* remains a defining moment in the annals of Hindi films, a cinematic triumph for all who teamed together in this scene. Earlier in the film, it was Waheeda who was attired to dance in a work of excellence: *Mose chhal kiye jaaye* had her decorated with a golden necklace and earrings, and an Amrapali-like blouse, the difference being, that she wore transparent sleeves here. The point to consider is, that this get-up predated *Amrapali* by a year, so it would not be altogether wrong to call it the Guide blouse. In the film, the lady was a dancer. Same as Vyjayanthimala in *Amrapali* a year later.

Bhanu Athaiya
with her Gandhi

As Rajnartaki of a mythical kingdom, Vyjayanthimala wore the famous sleeveless blouse in many variations, with a bunch of golden spaghetti straps too as in *Neel gagan ki chhaon mein*, in *Amrapali* (1966). But think also of Vyjayanthimala before this, in *Ganga Jamuna* (1961), when she went *Dhoondo dhoondo re saajna more kaan ka baala*. The lost earring she spoke about was the subject of all the verses in that song, engaging an accessory planned by the costume designer without naming her.

Athaiya went on to design costumes in dozens of features, on hundreds of actors, big or small. Think of Sadhana in *Dulha Dulhan* (1964), *Anita* (1967) and *Inteqaam* (1969). Shammi Kapoor in *Dil Deke Dekho* (1959), *Janwar* (1965), *Teesri Manzil* (1966), and *Brahmachari* (1968). Sharmila in *Dastaan* (1972). Vyjayanthimala in *Leader* (1964). Dilip in *Ganga Jamuna* (1961). Guru Dutt in *CID* (1956), *Kaagaz ke Phool* (1959), and *Chaudhvin Ka Chaand* (1960). Hema Malini in *Johnny Mera Naam* (1970), *Tere Mere Sapne* (1971), and *Razia Sultan* (1982). Mumtaz in *Brahmachari* (1968). Zeenat Aman in *Satyam Shivam Sundaram* (1978). Helen in *Teesri Manzil* (1966). Meena Kumari in *Sahib Bibi Aur Ghulam* (1962). Aamir Khan in *Lagaan* (2001). And Gayatri Joshi in *Swades* (2004). All these and many more were outfitted by clothes and accessories created in Bhanu Athaiya's mind.

But what about her husband Satyendra Athaiya? Here's what he also wrote, apart from *Aeri main to prem deewaani:*

- *Kisi surat lagi dil ki behel jaaye to achha ho* (Talat/ *Naubahaar,* 1952)
- *Main dil hoon ik armaan bhara* (Talat/ *Anhonee,* 1952)
- *Sama ke dil mein hamaare zara khayaal rahe* (Talat, Lata/ *Anhonee,* 1952)
- *Bheegi bheegi raat aayi* (Meena Kapoor/ *Aakash,* 1953)
- *So gayi chaandni…tum mujhe aur bhi yaad aane lage* (Lata/ *Aakash,* 1953)
- *Jhilmil sitaaron ke tale aa, mera daaman thaam le* (Lata/ *Naaz,* 1954)
- *Tum kahaan tum kahaan…aankhon mein dil hai* (Lata/ *Naaz,* 1954)
- *Aesi bansi bajaaye main to kho gayi* (Lata/ *Radha Krishna,* 1954)
- *Suno nath dinon ke dukhiyon ke pyaare* (Lata/ *Tanhai,* 1961)
- *Ja re ja re qasam khaaye jhootthi, peetal ki anguthi* (Lata/ *Badi Maa,* 1974)

So much has changed since the time Satyendra wrote *Main dil hoon ik armaan bhara, Tu aake mujhe pehchaan zara.* If he were alive today Satyendra may have realized that *Ab aake koi pehchaanta naheen, khud ja ke pehchaan ka dhandora peetna padta hai. Ya phir award waapas de ke.*

~~~~

The above was originally published in DNA Jaipur on 22 November 2015. It has since been updated and enhanced.

~~~~

8

Let's Tighten the Booze Noose

For decades there has been debate as to whether India is the world's biggest democracy or the world's largest functioning anarchy. Of course, we have the pride of cradling many key religions—Hinduism, Sikhism, Buddhism, and Jainism. We have Parsis who have lived here for centuries and the Baha'is who number about 2 million and have a key presence in this country. The Dalai Lama and his flock have made India their home since 1959. We have Muslims, Jews, and Christians of all hues. We also have tantric and various other strains that make up the composite culture so unique to us. Since we have been co-existing more-or-less harmoniously, we can justifiably be proud of our tolerance levels. But are we a democracy, as the United States or France is? Can we safely say civil rights are the same for everyone, regardless of where they come from, and the law is equal for all?

It doesn't seem so. Certainly not, for example, when someone from the economically lower or middle class becomes a victim of a drunk's behaviour. For we have long had a tradition of the rich and famous cocking a snook at the less fortunate. This money-can-buy-anything attitude has raised its ugly head from time to time.

Do you recall Manu Sharma, the son of a politician who in April 1999 got drunk enough to pump lethal bullets into the brain of Jessica Lal, a celebrity model who was serving as a barmaid at a high-society party? They put him in jail, but he managed to buy his way out. After a public outcry years later, the law threw him back into Delhi's Tihar jail for a life term, and that's where he belongs. But is Sharma in? No, he spends much of his time outside prison, mostly in Piccadilly Hotel, the property owned by his politician father. Let's connect some dots now: a warden of Tihar Jail, PC Sharma, has a son named Neeraj Sharma who is employed by the killer's father, Vinod Sharma, a Member of Parliament from Haryana.

Many moons before that, in 1984, a politician with a high trajectory, with the promise of an even higher orbit, got sloshed on a flight to Germany. Maharashtra Minister Ramrao Adik molested a stewardess, demanded more alcohol than was good for him, and misbehaved enough to be finally stopped. There was a stink. His party, under pressure, asked him to resign, and he eventually did, but he and his cronies fought tooth and nail for his job. Here's what India Today reported: "When asked at the press conference after his resignation announcement about the possible impact on the country's image by his reported misbehaviour abroad, Ramrao Adik shot back indignantly, waving his hand: 'It was neither in this country nor abroad. It was in the air.'"[2] The same report cites him as calling the purser "an idiot" and "a bastard."

But ignominy or punishment don't seem to work as deterrents for others.

Early in 2010, a 27-year-old wealthy Mumbai girl called Nooria Haveliwala had some drugs and washed them down with six beers in about ninety minutes. She then drove her car senselessly and rammed into two people, including a cop, killing them on the spot. Earlier still, in September 2002, actor Salman Khan ran his 2-ton Land Cruiser over many people, killing one and permanently, seriously injuring four others. What's the actor doing, pray? Doing time? No, he's shooting. Not black bucks any more, that's too risky now, and that case of his is also sub-judice. But shooting for films, while successfully remaining an idol to many formative minds. He also runs an NGO called Being Human. Wow! (Update: Salman Khan was later acquitted of all charges).

More recently, in June 2019, a young hotshot corporate lawyer called Janhavi Gadkar visited two bars within four hours, met different people, and bent her elbow far more often than was good for her. She then drove her solid, armoured-tank-like German car on the wrong side of the road and into a hapless taxi, killing two people instantly. Is she going to do time? Most people don't think so. She's a hotshot and she's a lawyer, remember?

We shift our focus to Pune on May 19, 2024. A teenage son of a wealthy realtor drove his Porsche too fast and recklessly. He killed two young techies. It was reported that the boy's blood sample was swapped with that of one of the doctors who hadn't consumed alcohol.

Look at cinema too. Priyanka drinks, Katrina drinks, and most of them drink now. It's so cool man! I'll drink too, thinks the impressionable mind. In real life, many do drugs too, as was so clearly found in the aftermath of actor Sushant Singh's death. But that's another story. So yes, drinking. Remember all these actors drinking and looking smart as they sang?

- ➤ KL Saigal: *Piya bin naahi aawat chain* (*Devdas*, 1935)
- ➤ Dilip Kumar: *Aye mere dil kaheen aur chal* (the slow version in *Daag*, 1952)
- ➤ Bina Rai: *Muhabbat mein aise qadam dagmagaaye* (*Anarkali*, 1953)

- ➤ Ashok Kumar (as Nimmi sings to him): *Sharaabi ja ja ja* (*Bhai Bhai, 1956*)
- ➤ Vyjayanthimala: *Zaalim teri aankhon ne kya cheez pila di hai* (*Devta, 1956*)

- Motilal: *Zindagi khwaab hai* (*Jagte Raho*, 1956)
- Johnny Walker: *Jangal mein more naacha* (*Madhumati*, 1958)
- Ajit: *Main nashi mein hoon* (*Do Gunde*, 1959)
- Rajendra Kumar: *Maine peena seekh liya* (*Goonj Uthi Shehnai*, 1959)
- Nishi: *Maine to naheen pee* (*Main Nashe Mein Hoon*, 1959)
- Raj Kapoor: *Mujhko yaaro maaf karna* (*Main Nashe Mein Hoon*, 1959)
- Shammi Kapoor: *Maine pee hai, pee hai pee hai* (*Raat Ke Raahi*, 1959)
- Sunil Dutt: *Main kaun hoon* (*Main Chup Rahungi*, 1962)
- Meena Kumari: *Na jao saiyaan chhuda ke baiyaan* (*Sahib Bibi Aur Ghulam*, 1962)
- Leela Naidu: *Aaj ye meri zindagi* (*Ye Raaste Hain Pyaar Ke*, 1963)
- Bharat Bhushan: *Mehfil se utth jaane waalo* (*Dooj Ka Chand*, 1964)
- Dev Anand: *Saawan ke maheena mein* (*Sharabi*, 1964)
- Pradeep Kumar: *Dil jo na keh saka* (*Bheegi Raat*, 1965)
- Helen and Nanda: *Peeke hum jo chale* (*Gumnaam*, 1965)
- Raaj Kumar: *Chhoo lene do naazuk honthon ko* (*Kaajal*, 1965)
- Nazima: *Saaqiya thodi thodi bekhudi hai* (*Nishan*, 1965)
- Sadhana: *Qareeb aa ye nazar phir mile* (*Anita*, 1967)
- Babita: *Aao huzoor tumko* (*Kismat*, 1968)
- Dharmendra: *Hui shaam unka khayaal aa gaya* (*Mere Humdum Mere Dost*, 1968)

Hui shaam unka khayaal aa gaya

- ➤ Deven Varma: *Dost kahaan koi tumsa* (*Khamoshi*, 1969)
- ➤ Balraj Sahni: *Maine pee sharaab* (*Naya Rasta*, 1970)
- ➤ Waheeda Rehman: *Rangeela re* (*Prem Pujari*, 1970)
- ➤ Sanjeev Kumar: *Humse kiya hai sab ne dikhaawa* (*Priya*, 1970)
- ➤ Radha Saluja: *Tumhi rehnuma ho* (*Do Raha*, 1971)
- ➤ Shashi Kapoor: *Kaise kahen hum pyaar ne humko* (*Sharmilee*, 1971)
- ➤ Hema Malini: *Haan ji haan maine sharaab pi hai* (*Seeta Aur Geeta*, 1972)
- ➤ Rajesh Khanna: *Ye laal rang kab mujhe chhodega* (*Prem Nagar*, 1974)
- ➤ Uttam Kumar: *Na poochho koi humen* (*Amanush*, 1975)
- ➤ Amitabh: *Chal mere bhai tere haath jodta hoon* (*Naseeb*, 1981)

Tobacco is dangerous too, so in 2008 the government introduced the Prohibition of Smoking in Public Places Rules, which covers almost everything you can think besides your home, car, or street. Some enclosed places are exempt if they provide separate smoking areas or booths. Since tobacco use accounts for 40% of cancers in India, the Government is seriously considering a punitive fine of 20,000 Rupees for smoking in public places. Ten years ago, who would have imagined smoking would be banned in planes, airports and many offices? We need to get similarly tough about alcohol consumption since figures are scary. Consider them. The World Health Organization recently reported that at 196,000, India had the highest annual incidence of road fatalities, some 70% of these caused by drunken driving. That translates to about 375 deaths every day, which is over 15 per hour. Deutsche Welle, Germany's international broadcaster, substantiates that.

Earlier in this story we wondered if we had full-strength democracy. But another question begs an answer: Would we benefit from a full-strength democracy? Perhaps we need tougher legislation, as we have done for tobacco. Not to forget that in smoking you only kill yourself, while in alcohol you may even kill some else. Innocent lives.

Films can help. They are a great medium to show the consequences of irresponsible drinking, while we continue to enjoy music when an actor gets high. But we all need to know that the law will have no mercy if we drink without responsibility. In that situation, we'll have to face the music, not enjoy it.

~ ~ ~ ~

The above was originally published in DNA Jaipur on 28 June 2015. It has since been updated and enhanced.

9

Conceived Immaculately?

Sitting down to deconstruct a work of art such as a painting or film is sometimes not easy. The idea of art appeals more to the heart than to the head, so one cannot build an argument about it. Such aesthetic appraisal is particularly difficult for magnum opus films, plays or musical scores since these usually have huge contributions from multiple sources. Interestingly, while a film such as *Mughal-e-Azam* (1960) may be almost universally loved, it has elicited divergent takes from different critics, each intellectually celebrating or running down the different elements of the movie as he sees them. I say 'almost universally loved' because even such a film as *Mughal-e-Azam* can have detractors; the Filmfare magazine review just about trashed the film, most particularly the music of Naushad Ali, which many see as the engine behind the film's phenomenal success. The landmark feature film *Sholay* (1975) is another case. One critic called it a cheap Indian cowboy movie. One lives and learns. One also thinks of French philosopher Blaise Pascal who said it so well: "The heart has reasons that reason cannot know".

But critics and historians like this writer need a platform for their expression. They also need to make a living. That said, consider this. Like many millions, I marvel at the extraordinary and undying appeal of thousands of Hindi film songs, made decades before, melodies that in some way are a social glue to bind a nation as heterogeneous as ours. A key reason these songs have merit is because of the obsession our music-makers had with creating something of worth. Such an obsession is reflected in the words of John Ruskin: "Quality is never an accident. It is always the result of intelligent efforts. There *must* be the will to make a superior thing". Looking at the Hindi cinema through a 'retrospectoscope', it becomes clear that for decades in the middle half of the 20th century, all people who contributed to the making of music (i.e., singers, composers, lyricists, arrangers, instrumentalists, and sound recording engineers) just wanted to excel in what they did. This last observation explains why a high number of songs from that period were (and still are) loved, even if some of the films themselves were eminently unwatchable. The reverse of that—where the film was good and the music forgettable—was rare.

Let's close in now on a concept that can be called Immaculate Conception. It's about situational filming. But for that let's first read about a related concept I have written about before.

The Surrogacy of Transferred Emotions

A surrogate is a person who substitutes for another in a specific assignment. In an earlier anthology (Windows to the Soul) I penned an essay entitled "They're Singing My Feelings", in which we considered film songs that were lip-synched by some actors who were singing not so much their own feelings, but rather the sentiments of other actors who did not move their lips to the lyrics. Perhaps the latter were grieving a loss, so were too choked to sing; but the camera focussed on them for us to know whose feelings were being showcased. Sometimes, when the actor was struggling with the idea of right or wrong, he couldn't moralize out loud in front of others. His conscience was singing him a song through someone else. There were many other situations, for instance, one of inspiration or affirmation of faith. Such songs which carried a surrogacy of emotions were a clever directorial ploy which often brought about attractive results. Examples of such surrogate singing songs would be *Dil ka na karna aitbaar koi* (Lata/*Halaku*, 1956), where Helen articulates the feelings of a pensive Ajit, and *Jaane kahaan gayi* (Rafi/*Dil Apna Aur Preet Parai*, 1960), in which Raj Kishore sings the feelings of a grieving Raaj Kumar. In *Kinare Kinare* (1963), a sadhu and his daughter sing Dev Anand's conscience call, the song being *O pagle der na hogi pal-chhin ki ke jis din chal chal chal hogi* (Rafi, Usha).

But what if no actor is seen moving his lips to express the feelings of another? What if a song runs only in the background, representing the emotional condition of an actor who doesn't lip-synch? Since no human being is shown singing, we can assume it's not a surrogate song. This becomes a case of Immaculate Conception. It's a situation where divinity, nature, or destiny—call it what you will—is in empathy with the actor and gives birth to a song.

It is in just such a situation that we notice a song finding an entry in *Aakhri Dao* (1958), where Nutan and Shekhar become star-crossed lovers. *Humsafar saath apna chhod chale, rishte-naate wo saare tod chale* was duetted by Asha and Rafi in the studio, without anyone miming the words on the screen.

Ashok Kumar, the fine actor but reluctant singer, always preferred that someone should playback for him, so that he could just lip-synch the song on the screen. But it looks like he preferred to sit out even that lip-synch role in several songs that had extraordinariness oozing from them. Instances of him emoting without moving his lips to such beautiful songs conceived immaculately are *Apna hai phir bhi apna, badh kar gale laga le* (Rafi/ *Bhai Bhai*, 1956), *Ya meri manzil bata ya zindagi ko chheen le* (Rafi/ *Raakhi*, 1962) and *Chhupa lo yoon dil mein pyaar mera ke jaise mandir mein lau diye ki* (Hemant and Lata/ *Mamta*, 1966).

Need more immaculate conceptions for Ashok Kumar? Check out these: *Kismat bigdi duniya badli* (Mukesh/ *Afsana*, 1951), *Jeevan ke raaste hazaar* (Manna/ *Savera*, 1958), *Agar sansaar mein aurat na hoti* (Rafi/ *Grahasti*, 1963), *Aye mere dost aye mere humdum* (Rafi/ *Meherbaan*, 1967), and *Meri aankhon ke ujaale* (Rafi/ *Aabroo*, 1968). In a song brilliantly filmed, this actor was seen to have pangs of conscience about a crime he was committing, so we saw another Ashok Kumar—representing the intending criminal's conscience—to emerge and sing *Sab kuchh luta ke hosh mein aaye to kya kiya* (Talat/ *Ek Saal*, 1957).

Wahaan kaun hai tera musafir, jaayega kahaan, sang SD Burman in *Guide* (1966), his own tune setting Shailendra's poetry to divine music, but on the screen, these were the feelings of a confused Dev Anand, wondering if The Almighty was asking him a rhetorical question.

Consider such conceptions for several actors now:

- ➤ Raj Kapoor: *Main zindagi mein hardam rota hi raha hoon* (Rafi/ *Barsaat*, 1949)
- ➤ Nirupa Roy: *Bedard zamaana kya jaane* (Rafi/ *Bedard Zamana Kya Jane*, 1959)
- ➤ Mala Sinha: *Daaman mein daag laga baitthe* (Rafi/ *Dhool Ka Phool*, 1959)
- ➤ Guru Dutt: *Dekhi zamaane ki yaari* (Rafi/ *Kaagaz Ke Phool*, 1959)
- ➤ Waheeda Rehman and Guru Dutt: *Waqt ne kiya kya haseen sitam* (Geeta/ *Kaagaz Ke Phool*, 1959)

Waqt ne kiya kya haseen sitam

- ➤ Dev Anand: *Na tel aur na baati na qaabu hawa par* (Manna/ *Ek Ke Baad Ek*, 1960)
- ➤ Dev Anand and Waheeda: *Rim-jhim ke taraane le ke aayi barsaat* (Rafi, Geeta/ *Kala Bazar*, 1960)
- ➤ Sadhana: *Mere man ke diye* (Lata/ *Parakh*, 1960)
- ➤ Mala Sinha: *Wo dekho jala ghar kisi ka* (Lata/ *Anpadh*, 1962)
- ➤ Rehman and Mala Sinha: *Aaj ki raat naheen shikwe shikaayat ke liye* (Mahendra/ *Dharamputra*, 1962)
- ➤ Mala Sinha: *Main jab bhi akeli hoti hoon* (Asha/ *Dharamputra*, 1962)
- ➤ Asha Parekh: *Mujhe pyaar mein tum na ilzaam dete* (Asha/ *Phir Wohi Dil Laaya Hoon*, 1963)

- Guru Dutt: *Mere pyaar mein tujhe kya mila* (Rafi/ *Suhagan*, 1964)
- Raaj Kumar: *Hey neele gagan ke tale dharti ka pyaar pale* (Mahendra/ *Hamraaz*, 1967)
- Sanjeev Kumar and Suchitra Sen: *Tere bina zindagi se koi shikwa to naheen* (Lata, Kishore/ *Aandhi*, 1975)
- Farooq Shaikh: *Seene mein jalan aankhon mein toofaan sa kyoon hai* (Suresh Wadkar/ *Gaman*, 1979)
- Supriya Pathak: *Dekh lo aaj humko ji bhar ke* (Jagjit Kaur/ *Bazaar*, 1982)
- Naseeruddin Shah: *Karoge yaad to har baat yaad aayegi* (Bhupinder/ *Bazaar*, 1982)

Sometimes though, it seems it is not just the film's actor the Omniscient Power is singing for, maybe He is singing for all of us. That is because some feelings are common to the human race, regardless of our age or colour, or where and how we live. This is one such song, for when a loving companion departs:

Na jaane kyoon hota hai ye zindagi ke saath

Achaanak ye man kisi ke jaane ke baad

Kare phir uski yaad chhoti-chhoti si baat

Na jaane kyoon...

Wohi hai dagar, wohi hai safar

Hai naheen saath mere magar

Ab mera humsafar

Idhar-udhar dhoondhe nazar

Wohi hai dagar

Kahaan gayi shaamen madbhari

Wo mere, mere wo din gaye kidhar

This last song was penned by Yogesh Gaud and rendered by Lata Mangeshkar for Salil Chowdhury in *Chhoti Si Baat* (1976). The actors were Amol Palekar, Vidya Sinha and once again, Ashok Kumar whom we met so often in many songs earlier! This background song was as if immaculately conceived in the heavens and despatched to the earth.

~ ~ ~ ~

The above was originally published in DNA Jaipur on 10 December 2017. It has since been updated and enhanced.

♪♫♩♪

10

Arrogance Punished

Last week, as they were burning down an effigy of Ravana in my neighbourhood, I was wondering about this man who is seen as the embodiment of evil in much of India, even if he is worshipped in Sri Lanka, Indonesia, and in several other places, including by many here in India itself. That's because Ravana had his plus points: apart from being a scholar and an able king, he was also an ace veena player. But it was another trait of this giant that made me connect the dots with John Lennon, the leader of The Beatles, the English music band that rocked the world and changed it forever in the 1960s. That would be arrogance, a tragic flaw common to both musicians.

Ravana. Two heads are not always better than one

"Two heads are better than one" is a proverb we learnt early in life. But is that always the case? Even if both the heads are sick? If so, by an extension of thought, Ravana, who had 10 heads, should have been 10 times smarter than anyone with one head. But Lord Rama with his one head outsmarted and eliminated him. A body of thought also believes scores of curses killed Ravana, and it was he who invited death upon himself. That could be because of his famous arrogance, which had ticked many people off. Think of this song from *Insaniyat* (1955), with the 10-headed giant strutting about, singing these lines:

Main Ravana Lanka Naresh
Mere dus hain sees
Mere bus mein dharti aur paataal
Hai chaaron dhaam mera hi naam
Meri takkar le kis ki majaal
(Manna Dey, Rafi/ Rajinder Krishan/ C Ramchandra)

John Lennon. "I am Jesus Christ"

Many music aficionados know that The Beatles are the highest-selling artists in the history of music. Their singles, albums and music videos have sold more than anyone else's. While estimates vary, the number of Beatles records, CDs and digital downloads bought ranges anywhere between 300 and 600 million units. Whew!

For people who were around in the 1960s, the Beatles were everywhere, and so was their music. The hysteria that accompanied them during that decade can hardly be imagined by those who didn't live in those times. With so much uncontrolled excitement around them, they were mobbed everywhere they went. The smallest twitch of their eyes became sensational news. It is no wonder then that they started getting feelings of megalomania. Particularly infected was John Lennon. Let's visit him now.

Over fifty years ago, in 1968, Lennon called his teammates for a breaking news kind of announcement. When they sat down, he told them, "I have something very important to tell you". Then he added with gravitas, "I am Jesus Christ. I am back again". He proceeded to tell his small but stupefied audience that he was the reincarnation of Jesus Christ. The other members didn't know what to say. They had heard such hubris from him before, and they would hear it from him in the coming years again. But on those occasions, he would be talking to the Press. This was no Press Conference. It was more intimate. They asked for a coffee break. After the break, Lennon did not mention the subject.

John Lennon had first made such waves in an interview in early 1966. "We are more popular than Jesus" he had said, arguing that rock music was here to stay, even as Christianity was in terminal decline. Later, in his 1970 song, *God*, here are parts of what he sang: "I don't believe in Bible…I don't believe in Jesus…I just believe in me".

We don't know if there's a connection, but somebody shot John Lennon dead in 1980.

History has shown us many cases of arrogance, something that has rarely gone unpunished. Roman Emperor Julius Caesar was assassinated in March 44 BC, and German Dictator Adolf Hitler committed suicide in April 1945, only because his arrest, trial and punishment were imminent. Poetry offers examples as well. Shelley wrote a sonnet called *Ozymandias*, the name of an arrogant king:

My name is Ozymandias, King of Kings
Look on my Works, ye Mighty, and despair!

But not long after, the arrogant man's statue was dismembered and found in a desert somewhere.

Cinema is not far behind, not at all. In the opening scenes of BR Chopra's film *Waqt* (1965), Balraj Sahni is shown as an industrious dry-fruits businessman high on arrogance, since apart from his own arms, he has three sons who would take his business forward. But presently a huge earthquake visits them, and in a matter of minutes, he is brought down to zilch, his sons separated from each other and the parents.

That is why Shakeel advised us against excessive haughtiness:

Insaan bano kar lo bhalaayi ka koi kaam…
Laakhon yahaan shaan apni dikhaate hue aaye
Dum bhar ke liye naach gaye dhoop mein saaye
Wo bhool gaye the ke ye duniya hai saraaye
Aata hai koi subah to jaata hai koi shaam
Insaan bano…
(Rafi/ Naushad/ *Baiju Bawra*, 1952)

Many more songs tell us to be modest, dump that arrogance, and guard against punishment. *Maghroor na ho apne muqaddar pe o naadaan, Allah ki nazron mein baraabar hain sab insaan* (Rafi/ Asad Bhopali/ Chitragupt/ *Insaaf,* 1956) is one of them. *Maati ke putle itna na kar tu gumaan* is another. It is from *Sheroo* (1957), the crew being Rafi/ Kaif Irfani/ Madan Mohan. That is why we have poetry such as *Qasmen waade pyaar wafa sab baaten hain baaton ka kya...Aasmaan pe udne waale mitti mein mil jaayega* (Manna/ Indeevar/ Kalyanji-Anandji/ *Upkar,* 1967).

Qasmen waade pyaar wafa sab

Arrogance is different from vanity. In arrogance, it's about power and influence in a non-cosmetic way. In the latter, the focus is on one's looks and appearance. These songs would fit the bill of vanity: *Main bahaaron ki natkhat raani, saari duniya hai mujhpe deewaani* (Asha/ Hasrat/ Shankar-Jaikishan/ *Boot Polish,* 1953), *Main jo chaloon pashchim, purab chale duniya, Meri qismat pe jale saari duniya* (Lata/ Shailendra/ Shankar-Jaikishan/ *Mayur Pankh,* 1953), *Mujhe dekh chaand sharmaaye ghata tham jaaye, main nikloon to kahe haaye zamaana kahe haaye* (Lata/ Nirupa Roy/ Kalyanji-Anandji/ *Samrat Chandragupta,* 1958) and *Nazar bacha ke chale gaye wo warna ghaayal kar deta* (Rafi/ Hasrat/ Shankar-Jaikishan/ *Dil Tera Deewana,* 1962).

While here are some songs that take us on the road of arrogance, in the opening lines themselves: *Hum hain to chaand aur taare, jahaan ke ye rangeen nazaare* (Mukesh, chorus/ Hasrat/ Shankar-Jaikishan/ *Main Nashe Mein Hoon*, 1959), *Main hoon mast madaari, bina teer dil ghaayal kar doon aisa main hoon shikaari* (Mukesh, Lata/ Pt Madhur/ Kalyanji-Anandji/ *Madari*, 1959), *Hum jab chalen to ye jahaan jhoome* (Rafi, chorus/ Sahir/ Usha Khanna/ *Hum Hindustani*, 1960), *Hai aag hamaare seene mein hum aag se khelte jaate hai, Takraate hain jo is taaqat se wo mitti mein mil jaate hain* (Geeta, Mahendra, Mukesh, Lata, Manna Dey/ Shailendra/ Shankar-Jaikishan/ *Jis Desh Mein Ganga Behti Hai*, 1960), *Haseenon ke jalwe pareshaan rehte agar hum na hote* (Manna Dey, Sudha, Asha, Rafi/ Sahir/ Roshan/ *Babar*, 1960), *Jab tak hum hain, hum hi hum hain, Koi naheen duniya mein apne siwa* (Rafi/ Shakeel/ Ravi/ *Pyaar Kiya To Darna Kya*, 1963), *Aji hum se bach ke kahaan jaiyega, jahaan jaiyega humen paaiyega* (Rafi/ Hasrat/ Shankar-Jaikishan/ *Arzoo*, 1965).

All that lasers in on the fact that if people put a little humility into their lives, they won't end up as arrogant or vain as they do. Reading about Julius Caesar and Ozymandias can tell us where not to go. Listening to messages in songs is a wonderful way to learn to behave with justifiable pride that keeps some distance from arrogance. Sadly though, such people are so much into themselves, that they have no time for appreciating literature or music. They end up poorer for it. One thinks of that master, Shakeel, again. Here he is speaking about a woman who seems to have it all: *"Muhabbat choome jinke haath, jawaani paon pade din raat, sune phir haaye wo kiski baat ho…"*. He offers more about her: *"Roop nagar se aa kar chanda unka roop churaaye…Nainon mein unke kaajal ban ke rahe suhaani raat"*. This was Rafi for Naushad in *Aan* (1952).

~~~~

The above was originally featured in DNA Jaipur on 28 October 2018. It has since been updated and enhanced.

~~~~

11

The Irony of an Iron Building

Many of us know that the American Thomas Edison received more than 2000 patents worldwide. He also developed early motion pictures which were shown to people through Kinetoscope, his machine into which you peeped down to see the new invention. Sadly, Edison didn't see a future in this business, so it was the Lumiere brothers of France who grabbed the opportunity to develop the Cinematographe. This was a device that recorded and processed images, to finally project them as moving pictures on a screen. The brothers' first films were very short, which, after being first exhibited in Paris in December 1895, were taken to the road the next year. In July 1896, their work was shown to an exclusive, paying audience at what was called The Watson's Esplanade Hotel in Bombay, a five-minute walk from Gateway of India, from where the brothers entered the country.

The Watson's Esplanade Hotel (more famously just Watson's Hotel) was the pride of the city at the time. There used to be a successful English businessman named John Watson living in Bombay. He was running short of space for his flourishing tailoring and drapery business, so he sourced from England the design and all the prefabricated cast-iron frames for a building that would do fine for his trade and make him proud, especially among expatriates like him. Materials were brought into Bombay in the early 1860s, and as the structure began taking shape, Watson grew increasingly fond of it. Somewhere along the line, he converted the idea into a hotel for European guests. This had especially to do with the stunning, already-blueprinted 98 by 30 feet atrium, which was being built under a skylight. Yes, thought Watson, this would be a ballroom for guests to dance in. The hotel would have wide and long balconies all built around a courtyard, and the balconies would lead to individual rooms. The hotel was readied and it soon became the most stellar example of colonial opulence in India. It also became a whites-only place and remained so for decades.

Enter Jamshetji Tata. Or rather, the unable-to-enter Jamshetji Tata.

Businessman Jamshetji was the man who founded the Tata Group. He felt insulted for they didn't let him into Watson's (whites-only, if you remember). So he decided to set up his own hotel, a few minutes' walk away. This would become The Taj Mahal Hotel, arguably the most famous hotel in India today. He built it on the waterfront opposite the Gateway of India, bang across the landing where passenger ships arrived. One chuckles about an irony: when Watson's Hotel was top class, there was no Taj Mahal Hotel around, and today when the Taj is top class, Watson's has gone, both in name and as a hotel. It is now called Esplanade Mansion and primarily houses lawyers' chambers. We are in mid-2024 and for some two years, this now pathetic-looking structure is being restored under shrouds of cloth.

Watsons Hotel

But in the last quarter of the 19th century, it was high noon for Watson's Hotel, with even the first films shown there, as we just saw. The structure ceased to be a hotel in the 1920s when it was sold to new owners. After that, it changed hands as also names, including being called Mahendra Mansion. One chuckles again, this time for the fact that at one point the same Tata Group, whose founder was once spurned at Watson's entrance, went on to buy the hotel, only to sell it away later.

In recent years, India's oldest cast-iron building was in serious structural trouble. You didn't have to be a structural engineer to certify that; just a layman's glance at the exterior itself was enough. In 2005, parts of the building fell off, killing a person and damaging cars below. Another part fell off in mid-2018, resulting in that wing of the road being closed for months. The city's Municipal Corporation declared the building to be dangerous and advised occupants to vacate it at once, with redevelopment as an option. However, the occupants wouldn't move. Most of them are lawyers whose work engages them with the Bombay High Court which is just a few minutes' walk from the structure. The Mumbai City Civil & Sessions Court is closer still. The lawyers stalled the Municipality's efforts, by taking the matter to court. There was nowhere the municipal folks could turn to, while we had a disaster waiting to happen in South Mumbai's Culture District. That was such an irony because the very people who should have been helping the law take its course were the cause of coming in its way here.

On a different note, there's no signboard of any kind whatsoever that it was here that India's film history had started. This is a sad airbrushing of our history. Not to forget that we produce the highest number of films in the world.

Finally, we come not to an irony, but to a mystery. One wonders how the word hotel came to mean an eatery in Hindustani parlance. Forget about 30 or 40 years ago, even today, some people say, *"Chalo hotal mein khaana khaate hain"* (Let's eat in a hotel today). We still find restaurants named Ram Bharose Hindu Hotel or Allah Bux Hotel across towns in India. These are establishments that will give you food, but no room to stay.

Do you recall these songs engaging with the word?

Aao hamaare hotal mein chai piyo ji garam garam
Biscut kha lo naram naram
Jo dil chaahe maang lo humse
Sab kuchh hai Bhagwan qasam…
Garmi ho to sharbat pee kar kar lo dil ko thanda
Sardi ho to kha lo bhaiya is murghi ka anda
Is hotal ke andar ja kar le lo babu naya janam…
(SD Batish, Sudha Malhotra/ Shakeel/ Ghulam Mohammad/
Kundan, 1955)

This one is more recent:

Aaya main laaya chalta phirta hotal
Garma-garam pakode, tthandi-tthandi botal
(Manna Dey, Mehmood/ Anand Bakshi/ SD Burman/ *Naya*
Zamana, 1971)

And this is even more recent:

Kisi disco mein jaayen
Kisi hotal mein khaayen
Koi dekh le na humen yahaan
Kaheen ghoom ke aayen hum
Chalo ishq ladaayen, chalo ishq ladaayen, chalo ishq ladaayen sanam
(Udit Narayan, Alka Yagnik/ Sameer/ Viju Shah/ *Bade Miyan*
Chhote Miyan, 1998)

Until recently, the iron structure was under the scanner as one of the World's 100 Most Endangered Monuments, as listed by The World Monuments Watch. As the Watch website tells us, "The World Monuments Watch is a global, nomination-based program that uses cultural heritage conservation to empower communities and improve human well-being. Through heritage, the program seeks to improve the resilience of communities, enhance social inclusion, and build new capacities in the heritage conservation field and beyond. Through the Watch, World Monuments Fund partners with local stakeholders to jointly design and implement targeted conservation programs…" The operative words above are "to jointly design and implement". India successfully cooperated with the World Health Organisation to eradicate polio from her soil, and so we are polio-free. On the other hand, our neighbour Pakistan had elements who thought vaccination was a Western conspiracy to sterilize its children. Today, three nations, Pakistan, Afghanistan and Nigeria, are paying the price for coming in the way of progress. That makes me digress to a song that has nothing to do with a hotel. But it sure has to do with irony. Lots of it.

Chingaari koi bhadke to saawan use bujhaaye
Saawan jo agan lagaaye use kaun bujhaaye…
Maana toofaan ke aage naheen chalta zor kisi ka
Maujon ka dosh naheen hai ye dosh hai aur kisi ka
Manjdhaar mein naiyya dole to maanjhi paar lagaaye
Maanjhi jo nao duboye, use kaun bachaaye…

(Kishore Kumar/ Anand Bakshi/ RD Burman/ *Amar Prem*, 1971)

~ ~ ~

The above was originally featured in DNA Jaipur on 6 January 2019. It has since been updated and enhanced.

The Unhurried Flautist

The great bansuri guru Padma Vibhushan Pandit Hariprasad Chaurasia is going to be 75 years old on the 1st of July, 2013. He is going to be celebrated in India and abroad, and before we glance at his work, consider his first name, Hari, pronounced 'hurry' (to rush) in India, and 'harry' (to harass) abroad, neither of the two meanings doing him justice! In fact, the instrument that he plays so wonderfully has always stood for an unhurried and unharried existence. Of Lord Krishna and his frolics. Of pastoral shepherds leading their flock, with time slowing down. An hour of listening to Hariji's flute is an immersive experience in which he can as if retard our sense of time.

Pandit Hariprasad Chaurasia

Both in and out of cinema, his work has been extraordinary. Some classical musicians are not very happy about their association with Hindi cinema, essentially because our film music does not carry a great image, thanks partly to the crass commercialism many film folk demonstrate. Neither is it endorsed by the 'sophisticated' Indian, nor by aficionados in the West; the latter fact is understandable, because while instrumental music has a more-or-less universal air to it, lyrics are not similarly blessed, leaving foreigners with an incomplete listening experience, like a jigsaw puzzle with missing pieces.

But not all classical maestros are sheepish about their role in cinema. Because film music has taken financial care of many gifted musicians, a lot of them have sailed for a while in musical catamarans—boats with two hulls—to offer them an artistic outlet while the commercial inlet has let them run their homes. With Shivkumar Sharma, his music-making partner, Hariprasad Chaurasia also manoeuvred such a boat for many years. When the two became too busy on the concert stage, they didn't really need another commercial inlet, so they had to turn down film offers. But let's start with Hariji's do-re-mi.

The Allahabad born, young Hari was eight when he first learnt singing from Pt. Raja Ram of Banaras. It was to be a quick start-stop, because within a year he switched to playing the flute, after being mesmerized by the flute of Pt. Bholanath, at Banaras again. The young lad learnt from this his guru for 8 years, before becoming an AIR artiste in Cuttack, Orissa.

Much later he was tutored in music by Annapurna Devi, the wife of Pt. Ravi Shankar, the sister of Ustad Ali Akbar Khan, and the daughter of the legendary Ustad Allauddin Khan. This teaching began in 1970, and was unusual: since Annapurna Devi couldn't play the flute, she would sing, and he would follow on the flute. As he was learning, he was performing and growing in repute as an artist who in many ways defined what we call the Bansuri, or the North Indian flute.

This amazing flautist then went on to do hundreds of recordings and performed on the stage, in India and abroad, with the who's who of the music fraternity. He was the first Indian soloist to perform at Bolshoi Theatre in Moscow. He has achieved many such firsts and received several honours, apart from many platinum and gold discs, and so much adoration.

But let's restrict ourselves to his amazing flute in cinema now, both for other composers, as well as for himself, when he teamed with santoor maestro Pt. Shivkumar Sharma, as the Shiv-Hari team. In doing the latter, the duo offered both classical touches and popular tunes, depending on the situations the films warranted. It can be argued with much conviction that when our music was in its darkest tunnel—the 1980s—the music of Shiv-Hari shone to keep listeners optimistic and engaged.

These are the songs where Hariji played his flute for other composers, who are named first:

- Madan Mohan: *Aye sanam aaj ye qasam khaayen* (Talat, Lata/ *Jahan Ara*, 1964)
- Madan Mohan: *Phir wohi shaam* (Talat/ *Jahan Ara*, 1964)
- Kalyanji-Anandji: *Ek tu jo mila,* and *Ek tu na mila* (Raag Mishr Charukeshi/ Lata/ *Himalaya Ki God Mein*, 1965)
- Kalyanji-Anandji: *Chaand si mehbooba ho meri kab aisa maine socha* tha (Mukesh/ *Himalaya Ki God Mein*, 1965)
- Kalyanji-Anandji: *Main to ik khwaab hoon* (Mukesh/ *Himalaya Ki God Mein*, 1965)
- Khayyam: *Bahaaro, mera jeevan bhi sanwaaro* (Lata/ *Aakhri Khat*, 1966)
- Laxmikant-Pyarelal: *Suno sajna papeehe ne* (Raag Yaman based/ Lata/ *Aaye Din Bahaar Ke*, 1966)
- RD Burman: *Chingari koi bhadke* (Kishore/ *Amar Prem*, 1971)
- RD Burman: *Kuchh to log kahenge* (Raag Mishr Khamaj/ Kishore/ *Amar Prem*, 1971)
- RD Burman: *Raina beeti jaaye* (Raag Mishr Pilu/ Lata/ *Amar Prem*, 1971)

Raina beeti jaaye

- ➤ Madan Mohan: *Mast pawan dole re* (Lata/ *Bawarchi*, 1972)
- ➤ Madan Mohan: *More naina bahaayen neer* (Lata/ *Bawarchi*, 1972)
- ➤ Madan Mohan: *Tum bin jeevan kaisa jeevan* (Raag Bhinn Shadaj/ Manna Dey/ *Bawarchi*, 1972)
- ➤ RD Burman: *Gum hain kisi ke pyaar mein* (Kishore, Lata/ *Rampur Ka Laxman*, 1972)
- ➤ Ravindra Jain: *Door hai kinaara* (Rabindra sangeet based/ Manna Dey/ *Saudagar*, 1973)
- ➤ Shyamal Mitra: *Dil aisa kisi ne mera toda* (Kishore/ *Amanush*, 1975)
- ➤ RD Burman: *O maanjhi re* (Kishore/ *Khushbu*, 1975)

And his flute was featured solo in many songs composed by the Shiv-Hari combine:

- ➤ *Hum chup hain ke dil sun rahe hain* (Lata, Kishore/ *Faasle*, 1985)
- ➤ *Parbat se kaali ghata takraayi* (Asha, Vinod/ *Chandni*, 1989)
- ➤ *Tere-mere honthon pe meethe-meethe geet mitwa* (Lata, Babla/ *Chandni*, 1989)
- ➤ *Kabhi main kahoon* (Lata, Hariharan/ *Lamhe*, 1991)
- ➤ *Megha re megha re* (Lata, Ila Arun/ *Lamhe*, 1991)

Beyond the microcosm of these songs, the maestro's work can be enjoyed in many more ditties, even as his work off-cinema has for long been awesome. With him at 75, what do we fans wish for him? Where does this Krishna-bhakt go from here? Perhaps a Bharat Ratna would help. His own wish is summed up by this line: "I dare to dream that through my students my flute will be left behind as the memory of Krishna".

For hard-core music lovers like me, the acid test is the flute piece you hear in the first interlude of a tune made by Laxmikant-Pyarelal, *Suno sajna*, listed above. Pyarelal himself said it so well for upcoming flautists: "Hear this piece again and again; only after that, attempt to play it that way". Novices are requested to forget looking at their watches, for, learning to play The Master's way means "No Hurry!"

~~~~

The above was originally published in DNA Jaipur on 9 June 2013. It has since been updated and enhanced.

~~~~

13

Mera Naam Hai Shabnam...

If it's the last few days in December, and you are in Mumbai, driving along the curve between National Sports Club of India and Haji Ali, expect to be confronted with a huge, high-profile hoarding that shouts:

Bindu and Champak Zaveri wish you a Merry Xmas and a Happy New Year!

The board is two-sided, so the greeting appears to motorists on both sides. This has happened for over thirty years now. In the late 1980s, I used to wonder who these Zaveris were, and why they chose this unusual way of wishing people. It took many winters for my curiosity to increase and develop into a critical mass, enough for me to want to get to the bottom of this mystery. It turned out that this message was offered by the famous actress of Hindi cinema, Bindu, and her husband Champaklal Zaveri. The latter is in the outdoor advertising trade, so this can be an effective thing to do, especially if you are proud of your wife and her accomplishments.

So one day last week, on behalf of so many of us cinema and music buffs, I finally decided to wish the lady a Happy New Year too. Because who doesn't like to be greeted back? Especially film stars, whose *raison d'etre* can be recognition and approval by cinemagoers like us. Not that Bindu hadn't heard from her admirers. She even had people writing to her in blood, threatening suicide if she didn't accept their matrimonial proposal. But Bindu was married, very early too, before she was an adult. You wonder what happened to the rejected candidates, but we are getting ahead of the story.

~~~~

I get into her ocean-view apartment on the third floor of an upscale building in South Mumbai. Before the lady shows up, several servants appear, offering me tea and Shrewsbury biscuits and allowing me time to breathe in the ambience. The lady does live well, on an entire floor too, with remarkable furniture and some of the finest objects d'art from around the globe. In the living room sits an attractive, well-stocked bar—stools and all— in mute but eloquent testimony of the good life. Moreover, since the bar sits near the centre of the living room, its personified message is staring at us: Everything revolves around me.

The sun is going to set in minutes now, so a servant arrives to work on a remote control to retract two electrically activated roller-blinds, while two other blinds are commanded to come down instead. Clearly, these people know what they need to do. I keep hearing a high-decibel parrot from an adjoining room, and fully aware that pets mean a lot to their owners, I decide that's going to be my ice-breaker with the lady. Bindu arrives and the idea works. Peeku is of African origin and all of 15 years of age. He speaks, sings, whistles and is very friendly indeed. Ice broken, we get going about her.

Bindu was born at Grant Road, Bombay many moons ago, and she went to National High School near her home. At school, she participated in many plays and dances. Her father Nanubhai Desai used to manage Central Studio where Tardeo AC market stands today. In the studio, Nanubhai came in touch with many filmmakers such as Mehboob Khan, J. Om Prakash and Mohan Kumar. Still a teenager, she got her break ('via-via', she says), playing the daughter of Dharmendra and Mala Sinha in *Anpadh* (1962), and hitting the jackpot right away, with a decent role and a wonderful song filmed on her: *Jeeya le gayo ji mora saanwariya*. Created by the Lata-Raja Mehdi Ali Khan-Madan Mohan combine, the song was a dream start. Since songs from the golden era tended to outlive the films they were made for, most actors would be delighted with such a marvellous beginning.
~~~~

Nothing significant happened for the next six years (except marriage at age 17), because filmmakers still considered Bindu to be too young for significant roles, and she didn't want just *any* screen appearances. It was Raj Khosla who was to offer her an adult break for his upcoming film *Do Raaste* (1969), based on *Neelaambari*, a Marathi book by Chandrakant Kakodkar. Bindu was offered the role of *Neelaambari*, even as he changed the title because it sounded mythological. Now this was a big break, but she had to think about it because *Neelaambari* was a negative character. She went for it. She also showed up opposite newcomer Vinod Khanna in *Nateeja* in the same year.

Shakti Samanta was next, offering her a vamp's role in *Kati Patang* (1971). She not only had a negative role again but had to sing and dance to a cabaret. Thumbs up she went again. That's where *Mera naam hai Shabnam* happened. It clicked big time and the lady was high in space.

She featured in a few more films after which Hrishikesh Mukherjee came forward and surprised the industry by casting her in a positive role as Amitabh's sensitive confidante in *Abhimaan* (1973). The film clicked and Bindu's role was enjoyed. The actress had arrived.

Here are some songs—mostly cabarets, qawwalis, and mujras—filmed on her:

- *Dil karne laga hai pyaar tumhen* (*Nateeja*, 1969)
- *Waada tera waada* (Rajesh Khanna to Bindu/ *Dushman*, 1971)
- *Jiske liye mera dil jale haan saari raat* (*Haseenon Ka Devta*, 1971)
- *Ek to ye bairi saawan…O haaye main ki karaan* (*Dastaan*, 1972)
- *Pee meri aankhon se* (*Dhadkan*, 1972)
- *Maine honthon se lagaayi to hangaama ho gaya* (*Anhoni*, 1973)
- *Raaz ki baat keh doon to* (*Dharma*, 1973)
- *Aa ke dard jawaan hai* (*Pran Jaaye Par Vachan Na Jaaye*, 1973)
- *Sharma na yoon, ghabra na yoon* (*Joshila*, 1973)
- *Apne dil mein jagah deejiye* (*Hawas*, 1974)
- *Main ek ladki hoon* (*Nirmaan*, 1974)
- *Dilruba Dilli waale* (*Dus Numberi*, 1976)
- *Mera dil chura kar na aankhen chura* (*Shankar Shambhu*, 1976)
- *Arre aa gaye hum dildaar* (*Chalta Purza*, 1977)
- *Sau saal jeeyo tum jaan meri* (With Reena Roy/ *Heera Moti*, 1979)

Bindu--usually, but not always, a vamp

Bindu danced to songs in over one hundred films, while the features she acted in were well over twice that number. Clearly then, she cannot be seen as an item girl, the kind whose only function is to titillate or seduce in a song, and to make a quick exit soon after. Not at all. It's not only her ability to dance and titillate, but also her convincing acting that had major directors like Hrishikesh Mukherjee, BR Chopra, Mohan Sehgal and Raj Khosla sign her up for meaningful roles. They were able to celebrate the fact that she lent heavy conviction in her portrayals, which is why she was signed up as Dilip Kumar's wife, no less, in *Dastaan* (1972), as also Amitabh's confidante in *Abhimaan* (1973), as we saw above. Not to forget that in the same year (1973) as she played Amitabh's friend in a positive role in *Abhimaan*, Prakash Mehra cast her in *Zanjeer* to do a cabaret for the same Amitabh. She danced with much conviction to *Dil jalon ka dil jala ke, kya milega dilruba*. And as she lip-synced this, who was watching? Ajit, whose moll she was, remember? Mona darling! Yes, moll, vamp, seductress, the world came to see her largely as a negative woman, which was like validating her talent.

Her other notable films were *Aaya Saawan Jhoomke* (1969), *Ittefaq* (1969), *Haseenon Ka Devta* (1971), *Mere Jeevan Saathi* (1972), *Raja Jani* (1972), *Dharma* (1973), going on to *Hero* (1983), *Biwi Ho To Aisi* (1988), *Krishan Kanhaiya* (1990), and *Om Shanti Om* (2007); there were many more films over the decades.

The lady is ageing gracefully and has a healthy sense of humour. She also spends time in her pooja room, which she invited me to see. One doesn't normally see pooja rooms that have a dedicated air-conditioner, another eloquent witness in her home, this one suggesting the kind of time people spend here. Bindu and her husband do not have children. But she has several siblings, and the couple have many friends. Plus they have the gregarious Peeku.

As she sees me off at the lift, I ask her one last question: "So what's the message you'd like to give your fans Binduji?" Pat comes her reply, "Happy New Year!"

~ ~ ~ ~

The above was originally published in DNA Jaipur on 27 December 2015. It has since been edited.

14

Door Hai Kinara

Water sports on and near a beach can be such fun! Millions of people all over the world visit the thousands of beaches around the world for fun and frolic. They play Frisbee, prance around the shore, make sand castles, exercise with hula hoops, and pitch tents. Sun worshippers tan themselves, and cyclists do their cycling. There's so much more to do at the beach, like surfing, swimming, or just plain wading in the water. If you are in India, maybe you'll fly a kite, play football, hit a cricket ball, or ride an escorted pony. The annual Ganesh immersion ritual also loves the beach, and so do the 10 day Ramleelas, with an effigy of Raavan burnt in a grand finale.

Time has been good for beach reputations around the world, including in India, but that's not the story in some places like Mumbai. We'll consider why, but let's see some of the inviting sands first. And even before that, what exactly does a beach mean?

A beach is the soft land along the edge of sea or ocean water and is usually made up of any combination of these materials: sand (the main thing), gravel, pebbles, cobbles, rock, and shells. That permits us to do many of the fun things described above. A coast on the other hand is a wider term which refers to the junction of land and water, whether it's a beach or rocks or a cliff, even a man-made wall. Peninsular India with its huge 7500 kilometre coastline has hundreds of beaches, in so many states.

Here are some of the dozens of enjoyable beaches dotting the country: Mandvi, Porbandar, and Dwarka in Gujarat; Baga, Palolem, Calangute and Varca in Goa; Bangaram in Lakshadweep; Kovalam,

Cherai, Marari and Varkala in Kerala; Ramakrishna and Rushikonda in Andhra Pradesh; Mandarmani in West Bengal; Kashid and Alibag in Maharashtra; Puri in Odisha, Nagoa in Diu; Marina in Tamil Nadu; and Karmatang, Elephanta and Radhanagar beaches in Andaman and Nicobar.

Most of these beaches and many of the others are more or less in fine shape, without too much litter and pollution. However, the same cannot be said of 2 of the 5 key beaches in or near Mumbai, ie, the ones at Girgaum and Juhu (as against the ones at Shivaji Park, Alibag, or Madh Island). The nightmarish litter and pollution caused by the annual Ganpati immersions and Raavan burning puts many people off. Compound that with the heavy proliferation of the *bhel puri* and *kulfi* stalls with their high-pressure soliciting. Add to that the dubious kind of professionals who populate the area, such as snake-oil salesmen who have a cure for all your ills real or imagined, the shady pedestrian masseuses who carry a dhurrie and coloured lubricants in a dozen bottles, and the strange community of yellow turbaned fellows who will clean your ears with a dangerously long metal rod that has a scoop at the probing end. All that has made these two beaches places you want to avoid. Yes, both these beaches attract huge crowds, especially on holidays. But you are not likely to find too many discerning visitors here. In a 2010 survey by Tripadvisor, Juhu Chowpatty earned the dubious distinction of being India's dirtiest beach, with 65% respondents giving it the thumbs down. This unattractiveness has been scanned by our mainstream cinema, which runs away from beaches when shooting in Mumbai. It wasn't always so.

After all, it was about here that Jeevan and Cuckoo danced in *Afsana* (1951), the number *Chowpatty pe kal jo tujhse aankh matakka ho gaya* (Shamshad and Rafi for composing duo Husnlal and Bhagatram). Chowpatty of course means the beach. Here are some more songs that were shot on beach sands:

> *Zor laga ke haiyya, pair jama ke haiyya* (Geeta/ SD Burman/ *Jaal*, 1952)
> *Chori chori meri gali aana hai bura* (Lata/ SD Burman/ *Jaal*, 1952)

- *Chaandni raaten pyaar ki baaten* (Lata, Hemant/ SD Burman/ *Jaal*, 1952)
- *Pighla hai sona door gagan par* (Lata/ SD Burman/ *Jaal*, 1952)
- *Jaayen to jaayen kahaan* (Talat/ SD Burman/ *Taxi Driver*, 1954)
- *Ab wo karam karen ke sitam main nashe mein hoon* (Rafi/ N. Datta/ *Marine Drive*, 1955)
- *Muhabbat yoon bhi hoti hai* (Asha/ N. Datta/ *Marine Drive*, 1955)
- *Phir wahi chaand wahi hum wahi tanhai hai* (Lata, Chitalkar/ C Ramchandra/ *Baarish*, 1957)
- *Aankh khulte hi tum chhup gaye ho kahaan* (Lata/ SD Burman/ *Munimji*, 1955)
- *Chain naheen aaye kahaan dil jaaye* (Lata/ Madan Mohan/ *Samundar*, 1957)
- *Kya saath mera doge tum pyaar ki raahon mein* (Mukesh, Lata/ Madan Mohan/ *Samundar*, 1957)
- *Aa ja kaheen se aaja dil ka qaraar leke* (Lata/ Madan Mohan/ *Samundar*, 1957)
- *Jaan-e-jigar yoon hi agar hota rahe ishaara tera* (Asha, Rafi/ OP Nayyar/ *Mujrim*, 1958)
- *Aa bhi ja bewafa* (Asha, Agha Sarwar/ Bipin-Babul/ *Raat Ke Raahi*, 1959)
- *Maine pee hai pee hai pee hai* (Rafi/ Bipin-Babul/ *Raat Ke Raahi*, 1959)
- *Khwaab mein kahaan miloge* (Rafi, Lata/ Iqbal Qureshi/ *Bindiya*, 1960)
- *Dil apna aur preet paraayi* (Lata/ Shankar-Jaikishan/ *Dil Apna Aur Preet Parayi*, 1960)
- *Sheesha-e-dil itna na uchhaalo* (Lata/ Shankar-Jaikishan/ *Dil Apna Aur Preet Parayi*, 1960)
- *Jaane kahaan gayi* (Rafi/ Shankar-Jaikishan/ *Dil Apna Aur Preet Parayi*, 1960)
- *Dil aye dil bahaaron se mil* (Talat, Lata/ Shankar-Jaikishan/ *Ek Phool Char Kaante*, 1960)
- *Kabhi to milegi kaheen to milegi* (Lata/ Roshan/ *Aarti*, 1962)
- *Baar baar tohe kya samjhaaye* (Lata, Rafi/ Roshan/*Aarti*, 1962)

- *Saagar pe aaj maujon ka raaj* (Lata/ Shankar-Jaikishan/ *Rangoli*, 1962)
- *Ek dil aur sau afsaane* (Lata/ Shankar-Jaikishan/ *Ek Dil Sau Afsaane*, 1963)
- *Tumse maano na maano mujhe tumse* (Rafi, Asha/ Iqbal Qureshi/ *Cha Cha Cha*, 1964)

Tumse, maano na maano
mujhe tumse...

- *Chale ja rahe hain muhabbat ke maare* (Manna Dey/ Jaidev/ *Kinare Kinare*, 1964)
- *Har aas ashkbaar hai* (Lata/ Jaidev/ *Kinare Kinare*, 1964)
- *Is duniya mein jeena hai to* (Lata/ Shankar-Jaikishan/ *Gumnaam*, 1965)
- *Pehla pehla pyaar hai ye* (Suman/ Shankar-Jaikishan/ *Budtameez*, 1966)
- *Kis qadar zaalim ho qaatil* (Manna, Asha/ Kalyanji-Anandji/ *Dil Ne Pukara*, 1967)
- *Aaj puraani raahon se* (Rafi/ Naushad/ *Aadmi*, 1968)
- *Dil karne laga hai pyaar tumhen* (Rafi, Hemlata/ Usha Khanna/ *Nateeja*, 1969)
- *Zindagi kaisi hai paheli haaye* (Manna Dey/ Salil Chowdhury/ *Anand*, 1970)
- *Jhilmil sitaaron ka aangan hoga* (Rafi, Lata/ Laxmikant-Pyarelal/ *Jeevan Mrityu*, 1970)

> *Sundar ho aisi tum jidhar chalo* (Rafi/ RD Burman/ *Dil Ka Raja*, 1972)
> *Hum tumhen chaahte hain aise* (Anand Kumar, Manhar, Kanchan/ Kalyanji-Anandji/ *Qurbani*, 1980)
> *Zindagi mere ghar aana zindagi* (Bhupinder, Anuradha/ Jaidev/ *Dooriyan*, 1981)
> *Solah baras ki baali umar ko salaam* (Lata/ Laxmikant-Pyarelal/ *Ek Duje Ke Liye* (1981)
> *Tere mere beech mein* (Lata, SP Balasubramaniam/ Laxmikant-Pyarelal/ *Ek Duje Ke Liye*, 1981)
> *Bichhde abhi to bus hum kal parson…Lambi judaayi* (Reshma/ Laxmikant-Pyarelal/ *Hero*, 1983)
> *Kitne phool kitne ped kitne panchhi* (Kishore/ Bappi Lahiri/ *Teri Baahon Mein*, 1984)
> *Saagar kinaare dil ye pukaare* (Lata, Kishore/ RD Burman/ *Saagar*, 1985)
> *Panchhi nadiya pawan ke jhonke* (Sonu, Alka/ Anu Malik/ *Refugee*, 2000)

A few songs were filmed not on a beach but on a coast with rocks strewn about. That's not really the same thing, because such coasts have limited entertainment value. Do recall these five songs:

> *Ro-oon main saagar ke kinaare* (CH Atma/ Shankar-Jaikishan/ *Nagina*, 1951)
> *Sach hue sapne tere* (Asha/ SD Burman/ *Kala Bazaar*, 1960)
> *Aap ne yaad dilaaya to mujhe yaad aaya* (Rafi, Lata/ Roshan/ *Aarti*, 1962)
> *Nadiya chale chale re dhaara* (Manna/ Kalyanji-Anandji/ *Safar*, 1970)
> *Raat kali ek khwaab mein aayi* (Kishore/ RD Burman/ *Buddha Mil Gaya*, 1971)

As seen earlier, a beach or a coastline needs a body of water to justify its existence. But can a body of water exist without any contact with any coast, any land at all? A sea without a shore? I was stunned to find just one such sea. The Sargasso Sea, located in the middle of the Atlantic

Ocean, is remarkable for its serenity, surrounded by turbulence. Its contours, entirely within the big ocean, can be seen from the air, the hue changing dramatically where it starts, to a deep blue. Baffling scientists for decades, the Sargasso Sea is the strangest sea on the planet. Wonder why no one has made a film on these waters within waters. *Door Hai Kinara* would be such an apt Indian title.

~~~~

The above was originally published as *Tere Mere Beach Mein* in DNA Jaipur on 31 May 2015. It has since been updated and enhanced.

~~~~

15

Ameen Sayani—Voice Extraordinaire!

"Behno Aur Bhaiyo…main aap ka dost Ameen Sayani bol raha hoon! Aur kitne saalon se bol raha hoon…aap sunte rahe hain na? Ji haan main December 1952 se bol raha hoon, jab main bees saal ka tha. Aur aaj… lekin arre arre, maine to shaayad apni umar bhi bata di!…"

Ameen Sayani spoke the above lines one day when we were toasting him on a stage in Mumbai. This was in response to audience demand for him to say *Behno aur Bhaiyo* the way he used to start his popular radio shows that ran for decades. Ameen Saab not only obliged his fans, he went a bit further than that. In doing that extra bit, he made us focus on his remarkably long and fruitful career. Let's consider the extraordinary run of this broadcaster's life.

Ameen Sayani

Ameen was born on 21ˢᵗ December 1932 to Kutchi parents who had migrated to Bulsar. His brother was the celebrated Hamid Sayani who hosted the popular Bournvita Quiz Contest on radio in his wonderful rich baritone voice. Little Ameen learnt his early speech fundamentals like inflexions and breath control from his brother. When he was 7, they put him on the air, to participate in a children's show. Around this time, Mahatma Gandhi advised his mother, a strong Gandhian, to start a magazine to educate people, which she did. Her fortnightly, called *Rehbar* (meaning the guide), is where young Ameen became many things such as a peon, bill collector, and writer. This magazine used to be published in English, Hindi, Urdu and Gujarati, and here the impassioned lad learned languages. Somewhere along the line, Ameen also started loving the poetry of Rabindranath Tagore and becoming deeply immersed in Rabindra Sangeet too. We will revert to Tagore soon but first a digression.

As we know, sometimes small events cause huge repercussions. In France in September 1918, a British soldier refused to shoot a German Lance Corporal named Adolf Hitler, thereby saving his life. That was not a small thing by itself. But compared to what Hitler did in the run-up to the Second World War and during it, pales to insignificance. Later in October 1962, we almost had a nuclear war that would surely have destroyed our planet completely, had it not been for a Soviet officer commanding a submarine carrying nuclear weapons. His name was Vasili Arkhipov, and you can look him up in The Cuban Missile Crises.

As for Ameen Sayani, he could not have imagined that he would owe his phenomenal success in some part to a letter written in 1940 by Tagore—the man he admired. This letter, addressed to All India Radio, urged the authorities to desist from using the harmonium in their studios. This was a French instrument, and as such did not serve our cultural interests well. He told the British Manager of AIR that he had the instrument banished from Shantiniketan. Tagore knew that the French were not only controlling parts of India, such as Pondicherry, but they were also the enemies of the British for centuries. It was a plan that was unlikely to fail.

The harmonium was banished from the AIR studios for some 30 years. That was a mistake. This is a wondrous instrument that blends easily with our kind of music, i.e., ghazals, bhajans, qawwalis, film music, and also Rabindra Sangeet itself. That is why some of the most tenacious exponents of Rabindra Sangeet, like Pankaj Mullick and Hemant Kumar, always practised and performed on a harmonium. Despite that, after the 1952 elections, the new I & B Minister, BV Keskar, went even further. He banned film music from AIR. That was a huge mistake, except for Ameen Sayani for whom it was a miracle. Consider why.

In the 1940s our music was widening its welcome by including foreign instruments and their gifted players. A great number of Goan and Parsi musicians were having to give up the employment of their British bosses who were leaving India. These musicians with their Western influences were coming into the recording studios of composers Naushad and SD Burman, C Ramchandra and more, bringing with them their euphonic sounds in brass, guitars, violins, mandolins and more. All these were lifting our music into a high orbit. What a strange anomaly then that while people were enjoying the accordion in say, Naushad's *Dil mein chhupa ke pyaar ka toofaan le chale* (*Aan*, 1952), we couldn't get to hear it on AIR! Not just songs with foreign instruments, we couldn't listen to any popular songs on AIR. Think of the songs of *Mahal* (1949), *Babul* (1950), *Albela* (1951), *Awara* (1951), and dozens of such films with hundreds of their songs. No sir, not on All India Radio!

All India Radio's divorce from reality was why film producers rushed to Radio Ceylon, just as a young man was clearing his throat to become destiny's elected one. You wonder if it's a debatable point whether there would have been an Ameen Sayani had All India Radio not banned Hindi film music. As it turned out, the planets were arranged perfectly for the young man. In the heady days of the '50s, '60s and later, Ameen Sayani scripted, spoke on and helped produce several thousands of Geetmala shows coming out of Ceylon (later called Sri Lanka). These airwaves took our music and Ameen Saab's super interviews to millions of listeners in Asia and parts of Africa, and his music *paayedaans* became a rage. Come 8 p.m. Wednesday, people sat glued to their receivers, sometimes twiddling the dial for the shortwaves to behave!

Ameen Sayani also hosted hundreds of stage shows and conducted as many advertising workshops, while making many a cameo appearance in cinema too. His several CD sets called *Geetmala Ki Chhaon Mein*, tracing great songs that did not bust the charts, have kept him busy the past few years. But it was with his weekly heart-stopping *Behno aur Bhaiyo*, that he won us over. We are in 2012, and he still hosts a weekly show on a Mumbai radio station, and you can bet your last Rupee you can't figure out from his voice whether we are in 1962 or 2012! There is no question that a slew of his fans have been nannied from the cradle to the grave with his music shows.

~~~~

The above essay was originally featured in DNA Jaipur on 28 October 2012. It has since been updated and enhanced. This is different from my essay on Ameen Sayani in my book The Hindi Music Jukebox.

PS: Ameen Sayani passed away in Mumbai on 20th February 2024. The legendary broadcaster was more than just a radio host for decades. He ran an advertising company, lent his voice in thousands of commercials, conducted beauty pageants, and also appeared in films, in front of the camera. His was a life illuminated.

Isn't it time for the Guinness people to include him as by far the world's longest-serving radio broadcaster, with an expanse of some 60 years? It won't make a difference to him now that he has gone, but what about us, his admirers?

~~~~

16

Would You Like Some Tea, Your Majesty?

In November 2015, Indian Prime Minister Narendra Modi lunched with Queen Elizabeth II at Buckingham Palace. He took with him several gifts that included some fine Darjeeling tea. He has come a long way: at one time he helped his father make and sell tea to passengers at a railway station, and today he is Prime Minister of the world's most populous democracy.

Clearly, the country he leads loves tea because that drink is omnipresent across his land. Cutting economic barriers, tea is the favoured beverage among Indians. We have it in homes, offices, and restaurants but also drink it on the streets. *Cutting chai*, as it's called in Maharashtra, is served in small doses usually in vertically grooved glasses or disposable paper ones, not bone-china cups. Other places offer them in porcelain mugs or cups called *pyaalis*. On some railway stations and many places dotted around Orissa and West Bengal—as also in upscale restaurants in towns like Mumbai and Delhi—you can have it in *kulhads* (clay cups), the kind that offer a unique flavour of tea with the raw hint of mother earth.

Tiny tea stalls dot the landscape in huge numbers nationwide, even if Google Maps won't show them to you. We drink the beverage so often that we see ourselves as a nation of tea drinkers. But are we? Well, at least comparatively it doesn't seem so. Here are some stats:

In 2022, India was the second country (after China) in tea production. But in exporting the stuff, we were the fourth (behind China, Kenya, and Sri Lanka), because of a huge domestic demand. Amazingly though, when it comes to tea consumption per capita, we are not even among the top 55 countries of the world, with figures not available after that number!

Turkey heads the list of countries with the highest per capita consumption of tea (3.16 kilos), with Mexico being the 55th in the list (0.014 kilos). Hence we consume less than 0.014 kilos per head per year. That comes as a surprise to many of us. Even so, tea remains central to so much that we do. Not so coffee, not by a long shot. Stats from 2014 inform us that per capita, we are not even in the first 100 countries in the consumption of the beverage.

Our first Prime Minister Pt Nehru famously loved tea, almost as much as he loved wearing a rosebud on his jacket. India's last Viceroy Mountbatten loved it too. And it has for long been the favoured drink of the rich and famous. But it is the drink for the poor and unknown too. Like death, it is tea that is the great leveller.

Now consider our culture, which still has a lot to do with arranged marriages. When parents of the two sides meet formally for the first time, they usually meet over tea. A few people from the boy's side go to the girl's home on an initial recce mission, and there's nothing quite like tea to start conversations and wash down our observations. Such an invitation is called *chai pe bulaana*.

That is what happened when actor Dinesh Hingoo arrived with his nincompoop son, who wanted to marry Dilip Tahil's daughter Kajol in *Baazigar* (1993). It was a tea-on-the-lawns scene, bearer and all. Or take Tina Munim who couldn't have been more open when she sang to Rajesh Khanna these lines in *Souten* (1983): *Shaayad meri shaadi ka khayaal dil mein aaya hai, isi liye mummy ne meri tumhen chai pe bulaaya hai.* While he, sensing a trap, responded thus: *Panchhi akela dekh mujhe ye jaal bichhaaya hai, isi liye mummy ne teri mujhe chai pe bulaaya hai.* It's another thing that in her real life, Ms. Munim first declined a tea date with the wealthy Anil Ambani, and then later invited him home for it.

For some reason, we also associate the rains with tea. One wonders if the film *Shree 420* sowed the seeds to begin this happy association, or if the idea is older. Wanting to impress Nargis, downmarket but glib talking Raj Kapoor asks her if she'd like some tea, "Perhaps in the Taj Mahal Hotel or Greens Hotel?" Broke, of course, he proceeds to take her to a pavement tea vendor. "Footpath Palace Hotel" is what he calls the place where they sip tea before the rains come down. *Pyaar hua iqraar hua hai* was born just after such a 'tea moment', the first flush of love mixed with a good cuppa to create a divine melody.

An interesting element in the film *Grah Pravesh* (1979) has tea playing a subtle role. The unhappily married Sanjeev Kumar loves to drink coffee, but when he is seduced by Sarika, she converts him into a tea lover as well! The seduction is in fact triggered by her giving him tea, as the song *Aap agar aap na hote* plays in the background.

Since tea estates make for beautiful locales, hundreds of Hindi and regional features have been filmed in and around such estates found in the Nilgiris, Darjeeling and Munnar. We ignore those scenes today and focus on just odes to the beverage. Here are a few songs that make a specific mention:

- ➤ *Chai piyogi Rani, aao chai pilaayen* (Kishore Sahu, Pratima Dasgupta/ *Kunwara Baap*, 1942)
- ➤ *Aao hamaare hotal mein chai peeyo ji garam garam* (SD Batish, Sudha/ *Kundan*, 1955)

Aao hamaare hotal mein

- *O daata o daata de humko bhi ek pyaara bangla* (with its *Khule aankh aur bistar par chai mile/* Rafi, Asha/ *Aji Bus Shukriya*, 1958)
- *Do ghoont chai pee aur sair duniya ki* (Rafi/ *Sanjog*, 1961)
- *Ek ek ek, ek chai ki pyaali* (Rafi/ *Zamana Badal Gaya*, 1961)
- *Aahen na bhar thandi-thandi* (with its *Garam garam chai pee le/* Lata/ *Ban Phool*, 1971)
- *Pyaara ik bangla ho* (with its *Naukaron ke hote khaana khud banaoon, Chai bhi apne haathon se pilaoon/* Lata, Bappi Lahiri/ *Aap Ki Khatir*, 1977)
- *Garam garam chai* (Baba Sehgal/ *Dance Party*, 1995)
- *Ek garam chai ki pyaali ho* (Anu Malik/ *Har Dil Jo Pyaar Karega*, 2000)

Let's return for a bit to Mr. Modi who for his humble tea beginnings has been insulted multiple times in his life. One is reminded of a story about US President Abraham Lincoln. When he was elected President, his father was a shoemaker. That offended a lot of wealthy people with ambitions. "Mr. Lincoln", said one aristocrat in an assembly, "You should not forget that your father used to make shoes for my family". Everyone laughed. Lincoln looked the man in the eye and said, "Sir, I know that my father used to make shoes in your house for your family, and there'll be many others here. Because the way he made shoes, nobody else could. He was a creator. His shoes were not just shoes, he poured his whole soul into them. I want to ask you, have you any complaints? Because I know how to make shoes myself. If you have any complaints I can make another pair of shoes. But as far as I know, nobody has ever complained about my father's shoes. He was a genius, a creator, and I am proud of my father"

It cannot be very different for Mr. Modi, the son of a tea maker. The world community is now aware of this. Some time back, when US President Barack Obama and Mr. Modi met and settled into their sofas, the Prime Minister poured the visitor a cup of tea and handed it to him. "Prime Minister Modi, thank you for hosting me, including our *Chai Pe Charcha*", is what Mr. Obama said, eliciting ripples of merriment among those who understood his fine reference here.

So when he was having that royal lunch with Queen Elizabeth, perhaps Mr. Modi may have thought of the quite remarkable journey of his life, from a humble lad making tea to being an honoured guest of Her Majesty the Queen. Many people also know that he has a soft corner for Hindi film music though we don't know if he he aware of this song: *Wo bhooli daastaan lo phir yaad aa gayi,* with its line *Kahaan thi zindagi meri, kahaan par aa gayi* from *Sanjog* (1961). Couldn't be truer in Mr. Modi's case. Instead, the grapevine suggests that he joked thus with Queen Elizabeth: *"Your Majesty, thanks for the wonderful lunch. Would you like some tea now? They say I make it well"*

~~~~

The above was originally published in DNA Jaipur on 15 November 2015. It has since been updated and enhanced.

♪♫♩♪
~~~~

Balraj Sahni, Jailor to Prisoner in Sixty Minutes!

The results of the Prime Minister's slogan of *Sabka Saath, Sabka Vikas* (everyone's support, inclusive growth) warrant a review by him and his team. While India's parameters do show an increasingly uniform society and higher standards of living, all isn't hunky dory. On the social front, discrimination for reasons of caste is still around, even if not in great strength as it was, say in Gandhiji's days. Intolerance too keeps rearing its ugly head now and then, and financial growth seems to be lop-sided if we are to go by a study published earlier this year. Oxfam is an independent international group driven by its mission of reducing injustice and economic inequality by highlighting it worldwide. In January 2018, it submitted that in India, the richest 1% of the population controlled about 73% of the wealth generated the previous year, while the bottom 50% controlled just 1% of that wealth. Phew!

It is never easy to run a country, especially one as large and disparate as ours. Some have compared the job with stitching buttons on ice cream. Many even wonder how we are together to begin with. This writer has for decades known about these challenges, but has long considered that cinema and its music have been key social glues that bind us together. Even so, politicians can do with the help of watchdogs, never mind that sometimes, rulers consider such watchdogs to be hurlers in the ditch, people who give unwanted and incompetent advice to others, sometimes to incite a mass rebellion. Such a rebellion happened in Bangladesh on 5th August 2024, when the country was taken over by the Army and its Prime Minister Sheikh Hasina fled to India.

Balraj Sahni in Hulchal

But back to India and the collective benefits of the harvest. It is in the area of collective work and *sab ki* enjoyment of the fruits of work that the following songs were written, with visuals supporting the idea of community struggles and payoffs. Since the affirmations have to come from everyone, such narratives always include a chorus:

- *Aaj sookhe kheton mein aayi bahaar* (writer unknown/ *Dharti Ke Lal*, 1946)
- *Dharti kahe pukaar ke…mausam beeta jaaye* (Shailendra/ *Do Bigha Zameen*, 1953)
- *Saathi haath badhaana* (Sahir/ *Naya Daur*, 1958)
- *Mehnatkash insaan jaag uttha* (Shailendra/ *Insaan Jaag Utha*, 1959)
- *Aao jhoome gaayen* (Anand Bakshi/ *Paraya Dhan*, 1971)

The songs from *Dharti Ke Lal, Do Bigha Zameen* and *Paraya Dhan* above featured Balraj Sahni, who in real life was one of society's watchdogs. He was a member of IPTA (Indian People's Theatre Association), a leftist organization. Through his statements and roles, he kept sending out piercing messages to build his image as a leftist. But for their strong leftist thoughts or criticism of the powers-that-be, people like him, Majrooh Sultanpuri and Anil Biswas were put behind bars. In fact, during the days when *Hulchal* (1951) was on the floors, Sahni was in jail. It was producer K Asif who was able to get the judge's nod to take him under police escort for the shoots every day, a one-hour journey, and to deliver him back in the evenings. Ironically, Balraj Sahni was a jailor in the film!

In the same year as *Hulchal,* Balraj was cast in *Hum Log,* in the role of a have-not who during the narrative gets arrested for someone's murder. But his roles of deprivation started as early as in *Dharti Ke Lal* (1946), in which KA Abbas cast him as an impoverished farmer who eventually helped improve people's lives with his ideas of collective farming and harvesting.

It is in this spirit of criticism of an unjust society that Balraj Sahni belted out a message against the haves in *Sone Ki Chidiya* (1958). This movie is essentially about an actress (Nutan) who is conned by her family and later by the hero (Talat Mahmood). One day, she is about to commit suicide when the song *Raat bhar ka hai mehmaan andhera,* a remarkable Rafi-Sahir-OP Nayyar inspirer, lip-synched by Balraj Sahni, comes to her rescue.

The film was directed by Shahid Lateef, while it was produced by his wife, Ismat Chughtai, who also wrote the story. Like Balraj Sahni, both of them were known to harbour heavily-socialist leanings. Together, these three ended up sending a leftist message in the film, and Sahir, the lyrics writer of this film, was quite up to it too. Not to forget that in the same year (1958), he had written a remarkable message on socialism in *Phir Subha Hogi: Cheen-o-Arab hamaara, Hindustan hamaara, rehne ko ghar naheen hai, saara jahaan hamaara.* Even so, the makers of *Sone Ki Chidiya* asked a famous Red Flag House inhabitant, Kaifi Azmi, to write a scathing nazm, his only outing in the film. They even asked him to recite it, and that poem was lip-synched by Balraj Saab in the film. Here's the start of that nazm, entitled *Makaan:*

Aaj ki raat bahut garam hawa chalti hai
Aaj ki raat na footpath par neend ayegi
Sab uttho, main bhi utthoon, tum bhi uttho, tum bhi uttho
Koi khidki isi deewaar mein khul jaayegi…
(Scorching winds are afoot tonight, a time when sleep won't come to those on the pavement. Let us all rise and open up our windows to let such underprivileged in).

Years later, a film called *Garam Hawa* was made whose title was taken from the first line of this poem, and which film also starred Balraj Sahni. It gets juicier when you realize the film was based on a short story by Ismat Chughtai again. But it is interesting that while the words *garam hawa* (scorching wind) were expressed by Kaifi Azmi to underline the privileged vs the underprivileged, Ismat Chughtai's story highlighted the Hindu-Muslim divide in the wake of the Partition.

As we saw above, Sahni was a key member of IPTA, which was hounded by Prime Minister Jawaharlal Nehru's government. "The group was dispersed by the Indian National Congress government using police violence and repressive measures in 1947", says Wikipedia. In light of this fact, how ironic that Jawaharlal Nehru University, established in the Prime Minister's name by an act of Parliament, is itself a base of left-wing activities!

In the late 1930s, when Balraj Sahni was in his mid-20s, the top 1% of Indians earned 21% of the country's total income, a figure that came down to around 10% when he passed away in 1973, to touch a low of 6% in 1983, and then to rise gradually to where we are now, as mentioned earlier. Were Balraj Sahni alive today, one wonders what he would have thought of the current inequality. Maybe he would have felt the absence of sensitive filmmakers such as Bimal Roy, K Asif, Hemen Gupta and Shahid Lateef. In fact, in a world populated by the likes of Bhansalis and Johars, there may well be someone with Balraj

Sahni's temperaments and talents among us even now. Sadly, no one can deliver alone, not in films. Not even in a country.

~ ~ ~ ~

The above was originally published as *Jailor to Prisoner in Sixty Minutes* in DNA Jaipur on 20 May 2018. It has since been updated and enhanced.

♪♫♩♪

18

India's Doo-wop

In the 1940s and '50s, a genre called Rhythm and Blues was popular in the USA. This genre was almost completely dominated by African Americans who through such music expressed the oppression and discrimination—as well as the search for freedom and happiness—that they felt at the time. In parallel, its sub-genre was born that got its name, Doo-wop, much later in the mid-60s. Ironically, Doo-wop didn't last for many years after getting its name. Reason? The British music invasion of the USA started at this time, with bands such as The Beatles, The Rolling Stones, and Herman's Hermits changing our tastes and steam-rolling everything that couldn't stand the onslaught. But what is Doo-wop?

The sub-genre is characterized by a lead singer or two, with backing vocalists who support the lead singers by offering nonsense syllables in harmonic support of the melody. In such a vocal harmony, the backing vocalists may also use words that mean something, but they just have to sing something that has no meaning, i.e., nonsense words like *damu damu damu* or sounds like *ee ee ee, oo oo oo, zu zu zu zu zu*, and so on.

It started *a capella*

The movement was initiated among poor, black, and uneducated Americans with the talent and the sensitivity, but not much cash. So in the first few years, they went *a capella*, meaning without using any instruments. This was fine because using just one's voice was quite popular in the middle of the last century. Doo-wop bands often rehearsed in closed areas, like domes and hallways to get enriching feedback. They did not usually have a sponsor, so they performed on street corners, but when they got to sing in an auditorium, the results would be better. As time progressed, the genre added a few instruments. But even without these additions, several Doo-wop recordings sounded so rich in vocal harmony that not many listeners felt the absence of instruments.

Let's pause to consider that last point and think of an Indian example. Most Hindi film music lovers of yesteryear have heard of the song *More saiyaan ji utrenge paar ho nadiya dheere baho* from *Udan Khatola* (1955). Many of us have heard the song multiple times, but just a few have noticed that the song has used musical instruments minimally. Vocalists backing the lead singer, Lata, have furnished the musical interludes, with their *dheere baho, dheere dheere, dheere baho nadiya, haiya ho, haiya re haiya, haiya ho, hm hm hm hm hm hm hm hm, o o o o o o o o.* They have used meaningful words too, but they have also used meaningless ones and made other vocal sounds for harmonic support, thus making this a great example of Doo-wop in Hindi films.

If you would like to get an idea of the original examples of the American Doo-wop, do look for these on YouTube: *When You Dance* (by The Turbans), *If I Didn't Care* (by The Ink Spots), *Earth Angel (Will You Be Mine?)* (by The Penguins), and *This Is My Story* (by The Valentines).

While the following songs are the desi version of Doo-wop:

- *Nadi kinaare saath hamaare* (Talat, Shamshad, Rafi, chorus/ *Babul*, 1950)
- *Naiyya teri manjhdhaar hoshiyaar* (Rafi, chorus/ *Awara*, 1951)
- *Suno gajar kya gaaye, samay guzarta jaaye* (Geeta, chorus/ *Baazi*, 1951)
- *Do deewanon ka afsaana aye chaand kisi se na kehna* (Lata, Chitalkar, chorus/ *Khazana*, 1951)
- *Suno mere dil ki kahaani...dil dhak dhak dhak dhak* (Miss Chand, chorus/ *Madhosh*, 1951)

➤ *O zara jhoom le jawaani ka zamaana hai* (Geeta, Rafi, chorus/ *Naujawan*, 1951)

Zara jhoom le jawaani ka
zamaana hai

➤ *Khayaalon mein tum ho nazaaron mein tum ho* (Lata, chorus/ *Saiyaan*, 1951)
➤ *Aa gup chup gup chup pyaar karen* (Hemant, Sandhya Mukherji, chorus/ *Sazaa*, 1951)

Aa gup chup gup chup
pyaar karen

➤ *Keh rahi hai raat andheri* (Talat, chorus/ *Hyderabad Ki Nazneen*, 1952)

- *Thumak thumak, thumak thumak jab chaloon main balam* (Suraiya, chorus/ *Khubsurat*, 1952)
- *Aa nainon mein jhoom kar saajna sapnon mein baaje shehnai* (Lata, chorus/ *Daara*, 1953)
- *Do bol tere meethe meethe* (Lata, Hemant, chorus/ *Daara*, 1953)
- *Chaand se poochho, sitaaron se poochho* (Lata, Hemant, chorus/ *Daku Ki Ladki*, 1954)
- *O maanjhi re re nao badha le* (Hemant, chorus/ *Ferry*, 1954)
- *O zindagi ke dene wale* (Hemant, chorus/ *Nagin*, 1954)
- *Main ghareebon ka dil hoon* (Hemant, chorus/ *Aab-e-Hayat*, 1955)
- *Ye duniya ek saagar hai* (Hemant, chorus/ *Bandish*, 1955)
- *Zindagi hai zinda* (Geeta, chorus/ *Munimji*, 1955)
- *More saiyaanji utrenge paar ho* (Lata, chorus/ *Udan Khatola*, 1955)
- *Us paar saajan is paar dhaare* (Lata, chorus/ *Chori Chori*, 1956)
- *Loshe wai wai* (Sandhya Mukherji, Haridhan, chorus/ *Jagte Raho*, 1956)

Loshe wai wai

- *Duniya ke saath chal pyaare aise na haath mal pyaare* (Geeta, chorus/ *Pocketmaar*, 1956)
- *Kaali kaali ye ghata* (Sudha, Balbir, Jagmohan, chorus/ *Zindagi*, 1956)
- *Aaja raat beeti jaaye* (Usha, Kishore, chorus/ *Begunah*, 1957)

- *Chal mere dil ke udan khatole* (Rafi, chorus/ *Gateway of India*, 1957)
- *Haaye jhilmil jhilmil ye shaam ke saaye* (Lata, chorus/ *Lal Batti*, 1957)
- *Chinchan papalu chinchan papalu* (Asha, Manna, chorus/ *Baaghi Sipahi*, 1958)
- *Mini mini chik chik* (Geeta, Hemant, chorus/ *Police*, 1958)
- *Do ekam do* (Rafi, Asha, chorus/ *Dil Deke Dekho*, 1959)
- *Chala dildaar vai vai leke mera pyaar vai vai* (Lata, chorus/ *Duniya Na Mane*, 1959)
- *Andaaz mera mastaana* (Lata, chorus/ *Dil Apna Aur Preet Parai*, 1960)
- *Hum jab chalen to* (Rafi, chorus/ *Hum Hindustani*, 1960)
- *O Mr. Dil badi mushkil mein tu ne aaj daala* (Asha, Rafi, chorus/ *Jali Note*, 1960)
- *Aaja re aaja, laage na mora jiya* (Asha, chorus/ *Sarhad*, 1960)
- *Bachpan o bachpan pyaare pyaare bachpan* (Lata, chorus/ *Mem Didi*, 1961)
- *Chhan chhan paayal chhanke* (Lata, Manna, chorus/ *Maa Beta*, 1962)
- *Dim dim dim dim digo* (Asha, chorus/ *Rahul*, 1964)
- *Do do haath do do paanv* (Rafi, chorus/ *Sharabi*, 1964)
- *Man mora naache tan mora naache* (Lata, chorus/ *Do Dil*, 1965)
- *Main jo chali Hindustan se* (Lata, chorus/ *Jab Jab Phool Khile*, 1965)
- *Khayaalon mein wo ab to aane lage* (Asha, chorus/ *Sher Dil*, 1965)
- *Raat hai kitni suhaani* (Chitalkar, chorus/ *Sher Dil*, 1965)
- *Nazar badli zamaane ki* (Mahendra, chorus/ *Tasweer*, 1966)
- *Oh re taal mile nadi ke jal mein* (Mukesh, chorus/ *Anokhi Raat*, 1968)
- *Hum tum gum sum raat milan ki* (Kishore, Asha, chorus/ *Humshakal*, 1974)

You may have noticed some songs featuring meaningless words sung by chorus singers missing from the above list. Examples: *Ina meena deeka* (*Aasha*, 1957), *Ichak daana beechak daana* (*Shree 420*, 1955), *Jhuk jhuk jhola haaye jhuk jhuk jhola* (*Do Behne*, 1959), and *Lara loo lara loo* (*Jaadu*, 1951). In such songs, the lead vocalists have themselves initiated the meaningless words for the chorus to follow.

That brings us to Scat, a similar singing style that preceded Doo-wop. In this style, the singer offers non-lexical vocables like tabla or sargam bols in Indian music (like *Na dir deem ta na* or *Sa re ga ma pa*), or pause fillers (like *er, um*), or nonsense words, (such as *baabdi ka boobdi ka*), or no words at all (like humming). But in Doo-wop, such vocables are rendered by the backing singers to harmonise with the lead singers.

19

Bombay Returned

More than a hundred years ago, in 1918, Germany surrendered and World War I came to a merciful end. This was not India's war, but since we were a British colony, the British had recruited Indians to combat their enemies, the Japanese and Germans, in various war zones abroad. Towards this end, a million Indians were dispatched out of the country, of which over 74,000 laid down their lives. The fortunate ones who came back proudly called themselves England Returned, an epithet that had been coined earlier for Indians who had spent some time abroad—even if not in England—and returned home. There was a certain prestige, a sense of culture and sophistication when such words were appended to your name. That is why many returnees printed the two words just below their names on their personalized stationery like letterheads and business cards.

In this context, three years after the war ended, a silent Bangla film called *Bilet Ferat*, meaning Foreign Returned, was released. This became known as the first Indian film based on a love story, and also the first one to feature multiple kissing scenes in an Indian film. In the story, its hero Dhirendranath Ganguly goes to England and returns suitably impressed with Western civilization. He also awes everyone here with his new British-style affectation, for which people begin referring to him as *Bilet Ferat*. Ironically, this movie was promoted as "the first Bengali-produced and Bengali-acted film without any foreign assistance".

The film gave a boost to the England-Returned or Foreign-Returned tagline since more and more people were going abroad for various reasons, initially to the United Kingdom, and later to America or other places. A hundred years on, the words Foreign Returned have lost their mojo, just like the degree B. A. (Bachelor of Arts), but in the first half of the last century, it was huge.

At one time it was also a big deal if our actors went abroad and did some work in a foreign film. You may recall, for instance, IS Johar, Persis Khambata, and Kabir Bedi in their Hollywood appearances. Many followed their footsteps too. But most of them returned to do more work back home.

In a smaller way, it was prestigious if you had left small towns or villages and returned from large cities like Calcutta or Bombay, Delhi or Madras. You were then Bombay Returned, Calcutta Returned, etc. That was nice.

But like the actors who went abroad and came back, you must certainly know of many actors who came to Bombay to try their fortunes in Hindi films, only to go back to where they were known better. Most of these talents came from West Bengal or from "the South", which for uninformed North Indians generally means the erstwhile state of Madras. These are actors who did fine where they came from, but not so well in Bombay. Maybe they weren't accepted by the Hindi audiences, or perhaps they had come for a quick visit anyway. Our story is about such artists from the two areas mentioned, actors on whom songs were filmed too. We'll visit these actors alphabetically, mostly through the prism of their songs.

First from Bengal

We begin with Aparna Sen, so admired in Bengali cinema. She was seen in a few Hindi films too. Do recall *Vishwas* (1969), in which she lip-synced her part in two duets: *Aap se humko bichhde hue*, and *Le chal le chal mere jeevan saathi*. In *Imaan Dharam* (1977), we found her moving her lips to *Aye kaash main dekh sakti*.

We find Basant Chowdhury who acted in a few Bombay films. *Rahgir* (1969) was one. But his more famous film was *Parakh* (1960), in which he was paired with Sadhana.

Next comes Ruma Devi (nee Ruma Guha Thakurta), Kishore Kumar's first wife, who was an actress and singer in Bengali films. She acted in *Afsar* (1950), *Mashaal* (1950), and *Raag Rang* (1952). Do recall the song *Aankhon se door-door hain par dil ke paas jo* from *Mashaal*. It was filmed on her.

Sandhya Roy acted in *Asli Naqli* (1962), *Pooja Ke Phool* (1964), and *Rahgir* (1969). Her best-known song while acting was *Laakh chhupao chhup na sakega raaz ho kitna gehra* (*Asli Naqli*, 1962).

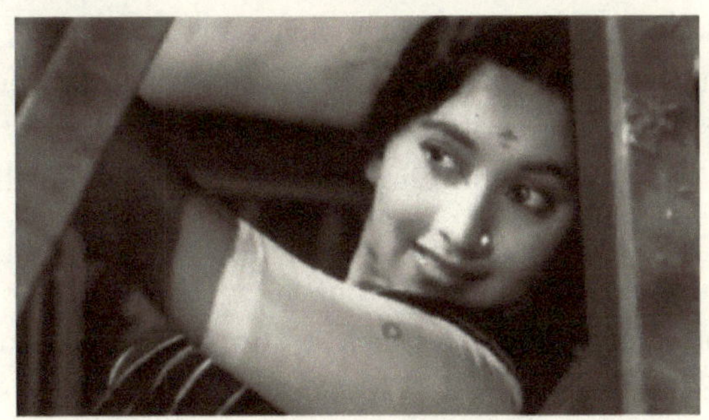

Laakh chhupao chhup
na sakega

Suchitra Sen (nee Roma Dasgupta) was huge in Bengal and also acted in Bombay in *Devdas* (1955), *Musafir* (1957), *Champakali* (1957), *Bambai Ka Babu* (1960), *Sarhad* (1960), *Mamta* (1966), and *Aandhi* (1975). Who can forget these songs filmed on her? *Chhup gaya koi re door se pukaar ke* (*Champakali*), *Deewana mastaana hua dil* (*Bambai Ka Babu*), *Rehte the kabhi jinke dil mein* and *Rahen na rahen hum* (both *Mamta*), *Is mod se jaate hain* and *Tere bina zindagi se koi shikwa to naheen* (both *Aandhi*).

Sumita Sanyal acted in *Ashirwad* (1968), *Anand* (1971), *Guddi* (1971), and *Mere Apne* (1971). Her better-known songs? *Ik tha bachpan* (*Ashirwad*, 1968), and *Na, jiya laage na* (*Anand*, 1971).

Supriya Choudhury performed to *Bulaati hai bahaar* in *Begaana* (1963), *Agar mujhse muhabbat hai* (*Aap Ki Parchhaiyan*, 1964), and *Khoya khoya chanda* (*Door Gagan Ki Chhaon Mein*, 1964).

Uttam Kumar—revered in Bengal—is remembered for lip-syncing Hindi songs *Chhoti si mulaaqaat pyaar ban gayi* (*Chhoti Si Mulaqat*, 1967), *Dil aisa kisi ne mera toda* (*Amanush*, 1975), *Saara pyaar tumhaara maine baandh liya hai* (*Anand Ashram*, 1977), and *Mere ghar aana zindagi* (*Dooriyaan*, 1981).

Let's Head South

We travel south to find many such talents too. Remember, there have been several stars from the South, as also from Bengal, who bought a one-way ticket to Bombay, those whose corpus in Bombay was larger than where they came from. Our narrative is only about the Bombay Returned kind.

A Nageswara Rao (popularly known as ANR), was an actor and producer of Telugu films. He acted in just one Hindi film, *Suvarna Sundari* (1958). *Kuhu kuhu bole koyaliya* was filmed on him.

Anjali Devi: *Baat chalat nayi chunri rang daari* (*Ladki*, 1953), *Aye chaand kal jo aana*, and *Do nainon ka bana jhoolna*, as also *Kaise aaoon Jamuna ke teer* (all three from *Devta*, 1956), *Ajab hai ye duniya ajab zindagi hai* (*Naya Aadmi*, 1956), *Kuhu kuhu bole koyaliya* (*Suvarna Sundari*, 1958), and *Taaron ki thandi-thandi chhaiyaan* (*Naag Devta*, 1962).

Arvind Swamy had a great entry in *Roja* (1993), with *Roja jaan-e-man*. Then *Tu hi re*, from *Bombay* (1995), *Door na ja mujhse, paas aa* (*Sapnay*, 1997), *Jhooth bol na, sach bol de* (*Saat Rang Ke Sapne*, 1998), *Mera dil chura ke wo chal di* (*Raja Ko Rani Se Pyaar Ho Gaya*, 2000).

B Saroja Devi was spotted essaying a role in *Paigham* (1959), singing *Hum rang rangili jobanvanti titliyaan re*. She was featured in the song *Saiyaan haaye haaye haaye tere gaon mein*, and *Dekho mausam kya bahaar hai*, as also *Balma maane na* in *Opera House* (1961). In *Ik sawaal main karoon* (*Sasural*, 1961). In *Muhabbat ka naghma zubaan par na aata* (*Pyaar Kiya To Darna Kya*, 1963). She moved her lips to *Agar teri jalwa-numaayi na hoti* in *Beti Bete* (1964), during the rain song *Pade barkha phuaar* in *Dooj Ka Chand*, (1964). And in *O jaane waale sun zara* in *Preet Na Jaane Reet* (1966).

Singing actress Bhanumati acted in *Nishan* (1949), *Mangala* (1950), *Rani* (1952) and *Chandirani* (1952). Her songs are *Teri meri ye kahaani* (*Nishan*, 1949), and *Khet mere babul ka khet lehraaye*, as also *Kabutar aaja re, tu kook kook bol* (both *Mangala*, 1950). She also rendered for herself on the screen *Nazar raseeli, qamar lacheeli* in (*Rani*, 1952). Not to forget the film *Chandirani* (1952) that featured her duet with Talat, *Chanda tale muskuraaye jawaaniyaan*, plus her solos *Maan ja jaan ja dil waale* and *Khilli khili chaandni chhaayi bahaar hai* and *O bholi si naar hoon, gaati bahaar hoon*.

Among other films, Gemini Ganeshan was spotted acting and singing in *Kisi se pyaar hai humko* (*Devta*, 1957) and *O raat ke musafir chanda zara bata de* (*Miss Mary*, 1957).

Jamuna was seen moving her lips to *Saiyaan lag ja gale* (*Miss Mary*, 1957), *Ajnabi se ban ke karo na kinaara* (*Ek Raaz*, 1963), *Mujhko apne gale laga lo, Karke jiska intezaar* and *Man re tu hi bata kya gaoon* (all from *Hamrahi*, 1963), *Aaj kal mein dhal gaya* (*Beti Bete*, 1964), *Mujhe yaad karne waale* (*Rishte Naate*, 1965), and *Bol gori bol tera kaun piya* (*Milan*, 1967).

KR Vijaya was a popular Indian actress who performed in Telugu, Tamil, and Malayalam films. She started her career in the '60s and acted for decades. She acted in only one Hindi film, *Oonche Log* (1965). Her duet *Aaja re mere pyaar ke raahi, raah niharoon badi der se* became quite famous.

Lakshmi hit the headlines in *Julie* (1975) which featured her on the screen during the song *My heart is beating*. She was also seen performing to *Saiyaan bina ghar soona soona* (*Aangan Ki Kali*, 1979).

The legendary singer MS Subbulaxmi sang and acted in several films. In Hindi films, she starred in the title role of *Meera* (1947). She rendered *Mere to Girdhar Gopal* and several other Meera bhajans in the film.

The South's huge actor Rajnikanth was seen performing to *Dim dim dim taara dim* (*Wafadaar*, 1985), and *Kisi ko muhabbat ki tension* (*Tyagi*, 1992).

We did see Sivaji Ganeshan in *Jhoome mori beliya preet re* (*Amar Shaheed*, 1960). While the future Chief Minister of Tamil Nadu, Jayalalitha was seen moving her lips and body to *Jaagi badan mein jwaala saiyaan tune kya kar daala* (*Izzat*, 1968).

Many actors from other points bought similar return tickets to Bombay, the Mecca of Indian Cinema. But why just actors? Composers, singers, lyricists too. Perhaps we'll put them under the scanner some other day.

~~~~

The above was originally published in DNA Jaipur on 18 February 2018. It has since been updated and enhanced.

~~~~

20

Nanda's Tunes

Recently, many of us read that the gifted actress Nanda passed away on 25th March 2014. Some of us knew that the unmarried lady was 75, and her father Vinayak Damodar Karnataki (the popular actor and filmmaker commonly known as Master Vinayak) helped her walk into cinema, even as she was just a little girl. When she matured, she developed an air of innocence and simplicity that we liked instantly and instinctively, making us believe in what she believed in, empathizing with her causes, and endorsing her worth as a credible performer. There was so much more to this actress.

Interestingly though, even as this lovely actress delivered remarkable performances in various roles, she remained glued to our minds as a sister. That's because when she started taking roles as an adult, she offered amazing performances as a sister, in films like *Toofan Aur Diya* (1956, as Satish Vyas's sister), *Barkha* (1959, as Jagdeep's sister), *Chhoti Behen* (1959, as the sister of Balraj Sahni and Rehman), and *Kala Bazaar* (1960, as Dev Anand's sister).

People generally overlook her various other roles because of her compelling performances in these films. Never mind that she teamed up romantically so many times with Dev Anand, Shashi Kapoor, Rajendra Kumar, and many others. As an aside, consider that in our scriptures Nanda was the name of the half-sister of Gautam Buddha. But the Buddha has such powerful images, that few people remember this other Nanda.

Nanda

But instead of going into Nanda's life and times, let's run through her songs and check out many of her films, co-stars, roles, situations in films, and who directed them, etc. Here we go:

- The chorus-backed Lata devotional *Piya te kahaan* was composed by Vasant Desai and filmed on Nanda in *Toofan Aur Diya* (1956). Mirabai penned this exceptional song.
- *Kaahe sharmaaye gori* (*Bandi*, 1957) was filmed as a *vivaah geet* on Nanda. Do you know which of the Ganguly brothers—Ashok, Kishore, and Anup acted in this film? All three.
- *Chali chali re patang meri chali re*, from *Bhabhi* (1957) featured the actress with Jagdeep flying a kite.
- *Wo door jo nadiya behti hai*, from *Barkha* (1959) was performed on-screen by Nanda and Jagdeep. As mentioned above, these two were brother and sister here.
- As Nanda and Rajendra Kumar are getting married in *Dhool Ka Phool* (1959), his ex Mala Sinha is in tears nearby. A background song in the voice of Rafi happens now. The song is *Daaman mein daag laga baithe*. Sahir wrote this gem for maestro N. Datta.
- *Pyaar bhari ye ghataayen* (*Qaidi No. 911*, 1959) saw her romancing the famous comedian Mehmood.
- *Ga rahi hai zindagi har taraf bahaar mein, kis liye* was a beautiful Asha and Mahendra duet in *Aanchal* (1960). Here Nanda was

romancing Sudesh Kumar, the same hero who was romancing Jayshree Gadkar in *Saranga* in the same year.

> *Apna Ghar* (1960) had a lovely patriotic number, *Aaram hai haraam*, inspired by a Pandit Nehru slogan. This was recorded in the voices of Rafi, Asha and a chorus. Prem Dhawan wrote this beauty and Ravi tuned it.

> In *Kala Bazaar* (1960) she offered an amazing devotional, sharing screen space with Leela Chitnis in *Na main dhan chaahoon*.

> *Aaha rimjhim ke ye pyaare-pyaare geet liye* was filmed on Nanda and Sunil Dutt in *Usne Kaha Tha* (1960). This story had to do with World War I.

> *Jaane waale sipaahi se poochho wo kahaan ja raha hai* (*Usne Kaha Tha*, 1960) had to do with the futility of war. It was filmed background on Nanda and Sunil at Ambala Cantonment, as the latter was leaving for military duty.

> The film *Aaj Aur Kal* (1963), in which she starred with Sunil Dutt and Ashok Kumar, had her lip sync awesome songs like *Maut kitni bhi sangdil ho magar, zindagi se to meherbaan hogi,* and *Mujhe gale se laga lo bahut udaas hoon main.* The film's story was adapted from a Marathi play called *Sunder Mi Honaar* by PL Deshpande.

> Nanda offered the exceptional Asha Bhosle mujra *Insaan muhabbat mein kuchh kaam to kar jaaye* on the screen. Nitin Bose directed its film, *Nartaki* (1963).

> *Manmohan man mein ho tumhi* (*Kaise Kahoon*, 1964) went SD Batish (On Manmohan Krishna), Suman (on Nanda) and Rafi (on Biswajit who fainted at the end of the song).

> *Tum humen pyaar karo ya na karo*, sang Nanda in *Kaise Kahoon* (1964). And she was looking at Biswajit's photo in this song.

> *Koi aane waala hai*, sang Nanda and Dharmendra in *Mera Qusoor Kya Hai* (1964). They were celebrating the impending arrival of their baby.

> *Mile to phir jhuke naheen nazar wohi pyaar ki, naadaan dil tujhe kya maaloom*, she went in *Akash Deep* (1965). The film's other heroine was Nimmi.

- ➤ *Yahaan main ajnabi hoon*, went Shashi Kapoor in *Jab Jab Phool Khile* (1965), while Nanda played the piano in the song.
- ➤ *Theheriye hosh mein aa loon to chale jaaiyega*, with its innovative 'unn hmm' was filmed on Shashi Kapoor and Nanda. Khayyam composed the music for the film *Muhabbat Isko Kehte Hain* (1965).
- ➤ *Aise to na dekho ke humko nasha ho jaaye*, sang Dev Anand to a delighted Nanda in *Teen Deviyan* (1965).
- ➤ *Waadiyaan mera daaman, raaste meri baahen* written by Majrooh for *Abhilasha* (1968) has a touch of Vedanta thought in it. It was Sanjay Khan who philosophised thus for Nanda on the screen.
- ➤ In *Gulaabi aankhen jo teri dekhi* (*The Train*, 1970), her consort was Rajesh Khanna.
- ➤ Talat's last recorded duet was with Lata in the film *Woh Din Yaad Karo* (1971). The song was *Muhabbat ki kahaaniyaan*. Nanda and Sanjay Khan lip-synced it on the screen.

There is no harm in recalling too that a few of the finest devotional songs from our films were filmed on Nanda. Apart from *Piya te kahaan*, as also *Na main dhan chaahoon*, and *Manmohan man mein ho tumhi* found above, she rendered on film two exceptional Lata gems, which remain very popular in our culture to this day: *Allah tero naam, Ishwar tero naam*, and *Prabhu tero naam*, written by Sahir and tuned by Jaidev in *Hum Dono* (1961). She also lip-synced *Tum to sab ke ho rakhwaale* in *Adhikaar* (1971).

Want to think of more beautiful songs filmed on Nanda? See these:

- ➤ *Taayi laga ke maana ban gaye janaab hero* (*Bhabhi*, 1957)
- ➤ *Ek raat mein do do chaand khile* (*Barkha*, 1959)
- ➤ *Jhukti ghata gaati hawa sapne jagaaye* (*Dhool Ka Phool*, 1959)
- ➤ *Chaand ko dekho ji* (*Chand Mere Aaja*, 1960)
- ➤ *Jhuk jhuk jhuk jhoom ghata chhaayi re* (*Char Deewari*, 1961)
- ➤ *Haule haule jiya dole* (*Kaise Kahoon*, 1964)
- ➤ *Kisi ki muhabbat mein sab kuchh bhula ke* (*Kaise Kahoon*, 1964)
- ➤ *Maine aye jaan-e-wafa tumse muhabbat ki hai* (*Bedaag*, 1965)

> ➤ *Humse hoti muhabbat jo tumko* (*Muhabbat Isko Kehte Hain*, 1965)
> ➤ *Likha hai teri aankhon mein kis ka afsaana* (*Teen Deviyan*, 1965)
> ➤ *Kajre badarwa re marzi teri hai kya zaalima* (*Pati Patni*, 1966)

Quite often many of us forget the films we have seen. But songs can often have a greater shelf-life. Here finally are even more long-life ditties that engaged with Nanda: *Machalti arzoo khadi baahen pasaare* (*Usne Kaha Tha*, 1960), *Mehndi lagi mere haath re* (*Mehndi Lagi Mere Haath*, 1962), *Ye sama, sama hai ye pyaar ka* and *Ek tha gul aur ek thi bulbul* (both from *Jab Jab Phool Khile*, 1965), *Jo hum pe guzarti hai, tanha kise samjhaayen* (*Muhabbat Isko Kehte Hain*, 1965), *Bheegi hui is raat ka aanchal* (*Neend Hamari Khwab Tumhare*, 1966), *Humsafar ab ye safar kat jaayega* (*Juari*, 1968), *Ja re kaare badra* (*Dharti Kahe Pukar Ke*, 1969), and many more.

Some of her roles are tattooed on our minds too. The sweet girl next door in *Teen Deviyan*, the wealthy, western chick Rita in *Jab Jab Phool Khile*, the morally-inspiring wife in *Hum Dono*, the wife who has an affair with a Police Inspector in *Ittefaq*, the child widow in *Bhabhi*, she won our hearts in all.

We will miss you, Nanda. You possessed a certain quiet dignity and innocence. And even more, character.

~~~~

The above was originally published in DNA Jaipur on 30 March 2014. It has since been updated and enhanced.

~~~~

21

If it's October it must be SD Burman

I have yet to find someone who hasn't liked the 1965 Hindi film *Guide*. Interestingly, I have yet to meet someone who has enjoyed the English version of that film. The Hindustani version stands tall among the best films ever made in our country. If a poll were held among cinema-loving people, it may even top the list today. Even now, almost every month one finds someone writing on some aspect of this milestone film: its music and dances, its power-packed dialogues and sets, its story of charm and betrayal, the spiritual message that is carried in the last quarter of the narrative, its costumes, and so on. Such assessments happen on social media sites too, those that did not exist when RK Narayan published his book The Guide, in 1958, or seven years later, when it was adapted for the screen. I too wrote a music-centric synopsis of the film, which was published in Saregama India Limited's emagazine, when I was a consultant with the music company many years ago. The story was carried out in 2006 and it was October, the month important for SD Burman, the composer Saregama was celebrating through the release of a CD. Maestro SD Burman was born on the first day of October in 1906 and passed away on the last day of October in 1975.

However, today I would like to offer a completely different story, not an essay on the film with its many layers, magnificent songs and dialogues, or its sensational dances and acting triumphs, but on just one fascinating, external aspect related to the film's music.

In the summer of 1974, when Nav Ketan was completing 25 years of filmmaking, Screen magazine (a now-defunct film weekly from the

Indian Express group), ran a two-page story of the Anand brothers, detailing from where they came, how and when they got together for cinema, their work, and much more. Embedded within these two pages was an absorbing story in a grey-shaded box, something specific to *Guide*, Nav Ketan's flagship feature. I made myself a nice tea to travel with a good hour's read.

It was a perfect day, partly cloudy but bright enough, with a gentle monsoon-time breeze coming in through the open windows. My tea ready, I plonked into my favorite chair by the window. But there came this irritating crow gutturally cawing more than a child crying during a night journey in a train! Somehow though I managed to start reading the Nav Ketan story. The grey-shaded box had a fascinating account of *Guide*, specifically about SD Burman. And who was recounting the tale to Screen? It was Dada Burman's son, RD Burman, himself a reputed musician by then.

Here is that story—as I remember it—from RD Burman's account.

During the early shoots of *Guide*, Dada Burman got a heart attack. So he had to undergo heart surgery. This meant that he stopped working for some time. In fact, so bad was his case that doctors advised him to forget about any rehearsals or even music meets for four months.

As you know, in films, first the song is recorded in a studio; later, during the shoots, it is 'played back' for actors to mime to it. As for *Guide*, its shooting was underway in full swing, so all its songs would be needed in about three months. When Dada Burman fell sick, only one song had been recorded for the film, the Lata-Kishore *Gaata rahe mera dil*. So a four-month wait? No one waits that long in filmmaking here, it's unthinkable. Everything is so crucially time-bound, actors' dates, studio availability, and post production work, so delays become a huge concern.

During the making of Guide, producer-actor Dev Anand was busy, and so was Vijay Anand who was directing the film. When Dada Burman was admitted to Breach Candy Hospital in Bombay, Dev was in the USA tying up things with Pearl Buck and Tad Danielewski, who were scripting and directing the English version of the film, respectively. When Dev heard about Dada's heart attack, he took the first flight home.

In a few days, when the recovering musician was in his room in the hospital, he told Dev that it would be difficult for him to compose for *Guide* anymore, so could he please take someone else instead? "Why dada, what's the problem?" asked Dev. "Because they are asking me to stay away from making music for at least four months. Who knows, it could be longer". "Dada, we have a tuning between us. You are already on board. You are going to make the music for *Guide*". "Dev look, if you are so keen, take Pancham here. He has now become an accomplished composer himself". "Dada, I love Pancham, he's very good. But this film is being made with a certain mission, a certain vision. You take your four months, we'll do the non-song shoots meanwhile. We'll shoot the songs later, and then just edit things afterwards". "But Dev, what if something happens to me? Your entire film…your planning… will be ruined!". "Dada, nothing will happen to you. You will come back soon. But God forbid, if something should happen to you, *Guide* will be released with just one song".

Dada Burman had tears in his eyes that day. But he got well, bounced back, and created unforgettable music for *Guide*. Perhaps his return—both in health and for the film's music—had to do not with just the film, its committed cast and crew, or the relevance of its story. Perhaps the fact that he was a wonderful composer was also not the full story. It is possible that his return and his music in the film had also to do in large measure with the guts and respect shown by Dev Anand during the days when there was no light in his tunnel.

As for my day, that lovely afternoon I was reading this illuminating story in my favorite armchair, I was so absorbed that I forgot to drink my tea. I also forgot to shoo away the crow. Very few people have understood Einstein's Theory of Relativity. For dummies like me, it has been simplified thus: If you are with someone you love, three hours seem like three minutes, because everything else goes out of focus. But three minutes near a furnace seem like a lifetime. For an hour on that remarkable day, Dev Anand's words offered me an example of the Theory of Relativity, making me forget the tea and the crow. That's because it showed Dev's character while saluting one of the greatest musicians Hindi cinema has experienced.

Here are the remarkable songs of *Guide*. All the lyrics were written by Shailendra.

- *Aaj phir jeene ki tamanna hai* (Lata)
- *Allah megh de paani de* (SD Burman)
- *Din dhal jaaye haaye* (Rafi)
- *Gaata rahe mera dil* (Kishore, Lata)
- *He Ram hamaare Ramchandra* (Manna Dey)
- *Kya se kya ho gaya bewafa* (Rafi)
- *Mose chhal kiye jaaye* (Lata)
- *Piya tose naina laage re* (Lata)
- *Tere mere sapne ab ek rang hain* (Rafi)
- *Wahaan kaun hai tera, musafir?* (SD Burman)

Tere mere sapne ab ek rang hain

Not to speak of Waheeda's incredible snake dance, which is backed with music, but has no words. That piece of choreography itself deserves detailed analysis.

~~~~

The above was originally published in DNA Jaipur in October 2017 as The Theory of Relativity for Dummies. It has since been updated and enhanced.

♪♫♩♪
~~~~

22

Proxy Love, Proxy War

Zindagi bhi patang hai o pyaare
Chal nikal ghar se pecha lada re
Haar se pehle mat haarja re
Chal nikal ghar se pecha lada re...
Dekh zara himmat hai kitni kaagaz ki kashti mein
Rang patang ke shaamil kar le tu apni hasti mein...
(Ravi Chopra's poetry set to music by Anand-Milind for singer
Amey Date in *Yeh Khula Aasmaan*, 2012)

Not Just the World's Oldest Toy

For thousands of years, human beings have marvelled at the flying
abilities of birds. After many such centuries of wonder China developed
the first man-made flying object. That was the kite. The Chinese
mounted silk on a lightweight frame of bamboo, both products the
region was famous for. Tethered to a person, such a heavier-than-air
contraption could be raised above the ground and manoeuvred to stay
there for some time. After that invention, their creators went about
improving the humble kite's structure for better aerodynamics. After
that was achieved, the simple toy evolved into multi-coloured designs
and complex shapes, including those of animals, birds and humans.
They made many other changes. For instance, by cutting notches in

the bamboo, the Chinese were able to make kites whistle as the breeze hit them. Such whistles were believed to drive away evil spirits, and so kites took on a religious and cultural significance in Chinese society. It is from here that kites migrated to the rest of Asia, and also to Europe and North America.

Today, kites are flown in dozens of countries, in some of which they have come to mean so much more than just a sport or pastime. The above song uses the kite as a metaphor for life, inspiring us to go wrestle our way out. In *Gattu* (2012), a black kite tethered to God-knows-whom has been scaring young children. When the eponymous 10-year-old finally cuts that kite and takes its possession, he furnishes his friends with the energy to think positively, not think failure. More recent examples of films which have featured kite-flying significantly include *Hum Dil De Chuke Sanam* (1999), *Fukrey* (2013), *Kai Po Che* (2013), and *Raees* (2017).

But if soaring in the sky and cutting off a rival's kite are positives, there's a reverse side to it too: the perspective of the person who has lost his kite in an aerial battle. Thus, in a mood diametrically opposite to the one we saw above *(Zindagi bhi patang hai o pyaare)*, we find disconnected desolation here:

> *Na koi umang hai, na koi tarang hai*
> *Meri zindagi hai kya, ek kati patang hai…*
> *Aakaash se giri main ik baar kat-ke aise*
> *Duniya na phir na poochho loota hai mujhko kaise*
> *Na kisi ka saath hai, na kisi ka sang hai*
> *Meri zindagi hai kya, ek kati patang hai…*
> (Lata/Anand Bakshi/RD Burman/*Kati Patang*, 1970)

Proxy war

Let's bear in mind that the person himself hasn't been defeated, it's only his kite that has been vanquished, but the owner of the kite personifies the toy he controls and then proceeds to identify himself with it, as if he has himself been defeated by a human rival. This is really like a proxy war, where the two belligerent parties have not engaged directly, but in a neutral space. In the reverse scenario of proxy love, we have a Punjabi song in which we see a woman flying a kite with her friends, as she sends indirect overtures to a man, who is flying his own kite with his male friends.

Meri patli patang tera peela-peela rang
Dole mere ang-ang-ang guddiye ni...
Chal naal-naal baadalaan de udiye ni...
(The lady is telling her kite what, roughly translated, means,
"My dear kite, so beautifully slim and bright yellow, you make
me swing so...let's go fly with the clouds").
(Shamshad Begum/ Verma Malik/ Sardul Kwatra/ *Koday Shah*,
1953)

In the song above, we watch and hear proxy love happening, perhaps because getting a direct no for an answer may hurt the lady's pride. This proxy concept is nice. Unsure of the mood of a girl, a man uses proxy by asking her out this way: "If I invited you for a musical performance, would you say yes?" If she agrees, then he will proceed to ask her. If she declines, no problem. He hasn't actually asked her yet.

Returning to kites, we find that other cultures derive much fun and inspiration from them as well. In *Mary Poppins* (1964), siblings Michael and Jane Banks have wealthy but laughter-less parents. Upon this scene, and to the delight of the kids, arrives a magical nanny called Mary Poppins, who proceeds to take the kids on many fantastic adventures. The influenced siblings pitch to rope in their parents into their new world of sunshine and happiness. The film ends with a waltz that offers a paradigm shift in the minds of the senior Banks. It highlights for them this message: that family is so much more important than the pursuit of wealth. During the song, all the Banks go to a festival where everyone flies a kite and enjoys himself.

Here's the essential part of the song *Let's Go Fly a Kite* from Mary Poppins:

With tuppence for paper and strings
You can have your own set of wings
With your feet on the ground
You're a bird in flight
With your fist holding tight
To the string of your kite
Oh, oh, oh
Let's go fly a kite
Up to the highest height
Let's go fly a kite
And send it soaring
Up through the atmosphere
Up where the air is clear
Oh, let's go fly a kite!
(David Tomlinson)

And here are some songs that romance with the idea of kites in Hindi films:

- *Aji aana zara ik udti patangiya* (Ashok Kumar, Devika Rani/ JS Kashyap/ Saraswati Devi/ *Jeevan Naiya*, 1936)
- *Meri pyaari patang chali baadal ke sung* (Shamshad, Uma Devi/ Shakeel/ Naushad/ *Dillagi*, 1949)

Meri pyaari patang chali
baadal ke sung

- *Ari chhod de sajaniya chhod de patang meri chhod de* (Hemant, Lata/ Rajinder Krishan/ Hemant Kumar/ *Nagin*, 1954)
- *Chali chali re patang meri chali re* (Rafi, Lata/ Rajinder Krishan/ Chitragupt/ *Bhabhi*, 1957)
- *Piya main hoon patang tu dor* (Asha, Kishore/ Jan Nissar Akhtar/ OP Nayyar/ *Ragini*, 1958)
- *Ye duniya patang nit badle ye rang* (Rafi/ Rajinder Krishan/ Chitragupt/ *Patang*, 1960)
- *Tumhaare sung main bhi chaloongi piya jaise patang peechhe dor* (Lata/ Shakeel/ Naushad/ *Sohni Mahiwal*, 1958)
- *Chunnu patang ko kehta hai kite* (Asha Bhosle/ Anand Bakshi/ S Mohinder/ *Zameen Ke Taare*, 1960)
- *Pyaar ke patang ki dor jis ke haath hai* (Kishore Kumar/ Rajinder Krishan/ Kalyanji-Anandji/ *5 Rifles*, 1974)
- *Patang jaisa dole re dupatta mera malmal ka* (Lata/ Dev Kohli/ Ram-Laxman/ *Mehboob Mere Mehboob*, 1992)
- *Patang jaisa hawa mein lehraaye dupatta mera malmal ka* (Kavita, Kumar Sanu/ Satish/ Bhoopi-Ratan/ *Koyal*, 1993)
- *Dheel de dheel de de re bhaiya* (Shankar Mahadevan, Dominique Cerejo, Jyotsna Hardikar, KK/ Mehboob/ Ismail Durbar/ *Hum Dil De Chuke Sanam*, 1999)

➤ *Udi-udi jaaye udi-udi jaaye dil ki patang dekho* (Sukhwinder Singh, Bhoomi Trivedi, Karsan Sagathia/ Javed Akhtar/ Ram Sampath/ *Raees*, 2017)

Makar Sankranti, celebrated on 14th January each year, has to do with elevated vision and high aspirations. It is also believed to get us a good dose of Vitamin D through sunshine. Moreover, it is a festival of harvest, of eating sesame sweets and flying kites. With so many positives, you wonder who invented the negative idiom Go Fly a Kite, which means "Go get lost".

~~~~

The above was originally published in DNA Jaipur on 14 January 2018. It has since been updated and enhanced.

~~~~

23

Naam Gum Jaayega

Two years ago, in 2016, British actor Michael Caine officially changed his name to Michael Caine. Now what was that, one name "changed"—to the same name? Was that a joke of some kind? It wasn't. We soon discovered that the octogenarian's real name was Maurice Joseph Micklewhite. He had hated that name. Before getting into films decades earlier, the young man had changed his name to Michael Caine, the name with which he had become successful over the years. But even as Michael Caine was recognized and celebrated worldwide, he hadn't bothered to change the name officially. His passport, like his other documents, still said Maurice Joseph Micklewhite. This was not a problem till 9/11 happened, followed by all the ghastly things Al-Qaeda and ISIS were doing. After such terror attacks and threats, everyone stepped up security, especially airports worldwide. So if it wasn't a big issue for Caine earlier, things had changed now. "Was Michael Caine travelling on a fake name?" officials wondered. In the new environment, the seasoned actor was detained at airports, with delays of an hour or more being quite common. The octogenarian couldn't take it anymore.

Do remember that in the same year, 2016, actor Shahrukh Khan was frisked and detained at a US airport too, not that this was the first time for him either. Such detention is interesting in the light of his film *My Name Is Khan* (2010), in which his key message to the President of the USA was "My name is Khan but I'm not a terrorist". One wonders if he too was fed up with all these detentions and if he ever considered changing his name, to say, Rajeev Saxena. Hmm. Maybe not, because this name could be shortened to Rajeev "Sucks" by his detractors. How about Rajeev Srivastava? That sounds nice, fresh and classy. Except that many Srivastavas themselves ran away from their surname, as we will shortly see. Meantime, how would his Indian fans react if the Khan changed his name? Perhaps not very positively one guesses. It seems Indians want you to be a Khan to put you up in high orbit, at least in part to show just how secular we are. But let's not go there today.

Anyway, all these name-change thoughts were fermenting in my mind earlier this week on Manna Dey's birthday, i.e., 1ˢᵗ May. A few of us were listening to him sing Madhushala, a long series of quatrains written by Harivanshrai Bachchan and composed by Jaidev. We know that Manna wasn't his real name, it was Prabodh Chandra, which he hated. At home, his elders called him by his pet name, Manna. "Bring me a glass of water, Manna". Or "Manna, get ready for school". The singer happily dumped his original first name. Harivanshrai's surname was Srivastava, but he too had a pet name, Bachchan, which means child-like. The poet dumped his original surname.

Many people like Michael Caine, Harivanshrai Bachchan and Manna Dey change their names. Here are some reasons why people do so:

- ➤ If they don't like the name their parents gave them.
- ➤ When their name evokes laughter among others.
- ➤ For reasons of acceptability in cinema or on the stage.
- ➤ When they want to visibly cut off ties with their parents.
- ➤ When they change their religion.
- ➤ If they want to stand apart from other people with the same name.
- ➤ If they want something that can sound better in their profession or something that can be pronounced more easily.
- ➤ For saluting their wife or mother by adding their names within their own. Sanjay Leela Bhansali's middle name is his mother's first name. After the Economist Swaminathan S Aiyar got married to Shahnaz Anklesaria, he changed his name to Swaminathan S Anklesaria Aiyar. These are rare, but not non-existent.
- ➤ When Asians go to live in the English-speaking world.
- ➤ For numerology, so that success comes their way.

Such name changes happen among ordinary folks too, but when high-profile celebrities change their names, it creates headlines. Even if they tweak the spelling a bit, it gets noticed virally.

If you think of poets in the West, they usually don't change their names. In our part of the world, though, they do so routinely. From Shakeel Badayuni to Hasrat Jaipuri, from Sahir Ludhianvi to Majrooh Sultanpuri, from Qamar Jalalabadi to Neeraj to Naqsh Lyallpuri, many poets have changed their names to adopt a *"takhallus"* (pen name). But since it is common among our poets, perhaps even expected from them, let's overlook them for now. Let's look instead at other kinds of celebrities, glancing first at famous people abroad who changed their name, without us going into specific reasons why they did so:

- Actress Norma Jeane Mortenson became Marilyn Monroe.
- Singer Bob Dylan was christened Robert Allen Zimmerman soon after his birth.
- Actor Kirk Douglas, of Russian-Jewish lineage, was born Issur Danielovitch Demsky.
- British singer of Indian origin, Freddie Mercury, was called first called Farrukh Balsara.
- Pugilist Cassius Clay changed his name to Muhammad Ali.

On the desi front too, there have been many such name changes:

- Filmmaker Sanjay Bhansali became Sanjay Leela Bhansali.
- Journalist Swaminathan Iyer renamed himself Swaminathan S. Anklesaria Iyer.
- Actor Rajesh Khanna was originally called Jatin Khanna.
- Actor Jaikishan Kakubhai changed his name to Jackie Shroff.
- Prolific actor Sanjeev Kumar had the name Harihar Jethalal Jariwala before he took on the new name.
- Johnny Walker was Badruddin Kazi before his work in films.

Does all this make you want to change your name too? If you officially want to change your name in any way, there's a procedure. You have to sign what they call a Deed Poll, which is a formal legal document in which you promise to give up your old name and take on another one for all purposes.

Arguably the most abandoned surname, Srivastava

Now let's get back to the great poet Harivanshrai Bachchan, whose original surname was Srivastava. Srivastavas are Kayasthas, a sub-caste of intellectuals spread across northern India. Many converted to Islam, so we have Muslim Kayasthas too, but one wonders whether they consider they have descended from Lord Chitragupt, who sits at the gates of Yamraj, the God of Death.

Apart from Harivanshrai, there have been other Srivastavas who have dropped or given up their surname, most notably the composer Chitragupt, at least in name the father of all the Kayasthas. Chitragupt preferred using only a mononym. We also had the lyricist-cum-director PL Santoshi whose real name was Pyarelal Srivastava before he changed his surname to Santoshi.

There was Lal Bahadur Shastri too, India's Prime Minister, who had issues with our caste system. So he first dropped the Srivastava surname, and later on, adopted Shastri instead. This was after he received a degree in Philosophy from Kashi Vidyapeeth. Shastri means the Wise One.

Independence activist "Loknayak" Jai Prakash Narain was another Srivastava who dropped his surname.

But perhaps the most drastic change from a Srivastava came from a certain Dhanpat Rai Srivastava, who went to a madrasa to learn Urdu and Persian and then wrote as Nawab Rai. When the British thought his writing was inflammatory, they went after both his books and him. He then changed his name to Munshi Premchand and is among other things known as the father of the Urdu short story, as also a great writer in Hindi.

Here are a few songs that in some way are associated with the five gifted ex-Srivastavas just mentioned.

- ➤ *Rang barse bheege chunariya* (*Silsila*, 1981. Bachchan wrote this)
- ➤ *Dil ka diya jala ke gaya* (*Akash Deep*, 1965. Chitragupt composed this song)
- ➤ *Pipra ke patwa sareekhe dole manwa* (from *Godaan*, 1963, a Munshi Premchand story)

- ➤ *Jai jawaan jai kisaan* (*Shankar Khan*, 1966. Lal Bahadur Shastri coined this motto)
- ➤ *Kahaan gayi wo teri Ahinsa* (*Nasbandi*, 1978. Jai Prakash Narain mentioned)

It is said that great people's work lives long after they have gone away. If we can recall their work, it's ok to say *"Naam gum jaayega, chehra ye badal jaayega, mera kaam khud hi pehchaan hai"*, with apologies to its writer Sampooran Singh Kalra, who too changed his name and became known as Gulzar.

The tailpiece of this story lists many other film people who changed their names. Surely you will add some more in your mind:

- ➤ Actor Ajit used to be Hamid Ali Khan
- ➤ Actor Balraj Sahani was Yudhishthir Sahani
- ➤ Actress Bina Rai was Krishna Sarin
- ➤ Actor Dilip Kumar used to be Muhammad Yusuf Khan
- ➤ Actress Geeta Bali was earlier known as Harkirtan Kaur
- ➤ Actor Jagdeep Syed was named Ishtiaq Ahmed Jaffery
- ➤ Actor Jayant's real name Zakaria Khan
- ➤ Actor Jitendra's real name is Ravi Kapoor
- ➤ Actress Kalpana Kartik used to be Mona Singha
- ➤ Actress Kamini Kaushal was Uma Kashyap before coming to films
- ➤ Singing actor Kishore Kumar was born as Abhas Kumar Ganguly
- ➤ Actress Kumkum's original name was Zaibunnisa Khan
- ➤ Madhubala was named Mumtaz Jahan Begum by her parents

Madhubala and Dilip Kumar

- Actress Mala Sinha's original name was Alda Sinha
- Actress Mandakini was originally called Yasmeen Joseph
- Actor Manoj Kumar had the name Harikrishan Goswami before cinema
- Actress Meena Kumari's name before coming to films was Mahjabeen Bano
- Actress Fearless Nadia's real name was Mary Ann Evans
- Actress Nargis was originally called Fatima Rashid
- Actress Nimmi was first known as Nawab Bano
- Actress Nirupa Roy was earlier named Kokila Kishorechandra Bulsara
- Actress Nivedita's real name was Libi Rana
- Actor Pradeep Kumar was Sital Batabyal before he entered films
- Actress Priya Rajvansh used to be Vera Sundar Singh
- Actress Reena Roy was Saira Ali before her film career
- Actress Rekha was originally Bhanurekha Ganesan
- Actor Sanjay Khan used to be Shah Abbas Khan earlier
- Music Director Saraswati Devi was originally known as Khorshid Minchor Homji
- Actress Shyama was named by her parents Khurshid Akhtar
- Composer Snehal Bhatkar's real name was Vasudeo Gangaram Bhatkar
- Actress Sulochana's real name Ruby Myers
- Actor Sunil Dutt was Balraj Dutt
- Actress Sumitra Devi was originally Nilima Chattopadhyay
- Actress Veena was named Tajour Sultana at her birth
- Actress Yasmin's real name was Vinita Bhat

~~~~

The above was originally published in DNA Jaipur on 6 May 2018. It has since been updated and enhanced.

♪♫♩♪
~~~~

24

White, Black and White, and Colour

Keralites are marvellously enterprising people. You find them in every sector, and you find them everywhere you go, Dubai, Hong Kong, Canada, you name it. Punjabis have made a great name for themselves too, especially in cinema and commerce. This story essentially flies over two men from Kerala, and two from Punjab.

Verghese Kurien spent the best part of his life in Anand (Gujarat), converting India from a deficit producer of milk to a surplus one by quadrupling our milk production. In time he came to be called The Milkman of India, and the Father of the White Revolution. Filmmaker Shyam Benegal made *Manthan* (1978), a movie inspired by Kurien's work. Another Malayali, named PK Nair, was in Pune (Maharashtra), 600 kilometers south of Anand around the same time Kurien was doing his remarkable work, i.e., the early 1960s. Nair began doing amazing work for the preservation of cinema. He founded the National Film Archive of Poona and set in motion the responsibility of sourcing, restoring, and cataloguing films from around the world.

In his time, Nair made out a list of the 21 Most Wanted Missing Indian Films, many of them firsts in one way or another. Among these Most Wanted were India's first talkie, *Alam Ara* (1931) and India's first banned film, *The Mill* (1934). The latter was a Munshi Premchand story about striking factory workers. In the film, the mill owner's daughter comes out to defend the cause of the striking workers. The powerful textile owners' lobby of the time was able to influence the British censor to ban the film, ostensibly because it "attempted to glamorize mutiny".

A short excursion into colour

One of the other films in Nair's Most Wanted list was *Sairandhri* (1933), a V Shantaram-directed venture which took a story from the Mahabharata epic. This was the only film that was processed in colour and yet released in black & white. The reason is that the colours came out as too garish. But that apart, this was actually the first Indian colour film, though it was processed in Germany. And yet, the history books mention *Kisaan Kanya* (1937), produced by Ardeshir Irani of *Alam Ara* fame, as India's first colour film. Perhaps "fully indigenous" would be stating it more correctly. If that is right, you wonder why *Aan* (1952), processed in Technicolor in London, is often cited as India's first Technicolor film.

To pick up the story after *Aan*, a few films started happening in colour, for example, *Mayur Pankh* (1954). But colour stock was expensive, so, to build a bridge between costs and attraction, filmmakers started offering "partly in colour" features in the 1950s. *Nagin* (1954) was a black & white film with some parts in Gevacolor. *Champakali* (1957) had some songs in colour too, even as Mehboob Khan went all-colour in Mother India in the same year. Meantime, V Shantaram, ignored by history as mentioned earlier, made *Jhanak Jhanak Payal Baaje* (1955) in colour, but, financially punished, reverted to monochrome in *Toofan Aur Diya* (1956) and *Do Ankhen Barah Haath* (1957). He went on to make *Navrang* (1959) in colour again, because, as he told us in a cameo at the start of the film, he had recently seen many dreams in colour. Here's why: he was nearly blinded when grappling with a bull in the last scene of *Do Ankhen Barah Haath*. They operated on his eye and blindfolded him for months, which is when he saw many colourful dreams and realized the value of vision, something he was very keen to share with us.

But colour was still the exception, not the norm, in much of the 1950s. In the early 1960s, however, when Kurien was focussing on white and Nair was mainly interested in black & white, a colour revolution of sorts was underway in Bombay. Many films like *Junglee* (1961), *Professor* (1962), *Phir Wohi Dil Laaya Hoon* (1963), *April Fool* (1964), *The Adventures of Robin Hood* (1965), and *Waqt* (1965) were being made in colour, even as several films were still being made in black & white in parallel. Examples of black & white movies from the 1960s are *Hum Dono* (1961), *Sahib Bibi Aur Ghulam* (1962), *Bandini* (1963), *Ghazal* (1964), *Shaheed* (1965), *Aakhri Khat* (1966), and *Khamoshi* (1969).

Let's pause here to see some colour songs that were from "partly in colour" films:

- *Oonchi oonchi duniya ki deewaaren saiyaan tod ke* (Lata/ *Nagin*, 1954)
- *Zaalim teri aankhon ne kya cheez pila di hai* (Lata/ *Devta*, 1956)
- *Kahaan le chale ho bata do musafir* (Lata/ *Durgesh Nandini*, 1956)
- *Ina meena deeka* (Asha/ *Aasha*, 1957)
- *Chhup gaya koi re door se pukaar ke* (Lata/ *Champakali*, 1957)
- *Tumhaare pyaar ka nasha hamaare dil pe chha gaya* (Lata/ *Madaari*, 1959)
- *Chaudhvin ka chaand ho* (Rafi/ *Chaudhvin Ka Chand*, 1960)
- *Pyaar kiya to darna kya* (Lata/ *Mughal-e-Azam*, 1960)

Pyaar kiya to darna kya

- *Tum jo aao to pyaar aa jaaye* (Manna Dey, Suman/ *Sakhi Robin*, 1962)

> ➤ *Wo jab yaad aaye, bahut yaad aaye* (Rafi, Lata/ *Parasmani*, 1963)
> ➤ *Mil ke bhi hum mil na sake* (Talat, Lata/ *Sunehri Nagin*, 1963)
> ➤ *Hum pyaar kiye jaayenge* (Lata/ *Aaya Toofan*, 1964)
> ➤ *Kya jaanu sajan* (Lata/ *Baharon Ke Sapne*, 1967)

New Delhi-based Sundeep Pahwa is something of an authority on films. His father Basant Kumar was an actor and film producer, known for his roles like opposite Manju in *Bahu* (1955), with two Talat and Geeta duets filmed on them: *Thandi hawaon mein taaron ki chhaon mein* and *Dekho dekho ji balam dheere dheere*. It was Basant Kumar who gave a directorial break to Shakti Samanta in the same *Bahu*. Sundeep Pahwa enlightens me that in the early '60s, Wadia Brothers was the first production company to announce a B-grade film entirely in colour. That was the Feroz Khan and Sayeeda Khan starrer *Char Darwesh* of 1964. This music and film buff also offered interesting information about another colour film released in 1964. That was J Om Prakash's *Ayee Milan Ki Bela*, which was to be made in black & white. The film was announced, the *mahurat* happened, the coconut was broken, and there was "Congratulations" and "Good Luck" all around. A week later, a unit member suggested to the producer to make it a colour film instead. "Yes", said the filmmaker, "that's it!" It was re-announced as a colour film. The film went on to become a Silver Jubilee hit.

Two Punjabi men

Now about the two Punjabi men mentioned at the start of this essay. J Om Prakash becomes the first of them. The other one is his namesake, Om Prakash, the comedian who was also a filmmaker. In 1964, both men released a colour film, J Om Prakash had *Ayee Milan Ki Bela*, while Om Prakash had *Jahan Ara*. But what release? *Jahan Ara* was such a commercial disaster that it had to be pulled away on its fourth day, from even its main theatre.

When *Jahan Ara* failed, many people attempted to understand what could have gone so wrong, why such a savage rejection of a film that had settled actors in Bharat Bhushan and Mala Sinha, a fine composer in Madan Mohan, sensational lyrics by Rajinder Krishan and awesome vocals by Talat and Rafi, Suman and Lata and Asha. Could it be that the time of historicals was over? Or maybe that colour was a bad idea, that Bharat Bhushan and Mala Sinha were both identified with their black & white films, so audiences would have loved them the way they had loved them till now.

One thing is certain. Had Om Prakash used black & white film, he may have saved a lot of money. As he scaled up to colour, he went on adding other costs, for instance on expensive sets and then upscale musicians like Ram Narain, Hari Prasad Chaurasia, Rais Khan, and Shiv Kumar Sharma. But that's fine. Because the music album did sell very well. Music is the main reason most people even remember that film.

~~~~

The above was featured as *To Each His Colour* in DNA Jaipur on 4 November 2018. It has since been updated and enhanced.

PS: Two 2023-related reports appeared in July 2024. One told us that with 2500 films annually, India was the largest producer of films in the world. The other informed us that with 87 million metric tons, India was the largest consumer of cow milk in the world. Some people's work has left a huge footprint.

~~~~

Visitors from 29028!

If you send a letter to 1600, Pennsylvania Avenue, it will be headed to the home of the world's most powerful man, the President of The United States. The Prime Minister of Great Britain lives at 10, Downing Street, while in India, the Prime Minister lives at 7, Race Course Road. For people who understand addresses, just a number with the street name is enough. You don't really have to append the city names, Washington, London, and New Delhi respectively, or their pin codes. Such short addresses are as well recognized as we know that the polar bear's natural habitat is in the Arctic Circle in the far north of our planet. The Alphonso mango is endemic to western India, and the many flora of Sri Lanka cannot be found anywhere else.

But suppose now that not just people, plants and wildlife, such an address was even needed by things we know don't exist conventionally. For example exceptional songs. We enjoy many wonderful songs, right? These accompany us on our travels and give us loads of happiness in our homes. Since they are with us in our joys and sorrows, they make for faithful companions. Plus they are truly *sufi*, in the sense that they offer their 'fruit' to whoever wants to take it, making their offering universal. For some of us, great songs are our best friend, guide, and philosopher, even if their communication is just one way. As such, they live in our hearts. But since 'our hearts' are vague addresses, maybe it's a good idea to give exceptional melodies a unique address that is an actual place on a map!

29028—just that number—can be such an address. That's the height in feet of Mount Everest, whose peak is the top of the world, a physical reference point which has become a metaphor not just for feeling good, but also for the showcasing of exceptional excellence. So we can say high art lives in the mountains, and very high art, like much of the work of Leonardo Da Vinci, Shakespeare and Ghalib resides high up there, at 29028.

Yes, for many of us, hundreds of wonderful songs from Hindi cinema's golden years have special attributes that give them this unique address location too. Let's meet just a few of them and see why they achieved such a position of eminence, even if our analysis may end up looking simplistic. But that's ok. After all, you can go on and on about the various attributes of the world's most admired painting, Mona Lisa, sitting in The Louvre in Paris, and why it is priceless, but there's always going to be some other x-factor in someone's else's mind. Let's anyway take one or two qualities of a few musical friends from Mt. Everest, all of whom are paragons of the peaceful coexistence of exceptional words, expression, and tunes—that is a given. We look at just one example per singer:

> *Panchhi baawra* (Khursheed/ Gyan Dutt/ DN Madhok/ *Bhakt Surdas*, 1942). This song of *Karuna Ras* (Essence of Compassion) is really about unrequited love. Look at the way she stretches *cha-aa-aa-aa-nd se preet lagaaye*…a class act!

> *Aye kaatib-e-taqdeer mujhe itna bata de* (Saigal/ Pankaj Mullick/ Pt. Bhushan/ *My Sister*, 1944). The whole "Why me, God? Why me?" experience does connect with us from time to time.

> *Akhiyaan mila ke jiya bharma ke chale naheen jaana* (Zohrabai/ Naushad/ DN Madhok/ *Rattan*, 1944). This has a ghoda gaadi rhythm, and a very different style of singing, thanks to Naushad, for e.g., on the *"haan"* in *Haan saiyaan ke paiyaan pad jaoongi roke kahoongi!*

> *Chhod babul ka ghar mohe pee ke nagar aaj jaana pada* (Shamshad/ Naushad/ *Babul*, 1950). A sensitive *bidaayi-geet.* Shamshad's vocals manipulate the maze to reach the centre of our hearts. Bull's eye!

> *Aaye bahaar banke lubha kar chale gaye* (Rafi/ Shankar-Jaikishan/ Hasrat/*Raj Hatth*, 1956). Rafi goes high, taking this beautiful ghazal up into the mountains. And the oboe joins the violins to have a great day.

➤ *Daane-daane pe likha hai khaane waale ka naam* (Chitalkar/ C Ramchandra/ Rajinder Krishan/ *Baarish*, 1957). Shampooing the song with a friendly harmonica and infectious rhythm, this is a beautiful ditty with a heavy message

➤ *Manzil wohi hai pyaar ki raahi badal gaye* (Subir Sen/ Shankar-Jaikishan/ Shailendra/ *Kathputli*, 1957). In the intro music, the piano and violins seem to be at war, but they calm down to allow the accordion to create a peaceful ambience. Why not, it's master craftsman Goody Servai on the instrument. What an intoxicant this song is!

➤ *Hum hain raahi pyaar ke* (Kishore/ SD Burman/ Majrooh/ *Nau Do Gyarah*, 1957). The whistle pitches for top billing, and so does the trumpet, but it's a Kishore win in this 'I love you all' sufi winner!

➤ *Rasiya re man baasiya re* (Meena Kapoor/ Anil Biswas/ Prem Dhawan/ *Pardesi*, 1957). The freshness of the lovely voice, with Pandit Pannalal Ghosh's bansuri flying almost solo in the first interlude while joining Ustad Ali Akbar Khan's sarod in the second…aah, manna to the ears! Check out the dramatic pauses too.

➤ *Jaane kya tune kahi* (Geeta/ SD Burman/ Sahir/ *Pyaasa*, 1957). The image of an alluring Waheeda, backed by Dada Burman's mystery-enhancing Chinese Temple Blocks for rhythm. The meta moments come in each stanza when after a couplet we hear a graceful, game-changing flute piece, to permit a killer third line to end the stanza. So for e.g.: flute piece, followed by *jaag utthe khwaab kayi, baat kuchh ban hi gayi!*

Jaane kya tu ne kahi

- *Hum pyaar mein jalne waalon ko* (Lata/ Madan Mohan/ Rajinder Krishan/ *Jailor*, 1958). The piano, and Lata's wonderful expression, especially when she articulates the stretched "*haaye*" in *haaye aaraam kahaan*. Ethereal!

- *Aansoo bhari hain ye jeevan ki raahen* (Mukesh/ Dattaram/ Hasrat/ *Parvarish*, 1958). The solo violin, the *raag Kalyan* that caresses your heart, and the alluring ten-beat, *jhaptaal* rhythm. *Barbaadiyon ki ajab dastaan hoon, shabnam bhi roye main wo aasmaan hoon*, exclaims Hasrat!

- *Sun mere bandhu re* (SD Burman/ SD Burman/ Majrooh/ *Bandini*, 1959). A touching and evocative boatmen's ditty, with the charming flute helping his story along.

- *Bekasi hadd se jab guzar jaaye* (Asha/ OP Nayyar/ Jan Nissar Akhtar/ *Kalpana*, 1960). Amazing use of the sarangi to echo the singer's pain, and four stanzas, all differently composed, all tugging at our hearts!

- *Kabhi tanhaiyon mein yoon* (Mubarak/ Snehal Bhatkar/ Kidar Sharma/ *Hamari Yaad Ayegi*, 1961). A beautifully crafted, haunting melody from the begum, qualifying to belong up there in the mountains!

- *Aye dil kahaan teri manzil* (Dwijen Mukherji/ Salil Chowdhury/ Majrooh/ *Maya*, 1961). The Western opera treatment, what with the chorus rising in pitch to underscore the loneliness that has to be conveyed. *Kis liye mil-mil ke dil toot-te hain, kis liye ban-ban mahal toot-te hain;* the chorus dramatizes the lines.

- *Dhadakte dil ki tamanna ho* (Suraiya/Ghulam Mohd./ Kaifi Azmi/ *Shama*, 1961). What incredible words of praise! *Khilao phool kisi ke, kisi chaman mein raho, Jo dil ki raah se guzri hai wo bahaar ho tum.* Fatal.

- *Na tum humen jaano* (Suman/ SD Burman/ Majrooh/ *Baat Ek Raat Ki*, 1962). Her voice shines in this tandem product, washed as it is by the violin ensemble, and the sensational *taar shehnai.*

- *Aap aaye to khayaal-e-dil-e-naashaad aaya* (Mahendra Kapoor/ Ravi/ Sahir/ *Gumrah*, 1963). It's between the singer, the writer and the violin ensemble here, the tabla keeping them excellent company.

> *Poochho na kaise maine raen bitaayi* (Manna Dey/ SD Burman/ Shailendra/ *Meri Surat Teri Ankhen*, 1963). The pain, the loneliness, the entire experience of this *Ahir Bhairav* work of class. Such songs define the golden age of our music.

> *Ashkon mein jo paaya hai* (Talat/ N. Datta/ Sahir/ *Chaandi Ki Deewar*, 1964). A ghazal by the King of Ghazals, and this one is beyond praise! *Jo taar se nikli hai wo dhun sab ne suni hai, jo saaz pe guzri hai wo kis dil ko pata hai?* No one can better the words or the voice.

> *Tum apna ranj-o-gham apni pareshaani mujhe de do* (Jagjit Kaur/ Khayyam/ Sahir/ *Shagun*, 1964). Jagjit Kaur sings the perfect *ardhangini* words for her husband's tune, and it's Enoch Daniels who starts and ends this melody with his euphonic piano.

> *Ya dil ki suno duniya waalo* (Hemant/ Hemant/ Kaifi Azmi/ *Anupama*, 1966). Hemant Kumar singing a ghazal? That's not his forte. But perhaps he just went up to the director and said, "Look here, Hrishi, I understand music, right? Leave it to me, and I will make Dharmendra look good. This song will get a visa for the mountains". And so it came to be recorded as an unforgettable melody with that famous address, 29028.

And don't we all know dozens of such lifelong visitor-turned-friends?

Enlightened men have said that happiness can be found at home, in a garden, or a library. Perhaps all that is true. Many others are most happy when they receive friends from the Himalayas, especially if these friends live high up at 29028!

~~~~

The above was originally published in DNA Jaipur on 29 December 2013. It has since been updated and enhanced.

~~~~

Second Sunday in May

God made mothers because he couldn't be everywhere—Yiddish proverb.

These days, it is said that if the United States sneezes, the rest of the world catches a cold. The reference is mainly to the economic strength of that country, but America has influenced the world culturally too, in music and cinema, in consumerism and language and much more. The idea of celebrating the second Sunday in May as Mother's Day started there in the early 20th century and by the end of the century had got a cultural hold in our country as well. So if your mother is around, make it extra nice for her today. It doesn't take much to make mothers happy.

In India, thanks to the power of cinema, it was Nargis who became the face of the ideal mother through her extraordinary portrayal in *Mother India* (1957). She played the role of a patient and industrious woman who suffers much, loves her children, maintains her dignity and holds high values. For a long time, she retained this image of the ideal Indian mother. For many, she is still number 1. But for most of the generation that came later, she was replaced by Nirupa Roy, the quintessential Indian mother, especially for the number of roles she came to essay in that capacity. Nirupa Roy died in 2004, aged 73 with about 200 films under her belt.

But other actresses in our films did admirable work as mothers too. We list them here, with just one film per person, along with who they played the mother to. The names are listed alphabetically.

➤ Achla Sachdev was the mother to Sunil Dutt, Shashi Kapoor and Raaj Kumar in *Waqt* (1965)

- Anjali Devi was Daisy Irani's mother in *Devta* (1956)
- Aruna Irani was Anil Kapoor's mother in *Beta* (1992)
- Bina Rai was the mother of Dilip Raj and Kashinath Ghanekar in *Daadi Ma* (1966)

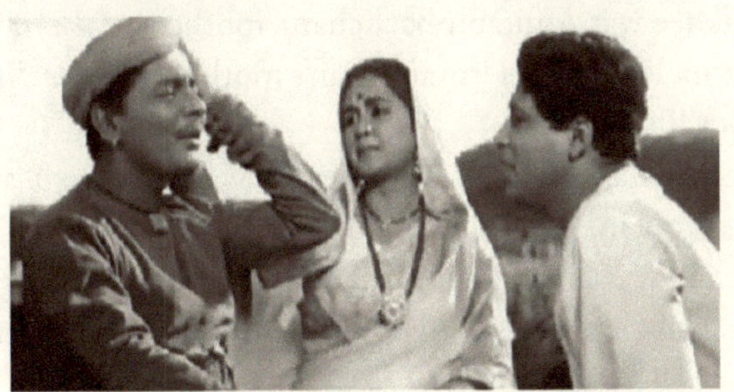

Bina Rai in Dadi Maa

- Dimple Kapadia was the mother to Salman Khan and Arbaz Khan in *Dabangg* (2010)
- Durga Khote was Dilip Kumar's mother in *Mughal-e-Azam* (1960)
- Farida Jalal was Kajol's mother in *Dilwale Dulhaniya Le Jayenge* (1995)
- Hema Malini was Master Alankar's mother in *Andaz* (1971)
- Kamini Kaushal was Manoj Kumar's mother in *Shaheed* (1965)
- Kirron Kher was Aishwarya Rai's mother in *Devdas* (2002)
- Lalita Pawar was Shammi Kapoor's mother in *Junglee* (1961)
- Leela Chitnis was Dev Anand's mother in *Kala Bazaar* (1960)
- Leela Mishra was Guru Dutt's mother in *Pyaasa* (1957)
- Mala Sinha was Bindu's mother in *Anpadh* (1962)
- Maushami Chatterjee was Akshaye Khanna's mother in *Doli Saja Ke Rakhna* (1998)
- Meena Kumari was Daisy Irani's mother in *Ek Hi Raasta* (1956)
- Nargis was the mother to Sunil Dutt and Rajendra Kumar in *Mother India* (1957)
- Nigar Sultana was Mala Sinha's mother in *Do Kaliyan* (1968)
- Nirupa Roy was the mother of Shashi Kapoor and Amitabh Bachchan in *Deewar* (1975)

- Nutan was the screen mother of Kumar Gaurav and Sanjay Dutt in *Naam* (1986)
- Pearl Padamsee was the mother of Tina Munim and Ranjit Chowdhury in *Baaton Baaton Mein* (1979)
- Rakhee was Amitabh Bachchan's mother in *Shakti* (1982)
- Ratna Pathak was Imran Khan's mother in *Jaane Tu…Ya Jaane Na* (2008)
- Reema Lagoo was the mother of Madhuri Dixit and Renuka Shahane in *Hum Aapke Hain Koun* (1994)
- Rekha was Hrithik Roshan's mother in *Koi Mil Gaya* (2003)
- Shabana Azmi was the mother of Urmila Matondkar in *Masoom*, 1983
- Sharmila Tagore: with Rajesh Khanna in a double role, she was the mother to one of them in *Aradhana* (1969)
- Suchitra Sen portrayed a double role, a mother and her daughter in *Mamta* (1966)
- Sulochana was Shashikala's mother, and Nutan's foster mother, in *Sujata* (1959)
- Waheeda Rehman was Jaya Bhaduri's mother in *Phagun* (1973)

Many of these ladies were lead or supporting actresses before they turned to playing maternal roles. For some like Sharmila Tagore and Shabana Azmi, the roles of a mother were just excursions before they came back to play in leading capacities. But whenever the idea of mothers comes up, the mind just has to think of Nirupa Roy.

This is the lady who is most remembered for a scene in *Deewar*, which doesn't even feature her in the frame. Her two sons—Shashi Kapoor and Amitabh Bachchan—are in serious conflict, and in one scene, confront each other. The unscrupulously successful son Amitabh announces to his unprosperous brother that he possesses so much—a villa, wealth, car, and bank balance. "What do you have?" he asks his sibling. After a pause, Shashi offers a disarming reply: *"Mere paas maa hai"* (I have mother). The line is followed by the shrill whistle of a train, with visuals of a compartment being jolted hard. All that dramatizes the dialogue, making the scene a meta moment not just in the film but outside as well; it has been universalized and immortalized for all of us, with people always thinking of the *maa*, Nirupa Roy here.

What an irony then that in real life too, Nirupa Roy gave birth to two sons who are now in serious conflict with each other. When she was doing well, she bought a flat in Embassy Apartments at Nepean Sea Road in South Mumbai. This was on the ground floor, a 3000 square foot, 4-bedroom flat with an attached lawn of about 8000 square feet. With increasing success, she bought another apartment in Gulmarg, one kilometre south of there, just above the flat owned by Shyama, to whom she was quite close. Across this home, in Poonam, stayed Waheeda Rehman. Nirupa didn't stay in Gulmarg, she had bought that apartment for the future of her family.

After her passing away in 2004, her husband and his sons continued to stay at Embassy Apartments. Then Mr. Roy passed away in 2015, which is when the real trouble started. Both flats are still there, but both her sons and their families stay unhappily together in Embassy Apartments. Not just unhappily, but with smashed windows, heated exchanges, and court cases on the front burner. The flat was bought in the same week as her film *Mujhe Jeene Do* was released, in 1963. It cost Rs. 10 lacs then and is valued at about Rs. 50 crores today. As such, the property—the structure and spaces—has multiplied an extraordinary 500 times. But what about the human beings in her *home*? Has the happiness multiplied among her survivors that many times? No, in fact, it has diminished, if it exists at all. Wonder if there's a message in there for all of us.

Perhaps we should respect the dead, especially if they have given us happiness of any kind, financial or otherwise. In recent years, there has been a controversy over the authorship of Bahadur Shah Zafar's ghazal, *"Na kisi ki aankh ka noor hoon"*. Mr. Javed Akhtar has staked a claim that it was written by his grandfather, Muztar Khairabadi. This ghazal was sung by Rafi in *Lal Qila* (1960). The film also featured another ghazal by the last Mughal King: *"Lagta naheen hai dil mera ujde dayaar mein"*. That ghazal ended with the couplet *"Kitna hai badnaseeb Zafar dafn ke liye, Do gaz zameen bhi na mili koo-e-yaar mein"*. (How unfortunate I am, that I could not even get to be buried in the land of my beloved). After news of this controversy, maybe the late Mughal Emperor is agitated and shaking his head in disapproval in his grave in Burma.

Nirupa Roy's soul too may be tormented these days. Wonder if her sons have thought about Mother's Day at all.

~~~~

The above was originally published in DNA Jaipur on 13 May 2018. It has since been updated and enhanced.

~~~~

27

Pets and Beyond

Each year, Forbes Magazine brings out a list of the world's richest people. Earlier this year, in January, it named Jeff Bezos of Amazon as the world's richest man with a net worth of 78 billion US Dollars. A billion is a thousand million, which is an awful lot of money. The person has to be doing many things right to create such fabulous wealth.

Amazon's philosophy is to efficiently sell us anything that answers a need as long as it's legal. That includes marketing whatever you have seen anywhere, even odd things that you may not have imagined, such as LED chopsticks to help you see the Chinese food you're eating or live cockroaches for pets. The latter are shiny little creatures called Madagascar Hissing Cockroaches, which make a cute *sh* sound when they are poked or in the mood. You can buy one for about 9 US Dollars, but for a couple of Dollars more, Amazon will send you a sexed pair instead, so you can breed a colony of roaches. One wonders who buys such creepy crawlies, but you'll be surprised how many of them are sold. We cannot order them in India yet, but who wants to buy them here anyway? We have so many; if animal rights activists allow it, we will even be able to sell these creatures, lacquered and all, on Amazon.

Cockroaches can be pets in the classical sense, but definitions of pets blur. In many people's view, pets are animals which are brought out of their natural habitat, tamed and looked after by an owner who expects recreation or protection in return. The question of commerce doesn't enter this equation. Cows, bulls, and goats are used for milking or farming so they are not considered pets. Horses neither, since they are used for transportation or racing. Elephants, bears, lions and monkeys are used for performing tricks in circuses or by solo operators, so they are not considered pets too. Hamsters and Guinea Pigs are laboratory animals, so they too don't get the nod. Poultry is used for eggs or for consumption, so the pet question doesn't arise. Camels are made to race by the Arabs and are also beasts of burden, like yaks, donkeys and llamas, so they are also denied the platform of pets. Also, Falcons, so popularly owned on the sands of Arabia, are almost exclusively used for hunting.

But then, importantly, it's also what you want from the animal you own that determines if it's a pet or not. If, for instance, a horse is owned only for pleasure—to ride on just for fun, rather than to check what's up on the ranch for instance—then it can become a pet. Hamsters are fun to play with, and in just that role they become pets. Several people in the West have a chimp as a pet too, when it entertains in a non-commercial environment.

Among the common animals, it's cats and dogs that lead as the most popular pets worldwide, followed in no particular order by rabbits, parrots, mynas, turtles, fish, frogs, snails, crabs, ducks, goldfish and lovebirds. Interestingly, what many of us treat as pests are kept by a few as pets, like worms, lizards and snakes.

Hindi cinema has had so much fun with such creatures too, even some wild ones like elephants and lions. For an early example, the mind goes to V Shantaram's *Shakuntala* (1943)—which he remade as *Stree* in 1961—on the story of a beautiful hermit maiden named Shakuntala who lives in the woods. A royal, Raja Dushyant, who is out hunting, sees her and in a couple of encounters, both of them are in love with each other. They get married secretly and soon he needs to go back to his kingdom, with a promise that he will return. Once in the palace, selective amnesia takes charge of the king, so he doesn't recall who she is. But she is already pregnant and presently she delivers a baby boy, who grows up in the jungle in the comfortable company of a pride of lions. In these happy times, the boy even asks a lion to open his mouth so he can count the animal's teeth. Now this would suggest that the lion is the boy's pet, right? But by classical definitions, that is still not so. The lion could have been a pet if he had been brought out of his natural habitat and domesticated in a human home. Here it's the boy who is not in his natural environment, so this becomes a case of peaceful coexistence, with no pet in the narrative.

Five years after the 1943-made Shakuntala was released, it was sent to the USA to become the first Indian film to be commercially screened there. A few years later, the Americans returned the favour by sending us their first actor, even if it was an animal. The chimpanzee named Zippy arrived to star in the film *Insaniyat* (1955). Zippy was already a celebrity in American films and television, and in *Insaniyat* he was given plenty of screen space. Not just that, filmmaker Vasan spent 55,000 US Dollars on the animal, more than he paid any one of the film's leading human stars, Dilip Kumar, Dev Anand and Bina Rai. *Insaniyat* was the only film in which Dev and Dilip acted together, but bearing in mind the above facts, we also need to consider that it was this landmark film in which both Dev and Dilip were upstaged by Zippy the Chimp.

At this point, a mention must be made of an animal that is a rarity in terms of ownership for protection. That honour goes to a mongoose in the film *Kohinoor* (1960). The animal's protective nature is highlighted at the end of the song *Madhuban mein Radhika naache re*, when the mongoose lashes out to destroy a snake let loose to kill his owner, Dilip Kumar. I owe a debt of gratitude to my film-crazy friend Bobby Sing, the author of the book "Did You Know", to reacquaint me with this fact.

So whether they were pets, pests or neither, here are some songs that featured a diverse range of creatures on our screen:

- ➤ *Jeevan ki nao na dole* (Lioness and Cubs/ *Shakuntala*, 1943)
- ➤ *Rumjhum rumjhum chaal tihaari* (Elephant/ *Tansen*, 1943)
- ➤ *Raja beta bada hoke jaayega school* (Chimpanzee/ *Insaniyat*, 1955)
- ➤ *Ghaayal hiraniya main ban-ban doloon* (Tiger/ *Munimji*, 1955)
- ➤ *Chhun chhun karti aayi chidiya* (Bear/ *Ab Dilli Door Nahin*, 1957)
- ➤ *Kaune rang mungwa* (Oxen/ *Heera Moti*, 1959)
- ➤ *Alhad jawaan mera jaage* (Bull/ *Amar Shaheed*, 1960)

Alhad jawaan mera jaage

> *Jhoome mori beliya preet re* (Deer, python/ *Amar Shaheed*, 1960)
> *Salaam-e-hasrat qubool kar lo* (Birds/ *Babar*, 1960)

Salaam-e-hasrat qubool kar lo

> *Ae baby, ae ji, idhar aao* (Dog, cockatoo, horse, ducks, rabbit/ *Love In Simla*, 1960)
> *Murghe ne jhootth bola* (Cock, goat, monkey, crow, sparrow/ *Manmauji*, 1960)
> *Angna mein suraj muskaaya* (Lions/ *Stree*, 1961)
> *Mera bandar chala hai sasural* (Monkey/ *Zindagi Aur Khwab*, 1961)
> *Meow meow meri sakhi* (Cat/ *Pooja Ke Phool*, 1964)

- *Pyaar ki manzil mast safar* (Elephant/ *Ziddi*, 1964)
- *Dil aye dil teri manzil* (Parrot/ *Laadla*, 1966)
- *Bahaaro phool barsao mera mehboob aaya hai* (Elephant/ *Suraj*, 1966)
- *Chal chal chal mere saathi* (Elephants/ *Haathi Mere Saathi*, 1971)
- *Aaj main jawaan ho gayi hoon* (Parrot/ *Main Sundar Hoon*, 1971)
- *Main jahaan chala jaoon bahaar chali aaye* (Elephant/ *Banphool*, 1972)
- *Dheere se jaana khatiyan mein* (Bedbugs/ *Chhupa Rustom*, 1973)
- *O kaali re kaali re* (Goat/ *Minoo*, 1977)
- *Kabootar ja ja ja* (Pigeons/ *Maine Pyaar Kiya*, 1989)
- *Dhiktaana tiktaana dhikhtaana* (Dog/ *Hum Aapke Hain Koun*, 1994)

The island of Madagascar has the most amazing bio-diversity of any country on earth. In fact, 90% of the country's wildlife cannot be found in any other place on this planet. With his current wealth at 96 billion, i.e., about 10 times the GDP of that country, one wonders if Mr. Bezoz is tempted by the idea of buying the whole place off. This wouldn't be the first time an individual has bought an island. Marlon Brando bought Tetiaroa Island in 1965. It would be the first time someone tried buying a country.

~~~~

The above was published in DNA Jaipur on 19 July 2018. It has since been updated and enhanced.

~~~~

28

The Original Mr. India!

Red Indians and other tribes existed in America before Christopher Columbus 'discovered' it, so isn't it interesting that an explorer who followed all of them—Amerigo Vespucci—has the continent named after him? Perhaps he had the first press conference!

In somewhat the same vein, there have been several India-lovers over the years, among them Rabindranath Tagore in the Arts, Subhash Chandra Bose in Politics, and V Shantaram in Cinema, etc. But Cinema's real 'Mr. India' of Tsunamic proportions happened upon us in the shape of Mahendra Kapoor, thanks mainly to his many patriotic songs covering several decades in our films. It was only later that Anil Kapoor (no relative of the singer) took control of the baton, and gave the title a new meaning and cinematic appeal through his role in *Mr. India* (1987). Looks like he too had the first 'press conference'!

Many examples abound of the patriotic nature of Mahendra's songs, right from his very debut year in cinema, that being 1959, with this song from Navrang:

Na raja rahega na raani rahegi

Ye duniya hai faani aur faani rahegi

Na jab ek bhi zindagaani rahegi

To maati sabhi ki kahaani kahegi!

The song, written by Bharat Vyas, goes on to celebrate the life of Rana Pratap, Shivaji maharaj, the Mughals, and The Rani of Jhansi. Clearly, this was grist for the mill for Mahendra Kapoor.

Over the years, Kapoor went on to sing many jingoistic songs for filmmaker-actor Manoj Kumar, often himself called Mr. Bharat. But Mahendra Kapoor didn't sign an exclusive contract for nationalistic songs with Manoj Kumar. He sang for a variety of actors. Here is a sampling of his songs dipped in love for India:

- *Qadam qadam se dil se dil mila rahe hain hum* (with Mukesh, Manna, Meena Kapoor/ *Char Dil Char Rahen*, 1959)
- *Chalo sipaahi chalo* (non-film song after the Chinese aggression, 1960s)
- *Jai janani jai Bharat maa* (*Dharamputra*, 1961)

Jai janani jai Bharat maa

- *Ye kis ka lahu hai, kaun mara, aye rehbar mulk-o-qaum bata* (*Dharamputra*, 1961)
- *Bharat bhoomi mahaan hai teerath iske praan* (*Kan Kan Mein Bhagwan*, 1963)
- *Mera rang de basanti chola* (with Mukesh and Rajinder Mehta/ *Shaheed*, 1965)
- *Mere desh ki dharti sona ugle* (*Upkar*, 1967)
- *Dil karta o yaara dildaara mera dil karta* (with Balbir and Joginder/ *Aadmi Aur Insaan*, 1969)
- *Dulhan chali, o pehen chali teen rang ki choli* (*Purab Aur Pashchim*, 1970)
- *Bharat to hai azaad* (*Aaj Ki Awaaz*, 1984)
- *Watan ke rakhwaale* (*Watan Ke Rakhwale*, 1987)

And of course that biggie from *Purab Aur Pashchim* (1970):

Hai preet jahaan ki reet sada, main geet waheen ke gaata hoon
Bharat ka rehne waala hoon, Bharat ki baat sunaata hoon

Consistent with his excessive love for India, the singer not only sang these and other songs in Hindi and Punjabi films, but spent a lot of time touring the border areas, rooting for troops in the 1960s after the Chinese aggression, and with his actor-son Ruhan even as recently as after the Kargil incursion. He also accompanied Prime Minister Vajpayee on the celebrated inaugural bus to Lahore, in February 1999.

As a direct consequence, Mahendra Kapoor's image became heavily associated with patriotic songs, but unfortunately—because he sounded like his idol Rafi—as a poor man's Rafi too. Neither image did him justice. But changing our minds is very hard, and changing others' minds is harder still.

Anyway, because these images clung to Mahendra Kapoor's persona, listeners rarely expected him to deliver much else. As a result, every song where he did not sound patriotic or like a Rafi clone was seen as really unexpected from him. As if *Arre, ye kya hua?* To borrow a cricketing neologism, these other songs are like *doosras*, signifying a special, unexpected delivery.

And so, just to get him out of our mental slot, let's slap the dust out of our sclerotic thoughts and go see some of the many nice songs this crooner gave us, those that don't position him as a *deshbhakt* or Rafi clone. Here we go:

- *Dhadakne lagi dil ke taaron ki duniya* (with Asha/ *Dhool Ka Phool*, 1959)
- *Tere pyaar ka aasra chaahta hoon* (with Lata/ *Dhool Ka Phool*, 1959)
- *Aadha hai chandrama raat aadhi* (with Asha/ *Navrang*, 1959)
- *Shamal shamal baran komal komal charan* (*Navrang*, 1959)
- *Ga rahi hai zindagi* (with Asha/ *Aanchal*, 1960)
- *Zara sambhaliye adaayen aap ki* (with Lata/ *Bada Aadmi*, 1961)
- *Aaj ki raat naheen shikwe-shikaayat ke liye* (*Dharamputra*, 1961)

> *Bhool sakta hai bhala kaun ye pyaari aankhen* (*Dharamputra*, 1961)
> *Jadoo bhare tore naina kateele* (with Asha/ *Jadoo Nagri*, 1961)
> *Aaj madhuvaataas dole* (with Lata/ *Stree*, 1961)
> *Dhoonde nazar-nazar* (with Asha/ *Dilli Ka Dada*, 1962)
> *Humne bhi muhabbat ki thi magar* (with Asha/ *Dilli Ka Dada*, 1962)
> *Badli-badli duniya hai meri* (with Lata/ *Sangeet Samrat Tansen*, 1962)
> *Aap aaye to khayaal-e-dil-e-naashaad aaya* (*Gumrah*, 1963)
> *O bedardi kyoon tadpaaye* (with Geeta/ *Godaan*, 1963)
> *Chalo ik baar phir se ajnabi ban jaayen hum donon* (*Gumrah*, 1963)
> *In hawaon mein in fizaon mein* (with Asha/ *Gumrah*, 1963)
> *Koi aane waala hai* (with Lata/ *Mera Qasoor Kya Hai*, 1964)
> *Chhod kar tere pyaar ka daaman* (with Lata/ *Woh Kaun Thi*, 1964)
> *Rangeen fiza hai* (with Asha/ *Bahu Beti*, 1965)
> *Chandrama ja unse keh de na bano itne katthor* (with Lata/ *Bharat Milap*, 1965)
> *Aaja re mere pyaar ke raahi* (with Lata/ *Oonche Log*, 1965)
> *Maine dekha hai ke phoolon se ladi waadi mein* (with Asha/ *Waqt*, 1965)
> *Dil laga kar hum ye samjhe* (*Zindagi Aur Maut*, 1965)
> *Humen to maar diya mil ke duniya waalon ne* (with Krishna Kalle/ parody in *Hum Kahan Ja Rahe Hain*, 1966)
> *Rafta rafta wo hamaare dil ke armaan ho gaye* (with Asha/ *Hum Kahan Ja Rahe Hain*, 1966)
> *Kalpana ke ghan baraste geet geele ho rahe* (with Lata/ *Amar Jyoti*, 1967)
> *Haath aaya hai jab se tera haath mein* (with Asha/ *Dil Aur Muhabbat*, 1969)
> *Andhere mein jo baitthe hain* (*Sambandh*, 1969)
> *Chand bhi koi deewaana hai* (with Asha/ *Apna Ghar Apni Kahani*, 1974)
> *Jigar mein dard kaisa* (with Kamal Barot/ *Apna Ghar Apni Kahani*, 1974)

That's not his entire repertoire; consider more of these exceptional 'doosras' offered by Mahendra Kapoor in several dozens of songs:

> *Jhukti ghata gaati hawa sapne jagaaye* (with Asha/ *Dhool Ka Phool*, 1959). This love song, exceptionally planned by N. Datta, has Asha going solo in the first half, with Mahendra's entry signalled by a change in tempo. Excellence obtained *in toto*.

> *Kaun ho tum, kaun ho* (*Stree*, 1961), in which Mahendra Kapoor goes uber-soft in love, the Vichitra Veena keeping him company.

> *Kho gaya hai mera pyaar* (*Hariyali Aur Rasta*, 1962), a medium-paced Shankar-Jaikishan work of class, the sad kind the composing duo normally gave to Mukesh.

> *Ye hawa ye hawa ye hawa* (*Gumrah*, 1963), the haunting raag Bhopali tune with its echoes achieved by moving the volume sliders up and down, before sophisticated electronics made such effects easy.

> *Tum nacho ras barse* (*Sati Naari*, 1966), a classical effort tuned by Pandit Shivram, the bold move producing winning results.

Amazingly, Mahendra Kapoor has a huge list of qawwalis that he rendered in his time. Here are many of them:

> *Ye masjid hai wo butkhaana* (with Balbir/ *Dharamputra*, 1961)
> *Muhabbat ke fasaane ko koi samjhe to kya samjhe* (with Asha/ *Elephant Queen*, 1961)
> *Jao ji jao badi shaan ke dikhaane waale* (with Asha, Sudha, and Balbir/ *Razia Sultana*, 1961)
> *Dil ka fasaana koi na jaana* (with Asha/ *Umar Qaid*, 1961)
> *Na ye ranj-o-alam hote, na ye zulm-o-sitam hote* (with Manna/ *Mehndi Lagi Mere Haath*, 1962)
> *Jo main tujhse poochhoon o dilruba* (with Shamshad/ *Ek Tha Alibaba*, 1963)
> *Aap se humko muhabbat ho gayi* (with Suman/ *Zingaro*, 1963)
> *Ek din ka baadshah yoon besahara ho gaya* (with Balbir, Kishore Sharma, and Surinder Kohli/ *Ek Din Ka Badshah*, 1964)

- *Husn waale dil na tadpa ab to kehna maan le* (with Usha/ *Rustom-e-Baghdad*, 1964)
- *Poochho na humen ishq mein kya-kya nazar aaya* (with Manna and Asha/ *Samson*, 1964)
- *Gar hata do aye sanam parda zara rukhsaar se* (with Asha/ *Tarzan And Circus*, 1965)
- *O bekhabar tujhe kya pata* (with Durrani and Bhupinder/ *Akalmand*, 1966)
- *Muraaden leke sab aaye hain* (with Manna/ *Johar in Kashmir*, 1966)
- *Ishq daulat se khareeda naheen jaata pyaare* (*Jab Yaad Kisi Ki Aati Hai*, 1967)
- *Jab aa hi gaye hain dar pe tere* (with Asha, Badri Pawar, and Shankar Dasgupta/ *Kaheen Din Kaheen Raat*, 1968)
- *Jo dil pe guzarti hai wo samjha naheen sakte* (with Lata/ *Jitni Door Utni Paas*, unreleased 1960s)
- *Ye hai apni chhail chhabili iski ada niraali* (with Jani Babu/ *Truck Driver*, 1970)
- *Ab ye chhod diya hai tujhpe chaahe zeher de ya jaam de* (with Manna Dey/ *Hamrahi*, 1974)
- *Hum to jhuk kar salaam karte hain* (with Bhushan Mehta, Aziz Nazan, Kishore/ *Fakira*, 1976)
- *Tum ja mile ho ghair se koi jhootth ya such much kahe* (with Asha, and Jani Babu/ *Mastan Dada*, 1977)
- *Ladki cycle waali de gayi raste mein* (with Asha/ *Pati Patni Aur Woh*, 1978)
- *Kaun hai mujrim kaun hai munsif* (with Manna/ *Chambal Ki Kasam*, 1979)
- *Aaye hain wo mazaar pe ghunghat utaar ke* (with Usha Khanna and Suresh Wadkar/ *Saajan Ki Saheli*, 1981)
- *Chehra chhupa liya hai kisi ne hijaab mein* (with Asha and Salma Agha/ *Nikaah*, 1982)
- *Sharafat Ali ko sharaafat ne maara* (with Mohd. Aziz, Kavita, and Jaspal Singh/ *Amrit*, 1986)

Plus he sang a very popular qawwali outside cinema: *Ajmer waale Khwaja, jhooli bharo hamaari.*

What a feast of melodies above! Of course, many of Mahendra's songs had sensitive poetry needing high-class expression. No filmmaker, composer, or songwriter would have liked to repeat working with him if that quality was lacking. But almost every composer repeated with this singer, which should tell us something.

The point in mentioning all this is to offer us thoughts about the heavy millstone slung around Mahendra's neck, not in small part because he sounded like the man he admired most. This talent of sounding like a successful singer works like a double-edged knife: it gets you more initial breaks, but it also creates enormous hurdles as you navigate the waters for newer opportunities. You are always branded as a no. 2 so-and-so.

Address this man's origins, and we can see how this burden of sounding like Rafi could hardly be lessened. To begin with, the obsessed young man famously ran away from home to go meet his idol. Later, young Mahendra's guru, Pandit Husnlal, was himself very fond of Rafi, having used that singer in several hits like *Muhabbat ke dhoke mein koi na aaye* (*Badi Behen*, 1949) and *Tune mera yaar na milaaya, main kya jaanu teri ye Khudaayi* (*Shama Parwana*, 1954). Later, when it came to participating in a high-profile music contest, young Mahendra sang the latter song before an august audience in which the judges were C Ramchandra, Naushad, Vasant Desai, Madan Mohan, and Anil Biswas. He got to be the best singer at the contest, earning himself breaks in cinema in *Sohni Mahiwal* (1958) and *Navrang* (1959).

Before long, he was singing away for many composers and lyricists, without pausing to reflect and change tracks. Pretty soon too, a rift between Rafi and OP Nayyar furnished him with invitations to sing in Nayyar's recording rooms. *Badal jaaye agar maali* (*Baharen Phir Bhi Ayengi*, 1966), *Laakhon hain yahaan dil waale* (*Kismat*, 1968), *Meri jaan tum pe sadqe* (*Sawan Ki Ghata*, 1966), and *Kahaan se laayi ho jaan-e-man ye* (with Asha/ *Dil Aur Mohabbat*, 1968), are just a few of these. With everything so hunky-dory, why upset the apple cart?

And that's the result of the road taken by Mahendra Kapoor, a successful singer who had the potential to offer so much more than we score him with.

Mahendra Kapoor was a fitness buff, and yet he got knee surgery done some time in 2006. But convalescing wasn't easy, and he soon lost his spirits. On September 27, 2008, this good singer and popular human being passed away.

He had given us some very good songs to enjoy. Many of us want to remember him through Sahir's poetry:

Na moonh chhupa ke jiyo, aur na sar jhuka ke jiyo
Ghamon ka daur bhi aaye to muskura ke jiyo…
Ghata mein chhup ke sitaare fana nahin hote
Andheri raat ke dil mein diye jala ke jiyo

~ ~ ~

The above was originally published in DNA Jaipur on 21 October 2012. It has since been updated and enhanced.

29

What's the Good Word?

The following is how part of the introduction happens in the song *What's The Good Word* (Peter Pan Orchestra and Chorus, 1963). "What's a good word? A good word is the right word in the right place at the right time. Each of the thousands of different words in our vocabulary has a special job of its own, and that's why it's important to learn as much as we can about the good words and how to use them. Are you ready to find out about some of them? Good! Let's go!"

There was also a popular Canadian word game show of the same name that was televised for four years from 1972. Soon after came India's first all-English television show of the same name again, hosted very professionally by Sabira Merchant on Doordarshan for 15 years. In this game, the host gives you a clue or two, and live participants guess the word. In the process, we viewers learn too.

Words are fun for many of us. Some people buy Reader's Digest just for their monthly vocabulary test page called It Pays to Increase Your Word Power. Others get newspapers featuring games where you make words from 9-letter wheels. Then there's Scrabble, the classic word game on a board for friends and family, now available on handheld devices, so you can play alone too. For word lovers like this writer, it can be great fun.

But besides the fun, there are rewards. A good vocabulary is a strong promise of a better future because studies have found links between intellectual depth and word power. Research has shown that the brain changes as you learn more words and express your thoughts with more refinement. You become smart, setting yourself up for improved professional chances. Such progress can be shown on a monitor.

This is not to say that people who have a problem with words are dumb or guaranteed to fail. Not at all. We know that dyslexia is a condition that challenges its victims to read and write. But when things are read out to them, some of them do not have a difficulty at all. Others improve with the help of phonics, a teaching approach that co-relates sounds with alphabets. Many people have combated dyslexia and gone on to have successful careers. This includes not only Singapore's ex-Prime Minister Lee Kuan Yew, but also entrepreneur Steve Jobs, painter Pablo Picasso, actor Tom Cruise, and physicist Albert Einstein. Why, even people working with words, like authors Jules Verne of France and John Irving of the United States have had such disabilities. Dyslexics often have other skills which can be exploited to advance their careers and enjoy a fulfilling life. It is just such a dyslexic child who has phenomenal painting skills that forms the subject of the film *Taare Zameen Par* (2007).

That's about people who have special skills. For the rest of us, the world of words can be beautiful. It is therefore delightful to know that Indian kids are doing so well in the spelling and meaning area. This is particularly true of Indian children in the USA, where such tests are calibrated and the winners are celebrated.

On 31st May 2018, for the 11th year running, Indian kids dominated the annual championships of the Scripps National Spelling Bee championship. The 96-year-old contest not only tests people for spellings but also the origins and meanings of words. The 2018 winner was 14-year-old Karthik Nemmani from Texas. His final correctly-spelt word was 'koinonia' meaning Christian communion. This was televised on ESPN in the USA and the boy took home an award of $42000. The runner-up was a 12-year-old girl named Naysa Modi, also of Indian origin, as was the 2nd runner-up, Abhijay Kodali. There were over 500 contestants in this event. The 2023 champion was another Indian, Dev Shah from Florida.

We are ignoring the success that came the way of children of Indian origin just a bit before the above. This was the National Geographic Bee

Scholarship, which tests knowledge of Geography and carries a prize of $50000. The winner here was Venkat Ranjan, followed by Anoushka Buddhikot and Vishal Sareddy. Phew!

That's great news, but now how about you? You are not being tested here for spellings or meanings of words, but do you recall these film songs in your unsupervised environment? They have to do with either words or spellings:

> *ABCDEF bhi jaane na hum* (Sabita Banerjee, Suman/ *Darwaza*, 1954)

> *ABC, ABC mere sapnon mein chori-chori aaya karo ji* (Asha, Kishore/ *Ilzaam*, 1954)

> *C-A-T cat, cat maane billi* (Kishore, Asha/ *Dilli Ka Thug*, 1958)

> *Likh padh padh likh, likh padh ke* (Geeta, Usha/ *Kangan*, 1959)

> *Ee se banti imli* (Rafi, Asha/ *Kya Yeh Bambai Hai*, 1959)

> *Likho padhoge to aage badhoge* (Lata, Rafi, Sheikh Mukhtar, Honey Irani/ *Barood*, 1960)

> *Alif zabr aa aa alif zer ae ae* (Rafi, Sudha/ *Love In Simla*, 1960)

Alif zabr aa aa

> *L-O-V-E, Love! Love ka matlab hai pyaar* (Rafi, Asha/ *Love In Simla*, 1960)

> *Ka se kul duniya hamaari* (Asha/ *Chandi Ki Deewar*, 1964)

> *Suno suno Miss Chatterji...B-E-T-T-E-R Better* (Rafi, Asha/ *Baharen Phir Bhi Ayengi*, 1966)

> *A for Apple B for Baby* (Manna Dey, Asha/ *Sadhu Aur Shaitan*, 1968)

- *ABCD chhodo nainon se naina jodo* (Lata/ *Raja Jani*, 1972)
- *L-O-V-E Love ka matlab prem* (Kishore, Usha Khanna/ *Bekhabar*, 1983)
- *Sa se banta hai saathi* (Kishore, Asha/ *Yaadgaar*, 1984)
- *ABCDEFG hum bolega* (Amit Kumar/ *Kasam Dhande Ki*, 1990)
- *ABCDEFG dil mera aake le lo ji* (Udit, Kavita/ *Anari*, 1999)
- *ABCDEFG are G se ghanti baj rahi hai* (Shailendra Singh, Usha Mangeshkar/ *Maqaar*, 1986)
- *ABCDEFG padh lo pyaar ki aa aa ee* (Alka Yagnik/ *Kanoon Apna Apna*, 1989)
- *ABCDEFGH PPPP piya* (Alka Yagnik, Udit Narayan/ *Prem Deewane*, 1992)
- *ABCDEFG…XYZ* (Udit Narayan, Hariharan, Shankar Mahadevan, Hema Sardesai/ *Hum Saath Saath Hain*, 1999)

Illiterate vs Functionally Illiterate

The inability to read and write isn't only about dyslexia. It may have to do with illiteracy or even functional illiteracy. The difference is this: a basic illiterate person does not know how to spell or read even easy words such as bat or cat in *any* language. A functionally illiterate person may know how to spell such words and what they mean, but will be unable to handle a sentence such as "The cat sat on Virat Kohli's bat". Functionally illiterate people cannot, for example, read the instructions on the back of a can of soup. Or articles such as this one. It's really about degrees here, with the functionally illiterate person better off than an illiterate person.

The above is easy to determine. It gets hard when you have to define literacy officially. The official definition in India is "people above the age of 7 who can read and write with understanding." According to 2023 figures, India's literacy rate was 77.7%, but global experts reckon that in fact we have 70% functionally illiterate people. That compares poorly with much of the West. The OECD (Organisation for Economic Co-operation and Development) is a body of a few dozen countries that aim to learn from each other and promote the social and economic lot of people around the world. It is famous for its statistical surveys on a wide variety of subjects like the perception of corruption, level of democracy and peace, human development, economic opportunities etc. Its 2013 survey tabled a startling discovery, that 47% of the adult population in Italy was functionally illiterate, the highest among its member countries. That accounts for the country's small circulation of newspapers.

But Italy's 47% is much better than India's 70%. One wonders if that's some consolation for persons of Italian origin who live in New Delhi.

~~~~

The above was originally published in DNA Jaipur on 17 June 2018. It has since been updated and enhanced.

~~~~

30

Singing in a Funny Way

Tony Ryman, my British colleague in Dubai several decades back, had no idea of Hindi film music. One evening, before going on a month's vacation, he dropped in unannounced at my home to say goodbye. I was in my shorts listening to music on my cassette player at the time, so I excused myself for a minute to wear something more presentable while he waited.

Upon my return, he asked me why I was listening to sad music. After all, things were going just so fine for me. Wasn't all well? I told him all was good, that I loved sad songs for they made me feel better in a way that I couldn't explain. But wait, where did he hear a sad song? It turns out that the song he meant was *Hum aaj kaheen dil kho baitthe, yoon samjho kisi ke ho baitthe*, from *Andaz* (1949). I told him that was in fact a romantic song. In the film, Dilip Kumar has just fallen in love, and while some people would go Yahoo about it, perhaps this actor was being understated since he had a sober kind of personality. "Really?" asked my colleague, "I heard hints of pathos, both in the voice and the violins. In fact even in the song's tempo". He may have had a point; the lyrics were telling us of incipient love, and the visuals were showing Nargis and Dilip Kumar smiling as the latter sang. But to someone who was denied the visual experience and had no idea of the language, the composition and voice were as if headed the other way.

When people cannot see the visuals and don't understand the lyrics of a song, it is the instruments and the voice that combine to become the language of communication. It is for such situations that the expression "Music is a universal language" gets meaning.

The *Andaz* song is not the only one in which all the elements of a song are not sending us a common message clearly. It is possible that for fear of overkill, many music makers may have even thought that every element is not needed to do so. And yet it is true that vocal elements can tell people like Tony Ryman the mood of the song. This becomes particularly clear in comedy songs if the singer is made to render a passage playfully. The musical description of such a passage is Scherzando, which is Italian. It comes from scherzare, to joke, and in music, it's an instruction to the singer to render a passage funnily.

Let's look at a few comic songs from Hindi cinema where the vocalist gave it a funny touch. In the few cases you may have a prima facie doubt, we have identified in brackets one passage sung that way. Such passages sometimes happen much after the start. The composer is mentioned along with the singer. Also, we leave out songs with yodelling since they are so predictably funny.

> *Qusoor aap ka huzoor aap ka (Left-right, left-right about turn)* (Shamshad or Kishore/ SD Burman/ *Bahar*, 1951)
> *Kabhi na bigde kisi ki motorrr raste mein* (Suraiya/ Hansraj Behl/ *Moti Mahal*, 1952)
> *Khaali peeli kaahe ko akkha din baitth ke bom maarta hai* (Kishore/ Manna Dey/ *Tamasha*, 1952)

Khaali peeli kaahe ko akkha din

- *Chaahe koi khush ho chaahe gaaliyaan hazaar de (Pi ke dhandhli karoon to mujhko jail bhej do)* (Kishore, Johnny Walker/ SD Burman/ *Taxi Driver*, 1954)
- *Daal kaise gale (Aise shaadi se hum to kunwaare bhale)* (Kishore/ C Ramchandra/ *Baap Re Baap*, 1955)
- *Dil ki umangen hain jawaan* (the Pran part is sung funnily) (Hemant, Geeta, Thakur/ SD Burman/ *Munimji*, 1955)
- *Dekh tere Bhagwan ki haalat kya ho gayi insaan (Sun kar is paapi ko taano)* (Rafi, SD Batish, Manmohan Krishna/ Madan Mohan/ *Railway Platform*, 1955)
- *Aal line kiliar (Papa! Are dhat teri ki)* (Rafi/ Shankar-Jaikishan/ *Chori Chori*, 1956)
- *Humko haste dekh zamaana jalta hai (Jalta hai jale koi yahaan hai fikar kise)* (Rafi, Durrani/ OP Nayyar/ *Hum Sab Chor Hain*, 1956)
- *Are bhai nikal ke aa ghar se (Kem oonghe chhe bhai Ghanshyam ji)* (Kishore/ Shankar-Jaikishan/ *New Delhi*, 1956)
- *Yaar tum shaadi mat karna (Chai pilaoon ke thanda mangaoon, ke murghi ke ande ki bhurji banaoon)* (Kishore/ Salil Chowdhury/ *Parivaar*, 1956)
- *Main ik shola aag babola (Baraf ka gola)* (Shamshad, Geeta Bali, Uma Devi/ Roshan/ *Rangeen Raaten*, 1956)
- *Aaj na jaane paagal manwa kaahe ko ghabraaye (Tabiyat bichki bichki jaaye)* (Kishore/ Shankar-Jaikishan/ *Begunah*, 1957)
- *Ye ho kar rahega (Abba ae abba!)* (Rafi/ Hansraj Behl/ *Changez Khan*, 1957)
- *Dekhta chala gaya main zindagi ki raah mein (Naheen hoti)* (Rafi, Lata, Johnny Walker/ Madan Mohan/ *Gateway Of India*, 1957)
- *Main hoon Mr. Johnny (Tum poochhoge kyoon? Main abhi bataata hoon)* (Rafi/ OP Nayyar/ *Mai Baap*, 1957)
- *Gaana na aaya bajaana na aaya (Kaheen ga ma pa dha ni hai)* (Kishore/ Hemant Kumar/ *Miss Mary*, 1957)
- *Tel maalish champi...sar jo tera chakraaye* (Rafi/ SD Burman/ *Pyaasa*, 1957)

- *Main sitaaron ka taraana (Dheere se jaana bagiyan mein)* (Asha, Kishore/ SD Burman/ *Chalti Ka Naam Gaadi*, 1958)
- *Zulf ke phande phas gayi jaan (Is dil ke armaan)* (Rafi/ OP Nayyar/ *Mujrim*, 1958)
- *Main Bangaali chhokra (Mur jaaye mur jaaye)* (Kishore, Asha/ OP Nayyar/ *Raagini*, 1958)
- *Kaise Diwali manaayen hum Lala (Daata teri akal ku he kaaye jhaala)* (Rafi/ C Ramchandra/ *Paigham*, 1959)
- *Aankhon se aankhon ka tu jaam liye ja* (Manna Dey, Kishore/ SD Burman/ *Bewaqoof*, 1960)
- *Dekh idhar dekh tera dhyaan kahaan hain, sar pe budhaapa hai magar dil to jawaan hai* (Asha, Manna/ SD Burman/ *Bewaqoof*, 1960)
- *Ye duniya gol hai (Ek photo ka sawaal hai baba)* (Rafi/ Ravi/ *Chaudhvin Ka Chand*, 1960)
- *Hum tum jise kehta hai shaadi (Mr. Iyer, are you there?)* (Rafi/ SD Burman/ *Kaagaz Ke Phool*, 1960)
- *Ye hai jeevan ki rail, ye hai toofaan mail (Mote-mote dil ke khote, Grand Hotel ke double rote)* (Kishore/ S Mohinder/ *Mehlon Ke Khwaab*, 1960)
- *Aaj ka din bhi pheeka pheeka gham mein tere beeta beeta* (Rafi, Asha/ SD Burman/ *Baat Ek Raat Ki*, 1962)
- *Aake seedhi lagi dil pe jaise katariya* (Kishore/ Salil Chowdhury/ *Half Ticket*, 1962)
- *Ye ras teri baton ka chaclate, ye jadoo teri ankhon ka aamlate* (Rafi/ Chitragupt/ *Ghar Basake Dekho*, 1963)
- *Aashiq hoon apne pyaar ke jauhar dikhaoonga (Apan to ghar ka aadmi hai na, aa?)* (Rafi/ Ravi/ *Kaun Apna Kaun Paraya*, 1963)
- *Duniya banaane waale…pyaar ki aag mein tan badan jal gaya* (Manna Dey/ SD Burman/ *Ziddi*, 1964)
- *Lori suna suna ke…muskura laadle muskura* (Mehmood/ Kalyanji-Anandji/ *Purnima*, 1965)
- *Yahaan bhi to naheen hai (Kamaal ho gaya)* (Kamal Barot, Rafi/ Kalyanji-Anandji/ *Preet Na Jaane Reet*, 1966)
- *Ek chatur naar (Aiyo ghoda bola)* (Kishore, Manna Dey, Mehmood/ RD Burman/ *Padosan*, 1968)

Want to think of some comic songs in which the vocals didn't carry the idea of fun? How about *Mere piya gaye Rangoon?* That was from *Patanga* (1949), with the singing by Chitalkar and Shamshad Begum for maestro C Ramchandra. Next year, in *Meena Bazaar*, the brothers Husnlal and Bhagatram composed for Ram Kamlani to sing *Suno buzurgon ka ye kehna, beta single single rehna*, without humour in the vocals. *Jaane kahaan mera jigar gaya ji* is another example. Tuned by OP Nayyar, it was duetted by Geeta and Rafi in *Mr. & Mrs. 55* (1955). *Do akalmand hue fikarmand* from *Akalmand* (1966) is another instance of non-humorous singing. This last ditty was sung by Rafi and Kishore for OP Nayyar.

As we saw, humour, when heard in a singing voice, is denoted by the Italian word Scherzando. Italians have contributed so much to the world in so many ways, in astronomy and gastronomy. In language, literature, and painting. In music and fashion. Many love the country for its tourist spots. They have done fairly in sports too, for instance finishing at no. 10 at the 2020 Summer Olympics. Sadly, twice consecutively they have not qualified for the football World Cup, first in Russia (2018), then in Qatar (2022). Wonder if they can manage humour in their voice and sing away their glaring absence from this game. The great Italian tenor Luciano Pavarotti would have managed that easily, but the world's most famous Opera star passed away over a decade ago.

~~~~

The above was originally published in DNA Jaipur on 1 July 2018. It has been updated and enhanced since then.

~~~~

31

Shyam—A Star Forgotten

Being a music lover, I had often heard a few songs filmed on an actor called Shyam, none more popular than *Tu mera chaand main teri chaandni* from *Dillagi* (1949). Then one day, I was amazed to hear what the film's composer Naushad said about this song in an interview. That effectively, *Dillagi* was perhaps the only film where the actor who played the villain had sung for the hero! Not just that, the villain's name was Shyam too—Shyam Kumar to be precise. In the film, both Shyam the hero, and Shyam Kumar the villain were wooing the heroine, Suraiya, so they were adversaries, with Shyam the hero getting Suraiya in the story. In the recording room though, there was no rivalry, since Suraiya was teaming up with Shyam Kumar, who was playbacking for Shyam! Then I had learnt about Shyam's premature death, triggered by a fall from a horse and being dragged for a distance. When it comes to sending a shudder down your spine, such imagery can hardly be bettered. Perhaps that is the reason why an overwhelming number of people who remember Shyam today first tell you it's the actor who fell off a horse.

Like everyone else, most Indian film personalities live normal life spans, i.e., 60 years or more. Some however have died too early. Such names include KL Saigal, Guru Dutt, Meena Kumari, Geeta Dutt, Madan Mohan, Madhubala, and Sanjeev Kumar, going on to Divya Bharati, and Sushant Singh Rajput in more recent times. But perhaps just two of our film celebrities have fallen off a horse. One was the Marathi actor and director, Baburao Painter, whose fall in the early 1920s left him with a permanent speech problem, and the other was

Shyam Chadha, for whom it was fatal. He was just 31 when his life was suddenly snuffed out in 1951.

Riding a horse was considered smart in those times. It was the mid-20th century equivalent of driving a sports car today. The filmmaker Mehboob Khan was just an 'extra' till he was admired for riding a wild horse, rodeo-style, in *Shirin Khusru* way back in 1929. Later on, action scenes with dashing men mounted on horseback were typically found in stories of dacoits (like Sunil Dutt in *Mujhe Jeene Do*, and Amjad Khan in *Sholay*, etc.). Since action scenes were hazardous, filmmakers often used trained doubles for them. But even for songs, just getting on a horse and being taken for a canter wasn't easy. And yet, many still preferred riding one themselves. Baby Tabassum and child actor Parikshit Sahni rode one during the song *Bachpan ke din bhula na dena* in *Deedar* (1951), Dev Anand went horseback in *Insaniyat* (1955) as he sang *Zulm sahen na, zulm karen ne, yehi hamaara naara hai*. Later still, both Dharmendra and Suchitra Sen rode horses during the song *In bahaaron mein akele na phiro* (*Mamta*, 1966). But the grapevine tells us that after Shyam's accident, most people were made aware of the dangers involved. They were informed, mainly through word-of-mouth, of the tragedy that had visited the debonair actor who was young, robust, and at the peak of his career. So if it could happen to Shyam, it could happen to anyone.

Shyam is an epithet of Lord Krishna, who famously loved butter, played his enchanting flute and wowed the girls. As I write this, my mind rushes to think of the film *Dillagi*, in which the opening scene introduces us to Shyam who plays his flute, mesmerising all the girls in the neighbourhood, Lord Krishna style. Not only that, but soon after, he has a spat with his bhabhi who won't give him any part of the butter she is making. He then proceeds to play the flute in many a song in the film.

Then I think of the popular KL Saigal song, *Ek raje ka beta lekar udne waala ghoda* from *President* (1937). There is a line in it that goes, *Itne mein honi ne apni bansi wahaan bajaayi* (where *honi* means fate; so this line means, 'fate intervened by playing its flute'). In this case, playing the flute is figurative, but taken in Shyam's context, with the horse and *honi*, one is prone to say, "Ouch, that hurt!"

Shyam

Shyam had an acting stint of just 9 years, and he was just 31 when he passed away. But he rocked, in his short life and career. These are his films, mentioned with his co-stars and directors:

- *Gowandhi* (1942). Punjabi film. This was Shyam's maiden outing. Co-star: Veena.
- *Khamoshi* (1942). He was credited as Shyam Sunder in this film. Co-star: Ramola. Director: RC Talwar
- *Bhalai* (1943). He had a small role in this film. The leads were Sitara Devi and Prithviraj Kapoor. Director: Nazir
- *Mazaq* (1943). He had a small role in this film. The leads were Madhuri and Pahadi Sanyal. Director: Zahoor Raja
- *Man Ki Jeet* (1944). From this film onwards, he was credited as Shyam. Co-star: Neena (wife of WZ Ahmed). Director: WZ Ahmed
- *Dhanwan* (1946). He had a small role in this film. The leads were Jairaj and Paro. Director: BM Vyas
- *Room No. 9* (1946). Co-star: Geeta Nizami. Director: Vedi
- *Aaj Aur Kal* (1947). He had a small role in this film. The leads were Neeta and Rashid Ahmed. Director: KA Abbas
- *Pehli Pehchaan* (1947). He had a small role in this film. The leads were Rajrani, Nihal, and Geeta Desai. Director: Raman B Desai
- *Majboor* (1948). Co-stars: Munawwar Sultana and Indu. Director: Nazir Ajmeri
- *Shikayat* (1948). Co-star: Snehprabha Pradhan. Director: Shahid Lateef

- *Bazaar* (1949). Co-star: Nigar Sultana. Director: K Amarnath
- *Chandni Raat* (1949). Co-star: Naseem Banu. Director: M Ehsan
- *Char Din* (1949). Co-star: Suraiya. Director: M Sadiq
- *Dada* (1949). Co-stars: Munawwar Sultana, Begum Para, Sheikh Mukhtar. Director: Harish
- *Dillagi* (1949). Co-star: Suraiya. Director: AR Kardar
- *Kaneez* (1949). Co-star: Munawwar Sultana. Director: Krishna Kumar
- *Naach* (1949). Co-star: Suraiya. Director: Ravindra Dave
- *Patanga* (1949). Co-stars: Nigar Sultana and Purnima. Director: HS Rawail
- *Raat Ki Rani* (1949). Co-star: Munawwar Sultana. Director: Jagdish Sethi
- *Roop Sundari* (1949). He had a small role in this film. The leads were Jamu Patel, Umakant, and Charubala. Directors: Narayan Patel and Ambalal Dave
- *Chhoti Bhabhi* (1950). Co-star: Nargis. Director: Shanti Kumar
- *Madari* (1950). Shyam was a guest artist in this Punjabi film. The leads were Om Prakash, Meena Shorey, and Suresh. Director: Rajinder Sharma
- *Meena Bazaar* (1950). Co-star: Nargis. Director: Ravindra Dave
- *Nirdosh* (1950). Co-star: Rehana. Director Najam Naqvi
- *Samadhi* (1950). He was in a supporting role in this film. Co-stars: Ashok Kumar, Nalini Jaywant, and Kuldip Kaur. Director: Ramesh Sehgal
- *Sangeeta* (1950). Co-stars: Nigar Sultana and Suraiya Chowdhury. Director: Ramanlal Desai
- *Surajmukhi* (1950). Co-stars: Rehana and Yashodhara Katju. Director: OP Dutta
- *Bhaiyaji* (1951). Punjabi film. Details not known.
- *Kale Badal* (1951). Co-stars: Meena Kumari and Pushpa Hans. Director: Anant Thakur
- *Shabistan* (1951). Co-star: Naseem Banu. Director: B Mitra

In those days, great songs were often a key to a film's success. Here is just one key song from some of the films listed above:

- *Gowandhi* (1942) (Punjabi): *Pagdi sambhaal jatta*
- *Man Ki Jeet* (1944): *Nagri meri kab tak yoon hi barbaad rahegi*
- *Majboor* (1948): *Ab darne ki koi baat naheen angrezi chhora chala gaya*
- *Bazaar* (1949): *O jaane waale chaand zara muskura ke ja*
- *Chandni Raat* (1949): *Chheen ke dil kyoon pher li aankhen*
- *Dillagi* (1949): *Tere kooche mein armaanon ki duniya leke aaya hoon*
- *Patanga* (1949): *Bolo ji dil logo, to kya-kya doge*
- *Raat Ki Rani* (1949): *Jin raaton mein neend ud jaati hai*
- *Meena Bazaar* (1950): *Maahi o, dupatta mera de de*
- *Samadhi* (1950): *Gore-gore, o baanke chhore*
- *Sangeeta* (1950): *Jo mujhe bhula ke chale gaye*
- *Shabistan* (1951): *Hai ye mausam-e-bahaar*

School, College, and Start of Career

Shyam was born in Sialkot on 20th February 1920. He was the eldest of four brothers and a sister. His schooling happened in various places because the family was moving about. He passed his Matric exam from Khalsa High School, Peshawar, in the first division. After his matriculation, Shyam expressed a desire to study further and do his graduate studies. It needs to be mentioned here that in those times, after matriculation, very few students opted to study further. But those who could graduate added their qualifications to their name. It was fashionable to do so. Shyam loved books and literature and wanted to write Shyam BA as his name. He sought admission to Gordon College, Rawalpindi, and went on to graduate from there. His photograph is displayed in the College Hall of Fame as a successful alumnus.

When he was at school and college, Shyam became fascinated by the performing arts in general, and theatre in particular. In college, he came across the actor Balraj Sahni and became good friends with him. Many of his other friends from this college were also inclined toward literature, arts, and culture. It was a flavour of the times, not different from studies in Management or IT in later years.

Shyam began playing roles in college plays and also got involved with theatre outside his college. Cinema was a relatively new medium and novelty during his college days, and it attracted Shyam. Lahore was a happening place, a crucible of culture, theatre, and filmmaking. He moved to Lahore in pursuit of his passion, hoping to find work in films.

Here he met the actor Om Prakash. They became good friends, especially because of their similar backgrounds and common interests. Both had similar struggles during these days. This friendship was to last a lifetime, even if Shyam's lifetime was quite short. It was Om Prakash who helped the handsome Shyam by scheduling a screen test for the Punjabi film *Gowandhi*, which got Shyam his much-needed entry into cinema.

Shyam was just 21 years old when he signed his first film. He was slim, tall, and a bit raw, but showing promise to become handsome and charming. As the shoots progressed, he picked up many ideas about acting and began working hard on his role. He improved in his work and made friends by the day. Of course, he was enjoying all this. And he was getting successful.

1949—A Great Year for Shyam

If you revisit the list of Shyam's films above, you will find that this man had 10 films released in 1949! The year was not only a great one for Shyam professionally, but he also fell in love with an aspiring actress named Mumtaz Qureshi (nicknamed Taji). The two solemnised their union by getting married on the 6th of July of the same year. They had a daughter, Sahira, who would go on to become a popular TV serial director in Pakistan, because after his death, Taji moved to that country. They would also have a son, Shakir, who would be born a couple of months after Shyam's death.

Shyam's death shocked the film world. It was too early for him to go. He was riding the crest in 1951. Perhaps in the 1950s and '60s, he would have been considered to be one of the quartet, along with Dilip Kumar, Dev Anand, and Raj Kapoor. We'll never know.

~~~~

PS: In February 2024, a book called *Shyam—A Star Forgotten* was launched in New Delhi. It was written by the actor's nephew, Bimal Chadha, and edited by me. Some of the content used in the above essay comes from that book.

♪♫♩♪
~~~~

32

Reluctant Singer?
Take a Boat Ride

In the world of comics, there is the fictional Superman, the famous crime-fighting cultural icon of the Americans. He can fix everyone, but he has one weakness: the sight of green kryptonite, a radiation-emitting mineral that instantly transforms the hero to zero. Another fictional comic character, Popeye the Sailor, is an uncultured, pipe-smoking, one-eyed young man. Typically, some problem visits him in every episode, but before he is finished, from somewhere appears magically a can of spinach, his source of strength. Popeye gulps down the spinach, and he instantly turns into a hero ready to handle every problem around him. You likely remember the story of Dr. Jekyll and Mr. Hyde too. That is the tale of a scientist who concocts a serum, and after consuming it, transforms into another person. Some of us real people may have our transformative turn-off or turn-on triggers too, even if not with such dramatic or instant results.

Take the mysterious case of a humourous man called Sultan Arshad Khan, who till he passed away in April 2023 headed Hum TV in Karachi. At one time, he was the Pakistan International Airlines chief in India for 9 years. Most of us who knew him thought of him as music personified. His knowledge and passion for songs and singing were legendary. He was incorrigible: you couldn't stop the man from singing and drumming his hands on whatever surface he could find, including coffee tables, car dashboards, books, you name it. Music is all he really cared about, so it was always a waste of his time and yours discussing fashion or politics; anything in fact that was not music-related. He was in Bombay for nine years, but within the first year itself, half the film industry got to know him and his affable nature. As for music people, he knew them all, from Anil Biswas to Babul Bose to Prasoon Joshi, Majrooh Sultanpuri, Naushad, Javed Akhtar and Gulzar, Asha Bhosle and more. You get the point. It was he who managed, with his childlike enthusiasm, to bring together many great maestros to have tea together, people like Anil Biswas, OP Nayyar, and Sajjad Husain, who were hardly known to give each other the time of day.

But he had a transformation point: the main door of his office in Mumbai. The amazing thing is, despite such a music obsession, and the nine long years, not a single person in his office had the foggiest idea that their boss knew anything about music, much less that he could whistle, hum, or sing! In light of this knowledge, none of us ever asked him what he actually did in his office, but that's another story.

Anyway, it is clear that for the music-obsessed Arshadbhai—as he was called by everyone—coming to the office and leaving it was as if executed under an invisible, magical arch that acted like a two-way trigger: non-musical after he entered, and utterly musical as he left. Some of us who also met him in his office noticed this amazing transformation in the man, and for this, he was the subject of much laughter amongst his friends.

Transformation on a boat

Interestingly, a transformation also happens to many people when they are on a boat that has left the shores as little as half an hour before. Please indulge me for a bit as I elaborate on this point. When we are on a boat—regardless of its size or sophistication—and after some time has elapsed, many of us start humming or singing to ourselves. Someone must do a study to find if there is any correlation between being at sea and getting musical. It has happened to many people. Only you wonder what triggers the singing mood. Maybe it's a feel-good thing resulting from being unhinged, pushing the right buttons in us. Perhaps it's the vastness of the sea that makes us realize how small we are in the cosmic scheme of things, making us philosophical, and goading us to reach higher planes of thought and feeling. Maybe the ripples create gentle waves of intoxication that make us go back to some memory that precipitates an urge to sing. You also wonder if the absence of hustle and bustle, or of a cultural vacuum in the waters triggers us this way.

Boatmen famously sing

It could be for any of these reasons that boatmen become singers once out at sea. It is such boatmen that we are toasting today. In Hindustani, such people who steer a sea vessel are called *maanjhi* or *khevaiyya,* whether they're controlling a *shikara*, dhow, sailboat, or fishing trawler. The following songs were sung by boatmen—at least partly—whether they were out fishing, ferrying passengers or plain having fun:

- ➤ *Katthwa ke naiyya* (Chitalkar, Lalita Dewoolkar, P Chandar, SL Puri/ C Ramchandra/ Moti/ *Nadiya Ke Paar*, 1948)
- ➤ *More raja ho le chal nadiya ke paar* (Lalita Dewoolkar, Rafi/ C Ramchandra/ Moti/ *Nadiya Ke Paar* (1948)
- ➤ *Kinaare kinaare chale jaayenge* (Suraiya/ SD Burman/ Yashodanandan Joshi/ *Vidya*, 1948)
- ➤ *Chanda re main teri gawaahi lene aayi* (Surinder Kaur/ Khursheed Anwar/ DN Madhok/ *Singaar*, 1949)
- ➤ *Nadi kinaare saath hamaare shaam suhaani aayi* (Shamshad Begum, Talat, Rafi/ Naushad/ Shakeel/ *Babul*, 1950)
- ➤ *Naiya teri majdhaar hoshiyaar* (Rafi/ Shankar-Jaikishan/ Shailendra/ *Awara*, 1951)
- ➤ *Ho kaali ghata ghir aayi re* (Rafi, Lata/ Shankar-Jaikishan/ Hasrat/ *Kali Ghata*, 1951)
- ➤ *Dharti azaad hai zindagi azaad* (Rafi, Chitragupt/ Chitragupt/ Anjum Jaipuri/ *Sinbad The Sailor*, 1952)
- ➤ *Pawan chale zor leher machaaye shor* (Pankaj Mullick/ Pankaj Mullick/ Satya Kumar/ *Zalzala*, 1952)

- *Maanjhi albele* (Geeta Roy/ OP Nayyar/ Majrooh / *Baaz*, 1953)
- *Toofanon se khele meri naav ho haiyya haiyya ho haiyya haiyya* (Shankar Dasgupta/ Madan Mohan/ Majrooh/ *Baghi*, 1953)
- *Nav badha le maanjhi zor laga le maanjhi ho* (Hemant Kumar/ Hemant Kumar/ Rajinder Krishan/ *Ferry*, 1954)
- *Maujon ka ishaara hai* (Shamshad, Lata, Rafi, S Balbir/ S Mohinder/ Tanvir Naqvi/ *Naata*, 1955)
- *More saiyaanji utrenge paar ho* (Lata/ Naushad/ Shakeel/ *Udan Khatola*, 1955)
- *Us paar saajan is paar dhaare* (Lata/ Shankar-Jaikishan/ Hasrat Jaipuri/ *Chori Chori*, 1956)
- *Wo dekhen to unki inaayat* (Kishore, Asha/ SD Burman/ Sahir/ *Funtoosh*, 1956)
- *Nadiya ke paani o re* (Lata/ Shailesh/ Shailendra/ *Savera*, 1958)
- *Jhuk jhuk jhola* (Lata, Mahendra/ Vasant Desai/ Pradeep/ *Do Behnen*, 1959)
- *Maanjhi re himmat na haar* (Mahendra/ Vasant Desai/ Bharat Vyas/ *Samrat Prithviraj Chauhan*, 1959)
- *Babam babam bam bam lehri* (Mukesh/ Chitragupt/ Majrooh/ *Ramu Dada*, 1961)
- *Le chal khevaiya naiyya le chal* (Lata/ Madan Mohan/ Rajinder Krishan/ *Senapati*, 1961)
- *Kho gaya hai mera pyaar* (Mahendra/ Shankar-Jaikishan/ Hasrat Jaipuri/ *Hariyali Aur Rasta* (1962)
- *Aag paani mein lagi* (Rafi, Lata/ Salil Chowdhury/ Rajinder Krishan/ *Jhoola*, 1962)
- *Aye meri jaan-e-wafa* (Mukesh/ Dattaram/ Gulshan Bawra/ *Neeli Aankhen*, 1962)
- *Ye chaand sa roshan chehra* (Rafi/ OP Nayyar/ SH Bihari/ *Kashmir Ki Kali*, 1964)
- *Pardesiyon se na akhiyaan milaana* (Rafi/ Kalyanji-Anandji/ Anand Bakshi/ *Jab Jab Phool Khile*, 1965)
- *Dil ne phir yaad kiya* (Rafi, Suman, Mukesh/ Sonik-Omi/ GL Rawal/ *Dil Ne Phir Yaad Kiya*, 1966)
- *Rula ke gaya sapna mera* (Lata/ SD Burman/ Shailendra/ *Jewel Thief*, 1967)

Rula ke gaya sapna mera

- ➤ *Saawan ka maheena pawan kare* sor (Mukesh, Lata/ Laxmikant-Pyarelal/ Anand Bakshi/ *Milan*, 1967)
- ➤ *Nadiya chale chale re dhaara…tujhko chalna hoga* (Manna Dey/ Kalyanji-Anandji/ Indivar/ *Safar*, 1970)
- ➤ *Maanjhi naiyya dhoondhe kinaara* (Mukesh/ Laxmikant-Pyarelal/ Anand Bakshi/ *Uphaar*, 1971)
- ➤ *Door hai kinaara* (Manna Dey/ Ravindra Jain/ Ravindra Jain/ *Saudagar*, 1973)
- ➤ *Naiyya meri chalti jaaye* (Rafi/ Naushad/ Hasrat Jaipuri/ *My Friend*, 1974)
- ➤ *Purwaiya leke chali meri naiyya* (Lata, Shailendra Singh/ Ravindra Jain/ Hasrat Jaipuri/ *Do Jaasoos*, 1975)

The above songs are not metaphorical references to life, like in *Maanjhi meri naiyya ko jee chaahe jahaan le chal* (Lata/ BD Burman/ Sartaaj/ *Char Paise*, 1955), and *Main tooti hui ik naiyya hoon mujhe chaahe jidhar le jao* (Rafi/ Naushad/ Shakeel/ *Aadmi*, 1968). We have also ignored just singing on a boat, as someone else propels it forward, like in *Meri daastaan mujhe hi mera dil suna ke roye* (Lata/ Usha Khanna/ Rajinder Krishan/ *Aao Pyaar Karen*, 1964), *O maanjhi re* (Kishore Kumar/ RD Burman/ Gulzar/ *Khushbu*, 1975), and *Do lafzon ki hai dil ki kahaani* (Asha, Amitabh, Sharad Kumar/ RD Burman/ Anand Bakshi/ *The Great Gambler*, 1979). Ignored too are songs where someone steers a speedboat and sings, as Raj Kapoor did in both these songs: *O mehbooba tere dil ke paas hi hai meri manzil-e-maqsood* (Mukesh/ Shankar-Jaikishan/ Hasrat/ *Sangam*, 1964), and *Chale jaana zara thehro* (Sharda, Mukesh/ Shankar-Jaikishan/ Hasrat/ *Around the World*, 1967). This list is a celebration of people who themselves manage to move a non-motorized sea vessel from one point to another.

So, the next time you get on a boat and feel like singing, do it. Others on the boat may be waiting for someone to help them start. Don't worry if you don't know how to sing well. Here's what Elvis Presley once said: "I don't know anything about music. In my line, you don't have to".

~~~~

The above was originally published in DNA Jaipur on 3 February 2019. It has since been updated and enhanced.

~~~~

33

Behno aur Bhaiyo!

Today is Raksha Bandhan day, a yearly moment when Indian sisters tie a sacred thread called raakhi to the wrists of their brothers, symbolising a bond that carries for the latter the responsibility of protection. It has also become obligatory for the brother to give his sister a gift on that day, preferably an expensive one if he can afford it.

The idea of Raksha Bandhan started in prehistoric times, and there are so many theories about its origins that it is best to forget them and get on with today. But perhaps it is true that raakhis have inspired the broader worldwide idea of Friendship Bands, which have become popular only in the last 50 years. The idea of raakhi has so much power that over the decades it has been snowballing into a silent movement that even accommodates Indian women who do not have real brothers or may want to add more. The reverse is equally true: for men who have no sisters or may want to add more. Raksha Bandhan has gone even farther, since girls send such threads to men they haven't met and may never do so, like heroes of sports or cinema. Virat Kohli, Amitabh Bachchan and such luminaries get plenty of raakhis from their female admirers. This is also true of politicians, who each year get raakhis tied by underprivileged women, orphaned children, or just plain ordinary ladies, in what routinely become nationalised photo-ops. All the Presidents of India, from Dr. Rajendra Prasad down, like Dr. APJ Abdul Kalam and Ram Nath Kovind have happily offered their wrists for multiple raakhis, mostly to unknown girls or ladies, no matter how young or old they are.

Like before, this year Prime Minister Narendra Modi will have many girls and women tying him a raakhi. One of the people who will be wearing a raakhi on him today is a lady of Pakistani ancestry. Qamar Mohsin Shaikh is originally from Karachi but has settled down in Ahmedabad after marriage. She has been wearing him a raakhi for an uninterrupted 23 years, and nothing has changed for her; the love for her caring and nominally-adopted brother remaining the same. But since he is so important and busy now, she is surprised he finds the time to meet her; he does so, at least on this day of the year.

This love between a Muslim woman and her Hindu brother is heart-warming, and it takes one to the great poet Rabindranath Tagore and the beginning of the 20th century. The British wanted to divide Bengal ("for administrative purposes"), so the state was cut up into a Hindu-majority part and a Muslim-majority part in 1905. That pained Tagore to no end. He thought of using raakhis as a bond of Hindu-Muslim brotherhood. He ran a strong campaign championing the cause of this amity, repeatedly urging people from both faiths to come and tie the thread of love on each other's wrists and send a message to the British. Here's a poem that he wrote:

The love in my body and heart
For the earth's shadow and light
Has stayed over years

With its cares and its hopes it has thrown
A language of its own
Into blue skies

It lives in my joys and glooms
In the spring night's buds and glooms
Like a Rakhi-band
On the Future's hand

His efforts paid off. To Tagore's delight, the British reversed their decision and reunited Bengal in 1911. Later, in 1947, they divided Bengal again, when the country got its freedom. It is good that Tagore passed away in 1941 because he may have wept to see what happened. We will meet Tagore again later, but for now, let's consider some film songs that feature a brother and sister. The actors are mentioned.

> *Chhota sa ghar hoga... "Chaandi ki kursi pe baitthe meri chhoti behna"* (Kishore to Noor) (Kishore Kumar, Shaila Belle/ *Naukri*, 1954)

> *Meri chhoti si behen dekho gehne pehen* (Nanda and Satish Vyas) (Lata, Geeta/ *Toofan Aur Diya*, 1956)

> *Wo door jo nadiya behti hai... "sun bhaiya mere"* (Nanda and Jagdeep) (Rafi, Lata/ *Barkha*, 1959)

> *Mere bhaiya ko sandesha pahunchaana* (Jaishree about Sunil Dutt) (Lata/ *Didi*, 1959)

> *Mere bhaiya mere chanda mere anmol ratan* (Meena Kumari to Shailesh Kumar) (Asha/ *Kaajal*, 1965)

> *Meri pyaari beheniya banegi dulhaniya* (Rajesh Khanna to Naaz) (Kishore Kumar/ *Sachcha Jhootha*, 1970)

> *Phoolon ka taaron ka sab ka kehna hai* (Dev Anand to Zeenat Aman) (Kishore Kumar/ *Hare Rama Hare Krishna*, 1971)

> *Behna o behna teri doli main sajaoonga* (Amitabh to Heena Kausar) (Mukesh/ *Adalat*, 1976)

> *Chanda re mere bhaiya se kehna behna yaad kare* (Farida Jalal for Raaj Kumar) (Lata/ *Chambal Ki Kasam*, 1980)

While these songs featured Raksha Bandhan:

> *Raakhi ka mausam aaya re* (Actors unknown) (Geeta Roy/ *Jeene Do*, 1948)

> *Rakhi ka aaya tyohaar* (Actors unknown) (Lata, Shamshad/ *Rakhi*, 1949)

> *Bhaiya mere raakhi ke bandhan ko nibhaana* (Nanda to Balraj Sahni and Rehman) (Lata/ *Chhoti Behen*, 1959)

Bhaiya mere rakhi ke bandhan ko nibhaana

- *Rang birangi raakhi leke aayi behna* (Mala Sinha to Balraj Sahni) (*Anpadh*, 1962)
- *Bandha hua hai ik dhaage mein bhai-behen ka pyaar* (background on Ashok Kumar and Waheeda Rehman) (Rafi/ *Raakhi*, 1962)
- *Rakhiya bandha lo bhaiya* (Indrani Mukherjee to Ashim Kumar) (Lata/ Bhojpuri film *Laagi Naahi Chhoote Rama*, 1963)
- *Meri raakhi ki rakhiyo tu aan re* (Vyjayanthimala to Ashok Kumar) (Asha/ *Naya Kanoon*, 1965)
- *Hum behnon ke liye mere bhaiya aata hai ik din saal mein* (Nazima to Rajendra Kumar) (Lata/ *Anjaana*, 1969)
- *Ye raakhi bandhan hai aisa* (Nazima to Manoj Kumar) (Lata/ *Beimaan*, 1972)
- *Behna ne bhai ki kalaayi pe pyaar baandha hai* (Kumud Chhugani to Dharmendra) (Suman Kalyanpur/ *Resham Ki Dori*, 1974)
- *Meri behna ye raakhi ki laaj tera bhaiya nibhaayega* (Shreeram Lagoo to Shraddha Varma) (Mohd Aziz, Suresh Wadkar, Manhar/ *Ghar Dwaar*, 1985)
- *Maata bhi tu pita bhi tu* (Divya Rana to Dharmendra) (Anuradha, Rafi/ *Watan Ke Rakhwale*, 1987)

We saw how much Tagore loved the idea of raakhi and used it as a weapon to fight the British occupiers on our land. It was the same

Rabindranath Tagore who didn't like the harmonium because it was of foreign origin. Consequently, in 1940, he wrote a letter to the Director of All India Radio, then run by the British, informing him that the instrument had been taken out of Shantiniketan, and please could they get it out of the studios of All India Radio too? That was a smart move, because the harmonium is of French origins, and was brought into India by French missionaries. The French were also in control of parts of India, and the British hated them, so the idea appealed to the latter too. Thus, the harmonium was taken out of AIR in a ban that lasted 30 years. This banning also meant a ban on popular music, which is the reason Indians started playing their film music on Radio Ceylon, later called Sri Lanka Broadcasting Corporation. The most successful of hosts to emerge as a consequence of Tagore's appeal was an amazing man named Ameen Sayani, who for decades ran his Binaca Geet Malas on the radio. Ameen Sayani passed away in February 2024, but the words *"Behno aur bhaiyo!"* have got to be inseparably associated with him. One wonders how many of his listening brothers hugged him, and how many sisters sent him raakhis.

~~~~

The above was originally published in DNA Jaipur on 26 August 2-18. It has since been updated and enhanced.

~~~~

34

Three Recently Bereaved Sitars

Three great sitarists from the sub-continent, Rais Khan, Abdul Halim Jaffer Khan, and Jairam Acharya, passed away in just a bit over the first four months of this year. There have been many other gifted sitar players, even in cinema, but the enormous corpus and deep footprint of these three musicians in our films remain awe-inspiring and unsurpassed. Most of the other virtuosos—Nikhil Banerjee, Ravi Shankar, Shamim Ahmed, Vilayat Khan, Kartik Kumar, and more—either did not play in more than a few songs in films or perhaps we don't know of many songs they played in. Some sitarists who came later showed promise too, but stepping into the universe of mediocre music that followed the golden era, they had no way of leaving any indelible music patterns on our minds.

Pandit Jairam Acharya

But these three gents were something else. By way of an example, consider the song *O sajna barkha bahaar aayi* (composed by Salil Choudhury in *Parakh*, 1960). Lata Mangeshkar starts the song with just two words, *O sajna*, as if to lay out a red carpet for Jairam Acharya's *Khamaj*-laden sitar which takes over for nearly 10 seconds. The accomplished singer goes centre-stage soon, sometimes with that sitar too, but the instrument has already made a lasting impression on us.

Roll back a few years to find the same Lata Mangeshkar starting a *Bhimpalasi* aalaap in *Anarkali* (1953), in the song *Ye zindagi usi ki hai*, tuned by C Ramchandra. *Aa aa aa aa aa*, she goes, and in the opening bars, Abdul Halim Jaffer Khan's sitar wafts through the air.

Fast-forward 20 years from here, and find the same Lata Mangeshkar in the studios with Rais Khan, both performing for Madan Mohan in *Haste Zakhm* (1973). Only in this ghazal, *Aaj socha to aansoo bhar aaye*, the lady will have to hold her voice, till the sitarist has played out his part for a good 30 seconds.

Needless to add, all the above songs featured the sitar in a most euphonious way. Each sitar must be grieving over her master's loss this year.

We will soon see a small list of the work of these three great gents, mostly alone, but sometimes in collaboration with others. But first, here are brief sketches of these gifted men, and my interactions with two of them.

Ustad Rais Khan

Ustad Rais Khan was born in Indore, on 25 November 1939, and passed away in Karachi, Pakistan on 6 May 2017. Belonging to a family of singers, Rais Khan became known for his elevated *"gayiki ang"* style (meaning making the sitar sound as if it was 'singing'). In the mid-

1980s the Ustad decided to migrate to Pakistan, even if he visited India now and then. He had four wives, three in Pakistan and one in India.

My solo meeting with him was in November 2006, when he was being felicitated at a show in an auditorium in Bandra, a suburb of Mumbai. After the show, Ameen Sayani introduced us, and I said, *"Rais Saab, main aapse milna chaahta tha"*. *"Kaunse silsile mein saahab?"* *"Sir aap ke sangeet ke baare mein poochhna tha"*. *"Haan haan, abhi poochhiye"*. *"Rais saab, aap Pakistan mein ja base hain. Kya farq hain wahaan aur yahaan mein, sunne waalon ke adab mein, ya phir…"* He cut me short, *"Saaf-saaf kyoon naheen poochhte ke India mein aapke itne ghane baal the, ye saare kahaan chale gaye? Are saahab main bataata hoon. Biwiyon ki wajah se ud gaye"*. Ripples of laughter. End of interview.

Think of just a few songs that featured his sitar. The composer finds mention.

- *Ishaaron-ishaaron mein dil lene waale* (OP Nayyar/ *Kashmir Ki Kali,* 1963)
- *Tora man darpan kehlaaye* (Ravi/ *Kaajal,* 1965)
- *Dil ki awaaz bhi sun* (OP Nayyar/ *Humsaya,* 1968)
- *Chandan sa badan* (Kalyanji-Anandji/ *Saraswatichandra,* 1968)
- *Baiyaan na dharo* (Madan Mohan/ *Dastak,* 1970)
- *Rasm-e-ulfat ko nibhaayen* (Madan Mohan/ *Dil Ki Raahen,* 1973)

Ustad Abdul Halim Jaffer Khan

Ustad Abdul Halim Jaffer Khan was born in Jaora, near Ratlam on 18 February 1927 and died in Mumbai on 4 January 2017. He had an energetic style of playing the sitar. He was introduced to cinema by composer Gobind Ram in *Doosri Shaadi* (1947), in the song *Man bhooli kathaayen yaad na kar,* rendered by Shamshad Begum, which has a long sitar prelude by the Khan saab. In the last several years of his life, the Ustad (along with his son's family) was practically living in Girnar, at the residence of Dr. Sushila Rani Patel. He also moved the Halim Academy of Sitar, set up in 1976, to this address. I was in touch with Dr. Patel for several years, but there was no opportunity to meet the sitarist one-to-one because he was either constantly busy or not on the premises. These are a few songs graced by Abdul Halimji's sitar:

- ➤ *Do naino ne jaal bichhaaya* (Roshan/ *Sanskaar*, 1952*)*
- ➤ *Jaag dard-e-ishq jaag* (C Ramchandra/ *Anarkali*, 1953)
- ➤ *Madhuban mein Radhika naache re* (Naushad/ *Kohinoor*, 1960)
- ➤ *Shama se koi keh de* (S. Mohinder/ *Jai Bhawani*, 1961)
- ➤ *Baalamwa, bolo na bolo na boo na* (S Mohinder/ *Picnic*, 1966)
- ➤ *Tthaare rahiyo o baanke yaar* (Ghulam Mohammed/ *Pakeezah*, 1971)

I was more fortunate with Jairam Acharya Hebbar, who was born in Salem district, Madras Presidency on 4 July 1928. He breathed his last in Mumbai on 4 April 2017. His grandfather used to sing devotional songs, that's how the music was kindled in the young boy. Jairam Saab wanted to become a singer, but couldn't get himself to sing well. So he began eyeing the musical instrument dilruba which was already there at his home, but his dad slammed the idea down. "You will learn to play the sitar, ok?" ordered his father.

Once we met for many hours in the studios during my stint with WorldSpace Satellite Radio. I asked him when he came to Bombay. He recalled his arrival as if it was only the day before. "Oh I arrived at Bombay on 17th January 1939…at 1.30 pm! The meter of the taxi was flagged down at 6 annas". Some recall that, 70 years before our interview.

Jairamji's father was a staff artiste under composer Saraswati Devi. Thus the young man, who did not know any Hindi or Marathi yet, got an opportunity to sing under her in a chorus in *Naya Sansar* (1941), in the song *Naya zamaana aaya logo.* But anyway, it was the sitar he was destined to play, and in time he played a lot of it. In time, he also got friendly with C Ramchandra, so much so that when the composer was selling his Shivaji Park residence, it was Jairam Saab who bought it from him. Much later the sitar maestro himself moved to Thakur Complex in the western suburbs of Mumbai, where I met him a few times. A huge statue of Sai Baba, gifted by C Ramchandra, sat prominently in the living room area.

Check out half a dozen songs he made his presence felt in:

> *Rasik balma* (Shankar-Jaikishan/ *Chori Chori,* 1956)
> *Saari-saari raat teri yaad sataaye* (Roshan/ *Aji Bas Shukriya,* 1958)
> *Tum saiyaan gulaab ke phool* (C Ramchandra/ *Navrang,* 1959)
> *Jyoti kalash chhalke* (Sudhir Phadke/ *Bhabhi Ki Chudiyan,* 1961)
> *Mujhko apne gale laga lo* (Shankar-Jaikishan/ *Hamrahi,* 1963)
> *Jo baat tujhe mein hai* (Roshan/ *Taj Mahal,* 1963)

If his sitar was amazing, and that statue was remarkable, even more awesome was Jairamji's sense of humour. In fact, he never took himself seriously. After a few meetings, one day over filter coffee I asked him, "Jairam ji, do you miss having no work, no shows, no phone calls?" Pointing upwards, he said, "No, that's because He is there. I take it easy. I never take anything seriously". "May I say something now sir?" I attempted. "Even I don't take you seriously. I have only come for the wonderful coffee". We laughed our hearts out for half a minute. We both knew I was lying.

~~~~

The above was published in DNA Jaipur on 21 May 2017. It has since been updated and enhanced.

~~~~

35

Hindi Filmdom's Dubious Distinction Songs

In an earlier compilation, Windows to the Soul, I had written a story about the world's most recognized song, Happy Birthday to You, defined that way by The Guinness Book of Records. While researching that story, I had wondered if it was possible for Guinness to also do a Dubious Distinction mention for the other side of the spectrum: the world's least recognized song. That would be really hard to do. Not that Guinness hadn't featured Dubious Distinctions in their lists. From Guinness, we had learned that the country with the dubious distinction for the most coups—numbering 188 between 1825 and 1982—was Bolivia. And the dubious distinction for the longest uninterrupted fart was achieved in 2016 by an Englishman named Bernard Clemmens. His timing? 2 minutes and 42 seconds. A constant tone that long. People may have needed plenty of air freshener during that demonstration.

Thoughts about the least recognized song visited me again when I was anchoring an event to celebrate yesteryear's singer Sudha Malhotra and legendary broadcaster Ameen Sayani on the stage on 9 December 2017. They had known each other for some six decades. I conceptualized a video performance that featured many of the lady's songs, followed by the two legends in a Q and A on the stage. The special takeaway from the absorbing show was many songs that even music specialists in the audience couldn't recall as being part of her films. Classic case: *Chalti Ka Naam Gaadi* (1958) had a mujra sung by Sudha and Asha, filmed on Helen and Cuckoo, *Hum tumhaare hain zara ghar se nikal kar dekho.* Now we know that this film was a musical hit, and don't we all sing its songs, and hear them all around us? But hello, what was *this* song? Was it actually there in the film? The song had a few hard-core music buffs reacting in delighted disbelief.

I proceeded by asking music lovers if they could think of popular old musical films that had a song as if forgotten even by reasonably informed aficionados. It turns out that there certainly were a few films and songs of this kind. We kept in mind that different people had different favourite songs, as also songs they easily liked the least. We widened the net and roped in 24 music lovers. We asked them to consider for instance the musical hit *Dil Deke Dekho* (1959), composer Usha Khanna's maiden outing which had 10 songs. We found that the film's song *Do ekam do* or *Pyaar ki qasam hai* paled before the likes of *Raahi mil gaye raahon mein, Hum aur tum aur ye sama,* or *Bade hain dil ke kaale,* to name a few.

So we made a survey among these 24 strong Hindi film music buffs of the vintage era. A list of 17 old musical films was made, with just one film per composer. In the first test, we gave them the names of just the films and requested them to recall their songs. Next, we listed all the songs from those films. Our judges were asked to choose which song in their opinion was their most popular song from that film, and which had the dubious distinction of being the least popular.

Before we proceed, let's remember that in fact the same Ameen Sayani we toasted on December 9 had been compiling CDs of songs that were very good but just missed being chart toppers in his own hit parades. Appropriately, the CDs were called *Geetmala Ki Chhaon Mein,* meaning songs that were very good, except that like runners-up in horse races or beauty contests, they had just missed the limelight. My question to these 24 music lovers went further. "Which songs do you music lovers consider to be your *most and least favorite* ones from a given list of films?"

Here are the collated results:

Film: *Arzoo* (1950)

Composer: Anil Biswas

Most popular song: *Aye dil mujhe aisi jagah le chal* (Talat) (this song was the unanimous choice)

Least popular song: *Humen maar chala ye khayaal ye gham* (Anil Biswas)

Film: *Albela* (1951)

Composer: C Ramchandra

Most popular song: *Shola jo bhadke* (Lata, Chitalkar)

Least popular song: *Haseenon se muhabbat ka bura anjaam hota hai* (Chitalkar)

Shola jo bhadke

Film: *Bhabhi* (1957)

Composer: Chitragupt

Most popular song: *Chal udja re panchhi* (Rafi) (unanimous choice)

Least popular song: *Jawaan ho ya budhiya* (Rafi)

Film: *Miss Mary* (1957)

Composer: Hemant Kumar

Most popular song: *O raat ke musafir* (Rafi, Lata)

Least popular song: *Aayi re ghir ghir pehli pehli baadariya* (Geeta)

Film: *Mother India* (1957)

Composer: Naushad

Most popular song: Tie between *Dukh bhare din beete re bhaiya* (Rafi, Manna, Shamshad, Asha), and *Duniya mein hum aaye hain to* (Lata)

Least popular song: *O mere laal aaja* (Lata)

Film: *Nau Do Gyarah* (1957)

Composer: SD Burman

Most popular song: *Hum hain raahi pyaar ke* (Kishore)

Least popular song: Tie between *Jaan-e-jigar haaye haaye* (Asha) and *See le zubaan* (Asha)

Film: *Madhumati* (1958)

Composer: Salil Chowdhury

Most popular song: *Aaja re pardesi* (Lata)

Least popular song: *Hum haal-e-dil sunaayenge* (Mubarak)

Film: *Phir Subha Hogi* (1958):

Composer: Khayyam

Most popular song: *Wo subah kabhi to aayegi* (the Mukesh-Asha duet)

Least popular song: *Do boonden saawan ki* (Asha)

Film: *Goonj Uthi Shehnai* (1959)

Composer: Vasant Desai

Most popular song: *Tere sur aur mere geet* (Lata)

Least popular song: *Teri shehnai bole* (Lata, Rafi)

Film: *Barsaat Ki Raat* (1960)

Composer: Roshan

Most popular song: *Na to caarvaan ki talaash hai* and *Ye ishq ishq hai* (Manna, Rafi, Sudha, Asha, SD Batish)

Least popular song: *Na khanjar utthega…pehchaanta hoon khoob* (Asha, Sudha, Balbir, Bande Hasan)

Film: *Chaudhvin Ka Chand* (1960)

Composer: Ravi

Most popular song: *Chaudhvin ka chaand ho* (Rafi) (unanimous choice)

Least popular song: *Baalam se milan hoga* (Geeta)

Film: *Jis Desh Mein Ganga Behti Hai* (1960)

Composers: Shankar-Jaikishan

Most popular song: Tie between *Honthon pe sachchai rehti hai* (Mukesh) and *Aa ab laut chalen* (Mukesh, Lata)

Least popular song: *Pyaar kar le* (Mukesh)

Film: *Jahan Ara* (1964)

Composer: Madan Mohan

Most popular song: *Phir wohi shaam* (Talat)

Least popular song: *Kisi ki yaad mein duniya ko hain bhulaaye hue* (Rafi)

Film: *Kashmir Ki Kali* (1964)

Composer: OP Nayyar

Most popular song: Tie between *Ye chaand sa roshan chehra* (Rafi) and *Deewaana hua baadal* (Rafi, Asha)

Least popular song: *Haaye re haaye ye mere haath mein tera haath* (Asha, Rafi)

Film: *Jab Jab Phool Khile* (1965)

Composers: Kalyanji-Anandji

Most popular song: *Pardesiyon se na akhiyaan milaana* (Rafi, happy version)

Least popular song: *Afoo Khuda* (Rafi)

Film: *Milan* (1967)

Composers: Laxmikant-Pyarelal

Most popular song: *Saawan ka maheena* (Mukesh, Lata) (unanimous choice)

Least popular song: *Tohe saanwariya, naahi khabariya* (Lata)

Film: *Kati Patang* (1970)

Composer: RD Burman

Most popular song: Tie between *Ye jo muhabbat hai* (Kishore) and *Ye shaam mastaani* (Kishore)

Least popular song: *Mera naam hai Shabnam* (Asha, RD Burman)

We looked at these results and smiled, because a few of the results surprised many of us.

Returning to Guinness, I am considering writing to them to suggest Helen's name for two records. Firstly, for appearing as a vamp in a record number of films, in excess of 300. And secondly, for the most artistic use of eyebrows, especially when she did one eyebrow at a time. From the point of view of raising one eyebrow while pinning down the other, the *Chalti Ka Naam Gaadi* mujra *Hum tumhaare hain* will certainly be on my suggested-watching list to them. Even if they treat it as a dubious distinction entry.

~~~~

The above was originally published in DNA Jaipur on 24 December 2017. It has since been updated and enhanced.

~~~~

36

Chashm-e-baddoor!

Celebrating Life

"Why do Indian female singers outlive their male counterparts?" Anchoring a music show in Mumbai in April 2009 to celebrate the 90th birthday of yesteryear singer Shamshad Begum, I asked this question of the lady herself on the stage of a packed auditorium. Before asking that question, I had observed that, from the golden era, except for Manna Dey, no significant male singer was around today. Talat, Mukesh, Rafi, Kishore, Mahendra Kapoor, Hemant, all had gone. While look, thankfully there were so many ladies around: Lata, Asha, Meena and Usha, Jagjit Kaur, Meena Kapoor, Suman Kalyanpur, Sudha Malhotra, Mubarak Begum, Madhubala Jhaveri, and of course, Shamshad Begum herself.

Shamshad Begum

Even as I was speaking, Shamshad Begum brought the house down by her instant response, something like Bruce Lee's quick response in martial arts: *"Dekhiye, aap hum sab par nazar mat lagaaiye! Chashm-e-baddoor!"* (Look here, keep that evil eye away!). Her mischievous expression said even more, which some in the audience interpreted as *"Buri nazar waale tera moonh kaala!"* Her point was made beautifully, as she converted a clinical situation into one of humour. As it was, the audience was only expecting to see her. Her speaking was a bonus! This was icing on the cake for some people who loved her voice but didn't know that the singer who was living in oblivion somewhere was still vibrantly alive!

That show is over, and the evening has gone away, but the thought I sought her answer for hasn't gone away. Expressed differently, why do men singers have shorter lives, short enough to be statistically significant? Indian women generally live longer of course, but not by so many years. I leave the thought to people with better knowledge. Meantime, let's celebrate life by thinking of songs that talk about the idea of a happy existence.

We begin with Khan Mastana with his two outings:

Zindagi hai pyaar se, pyaar mein bitaaye ja
Husn ke huzoor mein apna dil lutaaye ja
(Khan Mastana/ Pt Sudarshan/ Mir Saheb, Rafiq Ghaznavi/
Sikandar, 1941)

Zindagi zindagi zindagi, koi sapna naheen zindagi
(Khan Mastana/ Dewan Sharar/ Vasant Desai/ *Dr. Kotnis Ki*
Amar Kahani, 1946)

Here's KL Saigal, telling us to be a beacon in others' lives:

Jeene ka dhang dikhaaye ja,
Kaanton ki nok par khada muskuraaye ja
(Khursheed Anwar/ DN Madhok/ *Parwana*, 1947).

Jagjit Kaur offers a nice Shakeel love ghazal:

Khaamosh zindagi ko ik afsaana mil gaya
Bhanwre ko phool, shama ko parwaana mil gaya
(Ghulam Mohd./ Shakeel/ *Dil-e-Naadaan*, 1953)

This duet inspires with its ode to life:

Nayi zindagi se pyaar kar ke dekh
Iske roop ka singaar kar ke dekh
(Rafi, Lata/ Shailendra/ Shankar-Jaikishan/ *Shikast*, 1953)

Here is Lata, living for today:

Aye meri zindagi, aaj raat jhoom le, aasmaan ko choom le
Kis ko pata hai kal aaye ke na aaye!
(SD Burman/ Sahir/ *Taxi Driver*, 1954).

Here comes Talat with his divine expression, romancing Anil Biswas's piano:

Jeevan hai madhuban, tu is mein phool khila
Kaanton se na bhar daaman, ab maan bhi ja
(Anil Biswas/ Indeewar/ *Jaasoos*, 1955).

And Mukesh brings out a *piece de resistance* that lives in our hearts:

Zindagi khwaab hai, khwaab mein jhootth kya, aur bhala, sach hai kya!
(Salil Chowdhury/ Shailendra/ *Jagte Raho*, 1956)

The 60s are here, and here's what Majrooh pens for Rafi flying solo:

Zindagi hai kya, sun meri jaan, pyaar bhara dil meethi zubaan
(Rafi/ Majrooh/ Salil Chowdhury/ *Maya*, 1961)

Music has gotten faster, reflecting the speed of life in this ditty:

Zindagi mein pyaar karna seekh le
Jisko jeena ho marna seekh le
(Asha/ Shakeel/ Ravi/ *Phool aur Patthar*, 1966)

Zindagi mein pyaar karna
seekh le

While it's Asha again, suggesting the randomness of life:

Zindagi ittefaaq hai,
Kal bhi ittefaaq thi, aaj bhi ittefaaq hai
(Ravi/ Sahir/ *Aadmi Aur Insaan*, 1969).

Now let's see some of Shamshad's own recordings about a happy life

Do din ki zindagi mein ik baar muskura lo
(Shamshad, Rafi, Durrani/ Shakeel/ Ghulam Mohd./ *Ajeeb Ladki*, 1952)

Zindagi sanwar gayi, mastiyon se bhar gayi
Jab se pyaar ki nazar dil mein hai utar gayi
(Shamshad, Rafi/ Shyam Hindi/ Chitragupt/ *Sinbad The Sailor*, 1952)

Aye sanam ye zindagi aayi hai le kar khushi
Kar le baaten pyaar ki phaili hai dekho chaandni
(Shamshad/ Shakeel/ Ghulam Mohd./ *Laila Majnu*, 1953)

May you be the proud recipient of the Dadasaheb Phalke Award next year Shamshadji. And may you live to be 100 years of age. Thank you for your wonderful music and also for your disarming humour. I'll be more careful the next time!

~~~~

The above originally appeared in DNA Jaipur on 25 November 2012. It has since been updated and enhanced.

PS: Shamshad Begum passed away in her Powai, Navi Mumbai home on 23rd April 2013. She was 94 years of age.

~~~~

Riding in Masculine Style

Mr. Anand Mahindra must be a happy man. This week he travels to Detroit, USA to launch his "off-road" Sports Utility Vehicle, made in his US plant, for American buyers. The vehicle is named ROXOR (internet slang for 'Rocks' or 'Awesome') and will be unveiled on 2 March 2018. The automobile has 21st-century features of course, but it promises to look so much like the Jeeps that were imported from the USA, exclusively and for years by his company, starting 65 years ago. This week he will be returning the favour.

Sports Utility Vehicles—SUVs for short—are rough and tough automobiles that are so much in vogue these days. What sets these vehicles apart from others are key features like high ground clearance for best "off-road" use on unpaved terrain, a 4 Wheel-Drive system coupled with deep-groove tyres for better traction needed in say muddy waters or rocky streams, and a rugged body for its exteriors. Such vehicles are built on a light-truck chassis and have high seats. Today's SUVs are typically station wagons with air-conditioning, power steering and satellite navigation systems, but that wasn't the case at one time. These were mostly open-air vehicles, many without even doors. The appointments were spartan, so there was no question of air-conditioning. In fact, the ancestor of SUVs was the open Jeep.

It all started in the early 1940s, after the USA was forced to enter World War II. The Army wanted a robust vehicle it could depend on, especially where there were no paved roads. It put out tenders for tough cars that could be used in rough weather and not fall apart. Many companies sent out proposals and bids, and the winner was Willys-Overland. This auto-maker already had a head start in the business since it had earlier shown to an astounded audience of US Congressmen how their small, truck-like vehicles could ride up the steps of the Capitol Building in Washington DC. Since its off-road capabilities were already in place, winning the US Government contract was a foregone conclusion for them. The company sold well over half a million of these vehicles to the US Army. In the course of time, its ownership changed many hands, as did the Jeep's design. Over the years, the Jeep also went on to have many competitors, principally Land Rover, but the original Jeep is still in production.

In India, the early units were imported by Mahindra and Mahindra in knocked-down condition, then re-assembled and sold to the Indian Army and the Police. Many were bought by Princes, for whom the Jeep became the preferred mode of transportation when they went hunting—in their sport called Shikar—into the jungles. For this last job, the Jeeps were replacing the elephant as by far the more manoeuvrable of the two.

Shikars are not so hot now, and the Princes have all but gone too. But the Police still use such vehicles, as does the Army, which was spotlighted last year for inventing a new, out-of-the-box use: tying up a Kashmiri stone-pelter to the bonnet of just such a vehicle, for the safe passage of many innocents.

Jeeps are also popular among collectors, and so there have sprung up a few companies that make a living selling the refurbished kind. It is for the he-man, rough-and-tough image of these vehicles that filmdom too has engaged with them quite a bit. For instance in *Aayi Milan Ki Bela* (1964), Dharmendra forces Saira Banu to ride with him in a Jeep, with Rajendra Kumar in hot pursuit on a horse. In *Do Badan* (1966), we saw Manoj Kumar in one, working as he was in a lumbar estate owned by his sweetheart's father. Shashi Kapoor drove one too, as a Police Officer in *Deewar* (1975).

Actors have also been singing songs while driving a Jeep. Here are some cases of actors seen behind the wheel in a Jeep, with a song that either they were lip-synching or then someone accompanying them was, or even if the song was being filmed background:

> ➤ Shammi Kapoor in *Raahi mil gaye raahon mein* (Rafi/ *Dil Deke Dekho*, 1959)

> ➤ Sunil Dutt in *Soch rahi thi kahoon na kahoon* (Lata/ *Ek Phool Chaar Kaante*, 1960*)*

> ➤ Dev Anand in *Main zindagi ka saath nibhaata chala gaya* (Rafi/ *Hum Dono*, 1961)

> ➤ Johnny Walker in *Aashiq hoon apne pyaar ke jauhar dikhaoonga* (Rafi/ *Kaun Apna Kaun Paraya*, 1963)

> ➤ Vijay Anand in *Masti mein chhed ke taraana koi dil ka* (Rafi/ *Haqeeqat.* 1964)

> ➤ Manoj Kumar in *Aa tu aa zara dil mein aa* (Lata, Mukesh/ *Phoolon Ki Sej*, 1964)

> ➤ Biswajit in *Pukaarta chala hoon main* (Rafi/ *Mere Sanam*, 1965)

Pukaarta chala hoon main

> ➤ Firoz Khan in *Pyaar ka fasaana bana le dil deewaana* (Mukesh, Lata/ *Teesra Kaun*, 1965)

> ➤ Rajendra Kumar in *Kaun hai jo sapnon mein aaya* (Rafi/ *Jhuk Gaya Aasmaan*, 1968)

> ➤ Asha Parekh in *Tumhaare pyaar mein hum beqaraar ho ke chale* (Rafi/ *Shikar*, 1968)

Tumhaare pyaar mein hum beqaraar
ho ke chale

- Rajendra Kumar in *Main raahi anjaan galiyon ka* (Rafi/ *Anjaana*, 1969)
- Sujit Kumar in *Mere sapnon ki raani kab ayegi tu* (Kishore/ *Aradhana*, 1969)
- Dharmendra in *Dekha hai teri aankhon mein* (Rafi/ *Pyaar Hi Pyaar*, 1969)
- Deb Mukherji in *Chal akela chal akela chal akela* (Mukesh/ *Sambandh*, 1969)
- Anup Kumar in *Gham pe dhool daalo…Yaaro neelaam karo susti* (Bhupinder, Kishore/ *Prem Pujari*, 1970)
- Shashi Kapoor in *Aaha ha ha ha ye suhaana safar* (Rafi/ *Suhaana Safar*, 1970)
- Shammi Kapoor in *Re mama re mama re* (Rafi/ *Andaz*, 1971)
- Dharmendra in *Meri jaan meri jaan kehna maano* (Kishore/ *Do Chor*, 1972)
- Neetu Singh and Shashi Kapoor in *Keh doon tumhen ya chup rahoon* (Kishore, Asha/ *Deewar*, 1975)
- Firoz Khan in *Kya khoob lagti ho* (Mukesh, Kanchan/ *Dharmatma*, 1975)
- Vijayendra Ghatge in *Aaj se pehle, aaj se zyaada* (Yesudas/ *Chit Chor*, 1976)

As is clear from this list, a high percentage of Jeeps were driven by men. Most of these vehicles were also the Left Hand Drive kind. These are the ones that Mahindra and Mahindra had imported from the USA for sale in India. Later the company started making the Right Hand Drives right here. Later still, many other auto-makers entered the scene, like Maruti, which launched its Gypsy, a low-cost SUV, way back in 1985. Mahindra now has its Thar, a similar product. However, the thrill of driving a Willys Jeep, especially in the '60s and' 70s, can hardly be described. Nor can one current irony be nicely described: an Indian hiring American workers to make Jeep-like vehicles in USA, and then even selling these to Americans.

There's another irony too. While the company's boss, Anand Mahindra runs a huge car corporation in India, his own daughters are not among his buyers. In a recent interview with a TV channel, he announced that his daughters don't purchase cars. They don't even drive. "They use Uber", he said. One wonders if the script would have been different if he was selling jewellery. Or if he had a son. Because if diamonds are a girl's best friend, automobiles are a man's buddies.

~ ~ ~

The above was published in DNA Jaipur on 25 February 2018. It has since been updated and enhanced.

38

Doing Something Different This Baisakhi

This coming Saturday, 14th April 2018, is Baisakhi Day. It's a great occasion for the Sikhs, especially farmers who offer gratitude for the harvest and pray for a bright tomorrow. Baisakhi also sings Happy Birthday to the Khalsa faith, which was born way back in 1699. This is a family of soldier-saints from the Sikh faith, which itself was started much earlier, in the 16th century.

On this day, many places witness a *prabhat-pheri*, which is a morning procession of believers walking through the streets and singing hymns from the holy book, Granth Sahib. These singers typically go with hymns like, *"Tujh bin koi naahi, waheguru, waheguru, waheguru"* (There is no one but you, wonderful Lord), and *"Tera keeta jaato naahin"* (I have not appreciated your blessings). The lead singer reads from the holy book that he carries along, and the others repeat in *keertan* style, i.e., shared recitation of a religious thought. For all this, they carry a couple of basic microphones and some percussion instruments: cymbals, *chimtas*, *kartals*, and a *dholak* strung around the neck, along with some beaters and rattles. Everyone joins in.

My friend from Mumbai, Sardar Manjit Singh Kalsi has for decades been part of such early morning devotional processions and will be doing the same this year too. He also loves cinema, which is what binds me to him, and he informs me that later in the evening he will be thinking of wrestler and actor Dara Singh, though not for his work in cinema or in the wrestling arena. For the evening event, he has invited me too.

We will look at the Dara Singh part later, including why I have politely declined the invite, but for now, let's get a bit reacquainted with some of the Sikhs who did a good deal of work in Hindi films. Since there have been so many of them, and we don't have space here, we'll just look at the main names in a hurry. And we will make this a flying visit over a couple of their songs only, so that they appear on a common musical platform here, whether they faced the camera, wrote the songs, composed them, sang them, or filmed them.

> ➤ Dara Singh, actor: *Dil hai hamaara phool se naazuk* (with Kamran in *Faulaad*, 1963), and *Sooni-sooni lag rahi hai zindagi tere baghair* (with Meenakshi in *Chaalbaaz*, 1969)
> ➤ Dharmendra, actor: *Aap ke haseen rukh pe aaj naya noor hai* (*Bahaaren Phir Bhi Ayengi*, 1966), and *Bahaaron ne mera chaman loot kar* (*Devar*, 1966)

Two Punjabis, Dara Singh
and Dharmendra

> ➤ Geeta Bali (Harkeertan Kaur), actress: *Dil dhadke nazar sharmaaye to samjho pyaar ho gaya* (*Albela*, 1951), and *Hum pyaar mein jalne waalon ko chain kahaan* (*Jailor*, 1958)
> ➤ GS Kohli, composer: *Pyaar ki raah dikha duniya ko* (*Lambe Haath*, 1960), and *Agar main poochhoon jawaab doge* (*Shikari*, 1963)

- Gulzar, lyricist, filmmaker: *Mora gora ang lai le* (*Bandini*, 1963), and *Tum aa gaye ho noor aa gaya hai* (*Aandhi*, 1975)

- HS Rawail (Harnam Singh Rawail), filmmaker: *Ye nayi nayi preet hai* (*Pocket Maar*, 1956), and *Aye husn zara jaag tujhe ishq jagaaye* (*Mere Mehboob*, 1963)

- Jagjit Kaur, singer: *Tum apna ranj-o-gham* (*Shagun*, 1964), and *Kaahe ko byaahe bides* (*Umrao Jaan*, 1981)

- Jagjit Singh, singer, composer: *Tum itna jo muskura rahe ho* (*Arth*, 1983), and *Hosh waalon ko khabar kya* (*Sarfarosh*, 1999)

- Kabir Bedi, actor: *Jab bhi ye dil udaas hota hai* (with Simi in *Seema*, 1971), and *Waqt thoda sa abhi kuchh aur guzar jaane de* (with Simi in *Seema*, 1971)

- Kuldip Kaur, actress: *Gore-gore o baanke chhore* (with Nalini Jaywant in *Samadhi*, 1950), and *Abhi to main jawaan hoon* (*Afsana*, 1951)

- Neetu Singh, actress: *Ek main aur ek tu* (with Rishi Kapoor in *Khel Khel Mein*, 1975), and *Hum banjaaron ki baat mat poochho ji* (with Jeetendra in *Dharam Veer*, 1977)

- Poonam Dhillon, actress: *Aye saagar ki lehro* (with Sunny Deol in *Samundar*, 1986), and *Door naheen ja sakti tujhse* (*Hisaab Khoon Ka*, 1989)

- Rajinder Singh Bedi, writer, filmmaker: *Ye bahaaron ka sama chaand taaron ka sama* (*Milap*, 1955), and *Toote hue khwaabon ne humko ye sikhaaya hai* (*Madhumati*, 1958)

- S Mohinder (Mohinder Singh Sarna), composer: *Tera kaam hai jalna parwaane* (*Paapi*, 1953), and *Guzra hua zamaana aata naheen dubaara* (*Shirin Farhad*, 1956)

- Sardul Kawatra, composer: *Pyaar bhi aata hai kabhi gussa bhi aata hai* (*Goonj*, 1952), and *Tabiyat theek thi aur dil bhi beqaraar na tha* (*Mirza Saheban*, 1957)

- Simi Garewal, actress: *Ye kaun aaya roshan ho gayi mehfil kiske naam se* (*Saathi*, 1968), and *Teetar ke do aage teetar* (*Mera Naam Joker*, 1970)

- Uttam Singh, instrumentalist, arranger and composer: *Are re are ye kya hua* (*Dil To Paagal Hai*, 1997), and *Main nikla gaddi leke* (*Gadar*, 2001)

You may perhaps know that Baisakhi goes hand in hand with the folk dance bhangra, but there is no bhangra song in the list above. This is because the idea was to go away from the predictable, to see other cultural dimensions of the Sikhs here, even if we did so on Baisakhi day. This thought was sparked by the Dara Singh invite I declined, an event that has nothing to do with bhangra either. As many of us know, the man was also known for his voracious appetite, like consuming a dozen eggs, two chickens, and several glasses of milk in a single morning session, all of which he needed to keep his metabolism going, what with his workouts and all. Consistent with the late hero's polyphagous reputation, an inventive Sardarji from Mumbai has started offering a huge vegetarian and non-vegetarian platter for lunch and dinner. Called the Dara Singh Thali, the platter is there to be eaten in his restaurants called Mini Punjab in Powai and Thane. The Sikhs make it a cultural outing, especially on Baisakhi. The thali contains 40 different items: half a dozen non-veg dishes, 15 large bowls of dals and vegetables, soup, curds, *kachumbar*, *papads*, pickles, *biryani*, with a spread of 7 large *rotis* and *parathas*. It also contains 6 desserts. Still have room? They give you a few glasses of coolers to drink. If after all this, you still have room, you can wash things down with the 9" glass of *lassi*. You pay Rs. 1154 including taxes for this meal, and they let up to four people eat out of it. If however, you can finish eating it alone, you pay nothing.

As for why I'm not going, it's because I don't enjoy looking at people gorge so much. Somehow it lowers my own sense of self-esteem. Because this is not the kind of thali people eat. This is the kind of thali that eats people.

~~~~

The above was published in DNA Jaipur on 8 April 2018. It has since been updated and enhanced.

~~~~

39

A Eulogy that Touches the Heart

Three-quarters of a century back, a child prodigy from Punjab, the sensational vocalist named Master Madan used to electrify live audiences with his light classical singing of ghazals, thumris and Punjabi gurbanis. But before the boy became 15 years old, he passed away as a result of mercury poisoning, if the rumour is true. In his short life, he was able to cut 8 records, through which he is immortalized, especially for his rendering of two ghazals written by Sagar Nizami: *Yoon na reh reh kar humen tarsaaiye,* and *Hairat se tak raha hai jahaan-e-wafa mujhe.*

The gifted lad passed away in June 1942, around the time the political turmoil for India's freedom was sizzling up. The Quit India movement started two months later, in August 1942, and many were dispatched to jail immediately. Pandit Jawaharlal Nehru went in too, for the ninth and last time, which was also his longest time in prison, i.e., 34 months. We know Nehru loved children, but we do not know if he heard Master Madan's songs in jail, or if he even knew who this child prodigy was.

It's been ages since Pt Nehru too passed away, and as we celebrate his birthday this coming week on 14th November, one's thoughts go to this engaging man who was our first Prime Minister. Were he alive today, one wonders what he would have felt and thought about the current landscape, the political one mainly, but also the social and cultural one. Like us, maybe he would have been dismayed at certain things, and delighted with others. He loved education and kids. Very likely he may have been super happy with the way we were educating our people. One wonders if he too would be as pleasantly surprised as many of us are at the explosion of singing talent among children. That would mean singers who are below the age of 18 years, since most dictionaries and the United Nations Children's Fund (UNICEF) define children as people below the age of 18.

We hear such children on television and in stage shows and wonder how so many of them do such an exceptional job, offering classical raga-based songs, long *alaaps, taans* and vocal twists and turns. These new kids have sustaining lung power, and they stay faithful to the notes of the original compositions. Some of them are so good that they can offer a Master Madan level of performance. We are not talking about technology tweaking their vocals, not at all. And this is not to take away from Master Madan, who was a wonderful singer. It's just that parents have been giving a lot of attention to children who show early signs of singing, and then our audiences have been giving huge rewards to talent. Today's television can make you a celebrity in minutes.

Our films too have featured kids in hundreds of situations as well as songs. Let's see some songs now, but only those where children themselves sing, without any adults singing with them or to them. The songs are listed alphabetically, with the playback singer mentioned:

- ➤ *Aaj kal mein dhal gaya din hua tamaam* (Lata/ *Beti Bete*, 1964)
- ➤ *Aaj ki taaza khabar* (Shanti Mathur/ *Son Of India*, 1962)
- ➤ *Aayi pari rang bhari kisne pukaara* (Asha/ *Do Phool*, 1958)
- ➤ *Apne khaatir jeena hai apne khaatir marna hai* (Mahendra, Sudha/ *Dhool Ka Phool*, 1959)
- ➤ *Bachche man ke sachche* (Lata/ *Do Kaliyaan*, 1968)
- ➤ *Bachpan ka mora tora pyaar suhaana* (Lata/ *Do Phool*, 1958)
- ➤ *Bachpan ke din bhula na dena* (Shamshad, Lata/ *Deedar*, 1951)
- ➤ *Bade bhaiya laaye hain London se chhori* (Asha/ *Ek Hi Rasta*, 1956)
- ➤ *Bhaabhi aayi, badi dhoom dhaam se meri Bhaabhi aayi* (Usha Mangeshkar/ *Subah Ka Taara*, 1954)

➤ *Daadi amma daadi amma maan jao* (Asha, Kamal Barot/ *Gharana*, 1961)

Daadi amma, daadi amma maan jao

➤ *Dekh sakta hoon main kuchh bhi hote hue* (Lata/ *Majboor*, 1974)
➤ *Door desh se aayi naiyya* (Master Babu, Baby Boola/ *Ferry*, 1954)
➤ *Duniya mein aisa kahaan sab ka naseeb hai* (Lata/ *Devar*, 1966)
➤ *Ek do teen chaar bhaiya bano hoshiyaar* (Lata/ *Sant Gyaneshwar*, 1964)
➤ *Ek se do bhale, do se bhale chaar* (Asha/ *Hum Panchhi Ek Daal Ke*, 1957)
➤ *Hum panchhi ek daal ke* (Asha or Rafi/ *Hum Panchhi Ek Daal Ke*, 1957)
➤ *Is duniya se niraala hoon main* (Geeta, Asha/ *Ragini*, 1958)
➤ *Jab tak ke hain aakaash pe chaand aur sitaare* (Asha/ *Aap Ki Parchhaiyaan*, 1964)
➤ *Jyot se jyot jagaate chalo* (Lata/ *Sant Gyaneshwar*, 1964)
➤ *Kas ke kamar ho ja taiyaar* (Shamshad, Lata/ *Sangram*, 1950)
➤ *Laali laali doliya mein laali re dulhaniya* (Asha/ *Teesri Kasam*, 1966)
➤ *Lakdi ki kaathi, kaathi pe ghoda* (Vanita Mishra, Gurpreet Kaur, Gauri Bapat/ *Masoom*, 1982)
➤ *Lo har cheez le lo* (Sudha, Asha, Geeta/ *Ab Dilli Door Nahin*, 1957)

> *Maa mujhe apne aanchal mein chhupa le* (Lata/ *Chhota Bhai*, 1966)
> *Main bezubaan hoon panchhi mujhe chhod kar dua le* (Asha/ *Do Phool*, 1958)
> *Main ik nanha sa, main ik chhota sa bachcha hoon* (Lata/ *Harishchandra Taramati*, 1964)
> *Main to Raja bana hoon* (Singers unknown/ *Hum bhi Insaan Hain*, 1948)
> *Maine maa ko dekha hai, maa ka pyaar naheen dekha* (Lata/ *Mastana*, 1970)
> *Malik tere jahaan mein, itne bade jahaan mein koi naheen hamaara* (Sudha/ *Ab Dill Door Nahin*, 1957)
> *Mata o mata jo tu aaj hoti* (Sudha/ *Ab Dilli Door Nahin*, 1957)
> *Moochh waale daada, gol mol daadi* (Usha/ *Hum Kahaan Ja Rahe The*, 1966)
> *Mother Mary maa hum tere dulaare hain* (Lata/ *Bachpan*, 1970)
> *Mummy aur Daddy mein ladaayi ho gayi* (Asha/ *Shola Aur Shabnam*, 1962)
> *Murgha murghi pyaar se dekhe, nanha chooha khel kare* (Lata/ *Do Kaliyaan*, 1968)
> *Naani teri morni ko mor le gaye* (Ranu Mukerji/ *Masoom*, 1960)
> *Nanha munna raahi hoon* (Shanti Mathur/ *Son Of India*, 1962)
> *O albele panchhi tera door thikaana hai* (Asha, Usha Mangeshkar/ *Devdas*, 1955)
> *Phoolon ka taaron ka sab ka kehna hai* (Lata/ *Hare Rama Hare Krishna*, 1971)
> *Suno sunaate hain tumko hum ik dukh bhari kahaani* (Asha, Usha/ *Jeevan Jyoti*, 1976)
> *Tu kitni achhi hai, o maa* (Lata/ *Raja Aur Rank*, 1968)
> *Tumhi ho maata pita tumhi ho* (Lata/ *Main Chup Rahungi*, 1962)
> *Udan khatole pe ud jaoon tere haath na aaoon* (Shamshad, Zohra/ *Anmol Ghadi*, 1946)

Not everything that happens today would have pleased Pandit Nehru, but he may have been happy to see children doing well in sports, in spelling competitions especially in US schools, and musically in the new India inhabited by his great-grandchildren. There's the south Mumbai place named after his wife, Kamala Nehru Park. That's been renovated recently, with newer generations of children playing in and around the famous shoe house, now given new colours and a facelift.

Panditji was always associated with a rosebud fixed in the buttonhole or pocket of his jacket. Perhaps he would have been happy to see posters of him with that red rose for a movie named *Naunihal* (1967). The story had to do with an orphaned boy who wanted to meet him but missed meeting his "Chacha Nehru" by a whisker because the leader had just passed away. It is in the background of Nehru's funeral procession that a tribute to the loved leader was filmed. The lyrics of that eulogy, written exceptionally well by Kaifi Azmi, formed the basis for a great song. This nazm was tuned by Madan Mohan and sung feelingly by Mohammad Rafi:

Meri awaaz suno, pyaar ka raag suno

Meri awaaz suno

Maine ik phool jo seene se saja rakkha tha

Uske parde mein tumhen dil se laga rakkha tha

Tha juda sab se mere ishq ka andaaz suno

Meri awaaz suno, pyaar ka raag suno

Meri awaaz suno…

Kyoon sanwaari hai ye chandan ki chita mere liye

Main koi jism naheen hoon ke jalaoge mujhe

Raakh ke saath bikhar jaoonga main duniya mein

Tum jahaan khaoge thokar waheen paoge mujhe

Har qadam par hai naye mod ka aagaaz suno…

Meri awaaz suno, pyaar ka raag suno

Meri awaaz suno

Maine ik phool jo seene se saja rakkha tha

Uske parde mein tumhen dil se laga rakkha tha
Tha juda sab se mere ishq ka andaaz suno
Meri awaaz suno, pyaar ka raag suno
Meri awaaz suno…

~ ~ ~ ~

The above was featured in DNA Jaipur on 11 November 2018. It has since been updated and enhanced.

40

The Other Kishore

What are the first thoughts that come to your mind when someone mentions singing-actor Kishore Kumar? Chances are you will say yodeller, comic actor, or the voice of Dev Anand and Rajesh Khanna. Perhaps you will think of his eccentricities, and maybe even his multiple marriages. Many of us recall him fondly through his garage-mechanic's role and song *Ek ladki bheegi-bhaagisi* from *Chalti Ka Naam Gaadi* (1958). Others instantly mention his comic falsetto singing in *Aake seedhi lagi dil pe jaise katariya* from *Half Ticket* (1962).

People who are in love with his work and persona—and these are in the millions—know more about him, and so they see this man in his other avatars too, as a composer, filmmaker, editor, scriptwriter and even songwriter, yes! He is seen as a modern-day Leonardo da Vinci in our cinema, with an embarrassment of skills, many of them high-visibility. In his last ten years, he connected beautifully on the stage through his shows too. Surely we are talking about a people person. Now this hardly sits well with what we also know, that till his very end, Kishore Kumar preferred to be a recluse, ducking interviews, isolating himself for days in his home, and generally remaining a mystery to his friends and family. Kishore observers know that there were two Kishore Kumars, a happily connected one, and a sadly withdrawn one. And perhaps, essentially more sad than happy. Most people do not think of him in that way, but a certain theory of the case needs to be looked at.

Kishore Kumar, the family man

First: he disliked putting on greasepaint

Firstly, he was never happy acting in films. All he wanted to do was sing. What got the better of him was peer pressure, principally from his brother Ashok Kumar, a huge box office star when Kishore made his entry, and with a nineteen year age gap, old enough to be the beginner's father. It wasn't a bad idea of course, because in his early outings in films, apart from himself, Kishore was singing only for Dev Anand. That was surely not enough to keep him gainfully occupied. Hence he took to acting too. Interestingly, Ashok himself never wanted to sing; all he wanted to do was act. But when he was a young actor, playback singing hadn't matured yet, so he was forced to act and sing his own songs.

Second: four marriages, but a high failure rate

When his initial professional struggles were lessening, Kishore was finding the resources to sometimes reject greasepaint, but now he was getting periodically visited by discord in his personal life. His first wife Ruma left him to find a new career and husband in Calcutta. The second, Madhubala, was sick—and that for nine years, till she passed away. The third wife, Yogeeta chose an auspicious date—4th August, 1978—his 49th birthday, to walk out on him. Then she proceeded to marry a prominent actor. Hope winning over experience, Kishore finally found marital happiness with his fourth wife, Leena.

Third: not singing for Mrs. Gandhi

In between his marriages came huge success but also the Emergency. When Mrs. Gandhi's 'feelers' ordered him to sing for her 20-point plan during the Emergency, he shooed them away with a mouthful of choice Bengali expletives. The then I and B minister VC Shukla was offended enough to announce a ban on Kishore Kumar's voice on All India Radio. It was not a good time to be Kishore Kumar those days.

Fourth: Income tax issues

Around this time, he had plenty of issues with the Income Tax guys. Once he showed some tattered files to Pritish Nandy, editor of The Illustrated Weekly of India, who had called upon the legend for an interview. "What are these?" the journalist had asked Kishore. "They are my Income Tax records. Rats love to eat them. These are very effective as pesticide". Nandy loved the sarcasm, but missed the sadness in the story.

For people to take you seriously, you need an air of gravitas. Kishore was a singer with a wonderful expression, but when he spoke, perhaps he couldn't effectively convey the seriousness of the situation. When his route was sarcasm, they thought he was cuckoo. And when he used comedy, well, he was being funny!

Madness or Sadness?

Kishore didn't smoke or drink, and had no friends, so he didn't socialize either. By the late '60s, his distaste for people peaked, so he began treating his trees as pets, giving each one a name and talking to them. He once had an architect redesign his home like a moat, i.e., surrounded by water, so people who wanted access to him would be entirely turned off. Fortunately, that project was shelved. As for interviews, he would relent if people hounded him, then leave the scene with a regret note. His living room had skulls and bones with red lights and sounds backing them up to welcome unwelcome visitors! All these were his way of saying 'Please leave me alone'. Some people see this as the man's madness, while others see it as a case of sadness.

Kishore loved
being alone

Amazingly, all this was happening as he was producing unimaginable blueprints for some of the nicest fun songs and comic scenes that we have seen. His appearances in *Chalti Ka Naam Gaadi* (1958), *Jhumroo* (1961), *Half Ticket* (1962), *Manmauji* (1962), *Padosan* (1968) and a dozen more furnish us with plenty of examples of the fun and laughter that we associate with him. For other actors too, his songs of comedy and romance, as also of so many other vignettes of emotions were rendered so beautifully over the decades.

Jaate-jaate, since we are looking at Kishore's sadness, let's quickly fly over just a few soul-stirring sad songs that were rendered by the legend. *Marne ki duaen kyoon maangoon* (his first film song, from *Ziddi*, 1948), *Jagmag jagmag karta nika chaand poonam ka pyaara* (*Rim Jhim*, 1949), and *Husn bhi udaas udaas* (*Fareb*, 1953) were his early sad songs. Over the years he chased these with many more heart-rending ones. Here are some:

- ➢ *Dukhi man mere* (*Funtoosh*, 1956)
- ➢ *Aaj rona pada to samjhe* (*Girl Friend*, 1960)
- ➢ *Wo shaam kuchh ajeeb thi* (*Khamoshi*, 1969)
- ➢ *Zindagi ka safar* (*Safar*, 1970)
- ➢ *Kuchh to log kahenge* (*Amar Prem*, 1971)
- ➢ *Koi hota jisko apna* (*Mere Apne*, 1971)
- ➢ *Ghunghru ki tarah* (*Chor Machaye Shor*, 1974)
- ➢ *Badi sooni-sooni hai zindagi* (*Mili*, 1975)

Kishore Kumar passed away on 13th October, 1987. It was Ashok Kumar's birthday. The father-like brother couldn't have imagined a worse gift. Gone was the man who gave us so many wonderful compositions like *Raahi tu mat ruk jaana* (for Hemant in *Door Gagan Ki Chhaon Mein*, 1964). This was the hero who gave us our money's worth onscreen in *Nakhre waali* (*New Delhi*, 1956). Consider the romance through whom Shashi Kapoor wooed Rakhee in *O meri Sharmilee* (*Sharmilee*, 1971). His was the voice that graced Neeraj's nazm on a Pahadi tune by Dada Burman in *Phoolon ke rang se* (*Prem Pujari*, 1970). This was the golden hearted man who loved Mohd. Rafi, and had the latter playback for him the wonderful *Ajab hai dastaan teri aye zindagi* (*Shararat*, 1959).

They don't make his kind anymore. For, who can breathe expression into words like he did when he sang this philosophical one?

> *Humse mat poochho kaise mandir toota sapnon ka*
> *Logon ki baat naheen hai, ye qissa hai apnon ka*
> *Koi dushman tthes lagaaye to meet jiya behlaaye*
> *Man-meet jo ghaav lagaaye use kaun mitaaye?*
> *Chingaari…*
> (*Amar Prem*, 1971)

~~~~

The above was originally published in The Hindustan Times Bhopal on 3 August 2014. It has since been updated.

~~~~

41

Kuchh To Log Kahenge

When news travels in multiple lines of informal communication from person to person, it gets accidentally corrupted or is deliberately tweaked, along the way. After a while, it becomes somewhat unreliable, like a rumour, which we know has wobbly legs because it is an unverified observation. "Heard through the grapevine", is the disclaimer some people use for unverified statements.

Recently, in a brilliantly written piece ('The Power of Rumour', The Times of India, Saturday, May 14th, 2016), Chetan Bhagat wondered about the deliberately tweaked kind. For instance, the one against Indian Prime Minister Narendra Modi, where someone questioned the Prime Minister's bachelor's degree, and earlier for US President Barack Obama, that he wasn't a natural-born US citizen[3].

The relentless rapidity with which accusations can be generated, and then made to travel quickly over social media, makes it very difficult for the accused to respond in a clinching way, because no matter what the response, some people will always believe a story. If there's no response, many more will believe it. That's essentially the Power of Rumour. A negative power of course.

In my time as a Consultant with Saregama (earlier called Gramophone Company of India Limited, and generally referred to as HMV), my job among other things was to make CD compilations in varied categories, such as those based on raags or musical instruments, dances or moods, or then personalities. For these song selections, I would write relevant sleeve notes. On Raag Yaman and Shivranjani for example, or the saxophone and sitar, or on the dances Twist and Cha

Cha Cha, and on personalities like Naushad, Rajinder Krishan and OP Nayyar.

One day, Saregama's Nirjhar Mukherji asked me if I could write something as a release speech for a new CD of Lata Mangeshkar's eight Sanskrit Shlokas they were launching soon. "Please do mention that Lataji has sung some 25,000 songs for us and we are delighted to make a few more offerings", was Nirjhar's suggestion. "But I cannot write that, Nirjhar". "Why?" "Because she hasn't even sung 7000 songs yet—in all languages, from films and otherwise—so how could she have sung 25,000 for HMV alone?" Over the next hour or so, this became quite an issue in the office. I can only tell you that a few colleagues gathered around the open-plan offices, and if I could read their expressions, they were wondering if the company had made a huge mistake in hiring someone so much behind the curve. Hello, had I heard of The Guinness Book of Records?

I had. Guinness had credited Lata with "upwards of 25,000 recordings", and that for three consecutive years in the late '70s, till someone pointed its editors in the right direction. The misguided claim was pulled out from later editions. A decade later, in 1989, all of Lata's songs were itemised into lists, and have since been updated from time to time. The names who deserve credit for cataloguing her complete list of songs are Vishwas Nerurkar from Mumbai and Suman Chaurasia from Indore. But the fountainhead for all Hindi film songs is Harmandir Singh Humraaz, a man from Kanpur, whose unparalleled work is the source for Chaurasia and Nerurkar and the rest of us.

But let's return to Lata Mangeshkar. I requested my Saregama colleagues to get a fact check done in their databases. Could they find me the 25,000 songs? My colleagues could not get corroborative help from the Excel sheets in their computer database. Even so, everyone there continued to subscribe to the 25,000 plus theory. That was the power of rumour at full strength, which may have looked good for Lata, but sacrificing the truth brazenly, was also an insult to our intelligence. Now if the organization that has the copyrights to most of the nightingale's songs thinks she has rendered that many songs, how do we correct the layman who comes out with outlandish numbers?

But my next story is not about a layman. It's about an accomplished author and journalist. The kind who influences public thought. His name is MJ Akbar.

You must have heard of him. He has authored half a dozen books, written numerous articles, and been the Editorial Director of India Today, among several other assignments. He has also been a Member of Parliament.

Akbar wrote an article on Lata Mangeshkar some years ago (A Paean to India's Melody Queen, Times of India, October 4, 2009). Here's a part of what he wrote: "The 80th birthday of Lata Mangeshkar, surely the greatest popular singer of our lifetime and beyond, invites an irresistible question: which song is her best of her six-decade oeuvre? We are spoilt for choice of course, she has 30,000 on offer, which makes it about four a day, not counting holidays. Phenomena do not get more phenomenal than that".[4]

MJ Akbar was hardly to blame. If the Guinness Book of World Records had erred, and Saregama India Private Limited, the organization that receives royalties from those recordings refused to believe otherwise, why blame someone who was after all essentially a political writer? Music is not Akbar's core strength. We will go meet the writer again soon, but let's stay with Lata for a bit longer.

There are more rumours about Lata Mangeshkar, and these are the other kinds, the ones that don't make her look good. There are a few about her relationships, and the net is full of them. There is also a rumour about her aversion to Marathi-speaking folks. You wonder where that came from. Perhaps from such innocent experiences as the one I'm going to share now.

Some of my Maharashtrian friends were shocked that in my own long interview with Lata Mangeshkar (accessible on YouTube), the lady praised many composers, but made no mention of any Marathi music composer. Sudhir Phadke, C Ramchandra, N Datta, and Dattaram for example. I personally sensed no such animosity in her, nor any game plan. But it lent needless grist for the mill. Another rumour, alive and well for decades, was about her bringing down the competition, but not a single one of them has firm legs since no one ever has actually given specific examples. It has always been a vague, grapevine case. It's always "So-and-so has told me confidentially. He was an insider". My benefit of the doubt has always gone to her. Because fame comes at a price, giving credence to the line, "*Jo hai naam waala wohi to badnaam hai*".

That invites a question: why do people deliberately create rumours? Perhaps, sometimes there's someone who has an agenda. In Lata's case, it could be a spurned producer, or a family friend of a competitor. But some others create rumours to get a feeling of importance. They like to advance the idea that they are insiders with special information, the kind they are telling us now. That we are privileged to be among the first to know.

How much of what we want to take from such sources is entirely our call. Says Kim Harrison in CUTTING EDGE PR: "Research shows that grapevine information tends to be about 80% accurate. Since many rumours start from someone's account of an actual event, there are strong elements of truth in many rumours. However, grapevine information often contains big errors as people put their own interpretation onto an event or information they have seen, and then pass it on in a process of partial or selective recall".

On a different note, where did the expression From the Grapevine come from?

In the 1860s, the United States was engaged in a Civil War. The Morse Code of telegraphic communication had been invented, but the telephone hadn't been, yet. In this war, soldiers needed to communicate over a few miles, and also to move quickly. They would string their telegraph wires on grapevines. These plants also grow in North America and are just the right height for reaching up to rest wires on, while leaving the ground clear for unhindered movement. Stringing wires and sending messages was done in military haste, often resulting in garbled messages at the receiving end. This readied the platform for interpretation, giving birth to rumours caused by miscommunication.

Now about MJ Akbar again. Within a few days of his writing the Lata story, I was invited to the release of Jaswant Singh's book Jinnah

India-Pakistan-Independence, at the Oberoi in Mumbai. As I entered I was surprised to see many interesting people on the stage, filmmaker Mahesh Bhatt, writer Sunil Khilnani, and MJ Akbar among them. After the speeches and release, cocktails were announced. As Akbar stepped down, I started walking towards him to congratulate him on the nice Lata article but to also ask him where he got that 30,000 number from. But people had got to him before me. So I went and got myself a vodka and orange juice. Fifteen minutes later, people were still around him, but I approached him anyway. "Mr. Akbar, how are you? I am a music writer, and I love your work, especially the article you wrote on Lata Mangeshkar a few days ago. Just one thing though: where did you get that 30,000 number from?"

"Oh, I felt I was wrong, but I played safe. It's 50,000, right?"

"Cheers", I smiled and headed for the bar. I needed another drink.

~~~~

The above was published in DNA Jaipur on 22 May 2016. It has since been updated and enhanced.

♪♫♩♪
~~~~

42

Engagements with Shama

We must hand it to poets for lending new meanings to situations we normally don't make much of. In our part of the world, *choli* and *daaman* almost always go together, because *choli* is a midriff-exposing blouse worn by women, and *daaman* is part of the cloth that veils it. Our poets use the togetherness of these garments and hold them up as examples of inseparable buddies. *Phool* and *bhanwra* (flower and bee, respectively) have a symbiotic relationship in which two different organisms benefit from each other. Bees pollinate flowers, in exchange for which they receive the barter of nectar. Our writers turn them into lovers, no problem if one of them has a passive role in that narrative. But the most imaginative case, used hundreds of times in songs, is the hopeless love relationship between *shama* and *parwaana* (the flame and the moth). Their case is interesting, firstly because of the rivetting visuals that *shama* and *parwaana* offer, especially when their identities emerge in the dark. The darker the better. Secondly, while *parwaana* is a living being, *shama* is only a personified one. And yet these two are seen as doomed lovers. The moth—poetically imagined as a male—gets attracted to the flame, comes dangerously close to it and burns to his death.

The idea that the moth is a male and not a female is a very old one. From time immemorial, women have been known as the attractive sex. Popular culture has also seen them to be weaker, along with other attributes such as that of suffering silently, while lighting up the world for everyone. They are also suspected to symbolize greater patience than men. On the other hand, men are seen as hunters who run after women. In such a chase, they are also sometimes seen as mad, unthinking idiots. The book Men Are From Mars, Women Are From Venus validates some of these differences.

But *shama* also has other names like *diya*, *chiraag* and *deepak*, in which avatars we see her other roles, away from the *parwaana*. That other roles part does remind me of a song that had vexed me for decades: *"Jalte hain jiske liye teri aankhon ke diye, dhoondh laaya hoon wohi geet main tere liye"*. This was written by Majrooh Sultanpuri for SD Burman's music and Talat Mahmood's voice in *Sujata* (1959). Among the first things I asked Majrooh saab when meeting him was the meaning of the opening lines. "What *is jalte hain aankhon ke diye?*" Here's what he said, with the translation being mine: "When an important guest is expected, we light up lamps to welcome him with respect. In this film's story, Sunil Dutt is in love with Nutan. He is also a writer and an intellectual. He can use such imagery, because he has just found the song that Nutan was waiting for, with her eyes figuratively lit up like lamps-in-waiting. The excitement of the song's discovery electrifies him on so much that he calls her on the phone, right then, without waiting for the morrow. This was Bimal Roy's greatness."

This idea of the flame waiting for a guest can be found in these songs too:

Diya to jala sab raat re baalam par tum laut na aaye
(CH Atma/ Saroj Mohini Nayyar/ OP Nayyar/ *Dhake Ki Malmal*, 1956)

Mera jala raat bhar diya na aaye piya
(Sudha/ Qamar Jalalabadi/ Sardar Malik/ *Chamak Chaandni*, 1957)

Ik na ik shama andhere mein jalaaye rakhiye, subha hone ko hai mahaul banaaye rakhiye
(Chitra Singh/ Tariq Badayuni/ Jagjit Singh/ Non-film)

Here's the moth in a crazed lover's role:

> *Deewaana ye parwaana shama pe aaya leke dil ka nazraana…*
> with its *jaan jalaaye sukh paaye, jalne mein maza aaye*
> (Chitalkar, Lata/ Rajinder Krishan/C Ramchandra/*Albela*, 1951)

> *Shama jali parwaana aaya, pyaar ki aag mein jal jaane ko aaj koi deewaana aaya*
> (Rafi, Lata/Shakeel/Ghulam Mohammad/*Amber*, 1952)

> *Aaj ki raat mere dil ki salaami le le, Kal teri bazm se deewaana chala jaayega, Shama reh jaayegi parwaana chala jaayega*
> (Rafi/Shakeel/Naushad/*Ram Aur Shyam*, 1967)

Anup Jalota sang these beautiful lines off-cinema, hitting out at the flame:

> *Kitne parwaane jale raaz ye paane ke liye*
> *Shama jalne ke liye hai ya jalaane ke liye*

But Anand Bakshi sympathized with the flame in *Aaya Saawan Jhoom Ke* (1969):

> *Ye shama to jali roshni ke liye*
> *Is shama se kaheen aag lag jaaye to ye shama kya kare*
> (Rendered by Rafi for Laxmikant-Pyarelal)

Bakshi cemented it beautifully next year for Kishore and RD Burman in *Kati Patang* (1970):

> *Pyaar deewaana hota hai mastaana hota hai*
> *Har khushi se har gham se begaana hota hai…*

In the above song, the flame issues the moth an advisory:

Shama kahe parwaane se pare chala ja
Meri tarah jal jaayega yahaan naheen aa
Wo naheen sunta usko jal jaana hota hai

The above tells us that everyone has to execute his role on this planet, his *dharma*. It is ordained that the moth must die this way.

But it was writer Mulkraj Bakhri, who decades before the above had wonderful thoughts in this regard. He placed this 'performing our roles' issue at the doorsteps of Mother Nature:

Akela ishq ki duniya mein kab deewaana jalta hai
Ke pehle shama khud jalti hai phir parwaana jalta hai…
Na shama ka qusoor na parwaane ka qusoor
Ik jale aur ek jalaaye ye hai qudrat ka dastoor
(SD Batish/ Husnlal-Bhagatram/ *Bansuriya*, 1949)

While Shailendra was speaking about the havoc that love causes:

O shama mujhe phoonk de, main na main rahoon tu na tu rahe
Yehi ishq ka hai dastoor
(Mukesh, Lata/ Shankar-Jaikishan/ *Aashiq*, 1962)

The above sounds like Mutually Assured Destruction, a concept in which two nuclear powers have what it takes to destroy each other.

Remarkable poetry has emerged where the *shama parwaana* idea has been taken to extraordinary heights. In the following two songs, we find burning happening, but multiple times:

Tu pyaar kare ya thukraaye…
Mit-te hain magar haule-haule jalte hain magar ik baar naheen
Hum shama ka seena rakhte hain, rehte hain magar parwaanon mein
(Lata/ Rajinder Krishan/ Madan Mohan/ *Dekh Kabira Roya*, 1957)

Shama mein taaqat kahaan jo ek parwaane mein hai
Lutf jalne mein naheen, jal-jal ke mar jaane mein hai
(Rafi/ Hasrat Jaipuri/ Madan Mohan/ *Naya Qanoon*, 1965)

And of burning to death silently:

Dil ne phir yaad kiya…
Hum wo parwaane hain jo shama ka dum bharte hain
Husn ki aag mein khaamosh jala karte hain
(Rafi, Suman, Mukesh/ GL Rawal/ Sonik-Omi/ *Dil Ne Phir Yaad Kiya*, 1966)

Exemplary imagination was brought to the table by Majrooh in *Phir Wohi Dil Laaya Hoon* (1963). In one scene, Asha Parekh has a photo of Joy Mukherji in her hand and has gone bonkers over it! Majrooh just needed that to invert conventional imagery—of men going after women—to the other way around:

Aankhon se jo utri hai dil mein tasweer hai ik anjaane ki
Khud dhoondh rahi hai shama jise kya baat hai us parwaane ki
(Asha/ OP Nayyar)

Here is a small list of some more *shama-parwaana* songs:

- *Ja parwaane ja, kaheen shama jal rahi hai* (Hamida Bano, Mukesh/ Pandit Indra/ Bulo C Rani/ *Rajputani*, 1946)
- *Aye shama tu bata tera parwaana kaun hai* (Suraiya/ Shakeel/ Naushad/ *Dastaan*, 1950)
- *Mehfil mein jal utthi shama parwaane ke liye* (Lata/ PL Santoshi/ C Ramchandra/ *Nirala*, 1950)
- *O parwaane shama ko apni ruswa na karna* (Suraiya/ Majrooh/ Husnlal-Bhagatram/ *Shama Parwana*, 1954)
- *Sar-e-mehfil jo jala parwaana, kar gaya naam-e-wafa parwaana, shama se seekhe wafa parwaana, ye jali hai to jala parwaana* (Rafi, Suraiya/ Majrooh/ Husnlal-Bhagatram/ *Shama Parwana*, 1954)

235

> *Shama par jalke bhi parwaana fana hota naheen* (Asha/ Rajinder Krishan/ C Ramchandra/ *Meenar*, 1954)
> *Shama pe aake o parwaane jal jal jal jal jal jal jal* (Asha/ Rajinder Krishan/ C Ramchandra/ *Meenar*, 1954)

Shama pe aa ke o parwaane

> *Shama parwaana, ek diwaani ek deewaana* (Lata/ Sartaj Rehmani/ BD Burman/ *Char Paise*, 1955)
> *Shama se koi keh de ke tere rehte-rehte andhera ho raha* (Mukesh, Suman/ GS Nepali/ S Mohinder/ *Jai Bhawani*, 1961)

It is said that with his singing, the great vocalist Mian Tansen could light up lamps. Raag Deepak it is called. Today any singer can sing raag Deepak. All he needs is a remote control for LED lamps, which are the modern-day equivalents of the *chiraag, shama* and *diya*. But it is also believed that Tansen could sing Raag Malhar so well, it would bring down the rains. No singer, or any remote control else for that matter, has been able to achieve that feat yet.

~~~~

The above was originally published in DNA Jaipur on 29 April 2018. It has been substantially enhanced since then.

♪♫♩♪
~~~~

43

Horn OK Please

If you have been to a stylish casino, such as those in Las Vegas or Macau, you know how difficult it is to leave the premises. Unless you are cleaned out, casinos can rivet you. The thrill of making quick money in a universe of glamour and bright lights has cross-cultural magnetism. The throbbing music keeps visitors buoyed up, and the sometimes-free food and drink can turn most people into gluttons who lose all sense of calories and time. People want to behave like Humphrey Bogart playing Roulette in a casino in the movie Casablanca, even if they can play that role for only an hour or two. But the odds of winning are mathematically stacked against us players. Many of us know that; we just hope we are going to be the ones who will somehow beat the system.

So we stay back and play and play, but our bodies eventually get tired, and we begin to feel drowsy. The casino owners are aware of the body clock, so they adopt many strategies to hold us in there longer. They know that higher levels of oxygen keep us alert and rejuvenated, which for instance is what Pranayama does for us in Yoga. Hence, late at night, casinos introduce additional oxygen from pressurised cylinders to do the job. It works wonders.

There are other tricks these guys employ to keep us in there. For one thing, forte music is played, and that is done seamlessly, in a crossfade way so we feel no audio blemishes. Casinos are notorious for the absence of clocks or windows or anything that can be our moral compass, reminding us that we have responsibilities of time or of living in the real world. In this hermetically-sealed kind of universe, finding the exit becomes another issue, as is locating the counter to cash our chips. One of their cleverest ideas is to install psychedelic carpets, the kind that have strong, conflicting colours and garish designs. You just cannot feel serene looking at them; in fact, they zap you to stay alert.

Earlier this month, something like that last idea was installed in Pakistan, in the Baggage Claim area at Islamabad's new International Airport, but through paintings on the walls, not carpets on the floor. Most passengers who finish an air journey, especially a long one, feel tired and want to get home or to a hotel as soon as possible. The wait at Baggage Claim can feel very long. Three minutes can seem like thirty to a weary passenger dying to find a bed. The airport authorities figured that if that area could somehow be made colourful or funny, it could reduce sleep levels by engaging passengers for a while. It's a brilliant decision.

Pakistanis have not taken the idea from casinos; in fact, their idea predates the scientific findings made by casinos. Pakistan has an old and fairly developed 'Truck Art' culture, perhaps a unique one. This culture is the painting with messages, witticisms or images on all easily visible parts of trucks, and such painting is done in strong colours. Because it is important to truck owners, they let professionals take several months to paint their vehicles, paying the latter many lacs of Rupees to do so. But even this culture of painting trucks has an ancestor. Telling a story or outlining history is a tradition in that part of the world that began when camels were used to transport goods in British India. Camels would be decorated with bright colours and messages to attract customers. When trucks arrived on the scene, they simply continued the art on this new medium of transport. Over the decades, they went about improving the art and the paints used. It's the truck equivalent of tattoos on human bodies. It is such Truck Art that adorns the airport wall mentioned above.

Trucks (called Lorries in England) are goods-carrying vehicles, whose load-bearing areas can be covered or open-to-air. They come in many sizes and usually are fun to ride on, anywhere in the world. Truckers (long-distance lorry drivers), spend long days and nights away from home, so the vehicle becomes their second home, especially since they sometimes even sleep in it. Thus they decorate it with ribbons and tinsel, keep the tyres inflated, the radiator hydrated and the engine oiled. The vehicle's health and appearance are important for their lives. That is also the reason they paint messages of quick wisdom thoughts that can be read in a few seconds by vehicles behind them. In India, the most common message on trucks is Horn OK Please, in which you wonder why the OK is there at all. In fact for the decibel-level threatening times that we live in, the message should be Horn Not OK Please, which would even pass the grammar test better!

Many other messages can be found on the back of trucks. *"Buri nazar waale tera moonh kaala"*, *"Mera Bharat Mahaan"* (But a few also read *"Mera Bharat Mahaan, Magar 100 Mein 99 Beimaan"*) and funny ones too: *"Take Poison but Do Not Believe in Girls"*, and *"Has Mat Pagli, Pyaar Ho Jaayega"*.

What has Hindi filmdom done with trucks, as far as songs are concerned? Our story begins in 1957, when the Ajit-Nalini Jayant starrer *Miss Bombay* was released. The film's title itself was the name of the truck! Here are a few songs that were sung on these vehicles, with the names of actors who were on the truck:

- ➢ *Din ho ya raat hum rahen tere saath* (Rafi, Suman/ Hansraj Behl/ Prem Dhawan/ *Miss Bombay*, 1957) (Ajit and Nalini Jaywant)
- ➢ *Duniya ye kehti hai meri qismat mein likhi wo* (Rafi, Suman/ Hansraj Behl/ Qamar Jalalabadi/ *Miss Bombay*, 1957) (Ajit and Nalini Jaywant)
- ➢ *Le chala jidhar ye dil nikal pade* (Rafi/ Hansraj Behl/ Prem Dhawan/ *Miss Bombay*, 1957) (Ajit)
- ➢ *Hum hain raahi pyaar ke* (Kishore/ SD Burman/ Majrooh/ *Nau Do Gyarah*, 1957) (Dev Anand)
- ➢ *Kali ke roop mein chali ho dhoop mein kahaan* (Rafi, Asha/ SD Burman/ Majrooh/ *Nau Do Gyarah*, 1957) (Dev Anand and Kalpana Kartik)

Kali ke roop mein chali ho
dhoop mein kahaan

- *Balam bada jhoottha, sajan bada jhoottha* (Asha/ OP Nayyar/ Jan Nissar Akhtar/ *Farishta*, 1958) (Ashok Kumar, Meena Kumari, Smriti Biswas)

- *O mere pyaaro zameen ke taaro* (Asha, Sudha/ S Mohinder/ Pandit Indra/ *Zameen Ke Taare*, 1960) (Anwar Husain, Daisy Irani, Honey Irani)

- *Dil kehta hai zara to dam le lo* (Manna Dey/ Salil Chowdhury/ Shailendra/ *Sapan Suhaane*, 1961) (Balraj Sahni and others)

- *O gori aaja gaddi wich baitth ja* (Manna Dey, Lata/ Salil Chowdhury/ Shailendra/ *Sapan Suhaane*, 1961) (Balraj Sahni, Geeta Bali)

- *Subhanallah haaye haseen chehra haaye* (Rafi/ OP Nayyar/ SH Bihari/ *Kashmir Ki Kali*, 1964) (Shammi Kapoor, Sharmila Tagore and Pran)

- *Kaanton se kheench ke ye aanchal* (Lata/ SD Burman/ Shailendra/ *Guide*, 1965) (Waheeda Rehman and Dev Anand)

- *Do akalmand hue fikarmand* (Rafi, Kishore/ OP Nayyar/ Aziz Kashmiri/ *Akalmand*, 1966) (Kishore Kumar and IS Johar)

- *Kisi raah mein kisi mod par* (Lata, Mukesh/ Kalyanji-Anandji/ Anand Bakshi/ *Mere Humsafar*, 1970) (Jeetendra, Sharmila Tagore)

> *Mausam hai bahaaron ka* (Mahendra Kapoor, S Balbir/ Kalyanji-Anandji/ Anand Bakshi/ *Mere Humsafar*, 1970) (Jagdeep)
> *Raah pe rehte hain, yaadon pe basar karte hain* (Kishore Kumar/ RD Burman/ Gulzar/ *Namkeen*, 1982) (Sanjeev Kumar)
> *Tu le naam Rab ka, naam Sai ka, Ali Ali Ali Ali* (Jyoti Nooran, Sultana/ AR Rehman/ Irshad Kamal/ *Highway*, 2014) (Alia Bhatt, Randeep Hooda)

Jaate-jaate, here is a message found on the back of a truck:

Na mila hai na milega mujhe aaraam kaheen
Main musafir hoon meri subah kaheen shaam kaheen

In a Jaimala program on All India Radio, composer C Ramchandra informed listeners he had read these lines on the back of a truck. He loved the idea, and made the basic tune there and then, after which he gave these words to PL Santoshi to complete the poem. The full song was rendered by Chitalkar (ie, the composer himself), in a Marathi film called Dhananjay. We know that C Ramchandra couldn't make a tune without the lyrics. Words received, he was King. Never mind if the poetry was on the back of a truck. Geniuses look for sparks from anywhere.

~~~~

The above was originally published in DNA Jaipur on 23 September 2018. It has since been updated and enhanced.

~~~~

44

Not So 20th Century

We constantly excite ourselves with new products and processes. And during the last twenty years, one of the ways to be stylishly dismissive of old ideas and systems has been to brand them as 'Oh so 20th century'. As for what have rolled over from the last century—airplanes, cars, telephones, computers, cinema and its music, space technology, radio, television—these and more have been drastically transformed from their limited ancestral roles.

Such a change was not so drastic or rapid in the earlier times. For centuries, we went about celebrating our festivals much the same way. Unani, homeopathy, Ayurveda, and Allopathy have for centuries been used to combat our diseases. Water used to come up artesian wells so we didn't need electric pumps, and we transported ourselves on wheeled vehicles like the bullock cart for a few millennia.

Many of these old ideas are still in use. The old methods of medical treatment are very much around. There still are wells—even in ultra-modern Mumbai—where you can draw water up without electric power. And you still see bullock carts here and there, never mind that it's neither smart nor time-saving to use such a mode of transportation. But there was something so serene about sitting on one. You kind of felt as if time had slowed down for you to recharge yourself. If the weather was good, a ride on a cow or bullock cart was like spoiling yourself in a spa. The breeze, the gentle rhythm of the steps, the soft jingle of the bells hanging from the necks of cows and bulls could be intoxicating and lull you to sleep.

Khataara

With the coming of motorized means of transportation, even the graceful horse-and-carriage got sidelined. Gradually, the car became king, and everything else diminished to a *khataara*. In fact, with the improvements in transport, anything that is relatively slow—even an old jalopy or temporarily non-functioning car—is branded a *khataara*. Do recall the film *Haathi Mere Saathi* (1971), in which Rajesh Khanna called Tanuja's vintage American car a *khataara*, because it wouldn't start: *"Chal chal chal mere saathi, o mere haathi, chal le chal khataara khench ke, chal yaar dhakka maar…bund hai motor car!"* *Khataara* was originally meant for bullock carts, but by association, a stalled car, and even anything that cannot zip across speedily has been called this name.

It wasn't always so in films too. Bullock-cart or cow-cart, perhaps you recall some of the stars that were romancing the idea in parts of these songs from the 'oh so 20th century':

- *Ghata ghan ghor ghor* (As Khursheed sings, she's on a bullock cart at one point, while Saigal is on horseback/ *Tansen*, 1943)
- *Kyoon unhen dil diya* (Naseem Banu's cart tows Surendra's convertible in a case of one *khataara* pulling another!/ *Anokhi Ada*, 1948)
- *Gaaye ja geet milan ke* (Dilip Kumar rides one/ *Mela*, 1948)
- *Main bhanwra tu hai phool* (Dilip Kumar and Nargis are on one/ *Mela*, 1948)
- *Aa gup-chup gup-chup pyaar karen* (Dev Anand and Nimmi on a haystack with a caravan of carts/ *Sazaa*, 1951)
- *Dekh tere sansaar ki haalat kya ho gayi Bhagwan* (Ajit is on a train, but all around him are people on carts, on foot, etc./ *Nastik*, 1954)
- *Mera dil ye pukaare aaja* (Vyjayanthimala's on one/ *Nagin*, 1954)
- *Chala kaafila pyaar ka* (Shyama and Deepak in a convertible car with a caravan of carts carrying others who sing the chorus/ *Shart*, 1954)
- *O saajna chhoota hai jo daaman tera* ('Heer' Nutan sings on a cart, as her 'Ranjha' Pradeep Kumar joins with his feet on the ground/ *Heer*, 1956)

> *Aaj suhaani raat re* (Village belle Kum Kum and friends sing, as buddies Kishore Kumar and Johnny Walker who are passing through pause their bullock cart to join in/ *Naya Andaz*, 1956)

> *Chal ud ja re panchhi* (Dispossessed of their home, a family walks on foot, as a bullock cart passes by to show the transportation contrast/ *Bhabhi*, 1957)

> *Ho umad ghumad kar aayi re ghata* (V Shantaram aboard/ *Do Ankhen Baarah Haath*, 1957)

> *Dukh bhare din beete re bhaiya* (Nargis and Raaj Kumar sing on a cart, with the villagers furnishing the chorus/ *Mother India*, 1957)

> *O gaadi waale gaadi dheere haank re* (Sunil Dutt and friends are on one cart, while Chanchal and friends are on another/ *Mother India*, 1957)

> *Bedard zamaana tera dushman hai to kya hai* (Kumar and Jayshree philosophising during a cart ride/ *Mehndi*, 1958)

> *Teer ye chhup ke chalaaya kisne* (Bharat Bhushan plays his flute on a cart, as Madhubala sings from afar/ *Phagun*, 1958)

> *Tum rootth ke mat jaana* (This time Madhubala is on one, and Bharat Bhushan is on the ground, as both sing/ *Phagun*, 1958)

> *Sun ja pukaar* (Madhubala on a moving vehicle, among a caravan of carts/ *Phagun*, 1958)

> *Chale hum kahaan* (Madhubala and Pradeep Kumar on a haystack-carrying cart/ *Police*, 1958)

> *Wo door jo nadiya behti hai* (Nanda and Jagdeep riding one/ *Barkha*, 1959)

> *Naach re dharti ke pyaare* (Nirupa Roy and Balraj Sahni in Munshi Premchand's story of two bulls/ *Heera Moti*, 1959)

> *Teri aankhon mein pyaar maine dekh liya* (Bharat Bhushan and Nanda/ *Chand Mere Aaja*, 1960)

> *Baaje paayal chhun chhun* (Nutan enjoys the bed of hay on a moving cart/ *Chhalia*, 1960)

> *Baaten kaheen aur banao* (Jabeen Jalil on one/*Batwara*, 1961)

> *Khush raho ahl-e-chaman* (Background on Meena Kumari in a slow ride/ *Main Chup Rahungi*, 1962)

- *Aa ra ra ra paayal meri chhanke ho* (Shalini drives a cart, as Ranjan watches from the haystack above/ *Sakhi Robin*, 1962)
- *Ab koi gulshan na ujde* (Harvesting farmers sing and move in a convoy of carts/ *Mujhe Jeene Do*, 1963)
- *Laali laali doliya mein* (Kids sing to Waheeda, who sits in the rear of a moving cart, with Raj Kapoor at the front/ *Teesri Kasam*, 1966)
- *Preet bana ke tu ne jeena sikhaaya* (the Suman flash version/ Waheeda and Raj Kapoor are both on a cart/ *Teesri Kasam*, 1966)
- *Sajan re jhootth mat bolo* (Raj Kapoor on a cart/ *Teesri Kasam*, 1966)
- *Sajanwa bairi ho gaye hamaar* (Raj and Waheeda on a bullock cart/ *Teesri Kasam*, 1966)
- *Ye dil na hota bechaara* (Dev Anand spends some moments on a bullock cart/ *Jewel Thief*, 1967)
- *Oh re taal mile nadi ke jal mein* (Sanjeev Kumar on a slow motion cart/ *Anokhi Raat*, 1968)

Oh re taal mile nadi ke jal se

- *Manzil ki use kuchh bhi na khabar* (Kishore Kumar on a bullock cart/ *Door Ka Rahi*, 1971)
- *Tum bin jeevan kaisa jeevan* (Rajesh Khanna and Jaya Bhaduri on a bullock cart/ *Bawarchi*, 1972)

In fact, the bullock cart is not 'oh so 20th century'; it is several centuries older. In 1931, when speaking films came to India, the bullock cart was for long alive and well, and not just for transporting goods and people. Original thinkers created innovative platforms for it. For example, in Madras in that year, Dr. SR Ranganathan, the Father of Library Science in India, started the world's first mobile library, which carried books and journals using a specially-designed, hooded carriage pulled by a pair of bulls.

So yes, the bullock cart is still around, though in reduced strength. It's going to be many years before we retire it from our landscape completely. Our films may have put this mode of transportation out to pasture, but like its slow motion approach to life, in real life the bull may be in no hurry to be decoupled from its cart. Should we do that anyway, there's no saying what this animal will do if it decides to go after us. Many have realized this, including Juan Padilla, when a bull went after him in 2011, breaking his jaw and skull, and destroying his left eye permanently.

~ ~ ~

The above was originally published in DNA Jaipur on 7 September 2014. It has since been updated and enhanced.

Sleeping Beauties

Sleep is vital to human existence. Perhaps that's why we sleep about a third of our lives. We need to sleep to feel healthy, look good, and recharge ourselves. Skin doctors often speak about the benefits of an extra nap, a condition called beauty sleep. Many successful men speak similarly about the invigorating benefits of power naps, short sleeping spells that can refresh us. Such people have included British Prime Minister Winston Churchill, American inventor Thomas Edison, and Spanish artist Salvador Dali. This last artist just loved his siesta, and even wrote a story called "Slumber with a Key". Here's what he advised: Sit on a chair, one arm hanging out with a key held between your fingers. Below the key, keep a dinner plate inverted on the floor. Now try to sleep. As you doze off, the key will fall. The clang will wake you up inspired, even if the sleep happened for only a fraction of a second!

Diametrically opposite to power naps sit several stories in mythology and fairy tales, where many people have been said to sleep for incredibly long durations. In Hindu mythology, Kumbhakarna, the evil brother of Ravana would sleep for six months before waking up to eat up monkeys and everything else that crossed his path. In an American fictional tale, Rip Van Winkle shut his eyes in the Catskill Mountains, New York State for twenty years. In the European fairy tale Sleeping Beauty, a cursed princess hibernated for a hundred years before she was woken up by a kiss from a Prince.

In real life though, more than sleeping too much—called hypersomnia—there is the problem of insomnia, ie, sleeping too little. This is precisely what happens to Nutan, who is a princess in the film

Shabab (1954). Her father the king has tried various doctors and also unconventional ideas to get her some sleep, but nothing has worked. But the film is predicated on the miraculous powers of music. In fact, the leitmotif of this film is a rendering of the lines: *"Sangeet hai shakti Ishwar ki, har sur mein base hain Ram, Raagi ko sunaaye raag madhur, rogi ko mile aaraam"*. Consequently, enter Bharat Bhushan, a sitar-toting vocalist, who sings the Hemant version of *"Chandan ka palna resham ki dori, jhoola jhulaoon nindiya ko tori"*. Voila, the princess gets her sleep.

Under the scanner: Actresses in Sleep

Many of our lullabies are meant to put children to sleep. We are giving them a miss. Instead, our story today looks at adult actresses whose eyes were shut during a song, regardless of whether it was a lullaby or not. Some of these ladies were trying to sleep, or pretending to doze off, or then showing their nirvanic delight briefly that way. But all the songs we are listing below show us ladies whose eyes were shut for longer than a blink. The singers' names are mentioned too.

> ➤ Jamuna: *Soja Rajkumari, soja* (KL Saigal/ *Zindagi,* 1940)
> ➤ Shobhana Samarth: *Beena madhur-madhur kachhu bol* (Saraswati Rane/ *Ram Rajya,* 1943)
> ➤ Swaranlata: *Angdaayi teri hai bahaana* (Manju/ *Rattan,* 1944)
> ➤ Mumtaz Shanti: *Dheere dheere aa re, baadal dheere* (Amirbai Karnataki with Ashok Kumar in the film, with Arun Kumar on 78rpm records/ *Kismat,* 1943)
> ➤ Geeta Bali: *Mehfil mein meri kaun ye deewaana aa gaya* (Lata, Rafi/ *Albela,* 1951)
> ➤ Vyjayanthimala: *O zindagi ke dene waale* (Hemant Kumar/ *Nagin,* 1954)
> ➤ Nalini Jaywant: *Aankh khulte hi tum chhup gaye ho kahaan* (Lata/ *Munimji,* 1955)
> ➤ Nutan: *Allah teri khair kare* (Rafi/ *Heer,* 1956)
> ➤ Madhubala: *Mere sapne mein aana re sajna* (Lata/ *Raj Hatth,* 1956)

- Bina Rai: *Muhabbat zinda rehti hai* (Rafi/ *Changez Khan*, 1957)

- Madhubala: *Main soya akhiyaan meeche* (Rafi, Asha/ *Phagun*, 1958)

- Mala Sinha: *Ho sakta hai kaanton se bhi phool ki khushbu aaye* (Manna Dey/ *Duniya Na Maane*, 1959)

- Waheeda Rehman: *Chaudhvin ka chaand ho* (Rafi/ *Chaudhvin Ka Chand*, 1960)

- Waheeda Rehman: *Apni to har aah ik toofaan hai* (Rafi/ *Kala Bazaar*, 1960)

- Madhubala: *Prem jogan ban ke* (Bade Ghulam Ali Khan/ *Mughal-e-Azam*, 1960)

- Madhubala: *Dheere chal dheere chal aye bheegi hawa* (Rafi/ *Boy Friend*, 1961)

- Madhubala: *Salaam aap ki meetthi nazar ko salaam* (Rafi/ *Boy Friend*, 1961)

- Waheeda Rehman: *Na tum humen jaano* (Hemant Kumar/ *Baat Ek Raat Ki*, 1962)

- Shakila: *Dekho ji ik baala jogi* (Rafi/ *China Town*, 1962)

- Mala Sinha: *Main jab bhi akeli hoti hoon* (Asha/ *Dharamputra*, 1962)

- Sadhana: *Aye husn zara jaag tujhe ishq jagaaye* (Rafi/ *Mere Mehboob*, 1963)

- Leela Naidu: *Koi mujhse poochhe ke tum mere kya ho* (Rafi/ *Ye Raste Hain Pyaar Ke*, 1963)

- Helen: *Subah na aayi, shaam na aayi* (Rafi/ *Cha Cha Cha*, 1964)

- Mala Sinha: *Mere pyaar mein tujhe kya mila* (Rafi/ *Suhagan*, 1964)

- Nutan: *Ram kare aisa ho jaaye* (Mukesh/ *Milan*, 1967)

- Jyotilaxmi: *Aye mere soye hue pyaar zara hosh mein aa* (Kishore Kumar/ *Paayal Ki Jhankaar*, 1968)

- Moushumi Chatterjee: *Sansaar hai ik nadiya* (Mukesh/ *Raftaar*, 1975)

- Ranjeeta: *Is reshmi paazeb ki jhankaar ke sadqe* (Rafi, Lata/ *Laila Majnu*, 1976)

- ➤ Hema Malini: *Khwaab ban kar koi ayega* (Lata/ *Razia Sultan*, 1982)
- ➤ Sridevi: *Surmayi akhiyon mein nanha-munna ik sapna de ja re* (Yesudas/ *Sadma*, 1983)

There have also been situations where the men had their eyes shut. In *Tarana* (1951), Madhubala, lip-synching Lata, was romantically putting Dilip Kumar to sleep in the song *Beimaan tore nainwa nindiya na aaye*. Such lullabies by women to men are unusual, but the odd ones have been spotted. Minoo Mumtaz achieved the result for Kishore Kumar during the song *Soja re chanda soja, chandaniya arz kare* (Asha/ *Aasha*, 1957). Mala Sinha was singing to Guru Dutt the song *Main jaagoon saari rain, sajan tum so jao* (Lata/ *Bahurani*, 1963). Madhubala witnessed Bharat Bhushan with his eyes shut at the start of *Main soya akhiyaan meeche* (Rafi, Asha/ *Phagun*, 1958), and Sadhana similarly watched Dev Anand with his eyes shut at the start of *Abhi na jao chhod kar* (Rafi, Asha/ *Hum Dono*, 1961). In another song from the same *Hum Dono, Jahaan mein aisa kaun hai*, it was Sadhana again singing to Dev Anand whose eyes were shut. And if Sunil Dutt tried to make Nutan sleep in *Ram kare aisa ho jaaye* (Mukesh/ *Milan*, 1967), he was perhaps returning the favour. She had put him to sleep in *Tumhi mere mandir* (Lata/ *Khandaan*, 1965), with the line *Bahut raat beeti chalo main sula doon, pawan chhede sargam, main lori suna doon.*

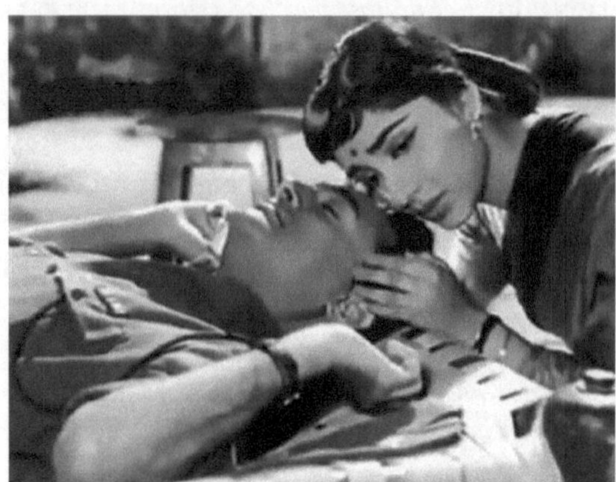

Jahaan mein ayesa kaun hai

We need more lullabies these days, because people stay awake longer these days than ever before in history. Insomnia has always been there, but these days we also have social media, with its chaos of constant connection. People's fear of missing out is so strong, no one has found a fix for it yet.

~~~~

The above was originally published in DNA Jaipur on 22 October 2017. It has since been updated and enhanced.

~~~~

R.I.P. Qawwali?

In June 2016, hardliners eliminated Pakistani qawwal Amjad Ali Sabri. His crime? Singing the qawwali *Ali ke saath hai Zohra ki shaadi,* live on Geo TV, which put him on the radar of people who thought the reference to Prophet Mohammad's family was blasphemy. And last week came news about a fatwa—a diktat of sorts—issued by Darul Uloom Deoband against a dozen Muslim women from Varanasi who had participated in an aarti (the devotional waving of a flame in front of a god) during the recent Diwali. What a far cry from another story that had featured the same city many moons ago. The great Urdu and Persian poet Mirza Ghalib once visited Varanasi (also known as Kashi and Banaras), and here's a translated extract from his poem called *Chirag-e-Dair* (meaning Temple Lights)[5]:

> *Morning and moon-rise my lady Kashi*
> *Picks up the Ganga mirror*
> *To see her gracious beauty, glimmer and shine.*
> *Said I one night to a pristine seer*
> *(Who knew the secrets of whirling Time)*
>
> *'Sir, you well perceive that goodness and faith,*
> *Fidelity and love*
> *Have all departed from this sorry land.*
> *Father and son are at each other's throat*
> *Brother fights brother*

Unity and federation are undermined.

Despite these ominous times, why has not doomsday come?

Why does not the Last Trumpet sound?

Who holds the reins of the final catastrophe?"

The hoary old man of lucent ken

Pointed towards Kashi and gently smiled.

"The architect", he said, "is fond of this edifice

Because of which there is colour in life.

He would not like it to perish and fall".

Hearing this, the pride of Banaras soared to an eminence

Untouched by the wings of thought.

If Ghalib were living today, it's likely the fundamentalists would have issued a fatwa against him for writing the above ode. He wrote many more things which would have ticked off intolerant minds. Consider this couplet from his ghazal *Baazeecha-e-atfaal hai duniya mere aage* (the world is a playground before me): *Imaan mujhe roke hai jo kheenche hai mujhe kufr, Kaaba mere peechhe hai kalisa mere aage* (Faith holds me back somewhat, but idolatry draws me, the Kaaba is behind me, as I face the Church). He went further in a thought that would surely have invited plenty of heat: *Jab ki tujh bin naheen koi maujood, phir ye hungaama aye Khuda kya hai?* (If no one but you is around everywhere, dear God what's all this commotion about?).

Ghalib was not the only bard who said challenging things. Great writings have been featured in many a qawwali. Trawl the qawwali waters and you'll find a lot of sensible but sensitive stuff. Habib Painter was an exceptional Sufi thinker and qawwal who ruffled many a religious feather. Look at this, from his poem *Sada chakkar mein rehta hai: Idhar Pandit akadte hain ke wo Kashi mein rehta hai, idhar hain Sheikhji naadaan ke wo Kaabe mein rehta hai...Habib ahl-e-nazar har shai mein usko dekh leta hai, wagarna dhoondne waala sada chakkar mein rehta hai* (The one with the vision finds God in everything, otherwise the seeker always remains confused). In fact, qawwalis question our basic beliefs with alarming periodicity. Remember Sahir Ludhianvi's long ode to love in *Barsaat Ki Raat* (1960)? The part where Rafi sings, "*...bande ko Khuda karta hai ishq*" (love turns a man into a god) is enough to tick off fragile minds.

What is qawwali?

It all started with Amir Khusro, the 13th-century musician and writer whose father was a Persian and mother an Indian. His bi-cultural heritage gave him a wide understanding of human nature, and he gained more depth after becoming a spiritual disciple of Sufi saint Nizamuddin Aulia of Delhi. Amir Khusro fused the music traditions of India with those of Persia and Arabia to kick-start the idea of the qawwali. Hence it is he who is known as the Father of the Qawwali.

The genre started as a spiritual offering, sung at dargahs, which are tombs where saints lie buried. They were not, and are not, sung in mosques because conservative Islam doesn't take kindly to any kind of music. Essential Islam doesn't even recognise dargahs, and as such there are none for example in Saudi Arabia and the United Arab Emirates. The idea is, that there should be no one between humans and the Almighty. Over the centuries though, the lyrical content of the qawwali has relaxed, allowing the use of other themes like alcohol and love between humans, with touches of sexuality as well.

The qawwali, unlike for instance the ghazal, is not a written form; it is about the musical way the lyrics are composed that sets it apart. Let's get close to the genre in its audio avatar. First of all, there is plenty of clapping for percussion. There's a harmonium in the equation, and sometimes there are two. Bulbul tarangs are euphonically juiced in this genre, while larger groups may use a clarinet too. The main percussion consists of a tabla and dholak. Choral singers are important to qawwalis, and everyone in the team sings, especially to repeat the key verses so that the main singer can arrive repeatedly with fresh thought, an *alaap*, a *taan* or a *sargam*. This call and response, lead-and-follow route is varied with dramatic stoppages of the rhythms to deliver key imageries positioned for high effect.

Now let's examine it visually. On the stage, there is a generally fixed protocol. There are typically 8 or more musicians in what is called a Qawwal Party. They sit cross-legged on a cushioned platform, on which the front row is occupied by the main and secondary singers as well as the harmoniumists, with the rear row taken up by the chorus and side rhythms.

Seating protocol and instruments in place, the qawwals often start slowly and rhythm-free, sometimes with a couplet or two thematically linked but not otherwise part of the main lyrics, and then they proceed to build energy and speed to induce both listeners and themselves into a kind of a trance.

That's about the genre in general. Now let's look at when the qawwali started showing up in films. Its first appearance was 3 years after sound came to our films. Ranjeet Movietone's 1934 film *Sitamgar* featured the first cinema qawwali, *Idhar dekhta hoon, udhar dekhta hoon, Khuda hi Khuda hai jidhar dekhta hoon*. This was sung by E Billimoria and Miss Khatoon, written by Pt. Narayan Prasad 'Betab' and its music was by Banne Khan and Revashankar Marwadi. The qawwali disappointed the aficionados of the time. Here's the reason. Off cinema, qawwalis are usually longish affairs, sometimes running into 15 minutes, or even 30 minutes when performed on a stage. That's because the frenzy that the qawwal is looking for cannot be achieved quickly. Also, the qawwal often lyrically radiates away from the central theme, only to return to it craftily. The idea of repeating lines and the concept of chorus so vital to qawwalis add to the time needed for the song to take effect. But when Sohrab Modi's *Sitamgar* featured this qawwali, they just had to shrink it, because the 78 rpm records on which songs were recorded in those days had a runtime of under 3.30 minutes. Cassettes came in the early 1950s and they fixed that issue, but we're in the 1930s just now.

The second qawwali appeared in *Barrister's Wife* (1935). *Nazariya taane hai teer kamaan, jaane legi ye kis kis ki jaan* was sung by comedian Charlie and his friends on and off the screen. Like the first qawwali, this too was written by Pt. Narayan Prasad 'Betab' and had music by Banne Khan and Revashankar Marwadi.

The genre is heavily populated by male musicians, but interestingly the first hit qawwali in our films was an all-women's affair in *Zeenat* (1945): *Aahen na bhari, shikwe na kiya, kuchh bhi na zubaan se kaam liya* was sung by Noor Jahan, Zohrabai Ambalewali and Kalyani. Penned by Nakhshab, its music was scored by Hafeez Khan. Over the years, significant and enjoyable qawwalis have featured many singers and actors, either mostly men or then men and women. But the odd women's-only qawwalis have shown up too, like *Jalwa jo tera dekha humne* (Meena, Usha, Asha, Shamshad/ *Gateway Of India*, 1957), *Sharma ke ye kyoon sab parda-nasheen aanchal ko sanwaara karte hain* (Shamshad, Asha/ *Chaudhvin Ka Chand*, 1960), *Teri mehfil mein qismat aazma kar hum bhi dekhenge* (Lata, Shamshad/ *Mughal-e-Azam*, 1960), *Dil gaya to gaya dilruba mil gaya* (Shamshad, Suman/ *Shama*, 1961), *Kehte hain jisko ishq tabiyat ki baat hai* (Shamshad, Usha/ *Aaj Aur Kal*, 1963), *Nigaahen milaane ko jee chaahta hai* (Asha/ *Dil Hi To Hai*, 1964), *Unse nazren mili aur hijaab aa gaya* (Lata/ *Ghazal*, 1964), and *Jab ishq kahi ho jata hain* (Mubarak Begum, Asha/ *Arzoo*, 1965).

Aahen na bhari, shikwe na kiye

In terms of fame as a composer of qawwalis, Roshan has been the King of Qawwalis in our films. His twin offerings, *Na to caarvaan ki talaash hai* and *Ye ishq ishq hai* remain unmatched in lyrical content, rendering and overall composition to this day. But maestro Ravi is not at all behind; his work, both in numbers and quality just cannot be dismissed away.

The genre, breathing freely once upon a time, is now on life support, at least in our films. But hardliners are not the only reasons why qawwalis may expire. Over the decades, our society itself has downgraded poetry, making it highly difficult for any writer to consider making a career of it. As society chokes the entire universe of poetry—ghazals, rubais and nazms—it cuts off the oxygen supply to music genres like the mujra and qawwali as well.

~~~~

The above was originally published in DNA Jaipur on 29 October 2017. It has since been updated and enhanced.

~~~~

47

Live Music While You Eat

You must have noticed that many of us are often different people in different settings. When alone (and without any electronic surveillance happening), we are completely ourselves, scratching wherever for instance, or farting without excuse, since no one is watching. On a one-to-one basis, the right social behaviour enters the equation. We appear to be somewhat honest with our spouses, our best friends, our siblings, acquaintances and colleagues. But when we are in a crowd mixed with these relationships, group dynamics take over; we transform into somewhat different people. Perhaps we tend to get a little smart-Alecy because now there's an audience to admire our wit. Maybe we are offering something like a common-minimum program to make the multiple interactions work during these meets.

Thus, when someone says, "My life is an open book", he is way off the reality unless he is in a very tiny minority. In other words, except in very rare cases, there's no such thing as a person being like an open book. Neither should the statement be taken seriously. Social scientists tell us that. They also tell us that there's nothing wrong in our being different people in different settings unless we compromise our core values. It is a part of being human to have so many facets to us, each making a strong pitch to make things work for us in specific settings.

In India more than in the Western world, such a transformation is quite noticeable when we are in a restaurant that has live musicians playing, especially the kinds who do the rounds of every table, stopping to serenade us with a couple of songs and taking requests too. Now you may be the sort who loves the Beatles go *Yesterday, All my troubles seemed so far away*, or Manna Dey's *Aye meri zohra jabeen*, but chances are, when the singer comes around with his guitar slung around his shoulder and the same song on his lips, you will avoid looking too much at him, subsuming the music with food, drink and conversation.

But there can be good reasons as well. Many people go out for the food and for sparkling conversation, some even for a business dinner. If someone trumps their agenda with music, they are not going to erupt in applause when a song ends. It's also possible that the singer may be going off-key, or he may be too much in the face. Some diners find the music too intrusive because being watched as we eat can be a turn-off.

But then again, maybe it's about you presenting a different face in a milieu in which most people are strangers seated at different tables. This is even if you may be enjoying the music.

Even so, many restaurants offer music to add to the dining experience; ghazals, popular film songs or pop, jazz, country western, etc. These establishments know the idea works for the bottom line. A book called *Gastrophysics: The New Science of Eating*, (Charles Spence of Oxford University), announces that music can make our food taste better. It lists many findings like patrons rate the quality of pasta and pizza higher when listening to Italian Opera. No wonder that a large number of eateries worldwide play recorded music or the radio. Several other restaurants feature even just a guitar or piano played live. There are even restaurants like The Lounge at Mumbai's National Sports Club of India, where a grand piano is played live, not by a human being, but by a programmed chip. You may hear a good tune and want to thank the pianist. You will find the keys being pressed down to play the tune, but won't find anyone sitting on the stool, or any hand doing the playing. This can seem quite spooky, but the food tastes awesome.

Back to live music bands in eateries. They have been around for as long as one can remember. Excluding restaurants and bars that feature cabarets and other dance acts, New York City leads the world with 1500 eateries that feature live music every day. Tokyo has less than 700 such restaurants. Mumbai clocks in at around 200, and Delhi is behind that figure.

In Mumbai, the Bar at Bombay Gymkhana features a live piano, as does The Yacht Club behind the Taj Mahal Hotel. The Taj itself features a live piano played unobtrusively at the Sea Lounge. Further south on the seafront from the Taj, find the Radio Club, whose bar can turn you into a gagged zombie on Wednesday nights. Gaylord at Churchgate has a pianist every weekend evenings. Then there is the Cricket Club of India also in Churchgate. It has a grand piano in its beautiful lobby where a couple of dozen guests can choose to sit and to listen before they go to the bar or any of the club's several restaurants. Such music-as-you-dine places are dotted in many places on our land.

Several musicians have played instruments or sung live in restaurants over the years. Chic Chocolate, who composed amazing songs like *Aa teri tasweer bana loon* (Talat/ *Nadaan*, 1951), and *Koi dard hamaara kya samjhe* (Lata/ *Rangili*, 1952), played his awesome trumpet in hundreds of songs but also ran an orchestra for years in the Apollo Room of the Taj Mahal Hotel in Bombay. Francisco Casanovas who composed Hemant Kumar's *Wo aankh se pila gaye* and *Jab chaand mera nikla* (besides arranging dozens of tunes), played in a band in The Grand Hotel, Calcutta. Biddu sang and played the guitar in Venice restaurant, at Astoria Hotel, Churchgate, Bombay, before going on to international stardom for composing *Aap jaisa koi meri zindagi mein aaye* (Nazia Hasan), and *Kung Fu Fighting* (Carl Douglas). Not far from Venice was a place called Talk of the Town, where Usha Uthup belted out songs for years. She is famous for singing *I Love You* (with Asha in *Hare Rama Hare Krishna*, 1971), and *Ramba ho Samba ho* (*Armaan*, 1981). It is here that Pam Crain crooned for years. Here again, Louis Banks played the keyboard while he sang away, after having done so at the Hindustan Hotel in Calcutta. Among his achievements is his arrangement of the music in *Mile Sur Mera Tumhara*. The gifted Manohari Singh was Louis Banks' first cousin; he not only graced hundreds of songs with his euphonious saxophone, flute and mandolin but also composed songs such as *Aa humsafar pyaar ki sej par* (Kishore, Lata/ *Chatpati*, 1983) and *Dono ke dil hain majboor pyaar se* (Lata, Jagjit Singh, non-film), along with his partner Basu Chakravarty. For years, Manohari Singh played the sax, trumpet and flute at the prestigious Firpo's restaurant in Calcutta. The pianist who put Hindi film songs into instrumental orbit, Brian Silas, played for years at the Dum Pukht restaurant at Delhi's Maurya Sheraton. There have been many others.

Consider these film songs where a person was seen singing in a restaurant. Not at a private party, and not essentially dancing and singing, because that becomes a story of song and dance. However, if the patrons get up to dance, that's ok.

- ➤ *Koi kisi ka deewaana na bane* (Lata/ *Sargam*, 1950)
- ➤ *Mere man ki dhadkan mein koi naache ta ta thai thai* (Manna Dey/ *Hamdard*, 1953)
- ➤ *Dil chhed koi aisa naghma* (Lata/ *Inspector*, 1956)
- ➤ *Kaun ye aaya mehfil mein* (Rafi/ *Dil Deke Dekho*, 1959)

Kaun ye aaya mehfil mein

- ➤ *Koi sone ke dil waala* (Rafi/ *Maya*, 1961)
- ➤ *Ajnabi tum jaane pehchaane se lagte ho* (Kishore/ *Hum Sab Ustad Hain*, 1965)
- ➤ *Aage bhi jaane na tu* (Asha/ *Waqt*, 1965)
- ➤ *Rut jawaan jawaan raat meherbaan* (Bhupinder Singh/ *Aakhri Khat*, 1967)
- ➤ *Hai preet jahaan ki reet sada* (Mahendra/ *Purab Aur Pashchim*, 1970)

Not all restaurants can afford live musicians. But a restaurant in Madrid, Spain uses a brilliant idea. It has been in the news for charging patrons during breakfast and lunch, and then giving away free meals to the poor at dinner. The place is called, not inappropriately, Robin Hood Restaurant, never mind that they don't rob the rich to pay the poor. Interestingly, lunch tables are booked for months, but the place still cannot afford live music. That is unromantic to some, so a message outside says you can sing inside, as long as you don't disturb the others. Reportedly, after such a meal, some deprived diners sang *Hasta Manana*, a popular ABBA song, in Spanish meaning see you tomorrow.

~~~~

The above was originally published in DNA Jaipur on 12 August 2018. It has since been updated and enhanced.

~~~~

48

Women in Proper Noun Roles

Most societies are patriarchal, meaning the male of the species is the boss in leadership areas. That is changing, more significantly in the First World than in countries like India. Such male dominance shows itself up in cinema as well, because cinema is often a mirror of our society.

A couple of years ago, a US-based digital publication called The Pudding did a seminal study of male dominance in Hollywood. The researchers made a primary list of 8000 films, and then shortlisted 2000 of them, in which they looked at screenplays and dialogues in detail. A strong yardstick of actors' importance in a movie is the number of words they speak, as a percentage of the total words in the feature. This is not very different from the percentage of time a team has possession of the ball in hockey or football. When the researchers examined the data, they found that only in 22% of American films did actresses have more spoken words than actors. The study also looked at the connection between dialogues and ageing. They discovered that after the age of 40, actresses had a sharp decline of dialogues written for them, while for actors it was the reverse: they spoke far more in the 42-65 years range than when they were 32 to 41 years old. It's a no-brainer then that men get to act in lead roles longer than women. The details of that study can be found in the footnoted link[6].

But what do we find here in India?

In the last two years, the Censor Board has had issues with two films, the eponymous *Padmaavat* (2018), and the mystifying *Lipstick Under My Burkha* (2016), both women-centric narratives. To see what was up, a study was conducted in late 2017 jointly by IBM Research India, Delhi Technological University, and Indraprastha Institute of Information Technology. They scanned roughly the last 50 years and found that in Bollywood, women-centric films have risen from just 7% during 1970-1975 to a still-small 12% today, while for male-oriented films, the figure is marginally down from 38% to 36% in the same years. In other words, nothing has changed substantially.

This means that one or more of these groups—the audiences, the filmmakers, or the male actors—have an issue when more importance is given to actresses. Male leads do not easily agree to work in women-centric films, where they will be subordinate to the fairer sex. The title of the story becomes of crucial importance in such films since it's easier for the male ego if it's a woman-centric film without the title suggesting such dominance. Examples are *Adalat* (1958), *Sadhna* (1958), *Anpadh* (1962), *Inteqaam* (1969) *Aandhi* (1975) and *Bazaar* (1982). One step harder are women's titles of the common noun kind, like *Badi Bahu* (1951), *Mem Sahib* (1956), *Bhabhi* (1957), *Sone Ki Chidiya* (1958), *Ardhangini* (1959), *Chhoti Behen* (1959), and *Didi* (1959). It is at the upper end, where the title of the film is a proper eponymous noun, named after the female protagonist that makes it hardest for the male actor. Examples of these would be films like *Anuradha* (1960), *Purnima* (1965), *Anita* (1967), and *Razia Sultan* (1982).

In the Indian statistical study, we can safely add a *desi tadka*, something having to do with music. Indian cinema has a key difference from films made in the West, in that we are essentially musical. Songs remain fundamental to the ethos of our films, even if more and more films are now being made without any music in them. Songs give enhanced value to the actor who is miming them. So, while we in India cannot find studies on dialogues, we certainly have almost complete knowledge of the songs lip-synched by actors and actresses.

Let's look at some songs now, all performed by actresses in 'Proper Noun Country', meaning in films named after their character, with their real name finding a mention after the movie title, and the singer's name after the song:

- *Mangala* (1950. P Bhanumati). *Jhanan jhanan jhanwa more bichhwa* (Geeta)
- *Anarkali* (1953. Bina Rai). *Aa jaan-e-wafa* (Geeta)
- *Miss Mala* (1954. Vyjayanthimala). *Dil na lagaana dil na lagaana* (Shamshad)
- *Champakali* (1957. Suchitra Sen). *Chhup gaya koi re door se pukaar ke* (Lata)
- *Miss Mary* (1957. Meena Kumari). *So gaya saara zamaana* (Lata)

So gaya saara zamaana

- *Rani Roopmati* (1957. Nirupa Roy). *Aaja aaja bhanwar sooni dagar* (Lata)
- *Sharda* (1957. Meena Kumari). *Jana gana mangal daayak Ram* (Lata)
- *Lala Rukh* (1958. Shyama). *Alvida jaan-e-wafa tera nigehbaan Khuda* (Asha)
- *Madhumati* (1958. Vyjayanthimala). *Zulmi sang aankh ladi* (Lata)
- *Sujata* (1959. Nutan). *Kaali ghata chhaaye mora jeeya tarsaaye* (Asha)
- *Anuradha* (1960. Leela Naidu). *Kaise din beete kaise beeti ratiya* (Lata)
- *Razia Sultana* (1961. Nirupa Roy). *Aaja re deewaane lagi dil ki bujhaane* (Asha)

- *Saranga* (1961. Jayshree Gadkar). *Koi ghar ayega, pyaar jataayega* (Lata)
- *Shama* (1961. Nimmi). *Dil gham se jal raha hai, jale* (Suman)
- *Aarti* (1962. Meena Kumari). *Kabhi to milegi, kaheen to milegi* (Lata)
- *Dr. Vidya* (1962. Vyjayanthimala). *Jaani tum to dole dagha dai ke* (Lata)
- *Benazir* (1964. Meena Kumari). *Gham naheen gar zindagi veeraan hai* (Asha)
- *Chitralekha* (1964. Meena Kumari). *Sansaar se bhaage phirte ho* (Lata)
- *Jahan Ara* (1964. Mala Sinha). *Haal-e-dil yoon unhen sunaaya gaya* (Lata)
- *Sati Savitri* (1964. Anjali Devi). *Jeevan dor tumhi sang baandhi* (Lata)
- *Purnima* (1965. Meena Kumari). *O is desh ke rehne waalo* (Lata)
- *Amrapali* (1966. Vyjayanthimala). *Jao re jogi tum jao re* (Lata)
- *Anita* (1967. Sadhana). *Main dekhoon jis ore sakhi ri* (Lata)
- *Noor Jahan* (1967. Meena Kumari). *Sharaabi sharaabi ye saawan ka mausam* (Suman)
- *Neel Kamal* (1968. Waheeda Rehman). *He rom rom mein basne wale Ram* (Asha)
- *Madhavi* (1969. Deepa). *Saanjh savere adharon pe mere bas tumra hai naam* (Lata)
- *Mahua* (1969. Anjana Mumtaz). *Pyaar mera jo tu ne loota* (Asha)
- *Jwala* (1971. Madhubala). *Dekho ji aankhon mein dekho* (Lata)
- *Seeta Aur Geeta* (1972. Hema Malini in a double role). *Haan ji haan maine sharaab pee hai* (Lata)
- *Anamika* (1973. Jaya Bhaduri). *Baahon mein chale aao* (Lata)
- *Archana* (1974. Mala Sinha). *Tan man tere rang rangoongi* (Lata)
- *Julie* (1975. Lakshmi). *My heart is beating* (Preeti Sagar)
- *Mili* (1975. Jaya Bhaduri). *Maine kaha phoolon se* (Lata)
- *Noorie* (1979. Poonam Dhillon). *Chori-chori koi aaye* (Lata)
- *Razia Sultan* (1982. Hema Malini). *Aye dil-e-naadaan* (Lata)
- *Umrao Jaan* (1982. Rekha). *Dil cheez kya hai* (Asha)

- ➤ *Henna* (1991. Zeba Bakhtiar). *Main hoon khushrang henna* (Lata)
- ➤ *Roja* (1993. Madhoo). *Dil hai chhota sa* (Minmini)
- ➤ *Zubeida* (2001. Karishma Kapoor). *Dheeme dheeme gaoon* (Kavita)
- ➤ *Padmavat* (2018. Deepika Padukone). *Ghoomar ghoomar ghoomar ghoomar ghoome re* (Shreya Ghoshal, Swaroop Khan)

Through the above songs, we are not just recalling women in meaty roles, but also in a sense celebrating all the actors who accepted subsidiary roles in these films. Also, it is interesting how some films mislead in their titles. We do not know for instance, how many words Prithviraj Kapoor had in his title role of The Great Mughal in *Mughal-e-Azam* (1960), but it seems certain that at least equal screen space belonged to Dilip Kumar and Madhubala. The lady even had a few songs to lip-synch, while these men had none. You wonder if this was a trade-off, a kind of win-win for all, with Prithviraj taking the title, Dilip arguably with the best-spoken words, and Madhubala the songs.

This Land is Mine: a fascinating story

Here's an exciting story. After working with filmmaker Mehboob Khan in *Andaz, Aan,* and *Amar,* Dilip Kumar learnt that the director was planning a remake of his super-successful film *Aurat* (1940). The remake was to be titled *Mother India*. Dilip was very keen to portray the role of the bad son Birju. But how could he play such a role in a film whose title announced that the lead role was a woman's? So he prevailed upon Mehboob to change the name *Mother India* to *This Land is Mine*. Interestingly, the heroine was still not taken for the film, but the mahurat was held anyway. Here is what the legendary film journalist Baburao Patel wrote[7]:

"On Friday, January 7, producer-director Mehboob performed the mahurat of *This Land is Mine* at Mehboob Studios, Bandra. The picture was originally titled *Mother India* but the new title *This Land is Mine* is equally dramatic. Mehboob, however, is still anxiously searching for a suitable girl who can play the heroine and also look the mother of Dilip Kumar."

But Mehboob couldn't find such a girl. And he couldn't change the script. Of course, he had introduced Nargis as a lead in *Taqdeer* way back in 1943. And later he directed her in *Andaz* (1949). He felt, as did his core team of colleagues (Faredoon Irani, cinematographer; S Ali Raza and Wajahat Mirza, dialogue writers) that it was Nargis who could do justice to the role. So Nargis it was. How Mehboob got Raj Kapoor—in whose camp Nargis was now more-or-less permanent—to agree releasing the lady for that film is itself a story, but she came aboard. However, now she had a problem with the casting. How could she play the role of Dilip's mother, having been romantically paired with him in *Mela* (1948), *Andaz* (1949), *Babul* (1950), *Jogan* (1950), and *Deedar* (1951)? Long story short: Dilip had to leave. The film's title was changed back to *Mother India*, and the film was a monster hit.

A fascinating sci-fi film

Talking about women-centric films brings to mind a wonderful science-fiction film called *The Last Man on Planet Earth,* released in 1999. In the story, World War III is in progress, when someone launches a biological weapon that selectively targets the Y chromosome, which is found only in men. Result: most of the world's men lie dead. In this environment, a female scientist, worried about the future of life on our planet, succeeds in cloning a man who is free from any violence or oppression.

Perhaps in such a balanced world, we can experience cinema that has no gender bias. Also perhaps then women can earn as much as men, a point of crucial importance not elaborated in the above surveys.

~~~~

The above was featured in DNA Jaipur on 17 October 2018. It has since been updated and enhanced.

~~~~

49

Dark Christmas

Many of us have no major quarrels with theologians, but calling the day Jesus Christ died Good Friday does seem like someone's idea of a cruel joke. It just has to be a terrible Friday, a holy Friday even, but a good one? Not the day they nailed Christ to his death. Something is seriously amiss here. You wonder if the followers of Jesus advanced such an idea, or was it in fact announced so by the Roman soldiers who crucified him.

Christmas Day is of course just the reverse. It is the birthday of Jesus the Saviour, and he's the reason for the season. People brighten up their homes, play music, eat goodies and share them, and go shopping if they missed it in the run-up till then. Kids are taken to meet Santa in stores and carnivals, people give and receive gifts, and Xmas trees with tinsel greet you everywhere. It's a time to be happy and grateful.

No Christian wants to be sad on this happiest of happy days. Much less, just no one wants to die on this day. But some do pass away. This is what happened to a not-yet-38, devout Protestant called Vinod. His real name was Eric Robert, and he was a highly gifted Hindi and Punjabi film music composer. Vinod passed away in Bombay after a prolonged illness way back on 25th December 1959. He was survived by his wife and two daughters, Veena and Veera, then aged twelve and nine respectively. Providence could have chosen another day.

This was the man who had given Lata Mangeshkar (singing with Rafi and Durrani) one of the early foot-tapping winners that catapulted her upwards: *Lara lappa lara lappa laayi rakhda*, from *Ek Thi Ladki* (1949). He followed up the Punjabiyat of this song by offering her another with that flavour: *Nee main kendi reh gayi, na na dhola na, hasde-hasde bedardi ne phad li meri baanh* (*Sabz Baagh*, 1951).

Why, he even made Talat—a quintessential Lucknowi—to croon in Punjabi. This happened twice, both times in duets, first with Sardarni Surinder Kaur (*Aa chanve*, in *Mutiyaar*, 1951), and later with Asha Bhosle (*Mere dil de sej di raaniye*, in *Lara Lappa*, 1953).

Vinod

Besides Punjabiyat, Vinod kept dressing up his poems with remarkably appealing charm. He understood poetry, and the composer permanently resided in Talat Mahmood's heart, especially because he had given some wonderful ghazal opportunities to the king of ghazals. These are just a few of them: *Ho gaye barbaad hum unki khushi to ho gayi* from *Ramman* (1954), *Jab kisi ke rukh pe zulfen aake lehraane lagi* (*Anmol Rattan*, 1950), and *Ek dil hazaar gham* (*Aag Ka Dariya*, 1953). By repeating his name to me in our meetings, Talat made sure I understood where Vinod sat in his scheme of thoughts.

Let's trace Vinod's beginnings. We find that Eric Robert was fond of music from his boyhood in Delhi, so his parents let him learn the piano. He learnt the rudiments of other instruments from some other teachers, including Pandit Amarnath, the elder brother of Husnlal and Bhagatram, who also taught Khayyam. That was in Lahore.

While he was tutoring under Pandit Amarnath, Vinod got the job of playing the piano in Lahore's Carlton Hotel. He also got a composing break with a few songs in *Paraaye Bus Mein* (1946), and the entire score, with eleven songs, in *Khamosh Nigahen* (also 1946). These were forgettable films, perhaps made more so by the political turmoil engulfing the sub-continent at this time. But success or not, Vinod wasn't going to have his core identity—his engagement with music—be snatched away from him. As such, he continued playing the piano at the hotel, lying low for better times. In Carlton, he had been spotted by filmmaker Roop K Shorey, who had named the young pianist Vinod, meaning happy, which reflected his personality. When the Partition happened, Roop K Shorey came to Bombay with many people. Vinod was one of them.

In the next twelve years, Vinod created music scores for some 30 Hindi and Punjabi films. Not bad at all, especially if you consider his tunes were so special; very likely they must have taken time to make. That is why hard-core music lovers keep soaking up many of his songs, so wonderfully planned and executed as they are. Lata in *Kaaga re ja re ja re* (*Wafa*, 1950); *Mere dil ke tadapne ka tamaasha dekhne waale* (*Sabz Baagh*, 1953); and *Meri ulfat soyi hai yahaan* (*Oot Patang*, 1955). Asha too shone in Vinod's *Lo phir chaand nikal aaya* (*Ek Do Teen*, 1953) and *Tera dard hai meri zindagi* (*Ramman*, 1954).

Vinod not only made his essential tunes appealing, he graced them beautifully with musical ornaments. The enchanting use of the clarinet and castanets in *Beqaraar kar diya* (Madhubala Jhaveri/ *Ramman*, 1954) is an example. Do hear the awesome trumpet played by Chic Chocolate in *Rakhna dil mein dil ki baat* (Sabita Chatterji, Rafi/ *Garma Garam*, 1957). The exceptional clapping and mandolin fillers in *Hum to aaya hai tere deedaar ke liye* (Shamshad/ *Shri Nakad Narayan*, 1955) spell artistic, long-shelf-life class. In *Titli* (*For Ladies Only*, 1951) Sulochana Kadam rendered the pleasing *Nigaahon ko jab aa gaya muskuraana*, the song riding on raag Bihag and a beautiful 6-beat pulse, with a piano and muted trumpet staying so seductively minimalistic. That muted trumpet is something he just loved, so he used it in many other songs, such as the euphonious Lata charmer *Taare wohi hain, chaand wohi hai* (*Anmol Rattan*, 1950).

But the way he conceived his duets? Intoxicating! Think of these: *Ik aag ka dariya hai*, rendered by Rafi and Asha in *Aag Ka Dariya* (1953), making us sing along, time and again. The same singers were featured in *Ek Do Teen* (1953) in *Tumhen chupke se dil mein liya jo basa*. Also his composition *Madhoshi mein, angdaayi mein* (Geeta and Durrani in *Sheikh Chilli*, 1956) is a charming wonder of a tune. So are the two Lata-Rafi duets from *Ek Thi Ladki* (1949), *Ab haal-e-dil ya haal-e-jigar kuchh na poochhiye*, and *Ye shokh sitaare*. Vinod also gave us, through the voices of Talat and Lata, exceptional duets in *Anmol Ratan* (1950): *Shikwa tera main gaoon dil mein samaane waale*, and *Yaad aane waale phir yaad aa rahe hain*. In *Makheechoos* (1956) Vinod tuned quite a few lovely duets for Talat, for instance with Sudha like *Dil le lo dil le lo dil le lo*, and this racy winner with Geeta: *O Arabpati ki chhori, gori-gori Dilli door naheen*.

One day Vinod accidentally cut himself while shaving. That turned into a wound that wouldn't heal. It then became septic, with an invasion of the bloodstream by virulent bacteria that can go attack the patient's vital organs. Tragically, they ravaged Vinod's kidney.

The composer spent nine months in Bombay Hospital before he left this world. He also knew that his end was near. "Consequently", his daughter Veena tells me, "he told my mother to get new clothes for me and my younger sister for Christmas Day". Veena and Veera did get those clothes and wore them, as their father lay dead in Bombay Hospital. That scene can better be imagined than described.

The dresses are still there for us to look at. The family's tears have dried. Veena has passed away too. But the others are unable to celebrate Christmas even today.

~ ~ ~ ~

The above was originally published in DNA Jaipur on 1 November 2015. It has since been updated and enhanced.

50

Behind the Human Curtain

France won the Football World Cup finals in Russia in July 2018, and while it was so well deserved, the ethnic profiles of its players celebrating on the field were surprising. A disproportionately large number of its players were dark-skinned or black, i.e., from North Africa or sub-Saharan Africa respectively, with either the players or their parents having been born on that continent. It is illegal to make a demographic assessment of one's ethnicity in France but learned estimates tell us that the coloured population of the country ranges between 13 and 16 per cent. With only five of the fourteen men in their football finals team being white, the government cannot be faulted for discrimination here.

Otherwise too, France has given so much to the world, in philosophy and culture, in fashion and cinema and the arts. Its national motto, *Liberty, Egalite, Fraternite* (Liberty, Equality and Fraternity) has inspired the world's community of nations. But recently, when it objected to people wearing a garment in public, the country precipitated an internationally polarized debate that refuses to sit on the back burner. The garment, called burkini—a portmanteau of the burkha and the bikini—is a new kind of swimwear for Muslim women, whose religion takes a stern view of women exposing their bodies in public. Respecting the Islamic traditions of modest dress, the burkini is a head-to-foot swimsuit, leaving only the face, hands and feet exposed. Made from lycra or polyester, it comes in many colours and three styles: modest fit, slim fit, and active fit. While the priests are not at all happy with the body-hugging necessities of the burkini, they have for now trained their guns in another direction: the French government. You wonder why, because the government has banned the use of the burkini in swimming pools.

Some people wonder how the ban comes from the same accommodating country whose national honour was crowned by a football team in which over half of the players were of African descent, as we saw earlier. They also wonder if it's the same country that has inspired the world, including in tenets of democracy and equality, which too we saw earlier. Others see no conflict of values here because it's like this: by creating a place that in the public space is religiously neutral, France wants to be a beacon to the world community. Its lawmakers argue that you must appear religiously similar—thus endorsing secularism—and only then expect equal treatment. It sees such outfits as a possible link to Islamic fundamentalism. The United States, on the other hand, allows you to wear what you want, do what you want, stand out like a sore thumb if you wish, and you may still expect equal treatment. Perhaps Americans are forgetting what their own President, John Kennedy said in his inaugural speech: "Ask not what your country can do for you, ask what you can do for your country". Both countries allow you to practice and preach your religion, no problem. The difference is in the philosophies of how a state must be run when it comes to a public show of religion. Take your pick.

That said, let's return to the burkini which is not a halal piece of clothing for Muslim women only. Other ladies also like the idea, since it also gives them a good deal of sun protection. By creating an air of mystery, it is nice for aesthetics too. Moreover, women who are not delighted with their bodies want to downplay the exposure. It is for these reasons that the outfit is a hot favourite worldwide.

Different cultures have different coverings for women

Many cultures have veils of some kind, running from ancient times. The Hindus, Sikhs and Jains have the ghunghat, still worn by ladies when around men and elders. Christian nuns wear a habit that covers their heads, as a dedication to God. Parsi women wear a headscarf when entering a fire temple and Orthodox Jewish women also wear one.

The veil is most common in the Muslim faith though, where it has many avatars and names. Hijaab covers a woman's hair. Naqaab covers the head and face with a cut for the eyes. Abaya is a long cloak covering the body, except the face, feet and hands. Burkha or Chaadari has a slit or a grill only for the eyes. Al-Amira is a two-piece veil consisting of a close-fitting cap and a complementing scarf. Chador covers the entire body except for the face, and burkini as we saw is the newest addition to the family.

Hindi cinema has had quite a few tragedies of errors resulting from women in burkhas and naqaabs. In *Chaudhvin Ka Chaand* (1960), it was the burkha that caused serious misunderstandings between two buddies, played by Rehman and Guru Dutt, both in love with the same girl, Waheeda Rehman. We move to *Mere Mehboob* (1963), and here we see the burkha causing a mix-up between Ameeta and Sadhana, each of them thinking Rajendra Kumar is in love with her. Nutan was no stranger to modesty veils, wearing them in *Laila Majnu*, *Shabab*, *Dil Hi To Hai* and *Dil Ne Phir Yaad Kiya*. But before all this, when she was just 15 years old, she was the heroine in a murder mystery called *Nagina* (1951). The film was given the Adults Only certificate, so she wasn't permitted to watch her own film in a cinema hall. Shrouded in a burkha, she tried to sneak into one, but her idea was discovered and she was stopped at the entrance.

As for our poetry, we put all cloaks under the simplistic umbrellas of *ghunghat*, *parda* and *naqaab*. While by *parda* we also mean a curtain separating the women from the men, the result being the same. And in this collective simplification can be found several songs from Hindi cinema. Our list begins with Mukesh's first hit, from *Pehli Nazar* (1945):

Dil jalta hai to jalne de aansoo na baha fariyaad na kar,
Tu parda nasheen ka aashiq hai yoon naam-e-wafa barbaad na kar
(Roughly, "Stop complaining if you're hurting. Please don't reveal her identity and insult her loyalty")

Here are many more songs having to do with the modesty veil:

> *Gore gore mukhde se ghunghat hatao jo* (Chitalkar/ *Babooji*, 1950)

- *Beech ghunghat kaise keh doon ke tera mera pyaar maahi re* (Geeta/ *Biwi*, 1950)
- *Ghunghat ke pat khol re tohe piya milenge* (Geeta/ *Jogan*, 1950)
- *Rukh se parda to hata zara nazren to mila* (Rafi/ *Shahi Mehmaan*, 1955)
- *Laaj lage ghunghat na khol balma* (Rafi, Asha/ *Shiv Bhakt*, 1955)
- *Aye pardanasheen ye ishq kaheen pardon mein chhupaaya jaata hai* (Lata/ *Teerandaaz*, 1955)
- *Kab tak rahega parda, parde mein chhupne waale* (Lata/ *Heer*, 1956)
- *Ghunghat uttha de parda hata de* (Rafi/ *Zindagi Ke Mele*, 1956)
- *Gori zara mukhde se ghunghat hatao na* (Asha/ *Miss India*, 1957)
- *Ghunghat naheen kholoongi saiyaan tore aage* (Lata/ *Mother India*, 1957)
- *Parda utthao saamne aao* (Rafi, Shamshad/ *Pak Daaman*, 1957)
- *Pyaas kuchh aur bhi bhadka di jhalak dikhla ke, tujhko parda rukh-e-roshan se hataana hoga* (Talat, Asha/ *Lala Rukh*, 1958)
- *Aaj kyoon humse parda hai* (Rafi, Balbir/ *Sadhana*, 1958)
- *Ja tose naheen boloon, ghunghat naheen kholoon* (Lata, Rafi/ *Samrat Chandragupta*, 1958)
- *Sharma ke ye kyoon sab pardanasheen* (Asha, Shamshad/ *Chaudhvin Ka Chand*, 1960)

Sharma ke ye kyoon sab
pardanasheen

- *Gori ghunghat mein mukhda chhupao na* (Asha/ *Ghunghat*, 1960)
- *Ghunghat hata na dena goriye chanda sharam se doobega* (Lata/ *Sapan Suhaane*, 1961)
- *Mat kholo ghunghat ke pat saiyaan* (Asha/ *Senapati*, 1961)
- *Parda utthe salaam ho jaaye* (Manna Dey, Asha/ *Dil Hi To Hai*, 1963)
- *Rukh se parda hataaya to pachhtaoge* (Asha, Manna Dey/ *Dil Ne Phir Yaad Kiya*, 1966)
- *Rukh se zara naqaab hata do mere huzoor* (Rafi/ *Mere Huzoor*, 1968)
- *Parde mein rehne do* (Asha/ *Shikar*, 1968)
- *Ye parda hata do, zara mukhda dikha do* (Rafi, Asha/ *Ek Phool Do Mali*, 1969*)*
- *Parda hai parda* (Rafi/ *Amar Akbar Anthony*, 1977)
- *Ghunghat ki aad se dilbar ka deedaar adhure rehta hai* (Alka, Kumar Sanu/ *Hum Hain Rahi Pyaar Ke*, 1993)
- *Sun gori khol zara ghunghat ka dor* (Rafi, Kamal Barot/ *Phool Bane Angaare*, 1963)

An interesting take on the *parda* was offered in a quatrain by poet Akbar Allahabadi, which could become a fun song if set to music:

Bepardah nazar aayin jo kal chund bibiyaan
To 'Akbar' zameen mein ghairat se gadh gaya
Poochha jo unse aap ke parde ko kya hua
Kehne lagi, wo mardon ki aql pe pad gaya

(When Akbar, the writer, espied a few uncovered women yesterday, he was scandalized! "What happened to your cloak?" he asked. They replied, "The cloak is now masking men's wisdom").

That was a commendable repartee. More seriously, perhaps it can be extended to mankind in general, because an invisible cloak often envelopes our minds.

~~~~

The above was originally published in DNA Jaipur on 19 August 2018. It has since been updated and enhanced.

~~~~

51

Two of a Kind

The poet Saleem Kausar wrote an unforgettable ghazal that has been rendered by several vocalists, including Mehdi Hassan and Jagjit Singh, from time to time:

> *Main khayaal hoon kisi aur ka mujhe sochta koi aur hai*
> *Sar-e-aina mera aks hai, pas-e-aina koi aur hai*

This is what the poet is saying, in essence, "Two people have me in their thoughts; while to one I appear as a reflection in a mirror, the other sees the real me".

Perhaps inadvertently, the poet is by extension suggesting a duality that lives in many of us. This duality of personas reminds you of the recent #MeToo scandals which have cast a shadow on the characters of several powerful men in India, some of whom have been summarily dispatched from their TV shows, films and important jobs. These exposés appear to be an effort to unmask and lay bare the dual identities of people who are one thing in public and quite another in private. They make you wonder about celebrities like the journalist turned politician MJ Akbar, the actor Nana Patekar, the director Vikas Bahl, the director Sajid Khan, and the actor Alok Nath, in the news for sexual accusations. But the list is longer than that. Much longer. It includes TV anchor Vinod Dua, singer Kailash Kher, actor Rajat Kapoor, Kathak dancer Birju Maharaj, composer Anu Malik and several more. Perhaps the second line, *Sar-e-aina mera aks hai, pas-e-aina koi aur hai* could fit them.

But this poem also has another beautiful line in it: *Teri daastaan koi aur thi, mera waaqiya koi aur hai.* Here, the poet is saying your narrative is different from mine. This thought makes you wonder if, in the aftermath of such allegations, accused persons like MJ Akbar and Alok Nath have exchanged notes with each other, to plot different landscapes of defence. But the accusations remain the same: their misuse of position and power to sexually exploit women. It is possible that in their private moments, some of the embarrassed men may now be wishing they had a kind of 'Erase History' option as is found in Photoshop and YouTube.

We leave these men with their scruples and move to the world of poetry, where two different poets have offered different expressions of the same key idea in two different songs. It would be as if one poet expressed an idea, and later, another poet said "*Me Too* thinks that way, even if our narratives are different!"

Such *humkhayaal* thoughts from different minds make for a fascinating study. Consider the commonality of the following snatches of thoughts.

We begin with the idea of living for others:

> *Kisi ki muskuraahaton pe ho nisaar*
> *Kisi ka dard mil sake to le udhaar,*
> *Kisi ke waaste ho tere dil mein pyaar*
> *Jeena isi ka naam hai...*
> (Shailendra/ Mukesh/ *Anari*, 1959)

Now compare it with this poem:

> *Apne liye jiye to kya jiye*
> *Tu jee aye dil zamaane ke liye...*
> (Javed-Anwar/ Manna Dey/ *Baadal*, 1966)

Apne liye jiye to kya jiye

Here's another set of fraternal poetic twins. The theme is 'Let each of us be happy in our own world'. Here are two of that kind:

> *Tumko mubaarak hon oonche mahal ye, humko hain pyaari hamaari galiyaan*
> (PL Santoshi/ Parul Ghosh, Suresh/ *Basant*, 1942)

And now look at

> *Tumhen zindagi ke ujaale mubaarak, andhere humen aaj raas aa gaye hain*
> (Gulzar/ Mukesh/ *Purnima*, 1965)

How about praising someone else's eyes? Here goes:

> *Teri aankh mein wo kamaal hai*
> (Anjaan/ Rafi/ *Mr. India*, 1961)

Which is in good company with:

> *Teri aankhon ke siwa duniya mein rakkha kya hai*
> (Majrooh/ Rafi or Lata/ *Chirag*, 1969)

Let's now go meet a narcissistic woman praising her own eyes:

> *Bachke kahaan jaoge in nigaahon se*
> (Hasrat/ Asha/ *Yakeen*, 1969)

And set it up with

In aankhon ki masti ke mastaane hazaaron hain
(Shahryar/ Asha/ *Umrao Jaan*, 1981)

Let's move on to the theme of 'Keep moving in life':

Nadiya chale chale re dhaara…tujhko chalna hoga
(Indeevar/ Manna Dey/ *Safar*, 1970)

And compare it with

Jeevan chalne ka naam, chalte raho subah-o-shaam
(Inderjit Singh Tulsi/ Manna Dey, Mahendra, Shyama Chittar/
Shor, 1972)

Yet another subject to receive an echo is the idea of 'Everyone is a thief':

Is duniya mein sab chor chor
(Rajinder Krishan/ Lata/ *Bhai Bhai*, 1956)

And its *humkhayaal* line:

*Humko haste dekh zamaana jalta hai…chor saari duniya humhi
ko mat gher zara*
(Majrooh/ Rafi, Durrani/ *Hum Sab Chor Hain*, 1956)

How about if you are feeling lonely when the weather is perfect?

*Mausam hai jawaan noor mein doobe hain nazaare…kaash tum
mere paas hote*
(Asad Bhopali/ Asha/ *Tower House*, 1962)

And its twin:

*Kitni jawaan hai zindagi kitni jawaan bahaar, aise mein koi aaye
kaheen se kar le humse pyaar*
(Rajinder Krishan/ Rafi/ *Shehnai*, 1964)

Here are a couple of poems invoking divinity for strength:

Hum ko man ki shakti dena
(Gulzar/ Vani Jairam/ *Guddi*, 1971)

And it's dual:

Itni shakti humen dena daata
(Abhilash/ Pushpa Pagdhare/ *Ankush*, 1986)

Under someone's magical spell?

Akhiyaan bhool gayi hain sona, dil pe hua hai jaadu tona
(Bharat Vyas/ Geeta, Lata/ *Goonj Uthi Shehnai*, 1959)

And

Kisi ne jaadu kiya main karoon kya
(Shailendra/ Mukesh/ *Chand Aur Suraj*, 1965)

Kisi ki muskurahaton pe ho nisaar

Now, how about one on someone coming into a room and one's heart goes aflutter?

Ye kaun aaya ke mere dil ki duniya mein bahaar aayi
(Sahir/ Geeta/ *Baazi*, 1951)

And its emotional soulmate:

> *Ye kaun aaya roshan ho gayi mehfil kis ke naam se*
> (Majrooh/ Lata/ *Saathi*, 1968)

Curses can come from everyone, but they sound scary coming from poets:

> *Jalta rahe tu hardam mujhko jalaane waale*
> *Phir main hasi udaoon sun-sun ke tere naale*
> (Asad Bhopali/ Balbir/ *Khul Ja Sim Sim*, 1956)

While its companion is:

> *Mere dushman tu meri dosti ko tarse*
> *Mujhe gham dene waale tu khushi ko tarse*
> (Anand Bakshi/ Rafi/ *Aaye Din Bahaar Ke*, 1966)

This was on the rich versus poor divide:

> *Ghareeb jaanke humko na tum mita dena*
> (Jan Nissar Akhtar/ Rafi, Geeta/ *Chhoo Mantar*, 1956)

Its fraternal twin being:

> *Mehlon ne chheen liya bachpan ka pyaar mera*
> (Prem Dhawan/ Lata, Mukesh/ *Zabak*, 1961)

Enchanted by someone? Think of

> *Teer ye chhupke chalaaya kisne*
> *Ye meettha-meettha jaadu jagaaya kisne*
> (Qamar Jalalabadi/ Asha/ *Phagun*, 1958)

To set it up against this one:

> *Ye kisne geet chheda*
> *Dil mera naache thirak thirak*
> (Shailendra/ Mukesh, Suman/ *Meri Surat Teri Ankhen*, 1963)

Consider these having to do with Coming of Age:

> *Rama kaahe main itni jawaan ho gayi*
> (Rajinder Krishan/ Asha, Usha/ *Saas Bhi Kabhi Bahu Thi*, 1970)

Which isn't too different in thought from

> *Aaj main jawaan ho gayi hoon*
> (Anand Bakshi/ Lata/ *Main Sundar Hoon*, 1971)

It's interesting to see how different writers have honed their craft so well as to be able to offer different imagery for the same idea. There are many thoughts with three or four, even more, different expressions. This, for instance, is about an *ardhangini*, one's constant companion, through good and bad times:

> *Ye jee chaahta hai kisi din main teri*
> *Nigaahon ki saari udaasi chura loon*
> (Rajinder Krishan/ Asha/ *Amar Deep*, 1958)

And its poetic echo here:

> *Tum apna ranj-o-gham*
> *Apni pareshaani mujhe de do*
> (Sahir/ Jagjit Kaur/ *Shagun*, 1964)

While another writer had his thoughts about such a person too:

> *Agar mujh se muhabbat hai*
> *Mujhe sab apne gham de do*
> (Raja Mehdi Ali Khan/Lata/ *Aap Ki Parchhaiyan*, 1964)

Consider too these three couplets that inspire us about a better time to come:

> *Wo subah kabhi to aayegi*
> *Wo subah kabhi to aayegi*
> (Sahir/ Mukesh, Asha/ *Phir Subah Hogi,* 1958)

In the same year, it was Sahir writing a similar thought elsewhere:

> *Raat bhar ka hai mehmaan andhera*
> *Kis ke roke ruka hai savera*
> (Sahir/ Rafi/ *Sone Ki Chidiya,* 1958)

And

> *Gham ki andheri raat mein dil ko na beqaraar kar*
> *Subah zaroor aayegi subah ka intezaar kar*
> (Jan Nissar Akhtar/ Rafi, Talat/ *Sushila,* 1966)

But even this one was written in the same vein:

> *Gham na kar khushi ka daur ayega*
> *Gham na kar zamaana aur ayega*
> (Tanvir Naqvi/ Talat/*Shahzada,* 1955)

And also this one, don't you think?

> *Kabhi to milegi kaheen to milegi*
> *Bahaaron ki manzil raahi*
> (Majrooh/ Lata/ *Aarti,* 1962)

But we will save such multiple groups of similar thoughts for another day.

Meantime, in conclusion, we can end with the immortal lines from the pen of the genius Sahir:

> *Jab bhi jee chaahe nayi duniya basa lete hain log*
> *Ek chehre pe kayi chehre laga lete hain log*
> (Lata in *Daag*, 1973)

Across the border in Pakistan, Mehdi Hassan rendered something similar in *Saza* (1969), to the poetry of Qateel Shifai:

> *Jab bhi chaahe ik nayi surat bana lete hain log*
> *Ek chehre pe kayi chehre saja lete hain log*

One is tempted to imagine that poets may have sometimes taken the imagery from someone else. But writing a similar thought in different words is still worth a salute.

~~~~

The above was originally featured in DNA Jaipur on 25 November 2018. It has since been updated and enhanced.

♪♫♩♪
~~~~

52

Chariots of Verse

You hear poorly made songs with dismal regularity these days. Everywhere you go, the vast majority of people tell you that our new music isn't fun, and that they find it hard to be optimistically engaged with the new crop of musicians. Such thoughts belong to all manner of people, up and down the social ladder, from captains of industry to cab drivers, from cultured housewives to their maids, mostly to the elderly but also to a sizeable number of the young. You wonder how composers and lyricists (with much encouragement from film producers) have lowered the bar to give us wave after wave of forgettable music. You wonder why there is such a huge disconnect between what we want to hear and what is currently being dished out. On a deeper level, you almost wonder if it was us, right here in Hindi cinema, who for decades made thousands of beautiful songs that refuse to die because they live in our hearts. Because in some ways, they define us.

One of the things harming music nowadays is a new novelty on the singing front, in which they have started bringing a strange foreign element into our songs. It's called Vocal Fry, a guttural croak produced at the back of the throat, which I am saving for a story for another day. But if you want to get some idea, listen to *Bol do na zara* from *Azhar* (2016), and *Tu pehla pehla pyaar hai mera* from *Kabir Singh* (2019). Meanwhile, the sounds of instruments have been ending up predictably similar and uniformly ersatz, driven by rhythms instead of melody. As for lyrical poetry, don't even go there. Barring a handful of lyricists, none would know, for instance, the original meaning of the word *sanam*, used so much even these days. Of course, it is Arabic for a statue, and it predates Islam.

Amateur Hour

The Urban Dictionary defines Amateur Hour as a sloppy performance. A large number of music lovers seriously think we are now experiencing Amateur Hour in Hindi cinema's music, especially its poetry. There is now a near-absence of imagery in a field which should have loads of it. *Jaanam, sanam, ishq, Rabba* and a hundred other words in a common pool are what our lyricists are routinely dipping into as words of final significance, rather than as props to convey an aesthetic idea. This does stand out in sharp contrast with the Axial Age of our cinema, mainly the middle 1940s to the late 1960s, when cinema and music reached heights of excellence that seem unachievable today. That age was exemplified not just by a wide range of words used, but by the high use of imagery too.

Let's take one element of the songwriters' art as an example. Sometimes, different poets of the past used different words or sentence structures to express essentially the same idea. It was as if a horse that was harnessed to a chariot could easily be replaced by another horse, who could race with equal felicity. A few pages ago, in the chapter called *Two of a Kind*, we looked at several examples of songs that expressed one idea in two different ways. Examples of such songs are as follows. When praising someone's eyes, the lyrics-writer Anjaan said *Teri aankh mein wo kamaal hai* (Rafi/ *Mr. India*, 1961), and Majrooh wrote *Teri aankhon ke siwa duniya mein rakkha kya hai* (Rafi or Lata/ *Chirag*, 1969). Elsewhere, Shailendra was advising us to live for others in *Kisi ki muskuraahaton pe ho nisaar* (Mukesh/ *Anari*, 1959) while a somewhat similar thought was advanced by Javed-Anwar in *Apne liye jiye to kya jiye* (Manna Dey/ *Baadal*, 1966).

As if such pairs of thoughts aren't rivetting enough, there are many thoughts—more or less of the same kind—that have been offered differently in 3 or more songs! Let's engage with such poetic chariots today, of three poems with similar attributes, even if sometimes the lyricist is common to two of them:

Everyone is a thief

- ➤ Rajinder Krishan: *Is duniya mein sab chor chor* (Lata/ *Bhai Bhai*, 1956)
- ➤ Majrooh: *Humko haste dekh zamaana jalta hai…chor saari duniya hai humhi ko mat gher zara* (Rafi, Durrani/ *Hum Sab Chor Hain*, 1956)
- ➤ Prem Dhawan: *Aenwe duniya deve duhaayi…apne dil ton puchh ke vekho kaun naheen hai chor* (Rafi, Balbir/ *Jagte Raho*, 1956)

Beauty is in the eyes of the beholder

- ➤ Shakeel: *Maan mera ehsaan…meri nazar ki dhoop na bharti roop to hota husn tera bekaar* (Rafi/ *Aan*, 1952)
- ➤ Shakeel: *Sharma ke kyoon sab pardanasheen…nazren jo na hoti to nazaara bhi na hota* (Shamshad, Asha/ *Chaudhvin Ka Chand*, 1960)
- ➤ Shewan Rizvi: *Meri nazren haseen hain ke tum ho haseen…jisko dil chaahe duniya mein hai wo haseen* (Asha/ *Ek Musafir Ek Haseena*, 1962)

What an entry!

- ➤ Sahir: *Ye kaun aaya ke mere dil ki duniya mein bahaar aayi* (Geeta/ *Baazi*, 1951)

Ye kaun aaya ke mere dil
ki duniya mein bahaar aayi

> Majrooh: *Ye kaun aaya roshan ho gayi mehfil kiske naam se* (Lata/ *Saathi*, 1968)

Ye kaun aaya roshan ho
gayi mehfil kiske naam se

> Sahir: *Kaun aaya ki nigaahon mein chamak jaag utthi* (Asha/ *Waqt*, 1965)

Kaun aaya ke nigaahon
mein chamak jaag utthi

The faithful woman

> Rajinder Krishan: *Ye jee chaahta hai kisi din main teri nigaahon ki saari udaasi chura loon* (Asha/ *Amar Deep*, 1958)
> Sahir: *Jahaan mein aisa kaun hai ke jisko gham mila naheen… tumse main juda naheen, mujhse tum juda naheen* (Asha/ *Hum Dono*, 1961)
> Sahir: *Tum apna ranj-o-gham apni pareshaani mujhe de do* (Jagjit Kaur/ *Shagun*, 1964)

A baby is coming

- ➤ Rajinder Krishan: *Chanda se hoga wo pyaara* (Lata, PB Srinivasan/ *Main Bhi Ladki Hoon*, 1964)
- ➤ Rajinder Krishan: *Koi aane waala hai* (Lata, Mahendra/ *Mera Qasoor Kya Hai*, 1964)
- ➤ Indeevar: *Saara pyaar tumhaara maine baandh liya hai aanchal mein* (Asha, Kishore/ *Anand Ashram*, 1977)

He has changed so much!

- ➤ Shakeel: *Badle-badle mere sarkaar nazar aate hain* (Lata/ *Chaudhvin Ka Chand*, 1960)
- ➤ Majrooh: *Wo jo milte the kabhi humse deewaanon ki tarah* (Lata/ *Akeli Mat Jaiyo*, 1963)
- ➤ Majrooh: *Rehte the kabhi jinke dil mein* (Lata/ *Mamta*, 1966)

There are several more such troikas. But there are chariots of four poems too, and even of five poems that carry somewhat similar thoughts. Let's see an example of this last group. It's about love at first sight:

- ➤ Jalal Malihabadi: *Mujhe kisi se pyaar ho gaya* (Lata/ *Barsaat*, 1949)
- ➤ Shailendra: *Unse pyaar ho gaya* (Lata/ *Baadal*, 1951)
- ➤ Zafar Raahi/ Naza Sholapuri: *Jabse dekha tumhen dil hai bechain sa* (Asha, Mahendra/ *Rustom-e-Rome*, 1964)
- ➤ Hasrat: *Unki pehli nazar kya asar kar gayi* (Lata/ *April Fool*, 1964)
- ➤ Hasrat: *Unse mili nazar ke mere hosh ud gaye* (Lata/*Jhuk Gaya Aasmaan*, 1968)

Consider these eight, all having to do with a girl coming of age

- ➤ *Aaj main jawaan ho gayi hoon* (Lata/ Anand Bakshi/ *Main Sundar Hoon*, 1971)
- ➤ *Aate hi jawaani ka mausam betaab nazar ho jaati hai* (Asha/ Shakeel/ *Mulzim*, 1963)

> *Bachpan o bachpan pyaare pyaare bachpan, O lalla sach batla kahaan gaya tu chhod ke* (Lata/ Shailendra/ *Mem Didi*, 1961)

> *Chocolate lime juice ice cream toffeeyaan, pehle jaise ab mere shauq hain kahaan…ye kaunsa mod hai umr ka* (Lata/ Dev Kohli/ *Hum Aapke Hain Koun*, 1994)

> *Dekho ji mera haal badal gayi chaal, dekho mohe laga solva saal* (Asha, Sudha, Rafi/ Majrooh/ *Solva Saal*, 1958)

> *Jeeya lehraaye aayi jawaani* (Nalini Jaywant/ Aah Sitapuri/ *Behen*, 1941)

> *Mat ja mat ja mat ja mere bachpan naadaan* (Asha/ Shailendra/ *Chhoti Si Mulaqat*, 1967)

> *Mere bachpan tu ja, ja jawaani ko le aa* (Lata/ Anand Bakshi/ *Kachche Dhaage*, 1973)

> *Rama kaahe main itni jawaan ho gayi* (Asha, Usha/ Rajinder Krishan/ *Saas Bhi Kabhi Bahu Thi*, 1970)

The idea of living for today also has so many avatars. Check these out, listed alphabetically:

> *Aage bhi jaane na tu…jo bhi hai bus yehi ik pal hai* (Asha/ Sahir/ *Waqt*, 1965)

> *Aaj ki raat mere dil ki salaami le le…kal teri bazm se deewaana chala jaayega* (Rafi/ Shakeel/ *Ram Aur Shyam*, 1967)

> *Aye meri zindagi aaj raat jhoom le…kisko pata hai kal aaye ke na aaye* (Lata/ Sahir/ *Taxi Driver*, 1954)

> *Guma ruma gelo…kal ki baaten kal pe chhodo aaj hi maza le lo* (Rafi, Suman/ Sahir/ Light House, 1958)

> *Jeene waale jhoom ke mastaana ho ke jee, aane waali subah se begaana hoke jee* (Lata/ Sahir/ *Vaasna*, 1968)

> *Har ghadi badal rahi hai dhoop zindagi…kal ho na ho* (Sonu Nigam/ Javed Akhtar/ *Kal Ho Na Ho*, 2003)

> *Kis ke liye ruka hai…karna hai jo bhi kar le, ye waqt ja raha hai* (Rafi/ Prem Dhawan/ *Ek Saal*, 1956)

> *Man more ga jhoom ke…rut ye bahaar ki, ye mauj pyaar ki laut ke na ayegi ghoom ke, ga* (Asha/ Majrooh/ *Mangu*, 1954)

- ➤ *Ye raat ye fizaayen phir aayen ya na aayen* (Rafi, Asha/ Majrooh/ *Batwara*, 1961).
- ➤ *Ye sama phir kahaan aa bhi ja* (Asha/ Jan Nissar Akhtar/ *Ustad*, 1957).

In Berlin, Germany, there is a spectacular sight for tourists called Brandenburg Gate, which is a key entry point to the city. The magnificent gate is crowned by the goddess of victory driving a chariot of four horses. Today the gate is a part of history, not too different from Hindi cinema's chariots of verse.

~~~~

The above was originally featured in DNA Jaipur on 16 December 2018. It has since been updated and enhanced.

~~~~

53

Daan Singh

Hindi film music composer Daan Singh passed away of liver complications in Jaipur at the age of 84 on 18th June 2011. Not many people have heard of this composer, mainly because of his small corpus. In fact, there is a joke in the music fraternity, that Daan Singh's unfinished films exceed the ones that were released. Let's quickly fly over this man's life and work.

Daan Singh was born in Jaipur in 1927. He showed an early interest in the musical instruments for which Rajasthan is famous, like the Ravanahatha and Sarangi. Barely in his teens, he ran away to Bombay and through an uncle, went and met another Rajasthani, the composer Khemchand Prakash, who was famous for his music in *Jaan Pehchaan* (1950), *Tansen* (1943), and *Bhartari* (1944). He assisted Khemchand Prakash for some years. Later, he had an exchange of words with the son-in-law of a film producer. He was so upset that he told his Guruji he was heading back to Jaipur. Daan Singh returned to Jaipur and began working with All India Radio in the music department. After some time, for some reason he left that job too.

Sometime in 1963, someone decided to make a film on the Chinese invasion of 1962 and how we fought them. The film was titled *Bhool Na Jaana* and Daan Singh was signed up as its composer. This was the break for Daan Singh, who was already in his mid-30s. He recorded many songs for this feature, including a sad song by Geeta Dutt: *Mere humnasheen mere humnavah, mere paas aa, mujhe thaam le.* Perhaps because her own marital life was at the time in an existential crisis, Geeta sang this poem as she best could. On a separate note, during the making of this film, in October 1964, her husband was found dead, thanks to an overdose of pills and alcohol in his body. That did not personally impact Daan Singh, but another development did: the box office response that was received by *Haqeeqat* around the same time, not to forget that *Haqeeqat* was the first film to be based on the same Indo-China war. We cannot be sure why the funds for *Bhool Na Jaana* dried up, but the jungle telegraph suggests it could be *Haqeeqat's* disappointing mild success, considering it had big-ticket names like Chetan Anand (director), Balraj Sahni, Priya, Dharmendra, Vijay Anand, Sanjay Khan, Jayant, Chand Usmani, and Achla Sachdev (actors), Kaifi Azmi (lyricist), and Madan Mohan (composer).

Wo tere pyaar ka gham

But Daan Singh soldiered on. Music historian Arunkumar Deshmukh records that Daan Singh signed up 3 more films, all of which were shelved. These are *Ret Ki Ganga*, *Matlabi*, and *Bahadur Shah Zafar*. Finally, his first complete film, *Toofaan* was released. This was in 1969 when the composer was 42 years old. First film at age 42? Seems like a record in our films.

After *Toofan*, his released films were *My Love* (1970), then, much later, *Bawandar—The Sandstorm* (2001), and the Rajasthani film *Bhobhar—The Live Ash* (2012). In the last two films, the music credits were shared with others.

Daan Singh was like a fast-traversing, low-intensity meteor that just showed up and sped away very very quickly. You wonder why. During my several visits to Jaipur in connection with music events, I did make the odd attempt to meet up with him (courtesy of fellow music aficionado Kushal Gopalka), but no meeting happened, either because the composer wasn't taking any calls, or they said he was out of station. The last time I called, he was quite unwell, so was in no mood to meet or talk. I would have loved to ask him about his meteoric passing through the Bollywood music skies, etc., but now it's too late.

Here was a man who descended upon the Bombay film music scene in 1963-64, to make music for *Bhool Na Jaana*. As we saw, sadly for him, the film was not released, and *Bhool Na Jaana* was forgotten. But he did make nice melodies in the film with Manna Dey going patriotic in *Bahi hai jawaan khoon ki aaj dhaara, uttho Hind ki sarzameen ne pukaara*. Daan Singh recorded Mukesh in the six-beat *dadra* song *Pukaaro mujhe naam lekar pukaaro…mujhe tumse apni khabar mil rahi hai*. And as we saw, Geeta Dutt rendered the wonderful *jhaptal*-braided, *shehnai*-laced, *Mere humnasheen, mere humnavah, mere paas aa mujhe thaam le*.

When 1969 came, in stormed *Aradhana* whose onslaught drowned every other melody, so there's no chance that people would recall songs from a Helen-Dara Singh film called *Toofan* (1969). However, Daan Singh's music was appreciated enough to get him some attention. In this film he recorded Mukesh and Asha in *Humne to pyaar kiya, pyaar pyaar pyaar*, and then Asha alone in *Laaga mohe ab ki baar*. The next year, Daan Singh created some wonderful songs in *My Love* (1970). By this time, he was absolutely in love with Mukesh's voice.

In *My Love*, Mukesh sang two super songs penned by Anand Bakshi: The ghazal *Zikr hota hai jab qayaamat ka, tere jalwon ki baat hoti hai*, as well as this one which was festooned with Manohari Singh's saxophone, *Woh tere pyaar ka gham, ik bahaana tha sanam*.

And that's it, Daan Singh's career paused for the next three decades. His failures, successes and long absences have left a mystery behind. Till someone can throw some light on that, we can offer only a frail tribute to a talented musician who remains undiscovered by the majority of music lovers.

~ ~ ~

The above was originally published on the site unboxedwriters.com on 21 June 2011. Here's the link. https://unboxedwriters.com/daan-singh-forgotten-melody/

The original has since been updated.

54

For the Love of a Goddess

Last week, on Monday the 4th of February, students of the Journalism stream at St Xavier's College, Mumbai were treated to an illuminating documentary called Music for a Goddess. This film was made by an American of Indian origin, Nazir Jairazbhoy, who is no more with us, along with his wife, Amy Catlin-Jairazbhoy, who curated the film at the college. Amy is a Professor of Ethnomusicology at the University of California at Los Angeles (UCLA), USA. She teaches the subject "Music of Bollywood and Beyond". A few months every winter, for as long as I can recall, she visits India to further explore the music forms of our culture. Every self-respecting musician in Mumbai has at least heard of her, if not known her. So much so, that if you are a serious musician in India and haven't heard of Amy, it argues yourself unknown. Ethnomusicologists like Amy look at musical instruments, their sounds and construction, and where these instruments belong—in the framework of an orchestra for example. They study the origins of musical instruments and the people who play them. But such experts go beyond that. They trace the social and cultural lives of specific people associated with music systems and consider the folk merit of such peoples' dance and music forms.

Music for a Goddess plots the amazing story of an Indian Goddess called Renuka, which is her name in southern parts of Maharashtra, or Yellama, as she is known in parts of northern Karnataka, Telangana and Andhra Pradesh. This Goddess has perhaps half a million devotees, mostly endemic to these regions. She is the goddess of the Dalit Devadasis and their families.

In the patriarchal society that we live in, giving birth to boys is a great thing, while the reverse is true if a girl is born. In some parts of India, particularly in economically deprived sections of society, births of girls lead to them becoming Devadasis. What happens is this: when girls achieve puberty, they are "married off" to God, which means they cannot marry any mortal being. But relationships are fine; there's no taboo there. So they are in effect sold to the highest bidder, who maintains them to begin with. Soon enough, they end up having multiple partners, effectively making them prostitutes. All this before they even begin to understand sexuality. Has the practice been outlawed? Of course, it has, from immediately after Independence. But in India's babel of anarchy, the Devadasi Abolition Bill has been enormously watered down to effectively render it meaningless. However, there is much more to the Devadasis than selling their bodies. They have their rituals. And they have their music. Which is where Amy and her husband come in for us.

Documented by the Jairazbhoys

Fascinated by the music, dance, culture and social lives of the Devadasi community, the Jairazbhoys toured deep into the regions of southern Maharashtra and northern Karnataka. They met with hundreds of Devadasi families, interacted with them, looked at their music and dance, and examined all that from up close. They filmed much, and in the film used the concept of fictive documentary, the technique involving the Goddess Renuka/ Yellama herself speaking to us, telling us about her origins and how she came to be. Also how she came to get so many followers.

Chaundka, Chondka, or Chaundke

The Goddess has followers called Jogtas and Jogtis—boys and girls who have been ordained by society to dedicate their lives to the service of a God. Such people sing and dance in praise of this Goddess. The main instrument these followers play is called the chaundka—

also called chaundke or chondka—a single-stringed variable-tension chordophone. Imagine a cylindrical container, typically about 6 inches in diameter and 8 inches in height, with a base but no lid. Make a hole at the bottom of the base, push a gut or metal string through it and tie the outer end around a wooden cross-bar that will effectively hug the base. Take the upper end and at about 10 inches, fasten it to another wooden cross-bar, which will become the handle. Next, tie a bunch of ghunghrus to this handle. Finally, hook it up with a strap to go over your shoulder, and voila you are good to play the instrument. You hold the drum between your arm and chest, with your non-dominant hand holding the wooden handle. As a finger of the dominant hand plucks the string, it sounds a pulse, which resonates in the chamber. If now the non-dominant hand pulls and relaxes the string, the pitch rises and falls respectively. With the ghunghrus also getting into the act, the aural experience becomes very nice to hear.

The chaundka sounds similar to the damru, the hand-held twin drum associated with Lord Shiva, but more commonly used by street performers like monkey trainers called madaris. The instruments are so similar in sound that even some percussionists get confused when differentiating between the two, though the absence or presence of the ghunghrus helps us get the right fix. Our cinema has used the chaundka in several songs. Here are some:

> *Hum kheton ke maharaj* (Geeta, Rafi, Pushpa Hans/ Nazim Panipati/ Vasant Desai/ *Sheesh Mahal*, 1950)

> *Gehri gehri nadiya mein bahi chali jaoon re* (Lata/ Shewan Rizvi/ Shivram Krishna/ *Surang*, 1953)

> *Teen deep aur chaar dishaayen* (Lata, unknown male voice/ PL Santoshi/ Shivram Krishna/ *Teen Batti Chaar Rasta*, 1953)

> *O balle balle din dhale hawa jab chale* (Kishore, Shamshad/ Rajinder Krishan/ Madan Mohan/ *Ilzaam*, 1954)

> *Shivji bihaane chale palki sajaaya ke* (Hemant/ Sahir/ SD Burman/ *Munimji*, 1955)

> *Tum sang preet lagaayi rasiya* (Lata/ Shailendra/ Shankar-Jaikishan/ *New Delhi*, 1956)

- *Meri chhoti si behen dekho gehne pehen* (Geeta, Lata/ Bharat Vyas/ Vasant Desai/ *Toofan Aur Diya*, 1956)
- *Aika ho aika dada* (Suman Kalyanpur/ PL Santoshi/ N Datta/ *Hum Panchhi Ek Daal Ke*, 1957)
- *Itne bade jahaan mein aye dil tujhko* (Lata/ Shailendra/ Shankar-Jaikishan/ *Kathputli*, 1957)
- *Dupatta mera malmal ka* (Asha, Geeta/ Rajinder Krishan/ Madan Mohan/ *Adalat*, 1958)
- *Such kehta hai Johnny Walker* (Asha/ Farukh Qaisar/ Roshan/ *Aji Bas Shukriya*, 1958)
- *Meri dulhan Bareilly se aayi re* (Asha, Usha Mangeshkar/ Khumar Barabankvi/ Ravi/ *Mehndi*, 1958)
- *Kaise bijli chamak gayi* (Manna Dey, Asha, Rafi, Chaand Kumari/ Majaaz Lucknowi/ Ghulam Mohammad/ *Do Gunde*, 1959)
- *Mera naam Raju gharaana anaam* (Mukesh/ Shailendra/ Shankar-Jaikishan/ *Jis Desh Mein Ganga Behti Hai*, 1960)
- *O chhalia re chhalia re man mein hamaar* (Asha, Rafi/ Shakeel/ Naushad/ *Ganga Jamuna*, 1961)
- *Zara si aur pila do bhang* (Rafi, Asha/ Sahir/ Ravi/ *Kaajal*, 1965)
- *Wo aa rahe hain saamne se* (Usha Khanna/ Rajinder Krishan/ Madan Mohan/ *Ladka Ladki*, 1966)
- *Gore gore mukhde pe matwaari akhiyaan hain* (Krishna Kalle, Rafi/ BD Mishra/ SN Tripathi/ *Shankar Khan*, 1966)
- *Patthar patthar par likh do re* (Mahendra/ Pradeep/ Shivram Krishna/ *Veer Bajrang*, 1966)
- *Bus yehi apraadh main har baar karta hoon* (Mukesh/ Neeraj/ Shankar-Jaikishan/ *Pehchaan*, 1970)

There is another instrument the Renuka/ Yellama devotees play, that can get somewhat close in sound to the chaundka. It is called tuntuna. But that is most often used as a secondary instrument, i.e., in addition to the chaundka. The tuntuna is also a drum, open at the top, but it has a long rod stuck inside the wall of the drum, a rod that typically rises about 12 inches from the rim. The top of this rod is where the string is tied, while the bottom of the string is tied to the cylinder's base as in the chaundka. Because you cannot pull or release the string while playing, the pitch cannot be varied, thus we hear just a drone to accompany the singers. Here is a YouTube link to both instruments in a quick demonstration: https://www.youtube.com/watch?v=FZJJhpPS654

Tuntuna at left, and Chaundka at right

For clearing the confusion in my mind as to which songs had the damru and which the chaundka, I owe a deep thank you to Deepak Borkar, arguably the country's leading percussionist. Thanks to Amy and Nazir, I now know what a tuntuna is too. That reminds me of Tuntun, the fat comedienne in old Hindi films. You wonder where she got her name from.

~~~~

The above was featured in DNA Jaipur on 10 February 2019. It has since been updated and enhanced.

~~~~

55

Lift Kara De!

In May next year, it will be a hundred years since an excited young man, DG Phalke, released a silent film called *Raja Harishchandra*. That path breaker went on to be called the father of Indian cinema, which leads the world in the number of films produced yearly, way ahead of Japan and the USA, at no. 2 and 3, respectively. Seen by so many in practically every part of the world, Indian cinema has become our de facto universal cultural ambassador. And riding the crest in this cultural embassy have been our songs.

These magical songs have been around for over 80 years (since *Alam Ara*, 1931), and the treat they offer is truly awesome, both in numbers and variety. Many of these melodies vitalize our spirits, in a sort of *'lift kara de'* way! This essay flies over just one such randomly chosen song per decade, if only to smell the fragrance of what was going on over the years. But of course everyone will have their own random list in their minds. It's all so subjective.

Anyway, happy or sad, here's one remarkable song per decade. This one is our winner from the 1930s:

Duniya rang rangeeli baba (singers Pankaj Mullick, Uma Sashi, and KL Saigal/ lyricist Pt. Sudarshan/ composer Pankaj Mullick/ *Dhartimata*, 1938). This medium-brisk song—allegro speed, in musical parlance—is remarkable for its celebration of the elements. Not only that, the planning is awesome, with blind actor KC Dey (playbacked by Pankaj Mullick) starting the celebration and praising—without a trace of irony, because let's remember that he can't see—the birds and flowers and what have you. Enter singing-actress Uma Sashi who first overlaps her voice with his, then relieves him and outlines the value of hope (with *qadam qadam par asha apna roop anoop dikhaati hai*). Upon this scene finally appears Saigal, as if in a baton race; he in turn overlaps the lady's vocals, to take the product to the end, at which point the three singers go ensemble. What a song this is, the first vocal trio from our films! The tune, heavily bathed in counter-melody, was arranged by Spaniard Francisco Casanovas who came to India in 1930 and stayed back for 26 years.

Our elevating song from the 1940s is a sad one, but what an experience this was and still is! A product that makes you say wow! A Majrooh work of class in which a spurned Nargis is boosting herself up. This, Lata's first ghazal in Hindi cinema, has quite exceptional use of the piano and guitar positioned by maestro Naushad. And her voice? *Kya kehne!* Here is that gem from *Andaz* (1949):

> *Utthaaye ja unke sitam, aur jeeye ja*
> *Yoon hi muskuraaye ja, aansoo peeye ja!*

In *Nausherwan-e-Adil* (1957), deeply-in-love Raaj Kumar and Mala Sinha render a lovely Rafi-Lata duet, *Bhool jaayen saare gham, doob jaayen pyaar mein, baj rahi hai dhun yehi raat ke sitar mein*. This one spells class for C Ramchandra, who tuned the words of one Parvez Shamsi. This songwriter wrote in only this film, and just about no one alive knows much more about him than that.

Bhool jaayen saare gham

> *Mora gora ang layi le, mohe Shyam rang dayi de*
> *Chhup jaoongi raat hi mein, mohe pee ka sang dayi de*

The above is how Nutan addresses the moon in *Bandini* (1963). But does she end it there? Nah! For infringing on her privacy, she showers on the moon a curse, a majestic one in fact.

Badri hata ke chanda, chupke se jhaanke chanda
Tohe Rahu laage bairi, muskaaye jee jalaayi ke!
(Lata/ SD Burman/ Gulzar).

In our random one song per decade fragrance, in 1975's *Uljhan* we find a married couple that is a victim of misunderstandings. Since they are not even communicating their problem, two tandem songs—both rendered background—find a situation in the narrative. *Apne jeevan ki uljhan ko kaise main suljaaoon, apnon ne jo dard diye hain, kaise main batlaoon,* goes Kishore for Sanjeev Kumar, while *Apne jeevan ki uljhan ko kaise main suljhaaoon, beech bhanwar mein naav hai meri, kaise paar lagaoon,* renders Lata for actress Sulakshana Pandit, a sore point with the actress who felt slighted that she was so often ignored as a singer who could playback for other heroines. But Lata playbacking for her, as in this case? That was taking it somewhat far! Kalyanji-Anandji took poignant words from MG Hashmat and dressed them up in raag *Ahir Bhairav* to craft this tune.

But Sulakshana did render a class ghazal a few years later, didn't she, for Khayyam in *Ahista Ahista* (1981)? *Maana teri nazar mein tera pyaar hum naheen, kaise kahen ke tere talabgaar hum naheen?* What a wow song this was, with its stanza…*Tan ko jala ke raakh banaaya, bichha diya, Lo ab tumhaari raah mein deewaar hum naheen!* Naqsh Lyallpuri, India's oldest songwriter alive today, wrote this marvelous poem[8].

Liberalization changed so much in India; the music too, which was becoming more and more Western in its poetry, choice of instruments and style of singing. Here is a landmark song from the '90s: *Main koi aisa geet gaoon ke aarzoo jagaoon, agar tum kaho.* What a lovely experience this song is! The whistle in the prelude sets a chirpy tone, and then comes Abhijit's voice chased by a lush of violins. By now you are singing along, and if you are shy, then at least your feet are tapping along! Javed Akhtar synthesized his poetry into Jatin-Lalit's melody (this tune was made first) to enchant our hearts here. The film was *Yes Boss* (1997).

Main koi aisa geet gaoon

Salaam Namaste turned it more westwards. Here is a romantic cheer-leader from the 2005 film: *Aati hai wo aise chal ke, jaise jannat mein rehti hai, Dekhti hai wo sab ko aise, jaise sab ko wo sehti hai, Par gusse mein jab wo aaye, aur aankhen jab dikhlaaye, ladte-ladte ghalti se muskaaye—My dil goes ummmm!* (Gayatri Iyer, Shaan/ Vishal-Shekhar/ Jaideep Sahni).

We have entered the new decade too, our ninth one in music, and a few meaningful songs do keep showing up now and then. *Club 60* (2013) will showcase a wonderful ghazal: *Rooh mein faasle naheen hote, Kaash hum-tum mile naheen hote* (Raju Singh/ Pranit Gedham/ Mahendra Madhukar). But we have lots of songs like *Character dheela*, and *Halkat jawaani* hitting the popularity charts. If art mirrors life, and life mirrors art, you sometimes wonder what's going on. Are we living in a society that is being reflected in this art? Of course in many ways, the world is a better place than it has ever been, and exciting times do lie ahead. But lyric writing in Hindi cinema? And originality in compositions? These seem to be on life-support. Is anyone listening?

~~~~

Originally published in DNA Jaipur in two parts, 13th and 18th November 2012. It has since been updated and enhanced.

♪♫♩♪
~~~~

56

Ornamented for Style

I have never hated a man enough to return his diamonds—Zsa Zsa Gabor, American actress.

The above remark has been associated with Ms. Gabor for well over half a century. It's unlikely to come unstuck from her name because of her long association with both men and diamonds. In her nearly 100-year-long life, she came to be friends with a slew of men and wore a lot of jewelry. In all, she had 9 marriages and loads of ornaments. But while she is known for that quote, she is by no means leagues ahead of millions of women across the world who have also had a strong bond with jewelry, especially diamonds. That fascination continues unabated, which is why they say diamonds are a woman's best friend.

Wearing jewelry is universal and predates recorded history. In ancient times, wealthy Egyptians wore all manner of gold and silver jewelry like crowns, bracelets, necklaces, collars, rings and earrings to attract the gods. In the process, they were also able to showcase their highness. Cleopatra, Queen of Egypt, is always associated with her heavy crown. If you were not of high rank or wealth, that was fine too; you could choose to wear many of the same things in base metals and stones. A similar fascination for jewelry could be found in many other cultures. In India too, the idea is ancient, and intricately woven with the idea of our classical dances, for instance, that also go back centuries.

As is evident from their images, even our gods wear ornaments. Why they should be wearing jewelry though, is something to wonder about. Upon such questions arrives informed opinion, telling us that the gods must wear them to attract our attention; humans that we are, we get propelled towards a decked-up person. The shimmer of gold and the sparkle of stones can be huge attractions. What a role reversal then, between what the Egyptians wanted from their gods, and what our gods want from us.

Within India, with its diverse culture, we have so many regional variations and styles of wearing jewelry. Kashmiri women can have several branches radiating out from a central core earring and coming down long, even as long as 12 inches. In Sidipet district of Telengana, women typically get 5 holes pierced in each ear to suspend that many earrings. They believe Ayurveda tells them gold is good for the body's hygiene, especially on the ear. Over the decades, their ears can become droopy.

Many other parts of the body get jewelry too, which is most observed during weddings. This is apart from the varnishes that go on the nails, liners applied to the eyes and eyebrows, henna that is used on the hands, arms and feet, etc. The idea is to highlight every part of the woman's body to dazzle everyone around.

Here are many of the other ornaments that are worn by women. *Maang tikka* is a pendant worn on the top of the forehead at the hair separation. A chain running from the pendant along the hair parting fastens the ornament to the hair behind. *Maatha patti* is more elaborate; it is a *Maang Tikka* combined with two chains running left and right from it, running over the forehead or over the hair to end up behind the ears. As for earrings, they can be in many styles and shapes, called *baali*, *jhoomar* or *jhumka* (meaning flower on the ear) which are quite popular. A choker is a close-fitting necklace worn around the neck, while a *mangalsutra* (sacred thread) is worn by a bride till her husband's death. *Paanchlada* and *saatlada* are necklaces of 5 and 7 strings respectively. *Chandrahaar* is a necklace of links that are shaped like the moon. *Choodi* is a bangle, *kangna* a bracelet and *haath phool* is an ornament that embellishes the back of one's hand. *Angoothi* or *mundri* is a finger ring. The small nose studs women wear are called *laung*, but a *nathni* is a nose ring, while *nath* is either just a hoop in many sizes or a hoop with a chain that goes back to be fastened to the hair behind the nearer ear.

Chhalla is a waist clip, usually to hang keys from, while *tagdi* is its smarter cousin, with its pearls and *jhumkas* meant only for aesthetics. *Baazubands* (corrupted to *bajubands*) are ornaments women wear on their upper arms. While *paayals* are ankle bells, toe rings address the lowest point where jewelry can and is worn.

A pair of baazuband
(arm bands)

Not all ornaments have found a mention in our songs, but many have. Let's put out the welcome mat for such songs.

- ➤ *Kaan mein baaliyaan, jhoomar waaliyaan* (Shamshad Begum, Ghulam Haider/ *Poonji*, 1943)
- ➤ *Naihar mein nathni gir gayi re* (Zohrabai Ambalewali/ *Gwalan*, 1946)
- ➤ *Chhalla de ja nishaani teri meherbaani* (Shamshad, Rafi, Batra/ *Bazaar*, 1949)
- ➤ *Jhanjhan jhanjhan paayal baaje* (Lata/ *Buzdil*, 1951)
- ➤ *Jhanan jhanan jhanan jhanan ghungharwa baaje* (Lata/ *Aah*, 1953)
- ➤ *Mohe la de naulakha haar* (Shamshad, Kishore/ *Naulakha Haar*, 1953)
- ➤ *La de mohe baalma aasmaani choodiyaan* (Shamshad, Rafi/ *Rail Ka Dibba*, 1953)

> *Baazuband khul-khul jaaye* (Lata/ *Baazuband*, 1954)
> *Chhalla de diya, humen yaad rakhna* (Asha, Rafi/ *Indra Sabha*, 1956)
> *Mori paayal geet sunaaye* (Lata/ *Baap Bete*, 1959)
> *Baaje paayal chhun chhun ho ke beqaraar* (Lata/ *Chhalia*, 1960)
> *Kaan mein jhumke…haath mein chhalla* (Rafi, Suman/ *Commercial Pilot Officer*, 1963)
> *Paayal waali dekhna* (Kishore Kumar/ *Ek Raaz*, 1963)
> *Le lo choodiyaan main laaya niraali* (Rafi/ *Ghar Ki Laaj*, 1960)
> *Mori chham chham baaje paayaliya* (Lata/ *Ghunghat*, 1960)
> *Mila hai kisi ka jhumka* (Lata/ *Parakh*, 1960)
> *Dhoondo dhoondo re saajna…more kaan ka baala* (Lata/ *Ganga Jamuna*, 1961)

Dhoondo dhoondo re saajna

> *Ho re ho re jhanan ghunghar baaje, mora man jhoome piya* (Lata/ *Ganga Jamuna*, 1961)
> *Khanke kangna bindiya hase* (Lata/ *Dr. Vidya*, 1962)
> *Chhanchhan chhanchhan paayal chhanke, khankhan khankhan kangna khanke* (Lata, Manna Dey/ *Maa Beta*, 1962)
> *Pag ghunghru bole chhana na na chhan* (Mahendra, Asha/ *Dev Kanya*, 1963)
> *Ghungharva mora chham chham baaje* (Asha, Rafi/ *Zindagi*, 1964)
> *Khanak gayo haaye bairi kangna* (Lata/ *Rishte Naate*, 1965)

- *Sone ke tere jhumke chaandi ki anguthi hai* (Rafi, Usha Khanna/ *Daku Mangal Singh*, 1966)
- *Maine dekha tha sapnon mein ik chandrahaar* (Lata/ *Gaban*, 1966)
- *Jhumka gira re Bareilly ke baazaar mein* (Asha/ *Mera Saaya*, 1966)
- *Jhanak jhanak tori baaje paayaliya* (Manna Dey/ *Mere Huzoor*, 1968)
- *Kaan mein jhumka* (Rafi/ *Sawan Bhadon*, 1970)
- *Choodiyaan bazaar se mangwa de re pehle saiyaan* (Asha, Rafi/ *Suhana Safar*, 1970)
- *Choodi naheen ye mera dil hai* (Kishore Kumar/ *Gambler*, 1971)
- *Nathaniya haale to bada maza hoye* (Shamshad/ *Johar Mehmood In Hong Kong*, 1971)
- *Nadiya kinaare heraaye aayi kangna* (Lata/ *Abhimaan*, 1973)
- *Ja re ja re qasam khaaye jhooti, peetal ki anguthi* (Lata/ *Badi Ma*, 1974)
- *Gori teri paijaniya* (Manna Dey/ *Mehbooba*, 1976)
- *Nathaniya ne haaye Ram bada dukh deena* (Shobha Gurtu/ *Sajjo Rani*, 1976)
- *Mere haathon mein nau nau choodiyaan hain* (Lata/ *Chaandni*, 1989)
- *Choodiyan khanak gayi* (Lata, Ila Arun/ *Lamhe*, 1991)
- *Mujhe naulakha manga de re* (Asha, Kishore/ *Sharaabi*, 1994)

Times are changing now. Up to a few generations ago, men typically wore perhaps just a ring. Some wore a bracelet, a tiepin or a necklace too. Now they too wear earrings. Like women, they now wear rings and stones on their eyebrows and tongues, as well as on their navels. They must be exploring more such places on their bodies, especially those that are not visible to the public at large. But the inspiring ornamentation may mean the wearers will have to change their privacy settings.

All that tells us not just that we need to invite attention, but we are attached to our valuables. Some even express a wish to be buried with them. The gifted trumpeter Chic Chocolate had his Selma trumpet buried with him. As for Zsa Zsa Gabor, we do not know what happened to her diamonds. Wonder if she requested to be buried with them. There's no question of her descendants returning them of course. But why individuals, even governments don't return them. The Kohinoor diamond is showcased in The Tower of London. But we'll keep asking for it.

The above was originally published in DNA Jaipur on 22 July 2018. It has since been updated and enhanced.

57

The Sublime Turned Ridiculous

The Oxford English Dictionary defines parody as an imitation that produces a ridiculous effect. For Cambridge Dictionary, the verb means "to copy the style of someone or something in a humorous way." Also called spoof or lampoon, parody is an imitative work created to poke fun, mock, or trivialize an original work, its subject, author, or style. The imitation can be in music, films, speech, literature, etc. Hegemon of Thasos, the comic writer of ancient Greece, is credited with inventing the parody. Aristotle said of him: "By slightly altering the wording in well-known poems he transformed the sublime into the ridiculous."

So for example when comedians go up to the stage to imitate Prithviraj Kapoor's style in *Mughal-e-Azam*, or Amjad Khan's lines in *Sholay*, they are parodying. Asrani was parodying Hitler in *Sholay*, with his moustache, hairstyle and general demeanour fashioned after the German dictator.

But wait, there's something called mimicry too. There's a thin difference between parody and mimicry. If an imitator uses humour when he is copying an original, it become parody. Just high fidelity imitation is mimicry.

Films are parodied too

While Hitler was parodied in *Sholay* to offset an essentially serious film (non-parody comedy was scripted for Dharmendra, Hema, and Jagdeep in the film), there have been entire Hollywood films parodying the German leader. Do recall Charlie Chaplin's masterly work in *The Great Dictator*. That in fact followed the first parody of the Nazis, *You Nazty Spy*, featuring The Three Stooges. Parodies existed in the silent era too, before Hitler and his Nazis arrived on the scene. Stan Laurel scripted and acted in several, including *Dr. Pyckle and Mr. Pryde*, an obvious take-off on *Dr. Jekyll and Mr. Hyde*, the book and two films that preceded Laurel's 1925 effort. Across our border in Pakistan, Moin Akhtar has a series of TV shows called Loose Talk, in which he parodies different stereotypes for show host Anwar Maqsood.

We Indians have many good qualities, but having a good laugh is perhaps not one of them. Laughing at ourselves is rarer still. Many outsiders have parodied abundantly and sometimes laughed at themselves too. That's called self-parody, a subset of parody in which artists laugh at their own work.

But we haven't fared too badly when parodying our film songs. Many of these musical parodies take a multiple jab at many popular old songs. But some are less scattered, choosing to spoof just a song or two. Coming up is an example of the latter, with Manna Dey singing Qamar Jalalabadi's spoof for Kalyanji-Anandji in the film *Raaz* (1967), with the song featuring comedian IS Johar. There are no prizes for guessing the original songs, both from movies released in 1960.

> *Pyaar kiya to marna kyoon*
> *Jab pyaar kiya to marna kyoon*
> *Are pyaar kiya koi jung naheen ki, pyaar kiya, aa aa*
> *Pyaar kiya koi jung naheen ki*
> *Chhuriyon se phir ladna kyoon*
> *Jab pyaar kiya to marna kyoon*
> *Jab pyaar kiya to...*

Pyaar kiya to marna kya

Aaj kahenge apna fasaana
Fillam bana de chaahe zamaana
Are aaj kahenge apna fasaana
Fillam bana de chaahe zamaana
Maut meri kyoon duniya dekhe, kyoon
Maut meri kyoon duniya dekhe
Maut se pehle marna kyoon
Jab pyaar kiya to marna kyoon
Pyaar kiya to marna kyoon…

He then switches to English for one line, with Manna Dey's faultless diction:

I am a lover, not a criminal; I am a lover, o-o o-o
I am a lover, not a criminal

And back to Hindustani, using Hinglish as a step:

Yaaro I should marna kyoon
Jab pyaar kiya to marna kyoon
Jab pyaar kiya to…

Dekho yaaro ishq hamaara

(Segues into a *Barsaat Ki Raat* song now)
Are ishq ishq ishq ishq
Ishq ishq hai ishq ishq hai
Ishq ishq hai ishq, haan

(Returns to *Mughal-e-Azam* next)
Dekho yaaro ishq hamaara
Chaaron taraf qaatil ka nazaara
Allah ne naheen marna likha
Bandon se phir marna kyoon
Jab pyaar kiya to marna kyoon
Jab pyaar kiya to marna kyoon

It is interesting that when Manna Dey sang the *Ishq ishq* part, he was in fact engaged in self-parody, because he too had sung in the original song in *Barsaat Ki Raat* (1960).

SD Burman would also execute such a self-parody. Twice.

Many moons ago, Burmanda had recorded a non-film song with compelling results, *Dheere se jaana bagiyan mein re bhanwra*. Taking off on himself, Burmanda had Kishore Kumar parody that same line in the song *Main sitaaron ka taraana* (*Chalti Ka Naam Gaadi*, 1958). To ridicule himself again, Burman had Neeraj write for him in *Chhupa Rustom* (1973), once again to have Kishore Kumar sing, this time tweaking the poetry to *Dheere se jaana khatiyan mein khatmal*. It's believed that Kishore Kumar was at first hesitant to parody someone he not just venerated, but who was alive and well. But here, Dada Burman was himself commissioning the young man with the assignment!

Reflecting the experience of using trains in India, qawwal Jani Babu sang a remarkable non-film qawwali in parody, *Ae bhai zara dekh ke chadho*, patterned after *Ae bhai zara dekh ke chalo* (*Mera Naam Joker*, 1970). It makes for fun listening!

In musical parodies, it is the words that are changed most of the time, while sometimes the poetry is left alone; instead, the singing is made to sound different. The essential tune remains the same. Here are a few more parodies that ridiculed earlier songs, with just one of the ridiculed songs mentioned in brackets, though parodies often lampoon multiple songs. We begin with 1948, which set the ball rolling:

- *Ik dil tera, ik dil mera* (*Hip Hip Hurray*, 1948, featuring *Afsaana likh rahi hoon*)
- *Duniya paglon ka bazaar* (*Chacha Choudhury*, 1953; *Duniya, duniya, toofaan mail*)
- *Dekh tere Bhagwaan ki haalat kya ho gayi insaan* (*Railway Platform*, 1955; *Dekh tere sansaar ki haalat*)
- *Diya bujhao jhatpat jhatpat* (*Taxi 55*, 1955; *Diya jalao jagmag jagmag*)
- *Ek roz hamaari bhi daal galegi* (*Bandi*, 1957; *Main ban ki chidiya ban ke*)
- *Hai bahut dinon ki baat* (*Bhabhi*, 1957; *Raat bhar ka hai mehmaan andhera*)
- *He baambo baambolo* (*Mausi*, 1958; *Ina meena deeka*)
- *Tu prem nagar ka sadhu* (*Masoom*, 1960; *Tere dil ka makaan saiyaan bada aalishaan*)
- *Khatmal aan baso khatiyan mein* (*Lucky Number*, 1961; *Baalam aaye baso more man mein*)
- *Tod diya chashma mera* (*Modern Girl*, 1961; *Tod diya dil mera*)
- *Ek ek ek, ek chai ki pyaali* (*Zamana Badal Gaya*, 1961; *Ina meena deeka*)
- *Ab tak mujhko Chowpatty ka yaad hai June maheena* (*Pathan*, 1962; *Mera joota hai Japani*)
- *Tum mard nikaaloge ghunghat jab raaz hamaara ayega* (*Reporter Raju*, 1962; *Bulbulo mat ro yahaan*)
- *Kha gaye phal ho gayi barbaadiyaan* (*Gul-e-Bakawali*, 1963; *Kya hua, ye mujhe kya hua*)
- *Ek din ka baadshah yoon besahaara ho gaya* (*Ek Din Ka Badshah*, 1964; *Afsana likh rahi hoon dil-e-beqaraar ka*)
- *Ja raha hoon zindagi se* (*Akash Deep*, 1965; *Tum mujhe bhool bhi jao*)

➤ *Muskura laadle muskura* (*Purnima*, 1965; *Muskura laadle muskura* from *Zindagi*, 1964)

➤ *Humen to maara hai* (*Hum Kahaan Ja Rahe The*, 1966; *Humen to loot liya*)

➤ *Suno suno kanyaon ka varnan* (*Haseena Maan Jayegi*, 1968; *Mere desh ki dharti*)

➤ *Chal-chal re naujawaan* (*Ek Phool Do Maali*, 1969; *Jo waada kiya wo*)

➤ *Chaahe mujhe koi bhoot kaho* (*Waris*, 1969; *Chaahe koi mujhe junglee kahe*)

➤ *Meri bhains ko danda kyoon maara* (*Pagla Kaheen Ka*, 1970; *Panchhi banoon udti phiroon*)

➤ *Jab pyaar kiya to darna kya* (*Raaton Ka Raja*, 1970; *Pyaar kiya to darna kya*)

➤ *Mere saamne waale kamre mein* (*Laakhon Mein Ek*, 1971; *Mere saamne waali khidki mein*)

➤ *Ye kaun hai ye kaun hai* (*Main Sundar Hoon*, 1971; *Teri pyaari-pyaari surat ko*)

➤ *Ghar apna Bangaal* (*Khoon Ka Badla Khoon*, 1978; *Sar par topi laal*)

➤ *Na maangen sona-chaandi* (*Mr. India*, 1987; *Saawan ka maheena pawan kare sor*)

Some parodies take the cake for the sheer number of songs they ridicule. *Nadi ka kinaara mendak kare shor* from *Shararat* (1972) targeted 13 songs: *Saawan ka maheena pawan kare sor, Bade armaanon se rakkha hai balam teri qasam, Ke hum tum chori se, Saajan saajan pukaaroon, Mere man ki ganga, Chaandi ki deewaar na todi, Ek bechaara pyaar ka maara, Meri dulhan aayi, Parde mein rehne do, Ek chatur naar, Main ka karoon Ram, Chaahe koi mujhe junglee kahe,* and *Aa mere humjoli aa.* And this one, as we discover, is the runner-up with 12 songs imitated: *Pa pa pa…Aaye na baalam* (*Main Chup Rahungi*, 1962). Here they are: *Aaye na baalam ka karoon sajni, Chaahe koi mujhe junglee kahe, Maa pyaari maa god mein teri khela bachpan mera, Itna na mujhse tu pyaar badha, Ehsaan tera hoga mujh par, Bikhra ke zulfen chaman mein na jaana, Daadi amma daadi amma maan jao, Husn waale tera jawaab naheen, Ek raat mein do-do chaand khile, Dhoondho dhoondo re saajna, Zara saamne to aao chhaliye,* and *Leke pehla pehla pyaar.*

Things haven't been so cheerful for this genre recently. In *Mohabbat* (1997), Akshay Khanna approaches Madhuri Dixit's home with a harmonium slung around his neck. Poor fellow, he doesn't have the foggiest idea of what he should play, as he sings a parody mix that includes *Tere dwaar khada ik jogi* and *Baba man ki aankhen khol,* etc. Featuring some very forgettable singing, the composers Nadeem-Shravan managed to plumb this parody to pathetic depths.

Parodies have almost disappeared from our films, so one more genre bites the dust, just like lullabies, songs on horseback, and qawwalis.

~ ~ ~

The above was originally published in DNA Jaipur on 2 November 2014. It has since been updated and enhanced.

58

The Male Advantage

Did you know that hurricanes (also called other names like typhoons) hit a few countries more or less once each year? China, the West Indies and Cuba, the United States, are hit by them at least once a year on average. Perhaps you know that weatherpeople have been naming hurricanes after people so that we can identify which hurricane is being talked about, especially since two hurricanes sometimes happen simultaneously. Now, most weather people are men, so till recently they named hurricanes after women. What was the logic behind this? This: the English playwright William Congreve famously wrote "Hell hath no fury like a woman scorned". And if nature keeps sending us samples of fury, then the comparison gets validated, and the argument settled. Ridiculous reasoning, that. Thankfully, with an increasingly-just society, this unkind naming has had to be given up, so that now hurricanes are named alternately, in a man-woman-man-woman way.

Let's turn our attention to the powerful world of our cinema, where too it's the men who have always been in the driver's seat. In production, direction, songwriting, music composing, story and dialogue writing, and so many aspects of filmmaking, men have been in charge. Consequently, they write better roles for men, give them more speaking lines—always a good barometer of importance in a film—and generally push the women into subsidiary roles. Not just that, many times they make it clear from the film's title that the story is about a man, so please come and watch his heroics.

Actors have no issues with that at all. Many of them do not want to play second fiddle to an actress in the narrative, or even be around in films whose titles tell you they are about the woman. But there are exceptions of actors who don't mind that at all, with Ashok Kumar leading that brigade. Here are some women-oriented films in which he showed up: *Achhut Kanya* (1936), *Najma* (1943), *Begum* (1945), *Padmini* (1948), *Jalpari* (1952), *Parineeta* (1952), *Ragini* (1958), *Kalpana* (1960), *Aarti* (1962), *Bandini* (1963), *Chitralekha* (1964), and *Mamta* (1966).

Dharmendra was easily one of them too, appearing in films that were making a prima facie announcement of the importance of ladies in the story: *Bandini* (1963), *Purnima* (1965), *Anupama* (1966), *Seeta Aur Geeta* (1972, with Sanjeev), *Dream Girl* (1977), and *Razia Sultan* (1982). Balraj Sahni was another, for instance in *Seema* (1955), *Kathputli* (1957), *Lajwanti* (1958), and *Anuradha* (1960). Manoj Kumar was another actor who accepted roles in women-centric cinema. *Dr. Vidya* (1962), *Anita* (1967) and *Neel Kamal* (1968) come to mind. Sunil Dutt was fine with the heroine getting more importance in *Sujata* (1959), *Amrapali* (1966), *Nartaki* (1963), and *Jwala* (1970). Guru Dutt was one too. He executed relatively minor roles opposite heroines in *Baaz* (1953), *Chaudhvin Ka Chand* (1960), *Sahib Bibi Aur Ghulam* (1962), *Bahurani* (1963), and *Suhagan* (1964). Pradeep Kumar let the ladies take more importance in *Anarkali* (1953), *Aarti* (1962), *Chitralekha* (1964), and *Noor Jahan* (1968). Shashi Kapoor did so in *Benazir* (1964), *Abhinetri* (1970), and *Sharmilee* (1971).

On the other hand, Dilip Kumar for one was not comfortable in doing subsidiary roles. He accepted being cast opposite Madhubala in *Tarana* (1951), which was Madhubala's name in the story, perhaps because around this time he was deeply in love with that woman. Their love story got over when she was replaced by Vyjayanthimala in *Naya Daur* (1958). And he did accept the role in *Madhumati* (1958), but you wonder if he was still trying to cope with his Madhu hangover. Neither was Dev Anand happy in executing subsidiary roles. The only occasions that he accepted being in films named eponymously on their heroine were in *Vidya* (1948) and *Jeet* (1949). But wait. Is it a coincidence that the heroine of both these features was Suraiya, who this hero was just now in love with? Surely it is not a coincidence.

That takes us to a story. We do know that Dev Anand and Guru Dutt were buddies, doing many films together. But they got into a spot of bother about even the hierarchy of credits once. It is generally agreed that the more important names of a film's cast are mentioned first. To Dev that was vital.

Here's what happened. In Guru Dutt's *Baazi* (1951), as the credits rolled, Dev was mentioned first, and Geeta Bali the heroine, after him. Guru Dutt reversed the order in *Jaal* the next year, crediting Geeta Bali first, and Dev after her. That did not go down well with the shocked hero. Next year director Guru Dutt himself appeared in *Baaz* with Geeta Bali, setting an example by mentioning her name first. He showed his magnanimity to his friend, who remained unconvinced. Later in 1955, Guru Dutt's chief assistant Raj Khosla directed *Milap* (starring Dev Anand and Geeta Bali again), where that director did not make the mistake of upsetting the hero. Finally, Guru Dutt asked Raj Khosla to direct *CID* (1956), with Dev at the top of the credits, Shakila after him, and Waheeda as the new lady being introduced in this feature. This is a case of male ego dynamics behind the screen.

On the other hand, there don't seem to be stories where actresses have had issues with billing credits or fewer dialogues, screen space, or even what the titles were indicating.

In this story, let's see a few songs from films whose title was a man's name. The male actor who lip-synched on the screen is named right after the film's year of release.

- *Chandidas* (1934. Saigal): *Tadpat beete din rain* (Saigal)
- *Devdas* (1935. Saigal): *Baalam aaye baso more man mein* (Saigal)
- *Bhakt Surdas* (1942. Saigal): *Nainheen ko raah dikha Prabhu* (Saigal)
- *Bhartari* (1944. Surendra Nath): *Prem bina sab soona hota* (Surendra)
- *Baadal* (1951. Premnath): *Main raahi bhatakne waala hoon* (Mukesh)
- *Baiju Bawra* (1952. Bharat Bhushan): *Man tadpat Hari darshan ko aaj* (Rafi)

> ➤ *Mirza Ghalib* (1954. Bharat Bhushan): *Ishq mujhko naheen wahshat hi sahi* (Talat)

Ishq mujhko naheen wahshat hi sahi

> ➤ *Azaad* (1955. Dilip Kumar): *Kitna haseen hai mausam* (Chitalkar, Lata)
> ➤ *Devdas* (1955. Dilip Kumar): *Mitwa laagi re ye kaisi anbujh aag* (Talat)
> ➤ *Hatimtai* (1956. Jairaj): *Parwardigar-e-aalam* (Rafi)
> ➤ *Samrat Chandragupta* (1958. Bharat Bhushan): *Chaahe paas ho chaahe door ho* (Rafi, Lata)
> ➤ *Kanhaiya* (1959. Raj Kapoor): *Mujhe tum se kuchh bhi na chaahiye* (Mukesh)
> ➤ *Kavi Kalidas* (1959. Bharat Bhushan): *Naye naye rangon se likhti dharti nayi kahaani* (Manna)
> ➤ *Jhumroo* (1961. Kishore): *Koi humdum na raha koi sahaara na raha* (Kishore)
> ➤ *Sangeet Samrat Tansen* (1962. Bharat Bhushan): *Jhoomti chali hawa* (Mukesh)
> ➤ *Badal* (1966. Sanjeev Kumar): *Apne liye jiye to kya jiye* (Manna Dey)
> ➤ *Suraj* (1966. Rajendra Kumar): *Bahaaro phool barsao* (Rafi)
> ➤ *Saraswatichandra* (1968. Manish): *Chandan sa badan chanchal chitvan* (Mukesh)
> ➤ *Gopi* (1970. Dilip Kumar): *Sukh ke sab saathi dukh mein na koi* (Rafi)

- *Anand* (1971. Rajesh Khanna): *Zindagi kaisi hai paheli haaye* (Manna Dey)
- *Rampur Ka Laxman* (1972. Randhir Kapoor): *Rampur ka vaasi hoon main Laxman mera naam* (Kishore)
- *Sagina* (1974. Dilip Kumar): *Saala main to saahab ban gaya* (Kishore, Pankaj Mitra)
- *Amar Akbar Anthony* (1977. Vinod Khanna, Rishi Kapoor, Amitabh Bachchan): *Anhoni ko honi kar de* (Mahendra, Shailendra Singh, Kishore)
- *Don* (1978. Amitabh Bachchan): *Khaike paan Banaras waala* (Kishore)
- *Hatimtai* (1990. Jeetendra): *Mere maalik mere daata* (Mohd Aziz)
- *Karan Arjun* (1995. Shahrukh, Salman): *Ye bandhan to pyaar ka bandhan hai* (Kumar Sanu, Alka Yagnik, Udit Narayan)
- *Asoka* (2001. Shahrukh Khan): *Roshni se bhare bhare naina tere* (Abhijit, Alka Yagnik)
- *Rowdy Rathore* (2012. Akshay Kumar): *Chinta ta ta chita chita* (Mika Singh, Wajid Ali)

The mind wanders, looking for titles where both the lead actors were named, such as in *Shin Shinaki Bubla Boo* (1952). The first two words were the name of actress Rehana, while the last two were about a male actor named Ranjan. *Heer Ranjha* (1970) was about the two lead actors too, and so was *Heera Panna* (1973). Weatherpeople could use this idea for hurricanes too. They can be called John-Mary, Susan-George, Raaj-Priya, and so on, to avoid ego issues.

~~~~

The above was originally featured in DNA Jaipur on 14 October 2018. It has since been updated and enhanced.

♪♫♩♪
~~~~

59

Wisdom in Swimwear

I often smile at beauty pageants. It's fine with me that they require women to wear swimsuits if not bikinis, never mind that most of these contests do not need women to swim or do water sports. Contestants need to show up with flat tummies and long legs, great manicure, rivetting eyelashes and hairdos, with hints of sexuality thrown into their voices and mannerisms. As blueprinted on the much-navigated roadmap to a crown, these women also need to conduct themselves with poise and charm, coupled with a million-dollar smile and attitude, which is also perfectly ok. I chuckle only when these women are asked their views on matters affecting the world. I chuckle not just for them, but also for the show hosts who ask them heavy questions, such as about the war in Eritrea or The GDP of certain countries, issues that are typically asked of important people like Amartya Sen, Muhammad Yunus or Larry Pressler on important platforms. It gets hilarious if these girls are brought onto the stage in swimwear and asked to speak their minds on such matters of gravitas in a quick-fire, 20-second philosophy round, just after they have finished showing off their bodies and strutted about for several minutes. It would be equally funny if, after a heavy interview, talk show gents such as Jay Leno or David Letterman took off their 3-piece suits and flaunted their bodies. People should stick to the knitting, at least for the sake of credibility.

It is not that beautiful women do not have brains. Many do. Some beautiful women have truly outstanding things to say about poverty in India, racism in America, or the glass ceiling around the world, and matters similarly significant for the human race. But many more women who do not participate in such pageants have a better understanding of issues of such importance, at least to qualify better for becoming brand ambassadors of a cause, a responsibility often given to winners of beauty events.

Not many of us take these ladies seriously either. Most people, beautiful or otherwise, do not have enough wisdom and knowledge at a young age. As such, expecting young girls who are heavily focussed on a two-dimensional existence, to promote universal peace and eradicate poverty with a few seconds' worth of wisdom can sound quite hilarious. You may have observed that some of the on-stage replies we have heard have lacked cerebral content or relevance. Here are just a couple of instances.

At the Miss World contest in 2000, Miss India Priyanka Chopra was asked, "Who do you think is the most successful woman living today, and why?" Her reply: "There are a lot of people I admire, but one of the most admirable people is Mother Teresa, who has been so compassionate, considerate and kind". Even if we accept her interchange between successful and admirable, Mother Teresa was not a living person when Ms. Chopra was questioned.

That was a minor faux pas. Here's a major one. At the Miss Panama pageant in 2009, contestant Giosue Cozarelli was asked, "Explain the following quote by Confucius: Learning without thought is labour lost". Her reply was classic: "Good evening Panama! Confucius was one of whom invented confusion, and that's why, er, one of the most ancient, he was one of the Chinese, Japanese, who was one of the most ancient. Thank you!"

Thanks, Miss, we learnt something today.

Unlike ramp models, film and stage actresses usually offer more depth. Typically, they are not only older than beauty pageant contestants, but the nature of their work makes it necessary for them to understand other people and cultures. That's how they can get under the skin of the character they're essaying. When such actresses expose more of their skin by wearing swimsuits, they receive more approval.

All the following actresses have been women of substance, and have worn swimwear in films: Lalita Pawar, Nutan, Nargis, Nalini Jaywant, Tanuja, Raakhi, Neetu Singh, Sharmila Tagore, Saira Banu, Zeenat Aman, Parveen Babi, Dimple Kapadia, Moon Moon Sen, Mandakini and there are plenty others. More recently, many actresses have been seen wearing bikinis, with Mallika Sherawat and Bipasha Basu taking the lead in such appearances. Some actresses have also been featured in songs while their swimsuits or bikinis are on. Here are instances as these ladies were singing or were sung to:

- Nalini Jaywant: *Ulfat ke jaadu ka dil mein asar hai* (*Sangram*, 1950)
- Nargis: *Tumko fursat ho meri jaan to idhar dekh to lo* (*Bewafa*, 1952)
- Saira Banu: *Aa gale lag ja* (*April Fool*, 1964)
- Vyjayanthimala: *Mere man ki Ganga* (*Sangam*, 1964)
- Tanuja: *Baag mein kali khili* (*Chaand Aur Suraj*, 1965)
- Helen: *Is duniya mein jeena ho to sun lo meri baat* (*Gumnaam*, 1965)
- Parveen Chowdhury: *Ye tune kya kaha* (*Insaaf*, 1965)
- Sadhana: *Surat haseen lagta hai deewaana* (*Budtameez*, 1966)

Surat haseen, lagta hai deewana

- Sharmila Tagore: *Aasmaan se aaya farishta* (*An Evening In Paris*, 1967)
- Helen (again): *Kis qadar zaalim ho qaatil* (*Dil Ne Pukaara*, 1967)
- Mumtaz: *Dil mera tumhaari adaayen le gayeen* (*Gauri*, 1968)

- ➤ Hema Malini: *Lehra ke aaya hai* (*Waaris*, 1969)
- ➤ Jaishree T: *Aana to sajni din ko aana* (*Raaton Ka Raja*, 1970)
- ➤ Aruna Irani: *Haaye haaye thanda paani* (*Bombay To Goa*, 1972)
- ➤ Leena Chandavarkar: *Sundar ho aisi tum chalo* (*Dil Ka Raja*, 1972)
- ➤ Zeenat Aman: *Main tasweer utaarta hoon* (*Heera Panna*, 1973)
- ➤ Nazneen: *Jaana kahaan hai, pyaar yahaan hai* (*Chalte Chalte*, 1976)
- ➤ Tina Munim: *Tu pee aur jee* (*Des Pardes*, 1978)
- ➤ Sharmila Tagore again: *O mere bechain dil ko chain tu ne diya* (*Aamne Saamne*, 1967)

And more recently:

- ➤ Kajol: *Zara sa jhoom loon main* (*Dilwale Dulhaniya Le Jayenge*, 1995)
- ➤ Mallika Sherawat: *Bheege honth tere* (*Murder*, 2004)
- ➤ Katrina Kaif: *Ooncha lamba kad* (*Welcome 2007*, 2007)
- ➤ Ameesha Patel: *Ye lazy lamhe* (*Thoda Pyaar Thoda Magic*, 2008)
- ➤ Anushka Sharma: *Chaska chaska laga hai chaska chaska* (*Badmaash Company*, 2010)
- ➤ Nupur Sharma: *Line laga, mind laga* (*Hey Bro*, 2015)

No dress code, no moves code for this beach party

The last few instances are a far cry from the cinema of 50 years ago, especially from the dance moves point of view. Let's take a case in point. Kishore Sahu was a very gifted director, and one of his films was *Dil Apna Aur Preet Parai* (1960). In the film, the song *Sheesha-e-dil itna na uchhaalo* was filmed on Meena Kumari, Shammi and their friends at the beach. It seems Sahu gave the picnicking ladies the option to dress and dance as they like. So, while Meena Kumari and a couple of girls came in a sari, Shammi and a few ladies arrived wearing swimming costumes, others wore shalwar-kurtas, and others yet wore hot pants. You could even spot skirts, capris, and backless dresses. There was no question of anyone offering pelvic thrusts either. Nowadays if you are on a beach, get yourself into a swimming costume, forget the sari, and forget even emoting. The camera won't train too much on your face anyway.

That makes me smile because another laughter round is coming to our screens next month, in Miss Universe 2017. If wisdom in swimwear also makes you laugh, do tune in to watch the Miss Universe event live, on 26th November, at Las Vegas, USA. But let's hope no girl messes up about the mass shootings that occurred in that city last week, on 1st October 2017. That was no laughing matter.

~~~~

The above was originally published in DNA Jaipur on 8 August 2017. It has since been updated.

~~~~

The FRS Factor

Can you guess what is common between these 10 Hindi film songs?

> *Chhod gaye baalam mujhe haaye akela chhod gaye* (Mukesh, Lata/ *Barsaat*, 1949)
> *Yaad kiya dil ne kahaan ho tum* (Hemant, Lata/ *Patita*, 1953)
> *Tu pyaar ka saagar hai* (Manna/ *Seema*, 1955)
> *Nakhre waali* (Kishore/ *New Delhi*, 1956)
> *Aiye meherbaan* (Asha/ *Howrah Bridge*, 1958)
> *Aa laut ka aaja mere meet* (Mukesh/ *Rani Rupmati*, 1959)
> *Sau saal pehle mujhe tumse pyaar tha* (Rafi, Lata/ *Jab Pyaar Kisi Se Hota Hai*, 1961)
> *Koi humdum na raha* (Kishore/ *Jhumroo*, 1961)
> *Phir wohi shaam* (Talat/ *Jahan Ara*, 1964)
> *Door rehkar na karo baat qareeb aa jao* (Rafi/ *Amanat*, 1975)

If you answer that they were all hits, you would be right, but only simplistically so. These songs were hits and continue to entertain us because they have no expiry date. But if you are an industry insider, you would probably also say "FRS". The full form of that is Famous Recording Studio, which used to be located in Mumbai's Tardeo area. It is this studio that recorded these ten and thousands of such songs for hundreds of films.

A Quick Story of the Group

After the sudden passing away in 1940 of the pioneering filmmaker Himanshu Rai who set up the publicly listed Bombay Talkies, a gentleman named Govindram Seksaria, popularly called India's Cotton King, bought majority shares in that company. Soon after, the Famous Cine Laboratory, located at Tardeo, virtually fell into his lap because of a court ruling. This was followed by the Famous Recording Studio next door. Excited by the prospect of a growing industry, Seksaria's company then proceeded to acquire Modern Studio at Andheri. This was a facility where films were shot. So, films could be processed at the cine lab, and their songs could be recorded in the recording facility next door. The shot footage of films would arrive at the cine lab. Here sound was synched with the captured visuals, and much of post-production work was done, including editing, dubbing, and Foley. From this, a final positive was readied, and that would become the master for the prints that were despatched to cinema halls for screening. The work of the lab technicians decided how good the final product appeared. *Anari*, *Mughal e Azam*, and *Hum Dono* are just a few of the 1500 feature films and documentaries that were processed at Famous Cine Laboratory.

This went on for decades until the 1990s came. With less open land, increased traffic and high property rates, South Bombay became unattractive to many filmmakers. A demographic shift resulted in people migrating to the Western suburbs of the city. This reminds you of the film business in the USA, where it was originally concentrated on the eastern side. When the Los Angeles Chamber of Commerce guaranteed filmmakers 350 days of the sun, the migration to Hollywood began.

But let's now turn to recording. First, a song is written or its basic tune is composed. The singer rehearses with the composer. An arranger is brought in, and he decides which instruments will be used, at what point and for how many bars. A "take" (recording) is done. Usually there is more than one take. And sometimes, several takes, till the composer thumbs-ups one of them. The longest it has taken to record a song is for the twin qawwalis, *Na to caravan ki talaash hai*, and *Ye ishq ishq hai* (*Barsaat Ki Raat*, 1960). Those qawwalis took multiple takes and 27 hours to be okayed!

Many other hallmark songs have taken a lot of time too. Take the case of the remarkable *Aa ab laut chalen* (*Jis Desh Mein Ganga Behti Hai*, 1960). For that, we first need to know a little bit about the story's background. The film was about dacoits, and it was made as a response to a call given by Acharya Vinoba Bhave, who was doing spectacular work in trying to get the dacoits to give up their armed existence, stop their crimes, and merge with the mainstream of Indian society. In the film, the dacoits have finally agreed to surrender, but only in exchange for a promise not to be punished. However, they can't be sure of the promises, so they are understandably agitated about their future. Raj Kapoor was an inspired filmmaker. He had Shailendra write rivetting lyrics to influence the dacoits, like *Tu jis maa ko bhool gaya tha, aaj usi ne yaad kiya hai* and *Laakh lubhaayen mahal paraaye, apna ghar phir apna ghar hai*. Kapoor had his composers Shankar and Jaikishan offer a massive charge with a huge chorus and dozens of instruments. All this as Mukesh sang the central message, and Lata repeated the *Aa ja re* part in a high pitch. This was a moment of truth for the dacoits and they were in turmoil, wondering if they were walking into a police trap. Their mental state was reflected in the song's agitato violins and the big orchestration. This is intelligent art, but it needed an intelligent studio to handle the assignment competently. Famous excelled at that.

For decades, many film and music professionals used to wonder what it was that made hundreds of songs come out of Famous to live in people's hearts for decades. Was it the mastery of ace recordist Minoo Katrak, and DO Bhansali who came later? Could it be the state-of-the-art acoustics and the equipment you found here? Was it for the way the owners ran the place, or the cosmic benevolence of Vastu? Perhaps it was all of these. When asked, composers OP Nayyar and Kalyanji would just say "The FRS Factor", with a smile.

It is the FRS Factor that created hits reflected in the people's choice radio programs hosted for decades by Ameen Sayani, the legendary broadcaster whose charts were a mirror to our tastes, as against the Filmfare awards, for instance, that became controversial because they were sometimes divorced from reality. Not just that, Filmfare awards just looked for one winner, rather than a list of great songs coming out each year. In three decades (1955 to 1984), from the total of 964 songs that were featured in Ameen Sayani's Geetmalas, 459 were recorded at FRS. That's roughly half of all the hits. The statistics are similar for Geetmalas' no 1 spot, as well as those that were in the *doosri* and *teesri paayedaans* (second and third place winners).

The group's current chief, Rajkumar Seksaria is an affable and giving man, dispensing CDs and pen drives of songs recorded at Famous to every music or film lover who visits him. He treats them to litres of tea or coffee, coordinated with sandwiches and cookies, and enthrals them with amazing stories of the many milestone recordings that happened as he was growing up here. For instance, about the song *Humko tumse ho gaya hai pyaar kya karen* from *Amar Akbar Anthony* (1977). This is the only time Rafi, Kishore, Mukesh and Lata came together in a song. The film had Amitabh paired with Parveen Babi, Vinod Khanna with Shabana, and Rishi with Neetu Singh. The song was to be lip-synched by all these six actors. After Kishore, Lata, and Mukesh came, Rafi who had also come, was seen to get impatient. Apparently, he had to go for another recording. He whispered to Mukesh, "Where are the other two female playback singers?" Kishore overheard this and said, "Rafi miyaan, they're not needed. This is Lata Mangeshkar. She is equal to three".

Composers Pyarelal and Laxmikant, at
left, with Rafi, Mukesh, Lata, and
Kishore. These 4 singers came together
for a song just once, for the film
Amar Akbar Anthony (1977)

Seksariaji tells me an interesting behind-the-scenes story about *Aa ab laut chalen*, already detailed above. "The film industry had many gifted people, but they were not without faults. Jealousy for example was very much around. It seems that the composer Naushad had recorded a remarkable song with huge instrumentation and chorus. But he had done the recording in a studio in Madras. Not to be left behind, composer Shankar had reservations about recording *Aa ab laut chalen* at Famous, because the studio just didn't have the space to handle the 110 musicians, plus the main singers as also the 60 chorus singers being planned for that remarkable song. Shankar informed Raj Kapoor of this difficulty. But Kapoor loved Famous, and he loved the engineering of its sound engineer, Minoo Katrak. The recording was finally done at Famous itself. Every inch of the studio was used intelligently. Guests and other VIPs were barred from attending. The 60 chorus singers were made to wait—and finally sing—outside the studio, on the main road. This being 1959, there wasn't too much traffic at night. The song ended up being okayed at around 3 in the morning". It was a triumph without peers before or since.

Things go better with Coke, goes a popular jingle. For me, things go better with coffee, especially with narratives like those from Rajkumar Seksaria. Never mind that he tells his stories so beautifully that my coffee often turns cold.

61

Garam Dharam's Musical Sizzlers!

Today is 8th December, and it's Dharmendra's birthday! In a career that has spanned 300 films across 50-odd years, this actor has touched our hearts with phenomenal performances, only to be rewarded with an award-less shelf to display in his living room. Some odd citations and last-minute Lifetime Achievement awards are there, sure, but they're like consolation prizes. Such late awards can often be just a way of signalling someone's way out. If you look at the facial expressions and body language of the person giving such late awards, you may find the message "Thank you for being around". Sometimes, such awards can also be a way of saying "Sorry we forgot you".

You forgot a lot. You forgot the bibliophile in *Anpadh* and his wonderfully underplayed performances in *Satyakaam* and *Bandini*. You forgot his comedy in *Sholay*, *Chupke Chupke* and *Pratigya*. You forgot his easy charm in *Blackmail* and criminality in *Phool Aur Pathar*, as also the writer in *Naya Zamana* and many other competent performances. We can't change all that you forgot. *Chalen*.

Instead, let us—his fans—remember him today through his music. Some of the best songs that emerged from our cinema were filmed on him, imprinting lasting images on our minds. Here first are some sad songs, those that can be heard repeatedly, with him striking pay dirt in his maiden performance, *Dil Bhi Tera Hum Bhi Tere*, mentioned below.

➤ *Mujh ko is raat ki tanhaayi mein awaaz na do* (Mukesh/ *Dil Bhi Tera Hum Bhi Tere*, 1960)

> *Jaane kya dhoondti rehti hain ye aankhen mujh mein* (Rafi/ *Shola Aur Shabnam*, 1961)
> *Aakhri geet muhabbat ka suna loon to chaloon* (Rafi/ *Neela Aakash*, 1965)
> *Tumhen zindagi ke ujaale mubaarak* (Mukesh/ *Purnima*, 1965)
> *Ya dil ki suno duniya waalo* (Hemant/ *Anupama*, 1966)

Ya dil ki suno duniya waalo

> *Aaya hai mujhe phir yaad wo zaalim* (Mukesh/ *Devar*, 1966)
> *Bahaaron ne mera chaman loot kar* (Mukesh/ *Devar*, 1966)
> *Hui shaam unka khayaal aa gaya* (Rafi/ *Mere Humdum Mere Dost*, 1968)
> *Hum bewafa hargiz na the* (Kishore/ *Shalimar*, 1978)

Dharmendra loved to romance his ladies! In these songs:

> *Ye waada karen, jahaan bhi rahen* (Mukesh, Lata/ with Kum Kum in *Dil Bhi Tera Hum Bhi Tere*, 1960)
> *Tumhen dil se chaaha, tumhen dil diya hai* (Suman, Rafi/ with Tanuja in *Chand Aur Suraj*, 1965)
> *Suniye jaana, kya pyaar mein sharmaana* (Mahendra, Lata/ with Nanda in *Aakash Deep*, 1965)
> *Aap ko pyaar chhupaane ki buri aadat hai* (Rafi, Asha/ with Mala Sinha in *Neela Akash*, 1965)
> *Tere paas aa ke mera waqt guzar jaata hai* (Rafi, Asha/ with Mala Sinha in *Neela Aakash*, 1965)

> *Humsafar mere humsafar* (Mukesh, Lata/ with Meena Kumari in *Purnima*, 1965)

> *Dil to pehle hi se madhosh hai matwaala hai* (Rafi, Asha/ with Tanuja in *Baharen Phir Bhi Ayengi*, 1966)

> *O main suraj hoon tu meri kiran* (Rafi, Asha/ with Nutan in *Dil Ne Phir Yaad Kiya*, 1966)

> *In bahaaron mein akele na phiro* (Rafi, Asha/ with Suchitra Sen in *Mamta*, 1966)

> *Rahen na rahen hum mehka karenge* (Rafi, Suman/ with Suchitra Sen in *Mamta*, 1966)

> *Mere sarkaar meri aahon ka asar dekh liya* (Mahendra, Krishna Kalle/ with Asha Parekh in *Shikar*, 1968)

> *Neele parbaton ki dhaara* (Mahendra, Asha/ with Saira Banu in *Aadmi Aur Insaan*, 1969)

> *Badra chhaaye* (Rafi, Asha/ with Asha Parekh in *Aaya Saawan Jhoomke*, 1969)

> *Ye dil deewaana hai* (Lata, Rafi/ with Sadhana in *Ishq Par Zor Nahin*, 1970)

> *Jhilmil sitaaron ka aangan hoga* (Rafi, Lata/ with Rakhee in *Jeevan Mrityu*, 1970)

> *Kuchh kehta hai ye saawan* (Rafi, Lata/ with Asha Parekh in *Mera Gaon Mera Desh*, 1971)

> *Chaahe raho door, chaahe raho paas* (Kishore, Asha/ with Tanuja in *Do Chor*, 1972)

> *Kaali palak teri gori* (Kishore, Lata/ with Tanuja in *Do Chor*, 1972)

> *Ek hi khwaab kai baar dekha hai maine* (Bhupinder, Hema Malini/ with Hema Malini in *Kinara*, 1977)

> *Jaan ki qasam such kehte hain hum* (Kishore, Lata/ with Hema in *Azaad*, 1978)

And if he wasn't singing love duets with his heroines, he certainly was pitching hard to them!

> *Main nigaahen tere chehre se hataoon kaise* (Rafi/ to Supriya Chowdhury in *Aap Ki Parchhaiyan*, 1964)

> *Yehi hai tamanna tere dar ke saamne* (Rafi/ to Supriya Chowdhury in *Aap Ki Parchhaiyan*, 1964)

> *Aap ke haseen rukh pe aaj naya noor hai* (Rafi/ to Mala Sinha and Tanuja in *Baharen Phir Bhi Ayengi*, 1966)

> *Ik haseen shaam ko dil mera kho gaya* (Rafi/ to Nutan in *Dulhan Ek Raat Ki*, 1966)

> *Na jaane kyoon hamaare dil ko tumne dil naheen samjha* (Rafi/ to Rajshri in *Muhabbat Zindagi Hai*, 1966)

> *Tumhen dekha hai maine gulsitaan mein* (Rafi/ to Meena Kumari in *Chandan Ka Palna*, 1967)

> *Chhalkaayen jaam* (Rafi/ to Sharmila in *Mere Humdum Mere Dost*, 1968)

> *Tumhaare pyaar mein hum beqaraar ho ke chale* (Rafi/ to Asha Parekh in *Shikar*, 1968)

> *Dekha hai teri aankhon mein* (Rafi/ to Vyjayanthimala in *Pyaar Hi Pyaar*, 1969)

> *Gar tum bhula na doge* (Rafi/ to Sharmila in *Yakeen*, 1969)

> *Mehbooba teri tasweer, kis tarah main banaoon* (Rafi/ for Sadhana in *Ishq Par Zor Nahin*, 1970)

> *Pal-pal dil ke paas* (Kishore/ to Rakhee in *Blackmail*, 1973)

> *Aaj mausam bada beimaan hai* (Rafi/ for Mumtaz in *Loafer*, 1973)

> *Dream girl, ik shaayar ki ghazal* (Kishore/ to Hema in *Dream Girl*, 1977)

And he was featured in a mixed bag of high-recall tunes:

> *Jeet hi lenge baazi hum-tum* (Rafi, Lata/ idealistic love with Tarla Mehta in *Shola Aur Shabnam*, 1961)

> *Chanda se hoga wo pyaara* (PB Srinivasan, Lata/ having a baby with Meena Kumari in *Main Bhi Ladki Hoon*, 1964)

> *Mujhe dard-e-dil ka pata na tha* (Rafi/ mixed feelings about being in love with Nanda, in *Aakash Deep*, 1965)

> *Koi aane waala hai* (Lata, Mahendra Kapoor/ having a baby with Nanda in *Mera Qusoor Kya Hai*, 1964)

> *Badal jaaye agar maali* (Mahendra Kapoor/ Sufiana philosophy in *Baharen Phir Bhi Ayengi*, 1966)

> *Ye dil tum bin kaheen lagta naheen* (Lata, Rafi/ love tinged with sorrow—with Tanuja in *Izzat*, 1968)

> *Duniya o duniya tera jawaab naheen* (Kishore/ a jab at society in general, in *Naya Zamana*, 1971)
> *Abhi to haath mein jaam hai, tauba kitna kaam hai!* (Manna Dey/ philosophy under the influence in *Seeta Aur Geeta*, 1972)
> *Zindagi hai khel koi paas koi fail* (Manna Dey, Asha/ comic philosophy with Hema in *Seeta Aur Geeta*, 1972)
> *Koi haseena jab rootth jaati hai to* (Kishore/ mischievously throwing himself upon Hema in *Sholay*, 1975)
> *Ye dosti hum naheen chhodenge* (Manna Dey, Kishore/ an ode to friendship, with Amitabh in *Sholay*, 1975)
> *Aayi zanjeer ki jhankaar Khuda khair kare* (Kabban Mirza/ a slave sings near his queen Hema Malini in *Razia Sultan*, 1982)

We can hardly forget the many songs Dharmendra lip-synced at parties, events where people are supposed to meet for happy reasons unless surprised by a different mood. Take a look:

> *Mere dushman tu meri dosti ko tarse* (Rafi/ choice curses sculpted for Asha Parekh in *Aaye Din Bahaar Ke*, 1966)
> *Kya miliye aise logon se jinki fitrat chhupi rahe* (Rafi/ about fakes in our society in *Izzat*, 1968)
> *Ye shama to jali roshni ke liye* (Rafi/ one man's food is another man's poison in *Aaya Sawan Jhoomke*, 1969)

In addition to the above party songs, there were others of this kind listed earlier, namely: *Ya dil ki suno duniya waalo* (*Anupama*, 1966), *Aaya hai mujhe phir yaad wo zaalim* (*Devar*, 1966), and *Bahaaron ne mera chaman loot kar* (*Devar*, 1966).

Born in Bikaner, Dharmendra first married Parkash Kaur in 1954. He was just 19 then. A quarter century later, in 1980, when he was 45, he married Hema Malini. He looked hot even later when he was in his 50s. Perhaps that's why his moniker is Garam Dharam. He went on to become a Member of Parliament from Bikaner, but there was nothing garam about his performance as a politician.

Happy birthday, sir! The awards may have escaped noticing you, but the question is, have we, your audiences, forgotten you and what you gave us? Nah! Neither scenes like *chakki peesing* in *Sholay* (1975), nor songs like *Mujh ko is raat ki tanhaayi mein awaaz na do* (*Dil Bhi Tera Hum Bhi Tere*, 1960).

~~~~

The above was originally published in DNA Jaipur on 8 December 2013. It has since been updated and enhanced.

♪♫♩♪
~~~~

62

Bombay to Hyderabad

Who says we don't know how to play badminton? Nandu Natekar, Prakash Padukone, Pullela Gopichand, Saina Nehwal, and now, India's most recent badminton champion, Olympic silver-medallist PV Sindhu, all these names have brought India much fame in the sport.

Even our film stars know how to play it well. In *Humjoli* (1970), Jeetendra and Leena Chandavarkar play the game under the lights. Something that particularly needs to be admired is a shot that the hero hits from between his legs. That deserves a salute. Leena and Jeetendra even sing as they dance and play! "*Dhal gaya din, ho gayi shaam*", they go, with the shuttlecock hits furnishing us the song's rhythm. PV Sindhu and her coach Gopinath must learn the art of playing while singing, from this song.

Jokes apart, we do play a few sports reasonably well. Not all of them get featured in the Olympics, the mother of most sporting encounters. Cricket, at which we generally excel, has shown up at the Olympics just once, in a feeble way and over a century ago. In 1900, the single time it was played in an Olympiad, the only two competing teams were Great Britain and France. No prizes for guessing who won the match here. Kho Kho is a traditional sport from our part of the world, which was played during the SAF games recently, between India, Bangladesh, Pakistan, Sri Lanka, Thailand, Japan, and Nepal. But it doesn't have the Olympic Committee's nod. Neither has Kabaddi ever been featured in Olympic competitions. Kite-flying is a sport too, if we accept this definition: A sport is an activity that involves physical exertion and skill in which an individual or team competes against others for entertainment, even in the absence of a scoring system.

In Tennis, we have had a slew of personalities over the years, such as Ramanathan Krishnan, Jaideep Mukherjea, Premjit Lall, Vijay Amritraj, Mahesh Bhupathi, Rohan Bopanna, Leander Paes, and of course the currently-popular Sania Mirza.

But just in case you were wondering why games of huge significance and following like Baseball, Squash, Sumo and Cricket—the de facto National Sports in some countries—are not part of the Olympics, the reason is this: to be considered for the Olympics, a sport must be played in at least seventy-five countries on at least four continents.

Let's come to India now, and just to our film songs showing a sport. For that, first let's honour one of the great sportsmen of India, the wrestler Dara Singh, who more than anyone represented the sports community in films. He showed us his wrestling in several films like *Pehli Jhalak* (1955), *Faulaad* (1963), *Rustom-e-Baghdad* (1963), and *Rustom-e-Hind* (1965). Here he is now, being celebrated by others, even as he remains topless and ready to wrestle, for you never know.

> *Aapne kya kaha, maine kya sun liya* (*Aaya Toofaan*, 1964)
> *Zara sambhaalna meri jaan apni nigaahen* (*Aaya Toofaan*, 1964)
> *Husn ikraar kare* (*Tarzan Comes To Delhi*, 1965)

Here now are some songs during sports that have been featured in Hindi films, even if not all have been done in a competitive environment:

> *Meri pyaari patang chali baadal ke sung* (Two groups of ladies in a kite-flying contest/ *Dillagi*, 1949)
> *Aa chhoo aa chhoo chhoo* ('Kabaddi dance' competition between two teams, led by Vyjayanthimala and Helen/ *Anjaan*, 1956)
> *Us paar saajan is paar dhaare* (Nargis swims in the sea/ *Chori Chori*, 1956)
> *Chali chali re patang meri chali re* (Jagdeep and Nanda flying a kite/ *Bhabhi*, 1957)
> *Jab din haseen dil ho jawaan* (Pradeep Kumar, Nargis and friends on cycles/ *Adalat*, 1958)

- *Ye bahaar ye sama* (Nutan and friends in a kind of synchronized swimming/ *Dilli Ka Thug*, 1958)
- *She ne khela he se aaj cirket match* (Dev plays cricket/ *Love Marriage*, 1959)
- *Jo hain deewaane pyaar ke* (Waheeda Rehman does *dombari*—slack rope walking/ *Baat Ek Raat Ki*, 1962)
- *Aye jaan-e-chaman tera gora badan* (Babita swims in a pond/ *Anmol Moti*, 1969)
- *Aa mere humjoli aa, khelen aankh micholi aa* (Jeetendra and Tanuja playing aankh micholi/ *Jeene Ki Raah*, 1969)
- *Zindagi hai khel koi paas koi fail* (Hema Malini does *dombari*—slack rope walking/ *Seeta Aur Geeta*, 1972)
- *Yahaan ke hum Sikandar* (Aamir Khan, Ayesha Jhulka and others across many sports like cycling, football, running/ *Jo Jeeta Wohi Sikandar*, 1992)
- *Chale chalo* (Aamir Khan and friends play cricket/ *Lagaan*, 2001)
- *Chak de, chak de India* (girls playing hockey/ *Chak De India*, 2007)
- *Bhaag Milkha bhaag* (Farhan Akhtar runs/ *Bhaag Milkha Bhaag*, 2013)
- *Dil ye ziddi hai* (Priyanka Chopra boxes/ *Mary Kom*, 2014)
- *Teri baari hai kamar kas le* (Akshay Kumar and Siddharth Malhotra doing boxing practice/ *Brothers*, 2015)

As PV Sindhu goes into the history books for being the first Indian woman to have won a silver medal at the Olympics, she joins the elite group of Indian women who achieved greatness in their fields of endeavour. These include Razia Sultana (the first woman to rule Delhi), Laxmi Bai, Rani of Jhansi (the first woman warrior of India's Independence), Vijaylaxmi Pandit (the first woman to become President of The United Nations General Assembly), Indira Gandhi (the first woman Prime Minister), PT Usha (the first Indian woman to reach the finals of an Olympic event), Kiran Bedi (the first woman officer in Indian Police Service), Mary Kom (the first Indian woman to get a Gold Medal for Boxing), and Kalpana Chawla (the first woman of Indian origin in Space).

With Sindhu's dramatic entry into the history books, it was only natural for people from Hyderabad, her home, to arrange a huge Victory Rally for her. For that, someone had a brilliant idea. They requested BEST (Bombay Electric Supply and Transport) Undertaking to lend them a double-decker open-air bus for the rally, the kind that is popular for birthday parties on the move, with streamers and balloons. Such mobile attractions also ply festively on Mumbai's scenic Marine Drive corniche, where you may sing and cut a cake in motion. Sindhu's victory convoy happened on Monday, 22nd August 2016, with herself, her coach Gopichand and important hosts waving out to the cheering masses from the open, upper deck as the bus passed through parts of Hyderabad, including the charming drive along Hussain Sagar Lake.

This bus from Bombay makes the mind go back to the one in the film Bombay To Goa (1972), which traced a riotous, music-filled journey of a bus over 600 kilometres. The distance from Bombay to Hyderabad is just 100 kilometres more than that. You wonder now, what if some of the main stars of that old film, like Amitabh, Aruna Irani, and Shatrughan Sinha had gone on a fun-filled bus trip called Bombay To Hyderabad, to salute the young girl personally? The man who produced Bombay To Goa, Mehmood is no more, but we do know of his leanings towards Hyderabad; why, in so many films he even used the Hyderabadi Urdu dialect for his comedy. *"Kaale se darr gayi kya? Hum kaale hain to kya hua dilwaale hain"*, he went Hyderabadi in *Gumnaam* (1965).

If that bus journey seems far-fetched, celebrities from Mumbai could have flown down to Hyderabad to receive Sindhu into the bus, to add national stardust to her glory. So many names from the celebrity circuit come to mind, Shahrukh, Kangana, Deepika, Chetan Bhagat, Boman Irani, and Shankar Mahadevan. Almost anyone in fact, except a certain gossip columnist, who made a sad comment about Indian sportspeople going to Rio only to take selfies. This is what the lady, famous for her sleazy pulp fiction, had tweeted: "Goal of Team India at the Olympics: *Rio jao. Selfies lo. Khaali haath waapas aao.* What a waste of money and opportunity." That was harsh. Let's not forget that players who bring medals vindicate themselves. A classic example is

Manu Bhaker who brought 2 bronze medals from the Paris Olympics in August 2024. But what about the vast majority of them who give it their best, and yet don't make it? The last thing they need, as they cry alone, is harshness from people who don't have the foggiest idea of how much the players tried. That it wasn't about taking selfies.

But Sindhu's admirers are many more than such pulp fiction detractors. Tweeted a delighted Amitabh Bachchan after Sindhu's win: #PVSindhu, *aap "khaali haath" nahein, medal leke waapas aa rahein hain…aur hum aapke saath 'selfie' nikalne chahate hain!!*

~~~~

The above was published in DNA Jaipur on 18th August 2018. It has since been updated and enhanced.

~~~~

63

Sunglasses Are Cool

Over the years, there have been many singers who have loved their drink. Some of them even drank before recordings and during live performances. The mind goes to the legendary KL Saigal, famously fond of the bottle. But he has company among the greats. Mukesh comes to mind as does Jagjit Singh. There is a story, perhaps apocryphal, of Jagjit Singh as he sang at a large private wedding party many years ago. An hour into the performance, he was in his spirited elements, rendering a class Sudarshan Fakir ghazal, *Gham badhe aate hain qaatil ki nigaahon ki tarah, Tum chhupa lo mujhe aye dost gunaahon ki tarah.* The audience, like him, was getting delightedly devilish. Soon he came to the line, *Har taraf zeest ki raahon mein kadi dhoop hai dost.* As is common with non-film songs in live performances, he repeated this line. Improvising it, he repeated the line again. *"Kadi dhoop hai aye dost, kadi dhoop hai..."* he kept ornamenting the line. At this time, a restless young man in the audience shouted, *"Kadi dhoop hai to kaala chashma pehen lo sir!"* Jagjit was known to be difficult on the stage, but this was a huge party, and everyone had started laughing, so he smiled and ignored the heckler. You wonder if the singer's gracefulness also had anything to do with the fact that he loved sunglasses. He had quite a collection. Many celebrities love sunglasses, especially when they don't want to be recognised and mobbed.

So, what is it about sunglasses that makes them cool? Why is it that they are seen more as style accessories than as protection for the eyes? When did they transform from a thing of function to one of fashion?

First, consider the benefits, which are many. When driving an open Jeep or two-wheeler, sunglasses protect us from the punishing gusts of the wind, as also from the dust in the atmosphere and exhaust fumes from passing vehicles. They protect us from the glare of horizontal reflections, especially if it's a flattish horizon. Such a glare can be painful on the sands in the Arabian Gulf, but a pair of Polaroids will set things right. They guard our eyes against radiation and harmful ultraviolet rays. Some people get a headache when out in the sun for some time. Sunglasses make such outings bearable for them. Goggles too offer protection, but the latter are not to be confused with sunglasses. Goggles are what come with a strap, and are worn by skiers and swimmers, to hug the face closely, which means even the sides.

But while some people wear sunglasses for reasons of health or comfort, many more people wear them for style than for these benefits. The transition from a health aid to a cool accessory started in Hollywood in the 1930s and refuses to die. Thanks to increasing fashion awareness around the world, designers have come up with hundreds of styles, while manufacturers have come up with a huge range of costs.

These are some of the popular shapes, and the celebrities associated with them: Wayfarer (Tom Cruise), Simple Black (Tommy Lee Jones, Will Smith in Men In Black, 1997), "Bug Eye" (Audrey Hepburn, Paris Hilton), Flat Top Visor (Kim Kardashian), Oversized (Jackie Onassis), Aviator (Elvis Presley), Browline (Malcolm X), and Wireframe (Emily Ratajkowski). We also have Cat Eyes, Mirrored, geometric shapes and dozens of other styles.

Such shades remain in high demand because almost everyone can buy them at a favourable price point, without sacrificing chic. Sunglasses can come from extremely cheap (say for 60 Rs, online in India, which is less than one US Dollar), to very expensive indeed. The costliest ones will set you back by 400,000 US Dollars. That's about 2.8 crores Rupees. This means virtually more than 99% of car models you can order from showrooms across India, or in fact anywhere in the world. That includes many models of a Ferrari. Whew!

These are the 10 costliest sunglasses of 2023:

1. $400,000: Chopard
2. $383,000: Dolce and Gabbana DG2017B
3. $200,000: Shiels Emerald

4. $159,000: Cartier Panthere
5. $65,000: Luxuriator Canary Diamond
6. $59,000: Bulgari Flora
7. $55,000: Gold and Wood 253 Diamond
8. $30,000: Gold and Wood 119 Diamond
9. $27,000: Lugano Diamonds
10. $25,000: Cartier 18K Gold

We don't know how many Indians own any of these, but we do know of several actors who were seen wearing sunglasses in a song. Here are some such songs, with the names of the actors wearing shades:

- Nigar Sultana: *Aye muhabbat unse milne ka bahaana ban gaya* (*Bazaar*, 1949)
- Ashok Kumar and Nalini Jaywant: *Ulfat ke jaadu ka dil mein asar hai* (*Sangram*, 1950)
- Pradeep Kumar: *Aankhon pe bharosa mat kar* (*Detective*, 1958)
- Premnath: *Main deewaana mastaana* (*Forty Days*, 1959)
- Ashok Kumar: *Dil dhoondta hai sahaare sahaare* (*Kaala Aadmi*, 1960)
- Sunil Dutt: *Jaane na jaane tu hi na jaane* (*Bhai Behen*, 1969)
- Moti Sagar: *Mausam ye pukaare masti mein le chal* (*Burma Road*, 1962)
- Shashi Kapoor: *Saawan ki raaton mein ayesa bhi hota hai* (*Prem Patra*, 1962)

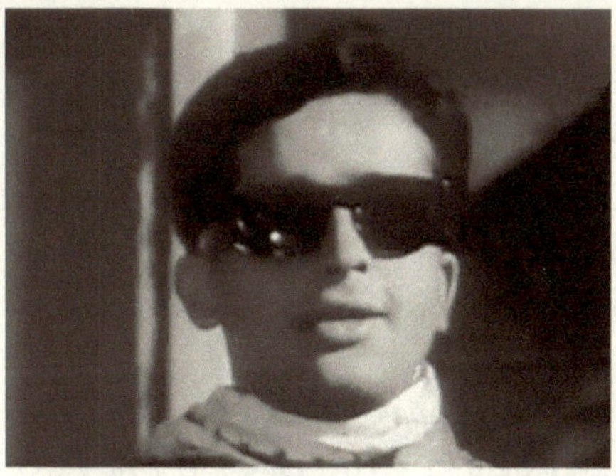

Saawan ki raaton mein

- Shashi Kapoor: *Ye mere andhere ujaale na hote* (*Prem Patra*, 1962)
- Chandrashekhar and Helen: *Tumse maano na maano mujhe tumse* (*Cha Cha Cha*, 1964)
- Joy Mukherjee: *Kya kehne mashallah nazar-e-teer aap ki* (*Jee Chahta Hai*, 1964)

Kayi baar yoon hi
dekha hai

- Mehmood: *Ajhun na aaye baalma saawan beeta jaaye* (*Saanjh Aur Savera*, 1964)
- Rajendra Kumar: *Chhalke teri aankhon se sharaab aur ziyaada* (*Arzoo*, 1965)
- Pradeep Kumar: *Tu mera jo naheen phir mujhko kya, ja kaheen* (*Bheegi Raat*, 1965)
- Ashok Kumar: *Chhupa lo yoon dil mein pyaar mera* (*Mamta*, 1966)
- Raj Kapoor: *Chale jaana zara thehro kisi ka dum nikalta hai* (*Around The World*, 1967)
- Rajesh Khanna and Hema Malini: *Zindagi ik safar hai suhaana* (*Andaz*, 1971)
- Rajesh Khanna: *Duniya mein logon ko dhoka kabhi ho jaata hai* (*Apna Desh*, 1972)
- Dinesh Thakur: *Kayi baar yoon hi dekha hai* (*Rajnigandha*, 1974)
- Govinda: *Pak chik pak Raja Babu* (*Raja Babu*, 1994)
- Shahrukh Khan: *Ye dil deewaana* (*Pardes*, 1997)
- Shahrukh Khan: *Chaand taare tod laoon* (*Yes Boss*, 1997)

- ➤ Saif Ali Khan: *Jise dhoondta hoon main har kaheen in* (*Dil Chahta Hai*, 2001)
- ➤ Akshay Kumar and Arjun Rampal: *Phatela jeb sil jaayega, jo chaahe mil jaayega* (*Aankhen*, 2002)
- ➤ Arshad Warsi: *Bole to bole to kaisi hogi bhai* (*Munnabhai*, 2006)
- ➤ Abhishek Bachchan: *Saiyaan chhed deve, nanad chutki leve, sasural genda phool* (*Delhi 6*, 2009)
- ➤ Siddharth Malhotra and Katrina Kaif: *Tenu kaala chashma jachda hai* (*Baar Baar Dekho*, 2016)

The idea of sunglasses is old and can be traced back to ancient China, where they were originally used to protect the eyes from glare. Somewhere along the line, the Chinese realised that sunglasses were useful not just for looking out, but for preventing others from looking in.

As such, Chinese judges began wearing them in courts to hide their expressions when interrogating witnesses. However, witnesses were not allowed to wear them in court. Today the rules have changed, and are different in different countries, or even their provinces. In general though, people in the dock should avoid wearing them, because studies have shown that you have a lower chance of convincing people of your innocence while wearing shades. Attorneys advise us to wear clear spectacles, even if they are not prescription glasses. You're seen to be more honest that way. Despite that, the Hollywood actor Johnny Depp wore sunglasses during his celebrated case against actress Amber Heard, and still won the case.

~~~~

The above was featured as *More than Meets the Eye* in DNA Jaipur on 30 December 2018. It has since been updated and enhanced.

~~~~

Two So Similar Qawwalis

Some questions don't have an answer, and some don't have an easy one. In the first kind we may find the logic type, such as this one that has always foxed people: "What happens when an immovable object meets an unstoppable force?" No one has a valid answer to that question. It's a paradox that has been dramatically promoted to market even events such as the Cricket World Cup, especially for Indian-Pakistani encounters. In the 1992 World Cup, it was used for Kapil Dev (the immovable object as a batter), versus Imran Khan (the unstoppable force as a bowler), and in the 2003 contest, it was the immovable object Sachin Tendulkar facing the unstoppable force of Shoaib Akhtar.

In the latter kind of questions, we can have those like why some people are so completely evil, or if there is a God, or if Man has a soul that lives after he passes away.

There are several such difficult questions to which many people have no honest answer, regardless of what they actually say. Recently, when hitmen gunned down Sufi Qawwal Amjad Sabri in Karachi, just such a question showed up for some of us again. When, if ever, will terrorism end? Yet, no sooner was the musician finished mid-career, than Bilawal Bhutto Zardari, the Pakistan Peoples' Party chief who runs Sindh province (whose capital is Karachi), promised the setting up of a 'Shaheed Amjad Sabri Sufi Music and Qawwali Institute'. Besides that, he promised the state encouragement of Sufi teachings in educational institutions. The question that begs an answer is, was Bhutto joking or was he serious? How could he risk saying what he did? To consider why we should ask such questions, let's see the history of violence from the perspective of just the Bhutto blood that has spilt over the years.

Bilawal's maternal grandfather Zulfiqar Ali Bhutto was hanged, something that the judiciary admitted in 2024 was a miscarriage of justice. His mother Benazir was assassinated, his maternal uncle Shahnawaz was fatally poisoned, and another maternal uncle Murtuza was killed. Interestingly, after they hanged Zulfiqar, it was Ghulam Farid Sabri, Amjad Sabri's father, who had sung a *marsiya* (an elegy to a departed soul), *Sada rahe aabaad, Bhutto Bhutto zindabad.* Was Bilawal only returning a salute to a dead man whose father had offered his grandfather a salute?

Two years earlier, Amjad Sabri had already got into trouble with the hardliners. His qawwali '*Ali ke saath hai Zahra ki shaadi*', shown on Geo TV, made him a target of people who thought the reference to Prophet Mohammad's family was blasphemous. (Zahra was Prophet Muhammad's daughter and Ali her husband). They had gone looking for Sabri a few months back, but hadn't found him at home, recalls his mother.

You wonder what Hazrat Amir Khusro, who fathered the qawwali 800 years ago, would have thought of all this. Sure, the genre is a musically pulsating form of mystical expression that stems from Islam, but emphasizes a personal connection with God, in addition to promoting peaceful coexistence. Khusro Saab may have been happy that in India and Pakistan, the qawwali still thrives. So much so, that in Karachi itself, there is an area called Qawwal Gali—actually a web of lanes—where live some two dozen families of professional qawwals, between them numbering some 600 performers, who make a living out of the art. Boys are only three to five years of age when they are brought to sit in during the mornings when adults do their riyaaz, and in a long journey of some twenty more years, they learn about dadra, thumri, ghazal and classical rendering. Into such a strict milieu was born Amjad Sabri.

My inability to answer the Bilawal Bhutto question ("Was he serious or was he kidding?") reminds me of another question—

this time about the birth of a qawwali, rather than the death of a qawwal—that I have no answer for. For many years, I used to host a bi-weekly show called *Nau Do Gyarah* on WorldSpace Satellite Radio. The programme was called as such not only because it was aired at 9 pm for two hours every Saturday, but also because *nau do gyarah* means absconding, or at large. We combined both meanings, identified songs that had got lost, and then played them for audiences in dozens of countries in Asia and Africa. Listeners would tune in to special satellite receiver sets, and some would respond with emails. One day, as a consequence of my airing the amazing twin qawwalis *Na to caarvaan ki talaash hai* and its follow-up, *Ye ishq ishq hai ishq ishq* (*Barsaat Ki Raat*, 1960), I got a mail from an upset listener in Indonesia. Didn't I know this was copied from a Pakistani original? If I didn't, I should have done my homework first. And if I did, why was I silent on it? "You Indians will never be graceful", he went on to say. As a parting gift, he sent me a link to a remarkable qawwali rendered by Sufi qawwal Nusrat Fateh Ali Khan, *Na to butkade ki talab mujhe*.

Na to caarvaan ki talaash hai

This was a long, wonderfully written and beautifully rendered qawwali and was remarkably similar in tune and meter to *Na to caarvaan ki talaash hai*. The words had enough in common as well. Its start was *Na to butkade ki talab mujhe, na haram ke dar ki talaash hai, Jahaan lut gaya hai sukoon-e-dil, usi rehguzar ki talaash hai.* (I need neither a temple, nor do I search for a mosque, I am looking for the street where I lost my heart).

There was too much similarity in the qawwalis in so many ways. The meter in the lines, the rhyming pattern called Kaafiya and Radeef (the *talaash hai* part), the tune itself and many of the keywords like rehguzar, Laila and Majnu, etc. Remarkably, midway through, both qawwalis romanced the word *Ishq*, and decided to shift their focus almost exclusively to the idea of love, with the frequent repeat of the line *Ye ishq ishq hai ishq ishq*. You could imagine whirling dervishes at this time. In the collective frenzy that followed, even the same classic rubai was heard:

Naaz-o-andaaz se kehte hain ke jeena hoga
Zeher dete hain to kehte hain ke peena hoga
Jab main peeta hoon to kehte hain ke marta bhi naheen
Jab main marta hoon to kehte hain ke jeena hoga

I was foxed. Whose was the original? Why did the imitator copy so much? I investigated.

Nusrat was only 12 when *Barsaat Ki Raat* (1960) came to the screen, so his version couldn't have predated the film. My friends in Pakistan, especially Sultan Arshad Khan, of Hum TV, said it was Nusrat's father, Fateh Ali Khan who had sung it before 1960. No one else I knew was aware of more than that. Additional search on the net offered me just a very basic recording, without visuals, by Fateh Ali Khan. This recording could equally have been from the late '50s or early '60s. How were we to be absolutely sure it was from before or after *Barsaat Ki Raat* (1960)? Not to forget that both Indians and Pakistanis had a healthy record of taking each other's tunes. But Nusrat and his father Fateh Ali Khan were too self-respecting to copy, and so were Roshan and Sahir. Difficult questions.

The big twist in the tale came when composer Khayyam announced on an Indian TV channel that he had refused to do *Barsaat Ki Raat* because the producer had brought with himself a spool recording of some music he wanted the maestro to copy. When I met Khayyam, I asked him if he had said that. "Yes, it's true", said the maestro. I probed further. "Did you hear what was on that spool, Khayyam Saab?" He said he didn't. Hmm.

All that brings me to questions that I am unable to answer. Does this mean Roshan, the composer of *Barsaat Ki Raat,* copied the tune? And also Sahir? He aped the lyrics? I remain foxed. But with whatever info I have, I would like to give Sahir and Roshan the benefit of the doubt. And this has nothing to do with my nationality.

Finally though, these are trivial matters. The bigger question many people are asking out there is, "Will the violence ever end?"

21st June is the longest day for much of the world. Amjad Sabri was gunned down on the next day, 22nd June 2016. None of the 600 qawwals from Qawwal Gali could sleep till the next morning. Arguably it was Qawwali's longest night.

~ ~ ~ ~

The above was originally published in DNA Jaipur on 3 July 2016. It has since been enhanced and updated.

♪♫♩♪

65

Happy New Year Ensemble!

An ensemble is a group of performers or musicians who sing or play together. Now consider this: later today, when it hits midnight, all of India will be lighting up the skies with fireworks, drinking up, dancing to happy music, hugging and shaking hands. Many of us will be sending WhatsUp messages. And some of us will be quietly making New Year's resolutions. In a sense, we will be exclaiming Happy New Year, ensemble.

Later, as midnight crawls westwards into different time zones across the globe, people in other regions will welcome the New Year too. For example, two and a half hours after we begin ours, celebrations will commence in Ankara, Turkey. Athenians in Greece will cheer an hour later, Parisians will be cheering sixty minutes after the Greeks, while Londoners will eagerly have to wait another hour still. Of course, that's because people in these cities live in different time zone slices. But wait, France with its dependencies has 11 time zones. This means people scattered in mainland France and its territories won't be right in singing *Bonne Annee* in a collective burst. It will be staggered 11 times. People living in the United Kingdom will have to echo their New Year outburst in 9 one-hour intervals since that country's dominions cover 9 time zones. This is somewhat like timed-release capsules, dissolving into our systems at one-hour intervals.

Interestingly, when you superimpose the map of India on one of Europe—so easily done on the net these days—you see how large we are. We are bigger than the UK and France put together. And there is enough left over to add half a dozen other European states. From wingtip to wingtip, our expanse is wider than the longitudes that pass through the 4 cities in different time zones listed above, i.e., Ankara, Athens, Paris, and London. Not just that, the number of languages and dialects we have far exceeds the diversity of Europe. And yet we remain one country. With one ethos. With one time zone and orchestrated effort, singing Happy New Year ensemble, in a *Mile sur tumhaara hamaara* 24/365 kind of way.

Interestingly, every significant religious group on our land has its own new year too, which too is celebrated. The Sikhs, Muslims, Hindus, Parsis, and Jains, all have their new year. Culturally considered as well, many have their own new year. For instance, Malayalis have their Onam, Sindhis celebrate their new year on Cheti Chand, while Maharashtrians do so on Gudi Padwa. Away from India too, such diverse celebrations apply to various nationalities such as the Chinese, Koreans, Tibetans and Japanese. But the excitement that accompanies the departure of December 31 has a universal electrical charge that dwarfs local festivities just about everywhere.

It wasn't always so, especially in India. It's the British who brought in this New Year enthusiasm, as recently as in the 1940s. In the United States, the public celebration of New Year's Eve began only in 1907, when several buildings in New York City's Times Square came together in an illuminated display. But now the idea has caught on, with Hindi films romancing this Western idea sufficiently in its songs. Here are a few songs sung at a New Year party, with the music crew in brackets:

> ➤ *Saal mubaarak aaya, ho jeeyo mere Raja* (Shamshad Begum, Trilok Kapoor/ Anjum Jaipuri/ Chitragupt/ *Toote Khilone*, 1954)

> ➤ *Sab ko mubaarak ho naya saal* (Asha Bhosle/ Rajinder Krishan/ Hemant Kumar/ *Samraat*, 1954)

> ➤ *Nineteen fifty-six, nineteen fifty-seven, nineteen fifty-eight, nineteen fifty-nine* (Lata Mangeshkar, Manna Dey/ Shailendra/ Shankar-Jaikishan/ *Anari*, 1959)

Nineteen fifty six, nineteen fifty seven

- *Jaani mujhe tu ne ye kya cheez pila di* (Sharda, Kishore Kumar/ Indeewar/ Shankar-Jaikishan/ *Naina*, 1973)
- *Happy New Year to you* (Shailendra Singh/ Writer unknown/ Ravindra Jain/ *Do Jaasoos*, 1975)
- *Saal mubaarak sahib ji* (Rafi, Mukesh/ Hasrat Jaipuri and Ravindra Jain/ Ravindra Jain/ *Do Jaasoos*, 1975)
- *Ye raaten nayi puraani* (Lata/ Anand Bakshi/ Rajesh Roshan/ *Julie*, 1975)
- *Naya saal haaye tamaasha dikhaaye* (Asha Bhosle, Amit Kumar, Anwar/ Nida Fazli/ Hemant Bhosle/ *Nazraana Pyaar Ka*, 1980)
- *Naye puraane saal mein ik raat baaqi hai* (Kishore Kumar, Asha Bhosle/ Anand Bakshi/ RD Burman/ *Raksha*, 1981)
- *Aane waale saal ko salaam* (Shabbir Kumar/ Anand Bakshi/ Laxmikant-Pyarelal/ *Aap Ke Saath*, 1986)
- *Aadhi raat aayi to khayaal aaya hai…naya saal aaya hai* (Suresh Wadkar/ Gauhar Kanpuri/ Ram Laxman/ *Baharon Ki Manzil*, 1991)

'Let the good times roll' is a fine thing to say, but it isn't always a happy new year for everyone. Every January 2, we get news of many mishaps that happened on the first day of the year. Much of the depressing news is associated with irresponsible alcohol consumption. Studies on alcohol drinking carried out abroad have observed that as a person consumes increasing quantities of it, his condition progresses through these five alliterated stages: Dry and Decent, Delighted and Devilish, Dizzy and Delirious, Dazed and Dejected, and Dead Drunk. Somewhere after the first drink they should have also added a Don't Drive stage.

Some of us can tell which of the five stages a person is in by watching him and hearing his speech. Consider in this context what some music lovers consider the ultimate song on New Year's Eve. *Haaye haaye haaye ye nigaahen* was rendered by Kishore Kumar for Majrooh's poetry and SD Burman's music in *Paying Guest* (1957). It was mimed by Dev Anand, clearly under the influence. How many did Dev had before the song? I'd say he was at the end of the Delighted and Devilish stage. What do you think?

As for in real life, many people get sloshed on New Year's Eve. Some of them have the good sense of not driving a vehicle in that state. However, some of the sad news doesn't have to do with alcohol either. Take the case of Dharmendra at a party on New Year's Eve in *Aaye Din Bahaar Ke* (1966). He is sober as a judge when he sees his old flame Asha Parekh, who has just picked up someone's cute child in her arms, only to feel happy for a few moments. In seconds and without determining whose baby it is, our hero showers highly poisonous verbal arrows on the lady through the song *Mere dushman tu meri dosti ko tarse* sung by Rafi, written by Anand Bakshi and composed by Laxmikant-Pyarelal.

~ ~ ~

The above was originally published in DNA Jaipur on 31 December 2017. It has since been updated and enhanced.

66

Dangerous Affairs

A couple of years ago, the popular American online dating site Ashley Madison had to shut down ignominiously, thanks to hackers who got into the website's sensitive database before dumping the information on the web. For many years before then, Ashley Madison had tempted and facilitated people already in relationships to have an affair. The successful outfit's tagline was "Life is short. Have an affair", and it famously ran hundreds of head-turning ads of an alluring woman with a wedding ring, a finger to her red lips promising secrecy with a silent shhh.

Their campaign was not without other attention-demanding messages. For a few days before February 18, 2013 which was Presidents Day, billboards in many cities across the USA featured Presidents Franklin Roosevelt, John Kennedy and Bill Clinton, all known to have had extra-marital affairs. "Who said cheaters never prosper? Happy Presidents Day" the ad said, with the three Presidents holding their index fingers over their mouths! A year later, the dating service took on Hillary Clinton, who had experienced being at the receiving end of her husband's misadventures, and who at the time was actively promoting her new book, Hard Choices. This time it was Ms. Clinton with a finger to her lips, accompanying the billboard message, "Harder Choices…lead to Ashley Madison.com".

Following the lives of celebrities of all hues is something many of us do, especially if such people are unable to stay faithful to one person. When they stray, they usually manage to keep things away from the public eye, but when the lid is off, it's fun! We Indians have known of our own adulterous celebrities too. The much-married Raj Kapoor had affairs with Nargis and Vyjayanthimala, avers the filmmaker's son in some detail in his autobiography, *Khullam Khulla, Rishi Kapoor Uncensored*. And who hasn't raised an eyebrow for seasoned politician ND Tiwari, having fun with three nude women, or Supreme Court lawyer Ram Jethmalani snapped kissing actress Leena Chandavarkar on the mouth?

If we focus on extra-marital affairs, they have existed across time and geography. What makes for fascinating reading too is how the laws look at them. The United States applies different laws in different states, with some 29 out of 50 states having decriminalized adultery. All the Islamic countries, including Pakistan, treat it as a crime. India too used to treat it as a crime, but that was changed in October 2018. But nowhere in Europe is adultery a criminal offence now. Europeans have turned it civil.

Such decriminalization has been taking place because of the universally growing agreement that adult consensual behaviour in private should not really be subject to harsh laws. The United Nations argues that the criminalization of sexual relations between consenting adults is a violation of their right to privacy. The organization also adds that provisions in penal codes don't often treat men and women equally, establishing harsher rules and sanctions for women. To fight such discrimination against women, the United Nations keeps asking member countries to decriminalize such relationships, allowing easier laws to take charge.

You wonder if the United Nations knows that in this regard women are so safe in India that they cannot be charged for adultery! That's because they are seen not as predators, but as their husbands' property. Amazingly, even they cannot press charges against their husband now. So say you are a married man and your wife has an adulterous relationship. You can press charges against her lover, but not against her. Also, under no circumstances can she frame charges against you or your paramour. Your wife's only hope is your lover is married so that her husband can take you to court!

Consider this February 2017 case. Upon returning home, a Hyderabad resident, C. Channaiah, found his wife Lalita in a compromising position with a police constable named Madhusudan

Reddy. Channaiah pressed charges against the man under Section 497 of the Indian Penal Code. But he could not use the law to punish his own wife, even as she filed a complaint against her husband and in-laws alleging domestic harassment, which resulted in a case against the latter under the same Indian Penal Code.

Way back in 1959, when one could charge one's wife for adultery, Navy Commander Kavas Nanavati didn't do so. He took a different route when he shot his wife's lover Prem Ahuja dead. He didn't harm her, hoping he would have a strong case that way. The film *Ye Raste Hain Pyaar Ke* (1963) was based on their story, and the recent *Rustom* (2016) was the same story too. But many film stories have dealt with infidelity--whether physical or emotional. These stories have been gripping, and perhaps the music in such narratives tends to be very spicy too. Without going into details of who was who in the cast, let's just consider one song each from Hindi films that have focussed on such questionable relationships. The listing is chronological.

- *Mahal* (1949): *Dil ne phir yaad kiya* (Lata)
- *Afsana* (1951): *Abhi to main jawaan hoon* (Lata)
- *Dharam Patni* (1953): *Lagi tumse lagan mere bhole sajan* (Asha)
- *Mayur Pankh* (1954): *Tandaana tandaana tandaana, mushkil hai pyaar chhupaana* (Lata)
- *Kaagaz Ke Phool* (1959): *Waqt ne kiya kya haseen sitam* (Geeta)
- *Ye Raaste Hain Pyaar Ke* (1963): *Aaj ye meri zindagi, dekho khushi mein jhoomti* (Asha)
- *Benazir* (1964): *Bahaaron ki mehfil suhaani rahegi* (Lata)
- *Jeene Ki Raah (1969): Aap mujhe achhe lagne lage* (Lata)
- *Dhund* (1973): *Uljhan suljhe na, rasta soojhe na* (Asha)
- *Doosra Aadmi* (1977): *Aao manaayen jashn-e-muhabbat* (Kishore, Lata)
- *Main Tulsi Tere Aangan Ki* (1978): *Main tulsi tere aangan ki* (Lata)
- *Pati Patni Aur Woh* (1978): *Tere naam tere naam tere naam* (Mahendra Kapoor)
- *Grah Pravesh* (1979): *Aap agar aap na hote* (Sulakshana Pandit)
- *Silsila* (1981): *Rang barse bheege chunar waali* (Amitabh Bachchan)
- *Masoom* (1982): *Tujhse naaraaz naheen zindagi* (Anup Ghoshal)

- *Aakhir Kyoon* (1985): *Saat rang mein khel rahi hai dilwaalon ki toli re* (Anuradha, Amit Kumar)
- *Ijaazat* (1987): *Mera kuchh saamaan tumhaare paas pada hai* (Asha)
- *Aastha* (1997): *Labon se choom lo* (Sriradha Bannerjee)
- *Biwi No. 1* (1999): *Aaja na chhoo le meri chunri* (Anuradha Sriram, Abhijit)
- *Astitva* (2000): *Chal chal mere sang sang* (Sukhwinder Singh)
- *Jism* (2003): *Jaadu hai nasha hai* (Shreya Ghoshal)
- *Joggers' Park* (2003): *Ishq hota naheen sabhi ke liye* (Adnan Sami)
- *Murder* (2004): *Bheege honth tere, pyaasa dil mera* (Kunal Ganjawala)
- *Kabhi Alvida Na Kehna* (2006): *Kabhi alvida na kehna* (Sonu Nigam, Alka Yagnik)
- *Rustom* (2016): *Dekha hazaaron dafa aap ko* (Arijit Singh, Palak Muchhal)

There are other classic examples of physical relationships, such as the one between Dev and Waheeda in *Guide* (1965). While there are also films that hint at an affair without physicality, such as *Gumrah* (1963), *Anubhav* (1971), and *Amar Prem* (1972)

So, do you subscribe to the notion "Life is short. Have an affair"? Just remember when it's time to pay, there's usually too much to pay, far more than we can afford. Most people who have been caught with their pants down regret they ever had an extra-marital relationship, no matter how exciting it was while it lasted. Precisely because life is too short, they advise us not to have an affair. But who is listening? If infants will have their infancy, adults will have their adultery!

~~~~

The above was originally published in DNA Jaipur on 2 April 2017. It has since been updated and enhanced.

~~~~

67

Never on a Sunday

Most of the people who gave us wonderful cinema and its unforgettable music in the golden age have gone away. Decades after such art was created, not only film and music historians but even plain aficionados sit down sometimes to repeatedly enjoy classic films and hear remarkable songs, as well as to appreciate the situations such songs were filmed in. Music buffs apply their minds to identify the different instruments used in songs, the charming lyrics brought to the table by our poets, and so many large and small facets of those wonderful melodies. This is not very different from the way archaeologists go about curating human culture from the past.

While revisiting a song filmed on Suchitra Sen on her birth anniversary a few weeks ago, a delightful discovery entered my thoughts. The song, from *Musafir* (1957), was *Man re Hari ke gun ga*, a Krishna bhajan that was so gracefully captured on celluloid. The lady was found watering a Tulsi plant. Before looking at my discovery, let's pause and reflect on this plant for just a bit.

The Tulsi (Holy Basil) is famous for its medicinal properties but is also worshipped by many people in our part of the world. According to Hindu mythology, there was a Goddess named Brinda who was a great devotee of Lord Vishnu. When she died, it was ordained that she would marry Vishnu in her next birth. They transferred her soul to a plant, which became the holy Tulsi. That is why lots of believers offer a Tulsi puja and do a circumambulation around the herb, in what is called parikrama. Every year, millions of people also celebrate her marriage to Vishnu. This happens after Diwali has gone, and it is only after this wedding of the gods that the auspicious months start for us mortals to get married.

It is for these reasons that the Tulsi is given the place of honour in people's homes. It is positioned well on the verandah or the parapet, and usually, no ordinary pots are assigned to this sacred herb. Most Tulsis are planted in square-shaped and decorative pots, sometimes on a chest-high pillar too, for they must ideally be distanced from and above the other plants. But now about that discovery.

In that devotional, Suchitra Sen was seen watering a Tulsi plant while singing a Lata Mangeshkar song. By filmic association, memories of another Lata Mangeshkar song rushed in now, a song where a heroine was also seen watering plants, including a Tulsi. That song was *Jaago Mohan pyaare* in *Jaagte Raho* (1956), and the leading lady was Nargis. That situation was just a year before the Suchitra Sen one. So, I switched to watching the *Jaagte Raho* song and was fascinated to find more dots waiting to be connected, one after another. Not only was the heroine watering a plant in both songs, and not only was the singer common, but the lyricist was the same for both songs (Shailendra), and so was the composer (Salil Chowdhury). The maestro even had the same assistants in both albums: Kanu Ghosh and Sebastian. My serendipity didn't stop there. Both the songs were even inspired by the same raag, Bhairav!

Jaago Mohan pyaare

There was hardly any time gap between the two films and there was too much in common here for this to be a pure coincidence. So then, who from the crew could be the pollinating agent in this case, taking the idea from *Jaagte Raho*, and offering it in a new avatar in *Musafir*? And if it was not them, could it be Suchitra Sen herself? Needless to say, the filming of the *Jaagte Raho* song was extraordinary and it remains one of the high points of Indian cinema to this day. Perhaps you will have thoughts on this.

Meantime, there have also been a few songs that have featured the heroine watering plants—if not just a Tulsi—as she sang. A film was even dedicated to the idea in *Main Tulsi Tere Aangan Ki* (1978), where we found Asha Parekh watering the plant while she sang the title song, *Main Tulsi tere aangan ki*. Here are a few more actresses with the songs they were singing. Singers, lyricists and composers also find a mention:

Meena Kumari in *Jap jap jap jap jap re* (Mukesh/ Rajinder Krishan/ C Ramchandra/ *Sharda*, 1957), Shyama in *Naihar ke geet main gaoon, babul ka baag sajaoon* (Lata/ Pt Indra/ BS Kalla/ *Do Dulhe*, 1959), Meena Kumari in *Jyoti kalash chhalke* (Lata/ Pt Narendra Sharma/ Sudhir Phadke/ *Bhabhi Ki Chudiyan*, 1961), Jaya Bhaduri in *Nadiya kinaare heraaye aayi kangna* (Lata/ Majrooh/ SD Burman/ *Abhimaan*, 1973), Nutan in *Tera mera saath rahe* (Lata/ Ravindra Jain/ Ravindra Jain/ *Saudagar*, 1973), and Jaya Prada in *De Tulsi maiya vardaan itna* (Anupama Deshpande/ Anjaan/ Bappi Lahiri/ *Ghar Ghar Ki Kahaani*, 1988).

In the above songs lies hidden a fascinating point that too awaits our thoughts. In *Saudagar*, Nutan was a Muslim from a poor background, as was Amitabh, for whom she sang *Tera mera saath rahe*. Interestingly, she was seen planting the Tulsi in her little compound outside her hut. Later on, they put a tikka on her forehead as she watered the Tulsi during that song. Now while such things are perfectly possible, they do seem somewhat unlikely for Hindi cinema. The mind goes to the film *Main Tulsi Tere Aangan Ki* released a few years earlier, in which not only was Nutan the main female lead, but for which she also received the Best Actress Trophy from Filmfare. However, the most popular song in that feature was filmed on the supporting actress Asha Parekh, the title song mentioned above. But even in that song, Nutan was given a lot of screen time. Perhaps she wanted more than that. A song in which she was watering a Tulsi, an act that helps sustain life in that most venerated of plants. That's a charming visual experience for filmgoers. Yes, that would be nice.

About the plant itself, we know that some people pluck Tulsi leaves to eat them for the preventive preservation of health and the positive treatment of diseases. But it is believed that while the holy plant can be plucked on most days, that's a no-no on Sundays. If you do so, you may invite a curse upon yourself. That does bring to mind a very popular English song called *Never on a Sunday*, rendered by lots of famous singers like Petula Clark, Andy Williams, and Connie Francis. Here's how the lyrics go:

Oh you can kiss me on a Monday, a Monday, a Monday is very very good
Or you can kiss me on a Tuesday a Tuesday a Tuesday in fact I wish you would
Or you can kiss me on a Wednesday a Thursday a Friday and Saturday is best
But never never on a Sunday a Sunday a Sunday coz that's my day of rest

Fair enough, if a holy plant needs a break on Sunday, we humans too can do with a day of rest.

~~~~

The above was originally published in DNA Jaipur on 22 April 2018. It has since been updated and enhanced.

~~~~

68

Arm Wrestling Equinox!

Today, 22nd September 2013, is the day of Autumn Equinox, when both day and night are of equal length for us. *Raat aur Din* in an arm wrestling situation, or *panja ladaana* as we call it in *desi* lingo. This is when day and night offer us an equal show of strength.

Imagine then if you were living in Norway, where the sun never sets for months and months. You could go play golf or ski down the slopes at 11 pm, or go for a midnight sun cruise on serene waters! If you are a sleep-deprived person, getting just 3 or 4 hours of rest, wow, then you should best be in Norway or anywhere above the Arctic Circle, and that can also be parts of Russia, Canada, and Alaska.

But then, in such a place, it would be hard to connect to a song like *Din dhal jaaye haaye, raat na jaaye, Tu to na aaye, teri yaad sataaye.* Perhaps more relevant would be lyrics like *Dhoop naheen jaaye, raat naheen aaye, neend sataaye, kya kiya jaaye, gaya pyaar bhara mausam deewaana* (sung to the tune of *Haaye re haaye neend naheen aaye,* from *Humjoli,* 1970)

That apart, if you are like most people, needing seven or eight hours of sleep daily, it would be difficult to stay in such a place for long. The result of extended periods of brightness combined with not experiencing darkness at night can cause hypomania, a clinical condition characterized by swings in mood.

Further, it can have religious issues for some people. For some Hindus it may mean too much *surya namaskaar,* for Muslims no eating or drinking during daylight hours in the month of Ramzan, for Jews too (their rites work around a twenty-four hour day/ night cycle), and certain strains of Christians who must stay holy, from sundown Friday to sundown Saturday. That's why it's so important to experience this interplay of light and shade. This interplay is needed even by poets. Because poetry loves to showcase contrasts; everything that has a yin and yang works fine for poets, such as *shama aur parwaana, subah aur shaam, dost aur dushman,* etc.

As such, let's look at songs that have been milked for their reference to both the day and night. For our spotlight, we take only *din* and *raat*, ignoring words like *subah, savera,* and *bhor,* as also *raen, raina, ratiya, shab,* and all their variants. It's only a microcosm of songs today, celebrating this single aspect of geography.

- *Tadpat beete din rain* (Saigal/ RC Boral/ Agha Hashr Kashmiri/ *Chandidas,* 1934)
- *Din se dugni ho jaayen raaten* (Saigal/ Gyan Dutt/ DN Madhok/ *Bhakt Surdas,* 1942)
- *Har din hai naya, har raat niraali hai* (Ashok Kumar, Amirbai/ SD Burman/GS Nepali/*Shikari,* 1946)
- *Din guzra raat aayi* (Suraiya/ Ghulam Mohd./ No idea/ *Kaajal,* 1948)
- *Beete hue din raat aye dil yaad na karna* (Suraiya/ Husnlal-Bhagatram/ Rajinder Krishan/ *Amar Kahani,* 1949)
- *Chaar din ki chaandni thi phir andheri raat hai* (Suraiya/ Naushad/ Shakeel/ *Dillagi,* 1949)
- *Lut gaya din-raat ka aaraam kyoon* (Mukesh/ Krishin Dayal/ Qamar Jalalabadi/ *Lekh,* 1949)
- *Wo din na rahe raaten na rahi* (Ila Ghosh/ Pankaj Mullick/ Pandit Bhushan/ *Manzoor,* 1949)
- *Wo raat-din wo shaam ki guzri hui kahaaniyaan* (Lata/ Sajjad/ DN Madhok/ *Saiyaan,* 1951)

Wo raat-din wo shaam ki

- *Raat ne aake din ko chooma saanjh suhaani aayi* (Sandhya Mukherjee/ Robin Chatterjee/ Vidyapati/ *Ratan Deep*, 1952)
- *Din aaye raat jaaye* (Madhubala Jhaveri, Harish, Balbir/ Hansraj Behl/ Prem Dhawan/ *Resham*, 1952)
- *Raat gayi phir din aata hai* (Manna Dey, Asha/ Shankar-Jaikishan/ Saraswati Kumar Deepak/ *Boot Polish*, 1953)
- *Ye raat din ka phera laga rahega* (CH Atma/ Bulo C Rani/ DN Madhok/ *Bilwamangal*, 1954)
- *Din raat jafaayen karte hain* (Asha/ Sajjad/ Khumar Barabankvi/ *Rukhsana*, 1955)
- *Din ho ya raat hum rahen tere saath* (Rafi, Suman/ Hansraj Behl/ Prem Dhawan/ *Miss Bombay*, 1957)
- *Kaari kaari kaari andhiyaari ki raat, ik din ki baat* (Chitalkar, Asha/ C Ramchandra/ Bharat Vyas/ *Navrang*, 1959)
- *Din-raat badalte hain, haalaat badalte hain* (Hemant/ Chitragupt/ Rajinder Krishan/ *Naya Sansar*, 1959)
- *Mujhe raat-din ye khayaal hai* (Mukesh/ Iqbal Quereshi/ Hasrat Jaipuri/ *Umar Qaid*, 1961)
- *Jumme ki raat ho ya din Jummeraat ka* (Mukesh, Lata/ Kalyanji-Anandji/ Haroun/ *Dulha Dulhan*, 1964)
- *Din dhal jaaye haaye, raat na jaaye* (Rafi/ SD Burman/ Shailendra/ *Guide*, 1965)

- *Waqt se din aur raat* (Rafi/ Ravi/ Sahir/ Waqt, 1965)
- *Tadap ye din-raat ki* (Lata/ Shankar-Jaikishan/ Shailendra/ Amrapali, 1966)
- *Kabhi raat-din hum door the* (Rafi, Lata/ Kalyanji-Anandji/ Anand Bakshi/ Aamne Saamne, 1967)
- *Raat aur din diya jale* (Mukesh or Lata/ Shankar-Jaikishan/ Hasrat Jaipuri/ Raat Aur Din, 1967)
- *Jeena-marna hai ab din-raat tere saath teri baahon* mein (Suman, Rafi/ Laxmikant-Pyarelal/ Anand Bakshi/ Suraj Aur Chanda, 1967)
- *Jaan-e-man jaan-e-man tum din raat mere saath is dil mein aji rehte ho* (Manna Dey, Usha Khanna/ No idea/ Haaye Mera Dil, 1968)
- *O tu kya jaane din-raat hum jeete hain* (Kishore/ Kalyanji-Anandji/ Anand Bakshi/ Mahal, 1969)
- *Jaane kahaan gaye wo din...Apni nazar mein aaj-kal, din bhi andheri raat hai* (Mukesh/ Shankar-Jaikishan/ Hasrat Jaipuri/ Mera Naam Joker, 1970)
- *Din raat jale akhiyaan, karoon yaad teri batiyaan* (Lata, Usha/ Chitragupt/ Majrooh/ Pardesi, 1970)
- *Muhabbat ke suhaane din, jawaani ki haseen raaten* (Rafi/ Kalyanji-Anandji/ Anand Bakshi/ Maryada, 1971)
- *Jeena-marna ab din-raat* (Rafi, Suman/ Laxmikant-Pyarelal/ Anand Bakshi/ Suraj Aur Chanda, 1973)
- *Din ja rahe hain ke raaton ke saaye* (Lata/ RD Burman/ Gulzar/ Doosri Seeta, 1974)
- *Main wohi, wohi baat...Mere liye to har din naya din, har raat nayi raat* (Rafi/ Laxmikant-Pyarelal/ Rajinder Krishan/ Naya Din Nayi Raat, 1974)
- *Tu mera din hai main teri raat* (Suman, Mukesh/ Shankar-Jaikishan/ MG Hashmat/ Sanyasi, 1975)
- *Hari din to beeta shaam hui, raat paar kara de* (Rajkumari/ RD Burman/ Gulzar/ Kitaab, 1977)
- *Chupke chupke raat-din aansoo bahaana yaad hai* (Ghulam Ali/ Ghulam Ali/ Hasrat Mohani/non-film, but included in Nikaah, 1982)

> *Kaate naheen kat-te ye din ye raat* (Kishore, Alisha/ Laxmikant-Pyarelal/ Javed Akhtar/ *Mr. India*, 1987)
> *Bole mera kangana tere bin sajna neend naheen aati...din-raat tadapta hoon, milne ko tarasta hoon* (Alka, Kumar Sanu/ Anand-Milind/ Sameer/ *Bandish*, 1996)

You can imagine if Prem Dhawan did not enjoy the day-night interplay, how would he write *Din ho ya raat, hum rahen tere saath ye hamaari marzi* (Rafi, Suman/ Hansraj Behl/ *Miss Bombay*, 1957)? Nature would have stolen the ink out of his poetry.

~~~~

The above was originally published in DNA Jaipur on 22 September 2013

♪♫♩♭
~~~~

Storytellers Par Excellence!

Here quickly is the story of Sultan Shahryar, the King of Persia, along with a bright girl in his kingdom called Scheherazade (pronounced Sheher Azaad, meaning the liberator of the city), and the tales she told him over three years. These stories have come to be called Tales of 1001 Nights. Legend has it that the King, suspecting his wife of unfaithfulness, had her beheaded. Turning his crazed revenge universal, he proceeded to marry a girl every day, only to have her killed the next morning. This became famous as his insanity. Soon the terror-stricken kingdom ran out of young girls, except for the vizier's daughter Scheherazade, who married the king, but managed to strike a deal with him: he would hear a story from her and only then order her execution. It turns out that she got him spellbound with her imaginative narrative, but cleverly left it unfinished so that by dawn, he was temporarily tuned out of his mission. The session continued the next night and more nights. Because she had her story so beautifully intermeshed with others, she would end one narrative in the middle of the night, cleverly making leaps of associations to start another one. This went on for 1001 nights, by which time she delivered three children, and he gave up his murderous run.

Many absorbing tales have been written in our films too, though they are not the story-within-a-story kind. They didn't have to be either, because our story writers were not weaving stories to stay alive, a situational imperative for Scheherazade. This is also true of our lyric writers. These latter penned several stories in our films as plain ballads, which are like a narrative of connected events—real or imagined—

and set to music. In simple Hindustani, they are *tarannum mein kahaaniyaan,* or stories in tune. There are some variations in ballads too, but let's keep it tight to our narrow filmy description for now. Here are some such stories in song, down the decades, with a brief description, and the names of the singers and lyricists:

- *Ik Raje ka beta lekar udne waala ghoda* (a winged horse, a fairy, and more in this children's story/ Saigal/ Kidar Sharma/ *President,* 1937)

- *Ek kali, naazon ki pali* (a beautiful young girl, hoodwinked and dumped by a charmer/ Shamshad/ Wali Saheb/ *Khazanchi,* 1941)

- *Panghat par paani bharne aayi thi gaon ki chhori* (village belle falls in love near the river bank/ SN Tripathi, Rajkumari/ Ramesh Gupta/ *Panghat,* 1943)

- *Suno sunaoon ek kahaani apni samjho ya begaani* (A girl is happy as a child but when she grows up, she falls in love and it doesn't work out with her beau/ Lata/ Rajinder Krishan/ *Bhai Bahen,* 1950)

- *Subhash Chandra ke naam se* (a celebration of the life and times of Netaji Subhash Chandra Bose/ Chitalkar/ Rajinder Krishan/ *Samadhi,* 1950)

- *Sun lo ek kahaani* (about a prince and an unknown girl/ Talat, Geeta Roy/ Pt Madhur/ *Ratnadeep,* 1952)

- *Rajguru ne Jhansi chhodi* (about the First War of Independence, 1857/ Rafi/ Pt. Radheshyam/ *Jhansi Ki Rani,* 1953)

- *Muhabbat ki daastaan aaj suno ye* (the great Moghul Shah Jahan, his wife Mumtaz Mahal and the Taj Mahal/ Lata/ Hasrat Jaipuri/ *Mayur Pankh,* 1953)

- *Suno Sita ki kahaani* (an innocent Sita is exiled/ Rafi/ Prem Dhawan/ *Biraj Bahu,* 1954)

- *Aao bachcho tumhen dikhaayen jhaanki Hindustan ki* (a conducted tour of Indian patriotism/ Pradeep/ Pradeep/ *Jagriti,* 1954)

- *Taaron ki nagri se chanda ne ek din* (Suraiya sings a lullaby to a boy/ Suraiya/ Qamar Jalalabadi/ *Waris,* 1954)

- *Murli Manohar Krishn Kanhaiya Jamuna ke tat pe viraaje hain* (the Krishna Radha story/ Ustad Amir Khan, Manna, Lata/ Diwan Sharar/ *Jhanak Jhanak Payal Baje*, 1955)
- *Shivji bihaane chale palki sajaike* (the Shiv Parvati wedding story/ Hemant/ Shailendra/ *Munimji*, 1955)
- *Suno chhoti si gudiya ki lambi kahaani* (a girl's chequered life starts sadly, and ends happily/ Lata/ Hasrat Jaipuri/ *Seema*, 1955)

Suno chhoti si gudiya ki

- *Suno suno nagri ke logo* (this one is about Marwar/ Asha, Manna Dey/ Bharat Vyas/ *Dhola Maru*, 1956)
- *Parwar digaar-e-aalam tera hi hai sahaara* (a hamd outlining Allah's kindness/ Rafi/ Akhtar Romani/ *Hatimtai*, 1956)
- *Kahaani badi suhaani hai* (the mythological account of Lord Rama/ Rafi/ Saraswati Kumar 'Deepak'/ *Sati Nagkanya*, 1956)
- *Hai bahut dinon ki baat* (a parody of the Laila-Majnu story/ Manna Dey, Rafi, Balbir/ Rajinder Krishan/ *Bhabhi*, 1957)
- *Suno sunaoon tumhen ek kahaani* (bad times come to a king, queen, and their son/ Kavi Pradeep/ Kavi Pradeep/ *Chandi Pooja*, 1957)
- *Suno-suno re kahaani ik bahut puraani* (a Rudyard Kipling-like Jungle Book account of birds and animals establishing a 'constitution' to coexist peacefully/ Shamshad, Asha, Suman, Usha/ PL Santoshi/ *Hum Panchhi Ek Daal Ke*, 1957)
- *Kuchh din pehle ek taal mein* (the story of a family of swans, used metaphorically to engage the attention of kids/ Asha/ Majrooh/ *Lajwanti*, 1958)

- *Thi ek shaahzaadi* (the story of a princess in love with a pauper/ Talat/ Kaifi Azmi/ *Lala Rukh*, 1958)

- *Bahut din hue taaron ke desh mein…Chanda ki nagariya mein rehte the ik Raja* (A happy princess stops smiling, so her father the king announces to give her and half his kingdom to the one who will make her smile/ Mahendra, Manna, Lata/ Shailendra/ *Anuradha*, 1960)

- *Gali gali Sita roye aaj mere des mein* (holding up the flag for fairness to women/ Rafi/ Qamar Jalalabadi/ *Chhalia*, 1960)

- *Aaj ki taaza khabar* (today's top headlines in four minutes!/ Shanti Mathur/ Shakeel/ *Son of India*, 1962)

- *Insaan tha pehle bandar* (Darwin's Theory of Evolution for dummies/ Shanti Mathur/ Shakeel/ *Son of India*, 1962)

- *Ek thi ladki meri saheli* (a girl's journey, and the advice she receives: "Don't fret about tomorrow, it's going to be fine"/ Asha/ Sahir/ *Gumrah*, 1963)

- *Ek tha Raja ek thi Rani* (childhood friends-turned-lovers losing each other/ Lata/ Shailendra/ *Hariyali Aur Rasta*, 1963)

- *Nayi Sita ki suno nayi kahaani* (extolling the virtues of Goddess Sita/ Rafi/ Bharat Vyas/ *Roop Sundari*, 1964)

- *Ek tha gul aur ek thi bulbul* (about two lovers who are interrupted by others, but unite finally/ Rafi, Nanda/ Anand Bakshi/ *Jab Jab Phool Khile*, 1965)

- *Main sunaata hoon tujhe ek kahaani sun le…Tu hoke bada ban jaana apni maata ka rakhwaala* (a father advises his son to take of his mother when he grows up/ Rafi/ Rajinder Krishan/ *Khandan*, 1965)

- *Caravan guzar gaya ghubaar dekhte rahe* (a self-deprecating memoir/ Rafi/ Neeraj/ *Nayi Umar Ki Nayi Fasal*, 1965)

- *Ek Raja ki sun lo kahaani* (about a man whose sons didn't stand by him, but a servant did/ Rafi, Lata/ Rajinder Krishan/ *Meherbaan*, 1967)

- *Ik tha bachpan…chhota sa nanha sa bachpan* (a young woman, separated since childhood from her father, remembers him/ Lata/ Gulzar/ *Ashirwad*, 1968)

- *Re mama re mama re* (a children's fun story/ Rafi/ Hasrat Jaipuri/ *Andaz*, 1971)

The stories that insiders to cinema wrote out of cinema got a great deal of attention too, and two were about huge personalities: Pt. Nehru and Mahatma Gandhi. This was about Nehru, and was rendered by a chorus-backed Mukesh:

Phool khilega baaghon mein jab tak gulaab ka pyaara
(penned by Shailendra)

And this was a huge Rafi elegy to Gandhiji in four parts (two back-to-back 78 rpm records): *Suno suno aye duniya waalo Bapuji ki amar kahaani.* Within months, the sales of these records zoomed out through the roof, so much so that Baburao Pai, the producer of these records, gifted an Austin car to its writer Rajinder Krishan for doing a wonderful job, so quickly after the Mahatma's demise too. The wealthy Pai was not just the partner of Famous Pictures Poona, he was also a huge Gandhi follower.

Could Scheherazade and the Tales of 1001 Nights be true? No one knows, it's all so lost in antiquity. We do know that many great narratives have been put to enjoyable musical form in our films, even if no writer has come close to Scheherazade's seemingly magical storytelling. But who knows, decades from now, the veracity of our lyric writers may itself be a subject of animated debate, considering their exceptional excellence in the golden years. Seen from the distance of time they too may appear as mythical as Scheherazade of the 1001 Nights fame.

~~~~

The above article appeared under the heading *Were Our Songwriters Real?* in DNA Jaipur on 16 March 2014. It has since been updated and enhanced.

~~~~

70

Raising Our Glass to India's Nightingale!

And why not? It's her birthday today

Let's pause to think of Lata Mangeshkar, arguably the most significant female singer in the history of Indian cinema. It's another matter that there was a time, many moons ago, when we had to pause to *stop* thinking about her. That's because she was everywhere, wasn't she? On the radio, in films, on our cassettes and records and CDs, as also on TV. In the extraordinary trajectory of her career which started in 1942, the lady has sung well over 7000 songs in over 70 years, translating to an average of about a hundred songs each year. This means roughly two songs every week, every year for seven decades! Think about that opus now, and maybe you want to mentally send her a Happy Birthday wish on her 85th special day today.

Since her work is too vast and complex, it constantly needs huge research. Not that that hasn't happened, nor that discographies or books on her have not been enjoyed either. But let's leave statistics out of our essay today. Instead let's host an imaginary party which has some of the best composers we have had over the decades, and ask them today, in retrospect, to celebrate Lata with one solo song they composed for her. And they have to tell us why they chose that one song, if not why they had Lata sing it.

Again, this is an imaginary meeting of just a few composers, some of whom I have had the good fortune of meeting, and be privy to their thoughts. But the statements that I attribute to these maestros may not in fact be entirely divorced from reality, because these thoughts reflect the views of a host of people who understand music. Let's go then, chronologically, film-year-wise.

Lata Mangeshkar

> ➤ *Dil mera toda* from *Majboor* (1948) (Ghulam Haider: *Maine is ladki mein hunar dekha, aur 1948 mein hi Lata ko recording studios mein bula liya. Aage ja ke inhone kya toofaan utthaaya, wo hum sab jaante hain!*)

> ➤ *Bahaaren phir bhi ayengi,* from *Lahore* (1949) (Sham Sundar: *Ye dard-o-alam mein doobi ghazal hai…kya mila judaai ka jazba inki expression se, wah wah*)

> ➤ *Ayega aane waala* from *Mahal* (1949) (Khemchand Prakash: *Although I didn't live to see this film's success, I gave Lata this, her first major hit*)

> ➤ *Taare wohi hain* from *Anmol Rattan* (1950) (Vinod: *I loved the way Lata sounded those days, like a fresh, pure waterfall!*)

> ➤ *Abhi to main jawaan hoon* from *Afsana* (1951) (Husnlal-Bhagatram: *Kya zamaana tha ji…Pran naayak ke roop mein, aur waltz dance kar rahe hain Kuldeep Kaur ke saath. Aap ko*

shaayad yaad hoga ki har Guruwaar ki shaam ko Radio Ceylon ke puraane geeton ka ye signature tune bhi ban gaya tha!)

➤ *Man mein kisi ki preet basa le* from *Araam* (1951) (Anil Biswas: *If the piano was perfect, and Madhubala was perfect, could we do with anything less than perfect?)*

➤ *Thandi hawaayen* from *Naujawan* (1951) (SD Burman: *Lata ka expression suno, Bangaali mitthaayi hai! Hum usko khushi se paan diya!)*

➤ *Sapna ban saajan aaye* from *Shokhiyaan* (1951) (Jamal Sen: *Janaab, pehle ek minute ke dohe mein hi Lata ne dil ko chhoo liya. Aur uske baad? Unhone 'Ye naina…bhar aaye…sharmaaye' jis ada se gaaya, uff!)*

➤ *Hai kaheen par shaadmaani* from *Aandhiyaan* (1952) (Ustad Ali Akbar Khan: *This challenging song was written by the great Pt. Narendra Sharma, and I played the sarod too. Nav Ketan also insisted on Lata)*

➤ *Dil matwaala laakh sambhaala* from *Bewafa* (1952) (Allah Rakha Qureshi: *Ye tandem gaane humne Talat aur Lata se alag-alag gawaaye. Dono nayyaab singers. Aur in dono gaanon ko bilkul alag treatment di. Itna ki Talat waale mein aap tabla sunte honge, aur Lata waale mein dholak)* (Tabla-nawaaz Allah Rakha composing and only dholak? Interesting!)

➤ *Bhool sake na hum tumhen* from *Tamasha* (1952) (Manna Dey: *Oh my God, what a singer, Lata! I have even sung many songs with her…)*

➤ *Kitna meettha hota hai* from *Teen Batti Char Rasta* (1953) (Shivram Krishna: *I had to think about this film that was loosely based on Lataji's real life. The song happened so easily)*

➤ *Na milta gham to* from *Amar* (1954) (Naushad: *Shakeel saahab was the best ghazal writer in our films. When he wrote this one, there was no doubt in our minds that Lata would do complete justice to this sufi kalaam)*

➤ *Wo chali gham ki hawa* from *Aaj Ki Baat* (1955) (Snehal Bhatkar: *Oh this was a song dipped in pathos. I put a muted trumpet and decorated Hasrat's words with plenty of violins. And I just didn't want to take chances with the voice, which was too vital!)*

> *Kho diya maine pa kar kisi ko* from *Bara Dari* (1955) (Nashaad: *Khaas rhythm hai, thoda alag qism ka keherwa. Gulookaara ka intikhaab aasaan tha*)

> *Rasik balma* from *Chori Chori* (1956) (Shankar-Jaikishan: *Arre bhai Shudh Kalyan ki baat hai, to humne studios mein bulaaya Pt. Ram Narainji ko, unhone sarangi bajaayi. Humne daavat di Jairam Acharyaji ko, jinhone khoob sitar bajaayi…aur dard ke liye humne invite kiya swaron ki malika Lataji ko. Ab aap hi kaho, dilko chhoota hai ya naheen*)

> *Guzra hua zamaana aata naheen dobaara* from *Shirin Farhad* (1956) (S. Mohinder: *O main kya, Farsi kahaani hai. Madhubala caarvaan mein rote-rote rukhsat ho rahi hai…is mein main kisi B grade singer ko le loon? Swaal hi naheen paida honda!*)

> *Jaago Mohan pyaare* from *Jagte Raho* (1956) (Salil Choudhury: *This was a landmark Raj Kapoor film about sleaze in the big city. We had to create an awesome song for Shailendra's immortal lyrics, urging people to see with their minds, more than with their eyes. 'Jisne man ka deep jalaaya, duniya ko usne hi ujla paaya. Mat rehna akhiyon ke sahaare!' I gave it the apt, morning-raag Bhairav treatment, and trained a chorus to heighten the impact. And handed it over to brilliant Lata. What you hear and see is a masterpiece*)

> *Chhup gaya koi re* from *Champakali (1957)* (Hemant Kumar: *Evocativeness at its best. With Pandit Pannalal Ghosh setting the mood with his flute…Lata is super!*)

> *Sab-kuchh luta ke hosh mein aaye to kya kiya* from *Ek Saal* (1957) (Ravi: *Aisa tha, ke beemaar Madhubala story mein marne waali hai. Is gaane ke doosre antre mein mujhe is baat ko dramatize karne ke liye singer ko bina melody khoye hue taar saptak mein le jaana tha. Yahaan: 'Aye maut jald aa zara aaraam to mile',. Lata ke siva humne kuchh socha hi naheen!*)

> *Unko ye shikaayat hai ke hum kuchh naheen kehte* from *Adalat (1958)* (Madan Mohan: *If it's a ghazal, why should the poetry and my tune both be wasted on someone who is not as good?*)

- *Haaye jiya roye* from *Milan* (1958) (Hansraj Bahl: *A solo violin, a few dramatic phrases, and it was naturally Lata that we decided on*)

- *Aurat ne janam diya mardon ko* from *Sadhana* (1958) (N. Datta: *Arre baap re! Sahir saab ne aisa likha, main to samajh gaya, yahaan music ko kam karo Datta, Lata didi ko expression ka platform do*)

- *Nadiya ke paani o re* from *Savera* (1958) (Shailesh: *Maine tez raftaar ka gaana banaaya, aur uske har antare mein brake bhi lagaayi, phir flute and dholak ka sundar upyog bhi kiya, theek hai? Aur sabke oopar Lata!*)

- *Meetthi-meetthi baaton se bachna zara,* from *Qaidi No. 911* (1959) (Dattaram: *Aap ne mera special rhythm pattern to suna hoga, jo Dattu Theka kehlaaya gaya. Is mein maine wohi bajaaya hai, aur Didi ne kya gaaya hai, bahut maza aaya*)

- *Aa laut ke aaja mere meet* from *Rani Rupmati* (1959) (SN Tripathi: *Sirf ek rani hi kisi rani ke liye ga sakti hai!*)

- *Haaye re wo din kyoon na aaye* from *Anuradha* (1960) (Pt. Ravi Shanker: *My attempts at Kalavati in its vocal form needed a great exponent*)

- *Itna na sata ki koi jaane* from *Bindiya* (1960) (Iqbal Qureshi: *Bhale hi parde pe film ki side heroine Vijaya Choudhury kyoon na ho, mera kaam to dekho miyaan!*)

- *Maanjhi meri qismat ke* from *Hum Hindustani* (1960) (Usha Khanna: *What a song! I created it using a stormy background, with Didi's voice as a stabilizing influence. It worked so well!*)

- *Jyoti kalash chhalke* from *Bhabhi Ki Choodiyan* (1961) (Sudhir Phadke: *With Pt. Narendra Sharmaji's incredible poetry, no other thought crossed our minds: only Lata Mangeshkar could do justice to this song!*)

- *Deewaane tum, deewaane hum from Bezubaan* (1962) (Chitragupt: *Dekho, main bezubaan ban jaata hoon. Aap Manohari Singh ki saxophone suniye, aur uske saath Lata ki awaaz ka sangam*)

- *Ja ja re chanda ja re* from *Private Secretary* (1962) (Dilip Dholakia: *A sleepless, forlorn Jayshree Gadkar is so bruised, even moonlight irritates her!*)

- *Bedardi daghabaaz ja* from *Bluff Master* (1963) (Kalyanji-Anandji: *This was a time when Saira Banu was trying everything to attract Dilip Kumar's attention. So if he could play the sitar so well in Kohinoor, she could play it well too. A wonderful Bageshri, and it had to be only Lata!)*

- *Har aas ashkbaar hai* from *Kinare Kinare* (1963) (Jaidev: *We had to set a six-beat dadra and control the violins to behave with restraint. The piano did some of that mediating, and Lata the rest)*

- *Aye mere watan ke logo* (non-film) *(first sung live in January, 1963)* (C Ramchandra: *Kavi Pradeep ne bol likhe, maine swar badd kiya, aur ye ghair-filmi gaana aetihaasik ban gaya!)*

- *Aye dilruba, nazren mila* from *Rustom Sohrab* (1963) (Sajjad Husain: *There were only two singers worth talking about, Noor Jahan and Lata. With the former gone, my decision on the singer was easy, very easy)*

- *Pankh hote to ud aati re* from *Sehra* (1963) (Ramlal: *Sarod, pakshi, Jaltarang, raag Bhopali, in sab ke saath mein Kumari Lata. Suniye to!)*

- *Aye dil machal machal ke yoon* from *Main Suhagan Hoon (1964)* (Lachhiram: *Hum bhi the is duniya mein. Humne bhi achha kaam kiya)*

- *Jeevan dor tumhi sang baandhi* from *Sati Savitri* (1964) (Laxmikant-Pyarelal: *Kya todenge is bandhan ko jag ke toofaan aandhi re aandhi. Lata bhi aisi hain, atoot, amulya!)*

- *Mere do naina matwaare* from *Namaste Ji* (1965*)* (GS Kohli: *Bhale hi small budget film ho, Lataji ne apna kaam hamesha top class kiya hai)*

- *Jogi hum to lut gaye tere pyaar mein* from *Shaheed* (1965) (Prem Dhawan: *Jee haan, kabhi-kabhi maine sangeet bhi banaaya, aur is gaane ke zariye Punjab ke bhangre ki khushbu laane ki koshish bhi ki hai)*

- *Rahen na rahen hum, mehka karenge* from *Mamta* (1966) (Roshan: *Pahadi tune, a high point in my musical life, and Lata at the crest)*

- *Maangne se jo maut mil jaati* from *Sunehre Kadam* (1966) (Bulo C. Rani: *I had worked with Lata before, but she saved her best for this, a wonderful ghazal for my last film)*

➤ *Ik tha bachpan*, from *Ashirwad* (1968) (Vasant Desai: *Hrishida bola 'Vasanta, kuchh ayesa banao ki story mein gaana chadh kar bole!' Gulzar ne nazm likhi, maine shehnai bajwaayi, female chorus shaamil kiya, aur Didi ko kaha, 'Aata tumchya warti'. Ab faisla aap ka hai*)

➤ *Kaanha re Kaanha* from *Truck Driver* (1970) (Sonik-Omi: *Krishna bhajan, flute, and Lata ji, bus*)

➤ *Raina beeti jaaye* from *Amar Prem* (1971*)* (RD Burman: *Jo kuchh main jaanta tha, usko maine Todi mein daal ke aap ke liye banaaya. Achha hai na?*)

➤ *Inhi logon ne* from *Pakeezah* (1971) (Ghulam Mohd.: *Aji saahab, is mujre mein humne kya naheen kiya…Majrooh ke kalaam pe Yaman tayyaar ki, khoob rhythm bajwaayi, ghunghru, kaanch tarang bhi. Aur kya gaayi hain Latabai! Kya kehne!*)

➤ *Ye raaten, nayi puraani* from *Julie* (1975) (Rajesh Roshan: *Filmfare award bhi mila is film ke liye, aur dhunen banaane mein bhi bahut achha laga*)

➤ *Zid na karo, ab to ruko* from *Lahu Ke Do Rang* (1979) (Bappi Lahiri: *Public decide karegi hamaara kaam, hamaara challenge hai*)

➤ *Jo tum todo piya* from *Silsila* (1981) *(*Shiv-Hari: *Lata ne Shivji ko harmonium pe iski dhun bajaate suna. Bahut mutassir hui. Agle hi din ye Meerabai bhajan record hua*)

➤ *Aye dil-e-naadaan* from *Razia Sultan* (1983) (Khayyam: *Razia Sultan was the only Queen of Delhi. There was no way Kamal Amrohi or I would consider anyone else to sing this amazing song…a certain greatness was needed!*)

➤ *Chitthiye ni dard firaaq vaaliye* from *Henna (*1990) (Ravindra Jain: *Punjabi folk ko Lata ne kaisa nibhaaya hai!*)

➤ *Yaara seeli-seeli* from *Lekin* (1990) (Hridyanath Mangeshkar: *Ah ha, kya gaaya hai Didi ne! Rajasthan ki ret ki khusbhu aati hai!*)

➤ *Dil hoom-hoom kare* from *Rudali* (1993) (Bhupen Hazarika: *Raag mishr Bhopali mein hum apna expression diya, aur Lata ne apna. Nasha sa ho gaya*)

➤ *Maayi ni maayi* from *Hum Aapke Hain Koun* (1994*)* (Ram Laxman: *In popular culture, when munder pe the crow caws, someone is coming. Hope you like it*)

> ➤ *Mere khwaabon mein jo aaye* from *Dilwale Dulhaniya Le Jayenge* (1995) (Jatin-Lalit: *Trumpets and Western rhythms, a new world is happening in our cinema, change is happening all around us, but Lata remains solid gold*)
> ➤ *Jeeya jale, jaan jale* from *Dil Se* (1998) (AR Rahman: *Lata was what I needed from my new sounds too*)

The above imaginary party was for composers only. But we still have to meet her lyric-writers. "Four score and seven years ago our fathers brought forth on this continent a new nation…" said Abraham Lincoln in his famous Gettysburg address. Let's wait for Lata Mangeshkar's four score and seven—her 87th birthday in 2016—to raise our glass for her magnificent opus with waves of songwriters. By that time she will hopefully have worked with a few more newcomers!

~~~~

The above was published in DNA Jaipur on 28 September 2014. The nightingale passed away on 6th February 2022.

♪♫♩♪
~~~~

Just a Spoonful of Sugar

Many moons ago, lyrics-writer Gulzar was at the center of a minor storm over his imagery using the word *mehek*, meaning *khushbu*, or fragrance. Now *mehek* is conventionally a function of smell, engaging the nose. But here was Gulzar linking the idea with the eyes: *Humne dekhi hai un aankhon ki mehekti khushbu* went Lata in *Khamoshi* (1969). Some folks from the literary universe thought this was over the top. As if he was enjoying the controversy so much, Gulzar put the idea into currency again nearly a decade later, with Kishore and Lata rendering *Aap ki aankhon mein kuchh mehke hue se khwaab hain* in *Ghar* (1978). Some people thought the songwriter had lost it. Had he?

A new idea has often been rejected at first. It can be about science and technology, and it can be about theology, but it can be about prose and poetry too. It's only that history sees virtue in recalling science and theology rejections more, so that gets hammered into our minds. After all, poetry and prose do not impact everyone's life. But rejections happen all round. As the German philosopher Arthur Schopenhauer said about a new idea, it must "endure a hostile reception before it is accepted".

Six hundred years back, Polish mathematician and astronomer Copernicus advanced the thought that the Sun, not the Earth, was at the center of our Solar System. He was greeted by raised eyebrows that wouldn't come down. Rudyard Kipling, the imaginative Bombay born writer of Jungle Book was sacked from The San Francisco Examiner in 1889. This is what the editor wrote to him: "I'm sorry Mr. Kipling, but you just don't know how to use the English language". Mr. Kipling went on to win the Nobel Prize for Literature.

In India, near the middle of the last century, aspiring musician Onkar Prasad Nayyar auditioned his tunes before filmmaker S. Mukherjee, who dismissed the wannabe composer for "lacking merit". OP Nayyar proceeded to ride the crest of waves for many years, including in some films made by Mukherjee himself. He shook the sober edifice of the prevailing music universe with unconventional concepts and treatments.

More recently, it was the invention of the personal computer that met with laughter. Steve Wozniak was working with Hewlett-Packard when he developed the idea of a computer for the common man. He took the prototype to his bosses at HP who thought the idea was ridiculous. He took it to them five times. They rejected him five times.

This makes you remember Albert Einstein, who said, "The great spirits have always encountered violent opposition from mediocre minds"

Many poets have taken liberties before

Let's rewind to before Einstein's time now, i.e., to about three hundred years ago. We find the poet Shelley saying, "Our sweetest songs are those which tell of the saddest thought". Now sweetness is a function of taste, decided by the tongue. How can songs be sweet? But wait, let's fly back even more, to meet William Shakespeare who said, "That which we call a Rose, by any other name would smell as sweet". A Rose *smelling* sweet? Perhaps in the time it was created, such outlandish imagery was denounced, but the fact that such quotes continue to impress us clearly suggests lasting value. That's why many such creators are idolised. It may be worth remembering here that no critics ever had statues erected in their honour, nor have they won the Dadasaheb Phalke Award, or an Oscar.

Sweetness—mostly beyond the sense of taste

So, if the above ideas of sweetness are a tough pill for you to swallow, here's a glassful of sweet content to wash it down:

- *Koi le lo main meettha doodh laayi* (Rajkumari/ *Brandy Ki Botal*, 1939)
- *Ek meetthi nazar ban ke aankhon mein sama jao* (Rajkumari/ *Sasural*, 1941)
- *Meetthi meetthi murali Shyam bajaaye* (Manna Dey, Sharda, Gayatri/ *Geet Govind*, 1947)
- *Meetthi meetthi loriyaan main dheere dheere gaoon re* (Madhubala Jhaveri/ *Apni Izzat*, 1952)
- *Meetthi meetthi baaton se bholi bhaali ghaaton se* (Lata/ *Parbat*, 1952)
- *Raat mohe meettha meettha sapna aaya re* (Geeta/ *Tamasha*, 1952)

Raat mohe meettha meettha sapna aaya re

- *Do bol tere meetthe meetthe* (Hemant, Lata/ *Daara*, 1953)
- *Kitna meettha hota hai kitna pyaara hota hai kisi ke pyaar mein kho jaana* (Lata/ *Teen Batti Chaar Rasta*, 1953)
- *Humse bhi kar lo kabhi kabhi to meetthi meetthi do baaten* (Geeta/ *Milap*, 1955)

- *Dekho ji dekho meetthi ada se* (Geeta, Rafi/ *Mai Baap*, 1957)
- *Bheeni bheeni hai meetthi meetthi hai bheeni bheeni hai kyoon hawa* (Lata/ *Nausherwan-e-Adil*, 1957)
- *Meetthi meetthi yaad teri dil tadpa gayi* (Manna Dey/ *Great Show of India*, 1958)
- *Meetthi meetthi baaton se bachna zara* (Lata/ *Qaidi No. 911*, 1959)
- *Dekha babu chhed ka maza, meettha meettha dard de diya* (Lata/ *Shararat*, 1959)
- *Salaam aap ki meetthi nazar ko salaam* (Rafi/ *Boy Friend*, 1961)
- *Zindagi hai kya sun meri jaan, pyaar bhara dil meetthi zubaan* (Rafi/ *Maya*, 1961)
- *Meettha meettha pyaar ka mausam* (Mahendra/ *Bombay Race Course*, 1965)
- *Meetthe bol bole, bole paayaliya* (Lata, Bhupinder/ *Kinara*, 1971)
- *Ek meetthi si chubhan* (Lata/ *Reshma Aur Shera*, 1971)
- *Mitwa bole meetthe bain* (Bhupinder/ *Parichay*, 1972)
- *Khatta meettha…ye jeena hai angoor ka daana* (Kishore, Usha/ *Khatta Meetha*, 1977)
- *Pyaar ka dard hai meettha meettha* (Asha, Kishore/ *Dard*, 1981)
- *Kori gagariya meettha paani* (Kavita/ *Zid*, 1993)

In the above list, just two songs—the first and the last—refer to sweetness experienced by the tongue. The rest have used imagination.

Sweetness is no longer in vogue

"Just a spoonful of sugar helps the medicine go down, in a most delightful way", went Julie Andrews in Mary Poppins. She was right. That's also why we have sugar-coated pills. But sweetness isn't otherwise so chic these days. People are getting fatter and sicker, so health awareness is up. Many of us use less sugar in our beverages and sweetmeats than before. Bitter and dark chocolates are getting more popular. And brown sugar or sugar substitutes can be found in every self-respecting restaurant around the globe. Diet Cokes are popular as they contain no sugar, but furnish the sweetness via the chemicals acesulfame-potassium and aspartame. Sweetness sans calories has made heroes out of artificial sweeteners which are helping a frustrated world trying to keep its waistline from bulging more and more.

But the imaginary kind of sweetness is still in vogue. When Rudyard Kipling was given the Nobel Prize in 1907, the citation extolled many of his virtues, including "originality of imagination". Just such originality of imagination brought sweetness to the sense of smell, and the sense of smell to the eyes, as we saw Shakespeare and Gulzar do above.

Jaate-jaate, let's spare a thought for Shakespeare again. Like all great thinkers, he must have faced so much criticism in his time. But there's no facet of human emotion he didn't touch, boldly and originally. "Sweet are the uses of adversity", he said, confounding critics even more.

The above was published in DNA Jaipur on 1 May 2016. It has since been updated and enhanced.

72

Socha Kya?

It is often said that poetry is the language of the heart. If it is, you wonder why it pitches so much at our heads too. That's why we have aesthetics, the philosophical study of beauty, which includes music, visual arts, and poetry. It is considered that when a poem is read or heard, it is processed in the brain before finding instructions on whether it qualifies to go to the heart. Reversing the route, consider what the great poet Robert Frost said: "Poetry is when an emotion has found its thought, and the thought has found its words." This suggests a symbiotic relationship between the heart, head, and poetic expression.

Sock and Buskin, comedy and tragedy respectively

In recent decades though, poetry has substantially surrendered its responsibility of knocking at the brain's door to get a visa for the heart. Let's consider why that has happened. Firstly, tragedy and comedy were for centuries considered the extremes between which lay various shades of feeling. The Greeks even invented masks for comedy and tragedy. Such masks, now commonly known as Sock (for comedy) and Buskin (for tragedy) adorned the walls in many cinema halls such as Golcha in Delhi and Liberty in Bombay until some 40 years ago. Those masks are no longer in vogue because filmgoers now just want to watch romance, wealth and happiness. No *rona-dhona*, thank you! Film themes, their songs, and their background music—so vital in influencing our emotions—are mostly geared to giving audiences a happy, even escapist experience. That has narrowed down poetry's bandwidth.

That's one thing.

Sock and Buskin

No thinking, so no visa!

The second thing is the challenge that cinema has had to face from Television and Social Media. Because TV is known for its emphasis on mindless entertainment, it is famously called the Idiot Box. Repeated exposure to mindless programs dumbs you down. However, studies after studies tell us that mental activity can prevent dementia. Thinking isn't easy, but is not thinking really an answer? Consider in this context sitcoms, which started in the USA and have now become popular in India as well. Somewhere down the line, the West introduced laugh tracks, which feign the appearance of a live audience, so that we, the real audience, are encouraged to laugh. You can hear such canned laughter in shows like Mr. Bean and Yes, Minister. If we don't laugh, we may appear odd. This can be fine in cerebral shows like Yes Minister. But Indian serials like *Taarak Mehta Ka Oolta Chashma*, with their inane jokes and funny-sounding music effects may have entertainment merit for many but offer little that you can use your brains for.

Anyway, since we are on the subject of thinking, let's consider a few songs that engage our minds by the use of the operative word *soch* and its variants.

Songs that make us think

Examine for a start Javed Akhtar's words in *Rock On* (2008), lip-synced by a spirited music band, and compelling us to use our grey matter:

> *Aasmaan hai neela kyoon?*
> *Paani geela-geela kyoon?*
> *Gol kyoon hai zameen?*
> *Silk mein hai narmi kyoon?*
> *Aag mein hai garmi kyoon?*
> *Do aur do paanch kyoon naheen?*
> *Socha hai ye tumne kya kabhi?*
> *Socha naheen to socho abhi…*
> (Farhan Akhtar/ Shankar-Ehsan-Loy)

The same writer had produced a thinking man's masterpiece a few years earlier, in *Refugee* (2000):

> *Panchhi nadiya pawan ke jhonke, koi sarhad na inhen roke*
> *Sarhad insaanon ke liye hai*
> *Socho tumne aur maine kya paaya insaan hoke*
> (Sonu, Alka/ Anu Malik)

Even when it's not so direct, the idea to make us think—as against feel, which we will see soon—is built into many a song. This one was conceived by Sameer in *Ghulam* (1998):

> *Ae, kya bolti tu? Aati kya Khandala—?*
> *Kya karoon aake main Khandala?—*
> *Ghoomenge phirenge naachenge gaayenge*
> *Aish karenge, aur kya?*
> (Aamir Khan, Alka/ Jatin-Lalit)

The idea of thought is not as recent as the above examples may suggest. It has been going on for decades. Here is a sampling of Hindi film songs that offer different positions on matters cerebral, our operative word being *soch* with its many variants:

- ➤ *Sharaabi, soch na kar matwaale* (Pankaj Mullick, Radharani/ Prem/ Pankaj Mullick/ *Mukti*, 1937)
- ➤ *Socha tha kya, kya ho gaya* (Suraiya/ Tanvir Naqvi/ Naushad/ *Anmol Ghadi*, 1946)
- ➤ *Na socha tha ye dil lagaane se pehle* (Shamshad/ Shakeel/ Naushad/ *Babul*, 1950)
- ➤ *Soch-samajh kar dil ko lagaana* (Geeta Roy/ Sahir/ SD Burman/ *Jaal*, 1952)
- ➤ *Socha hai sahenge door se gham* (Geeta/ Majrooh/ Dhaniram/ *Sholay*, 1953)
- ➤ *Sochne ko laakh baaten soche insaan* (Rafi/ Rajinder Krishan/ Madan Mohan/ *Baap Bete*, 1959)
- ➤ *Chal ri sajni ab kya soche* (Mukesh/ Majrooh/ SD Burman/ *Bambai Ka Babu*, 1960)

Chal ri sajni ab kya soche

- ➤ *Soch rahi thi kahoon na kahoon* (Lata/ Shailendra/ Shankar-Jaikishan/ *Ek Phool Chaar Kaante*, 1960)
- ➤ *Soch samajh le o parwaane jal jaana aasaan naheen* (Asha/ Prem Dhawan/ Ravi/ *Apna Ghar*, 1960)
- ➤ *Sochta hoon ye kya, ye kya kiya maine?* (Mukesh, Lata/ Kidar Sharma/ Snehal Bhatkar/ *Hamari Yaad Ayegi*, 1961)
- ➤ *Kya soch raha matwaale* (Rafi/ Jan Nissar Akhtar/ GS Kohli/ *Mr. India*, 1961)

- *Ishq mein kya sochna? Sawaal kya, jawaab kya?* (Asha/ Rajinder Krishan/ N Datta/ *Akela*, 1963)
- *Socha tha pyaar hum na karenge* (Mukesh/ Rajinder Krishan/ Kalyanji-Anandji/ *Bluff Master*, 1963)
- *Main ye soch kar uske dar se uttha tha* (Rafi/ Kaifi Azmi/ Madan Mohan/ *Haqeeqat*, 1964)
- *Sochta hoon ke tumhen maine kaheen dekha hai* (Krishna Kalle, Rafi/ Akhtar Romani/ Kalyanji-Anandji/ *Raaz*, 1967)
- *Soch ke ye gagan jhoome* (Lata, Manna Dey/ Anand Bakshi/ SD Burman/ *Jyoti*, 1969)
- *Na socha na samjha na dekha na jaana* (Asha/ Hasrat/ Shankar-Jaikishan/ *Shatranj*, 1969)
- *Aaj socha to aansoo bhar aaye* (Lata/ Kaifi Azmi/ Madan Mohan/ *Hanste Zakhm*, 1973)
- *Jaane kya soch kar naheen guzra* (Kishore/ Gulzar/ RD Burman/ *Kinara*, 1977)
- *Aaj socha hai khayaalon mein* (Sulakshana, Rafi/ Sahir/ N Datta/ *Chehre Pe Chehra*, 1980)

Many other songs don't push you to think right away, but they do so somewhere during the song! Examples:

Jo main jaanti unke liye mere dil mein kitna pyaar hai...
Jo main soch-samajh ke chalti, hadd se baat guzarti kyoon
(Lata/ Shailendra/ Shankar-Jaikishan/ *Aah*, 1953)

Chanda chaandni mein jab chamke
Kya ho aa mile koi chham se
Socho, poochhte ho kya humse?
(Geeta/ Majrooh/ OP Nayyar/ *Mujrim*, 1958)

Bolo-bolo kuchh to bolo...
Kum naheen tum, kum naheen hum, socho zara
(Rafi/ Majrooh/ Usha Khanna/ *Dil Deke Dekho*, 1959)

Ek thi ladki meri saheli…
Ye mat socho kal kya hoga, jo bhi hoga achha hoga
(Asha/ Sahir/ Ravi/ *Gumrah*, 1963)

Tum kamsin ho naadaan ho naazuk ho bholi ho
Sochta hoon main ke tumhen pyaar na karoon
(Rafi/ Hasrat/ Shankar-Jaikishan/ *Ayee Milan Ki Bela*, 1964)

Bujha diye hain khud apne haathon muhabbaton ke diye jala ke…
Na sochne par bhi sochti hoon, ke zindagaani mein kya rahega
(Suman/ Sahir/ Khayyam/ *Shagun*, 1964)

Bolo ji bolo kuchh bolo ji bolo parwaana teri mehfil mein aaya
hai, deewaana teri mehfil mein aaya hai
Socho ji socho, kuchh socho ji socho kyoon shamma ne tumko bulaaya hai
(Mukesh, Suman/ Javed-Anwar/ Usha Khanna/ *Nishaan*, 1965)

The feeling equivalent of thinking features words like *ehsaas, jazba, mehsoos,* etc. You are not likely to find too many of this kind, certainly not in comparison with the thinking sort. Here though is a Gulzar classic that reaches for the heart in *Khamoshi* (1969):

Humne dekhi hai un aankhon ki mehekti khushbu
Haath se chhoo ke ise rishton ka ilzaam na do
Sirf ehsaas hai ye rooh se mehsoos karo
Pyaar ko pyaar hi rehne do koi naam na do
(Lata/ Hemant Kumar)

And a Sahir Ludhianvi ghazal of excellence from *Ghazal* (1964):

Ishq ki garmi-e-jazbaat kise pesh karoon?
Ye sulagte hue din-raat kise pesh karoon?
(Rafi/ Madan Mohan)

And

Do jaasoos karen mehsoos
(Mukesh, Rafi/ Hasrat/ Ravindra Jain/ *Do Jaasoos*, 1975)

Let's finally turn away from poetry to briefly consider the world's most famous sculpture, The Thinker. This work of class by Rodin of France features a muscular man cast in bronze—there are twenty-eight statues of the same thinking guy in different parts of the world—resting his right elbow on his knee and his chin on the back of his hand, clearly lost in deep thought. But no one thought of (or perhaps felt like?) creating a statue called The Feeler. Perhaps the nearest image of that could be of a clown. That absence should tell us something.

~ ~ ~ ~

The above was originally published in DNA Jaipur on 19 May 2013. It has since been updated and enhanced.

73

Should They Let Their Hair Down?

In the romantic comedy *Ek Phool Char Kante* (1960), Waheeda Rehman was featured in an exceptional Krishna bhajan set in a public temple: *Banwaari re jeene ka sahaara tera naam re*. Not only was this devotional offering beautiful, Waheeda herself looked stunning rendering it, part of the reason being the importance given to her open, flowing hair, which all but covered her face when she began singing the song. This was in stark contrast with the other ladies in the temple, whose hair was tied up and covered by their saris. It was as if Vogue Magazine was going to feature the actress on its cover soon, in an "India's Ravishing Mendicant, Ms. Rehman" kind of way!

Banwaari re

You wonder what the right thing is for ladies when in a temple, especially if they are singing: should they keep their hair plaited or bunned up, or should they leave their tresses open in an informal way? In the manner our temples are run, as also from the customs that are followed in different places of worship, surely we would get an informed view. Here's an online opinion from www.hindujagruti.org:

"It is a common scene nowadays with women in every corner of the world trying to beautify themselves by leaving loose hair; some even go to the extent of styling their open hair. You must have noticed in horror movies where female ghosts have loose hair all the time while mythological movies show women with hair tied as plaits or buns. All female deities have their long hair tied up, except when they are on a mission to destroy demoniac forces.

"Superficially, loose hair might look good, but from a spiritual perspective, it is actually a very dangerous invitation to negative energies"[9].

Many family elders advise ladies to tie up their hair, even at home. They tell us how open hair has a symbiotic relationship with everything negative, like grief, suffering, poverty, sin, ill fortune and even revenge. The epic Mahabharata informs us of the time Draupadi was dragged by her hair in the Kuru Sabha by Dushasana, and how, out of obsessive revenge, the lady didn't tie her hair up for 13 years, till it was washed with Dushasana's blood. That was a clear case of open hair symbolizing vendetta.

And yet, in spite of such clear directives, filmmakers have sometimes shown positive emotions in bhajans or spiritual songs on actresses with open tresses, whether at home or in a temple. This includes the filmed-on-Meena Kumari masterpiece *Jyoti kalash chhalke*, from *Bhabhi Ki Chudiyan* (1961), finding special mention here because all the three main creators of this song, Pandit Narendra Sharma, Sudhir Phadke, and Lata Mangeshkar—its poet, composer, and singer, respectively—knew so much about our culture and code of conduct.

Here's more proof such cinematic coiffure has existed in fair supply when filming devotional or spiritual songs:

- *Tere phoolon se bhi pyaar* (Nalini Jaywant in *Nastik*, 1954)
- *Jaago Mohan pyaare* (Nargis in *Jagte Raho*, 1956)

- *Bade bhole ho haste ho sun ke duhaayi* (Meena Kumari in *Ardhangini*, 1959)
- *Prabhu tero naam jo dhyaaye phal paaye* (Nanda in *Hum Dono*, 1961)
- *Krishna o kaale Krishna* (Meena Kumari in *Main Bhi Ladki Hoon*, 1964)
- *Manmohan Krishna Murari* (Meena Kumari in *Sanjh Aur Savera*, 1964)
- *Jeevan daata jagat pita tum, main santaan tihari* (Indrani Mukherjee in *Sharafat*, 1970)
- *Chup chup Meera roye, dard na jaane koi* (Hema Malini in *Johny Mera Naam*, 1970)
- *Tum to sab ke ho rakhwaale* (Nanda in *Adhikaar*, 1971)
- *Manmohan se preet badhaayi* (Saira Banu in *Mera Vachan Geeta Ki Kasam*, 1974)
- *Jo tum todo piya* (Jaya Bhaduri in *Silsila*, 1981)

The conservative, safer way—where the actress has tied up her hair—exists in plenty of examples too. Here are instances:

- *Ab tere siwa kaun mera Krishna Kanhaiya* (Mumtaz Shanti in *Kismat*, 1943)
- *More to Girdhar Gopal* (MS Subbulakshmi in *Meera*, 1947)
- *Ghunghat ke pat khol re tohe piya milenge* (Nargis in *Jogan*, 1950)
- *Darshan pyaasi aayi daasi* (Madhubala in *Sangdil*, 1952)
- *Jai jai Ram raghurai…Kaun chhooega uski parchhain re* (Nalini Jaywant in *Nastik*, 1954)
- *Mere devta mujhko dena sahaara* (Meena Kumari *in Bandhan*, 1956)
- *Man re Hari ke gun ga* (Suchitra Sen in *Musafir*, 1957)
- *Tora manwa kyoon ghabraaye re* (Leela Chitnis in *Sadhana*, 1958)
- *Allah tero naam* (Nanda in *Hum Dono*, 1961)
- *Suno naath deenon ke* (Usha Kiran in *Tanhai*, 1961)
- *Daiya re daiya Yashodha maiya* (Ameeta in *Aasra*, 1966)
- *He rom rom mein basne wale Ram* (Waheeda Rehman in *Neel Kamal*, 1968)

Allah tero naam

> *Bada natkhat hai ye Krishan Kanhaiya* (Sharmila Tagore in *Amar Prem*, 1973)
> *Bole Radha Shyam deewaani* (Vidya Sinha in *Tumhare Liye*, 1978)

There is even a hybrid formula, where the hair is tied up in a knot, even as much of it is left open. This is visible in a few songs. *Meri pat raakho Girdhaari* (Bina Rai in *Ghunghat*, 1960) is one of them. *Sun le pukaar* (Meena Kumari in *Phool Aur Patthar*, 1966) is another. *Kaanha kaanha, aan padi main tere dwaar* (Saira Banu in *Shagird*, 1967), is another still. In *Tora man darpan kehlaaye* (*Kajal*, 1965), the director decided to leave Meena Kumari's hair open, but covered the open hair with a pallu.

Letting your hair down means forgetting your inhibitions or behaving in a manner that is away from social constrictions or codes of conduct. So if you were directing a bhajan for filming, would you go the conservative way, or would you ask the lady to let her hair down, literally? Or else, maybe go the hybrid route?

~~~~

The above was originally published in DNA Jaipur on 12th February 2017. It has since been updated.

♪♫♩♪
~~~~

74

Our Sweetest Songs

Many moons ago, during a fascinating couple of hours with songwriter Hasrat Jaipuri, I asked him to name one quality, just one if it had to be one, that was a prerequisite to writing good poetry. Within a second, he said "*Dard*, pain…*uske baghair baat naheen banti*".

That was amazing I thought. If Kaifi Azmi had said that, I wouldn't have blinked. Shakeel too yes, and here and there just about everyone. But here was the King of Romance in Hindi lyrics, not talking about the importance of love, but rather extolling the virtues of a pen dipped in pain and sorrow. I learnt something interesting that day and parked it in my mind, only to observe that over the past few decades, sad songs have been on a slippery slope. Of course, we now live generally better and longer than ever before, but perhaps we are also sadder than we ever were. Because while it's evident that opportunities, healthcare, education and the internet have vastly contributed to the plus side, we also have more frustrations, loneliness and inadequacy riding along with all that. So then, why are most of our filmmakers dumping sorrow, the salt and vinegar of our music and cinema, and opting to give us an overload of sugar and honey? Why is art not reflecting life in high fidelity? It seems most filmmakers have become brand ambassadors of Johnson's No More Tears shampoo!

Recently I learnt some more from a fascinating book whose writer, Eric Wilson, was a professor of English, teaching Film and Literature at Wake Forest University, North Carolina, USA. That book is called Against Happiness: In Praise of Melancholy. The author is exasperated by the shallow consumerist contentment pursued by the "Happy

American types", bathed in excessive doses of positive thinking. His thought-provoking cultural analysis pitches for the roller-coaster of the full spectrum of feelings, leading to creativity that the depths of melancholia can help generate. After all, says he, it is inauthentic and shallow to celebrate only happiness in a world that also has a lot of tragedy. Wilson argues that if you want to create beautiful art, emotional sorrow is critical to our work. Isn't that what Hasrat was also saying?

But as noted earlier, sad films and songs have shrunk to a very small size. This wasn't always so. To get a taste of more balanced times, let's consider just two sad songs by some of the key songwriters in our films down the years, and get a glimpse of the beautiful art Eric Wilson speaks about:

> ➢ Aah Sitapuri: *Dil jalta hai to jalne de* (Mukesh/ *Pehli Nazar*, 1945), and *Dum bhar daur khushi ka* (Mukesh/ *Maan*, 1954)

> ➢ Anand Bakshi: *Chingaari koi bhadke* (Kishore/ *Amar Prem*, 1971), and *Yaar jinhen tum bhool gaye ho* (Rafi/ *Wo Din Yaad Karo*, 1971)

> ➢ Anjaan: *Aaj tumse door ho kar aise roya mera pyaar* (Mukesh/ *Ek Raat*, 1968), and *Aa jao aa bhi jao* (Mahendra/ *Bandhan*, 1969)

> ➢ Anjum Jaipuri: *Aayi birha ki raat mora tadpe jiya* (Geeta/ *Nav Durga*, 1953), and *Manzil kahaan meri gulshan kahaan mera* (Kishore/ *Miss Mala*, 1954)

> ➢ Anjum Pilibhiti: *Kya mil gaya Bhagwan* (Noor Jahan/ *Anmol Ghadi*, 1946), and *Daaman ko haath se wo chhuda kar chale gaye* (Geeta/ *Kasam*, 1947)

> ➢ Arzoo Lucknowi: *Karoon kya aas niraas bhai* (Saigal/ *Dushman*, 1939), and *Prem ka naata chhoota* (Pankaj Mullick/ *Nartaki*, 1940)

> ➢ Asad Bhopali: *Awaaz de raha hai dil-e-beqaraar aa* (Madhubala Jhaveri/ *Jaggu*, 1952), and *Aye mere dil-e-naadaan* (Lata/ *Tower House*, 1962)

> ➢ Behzad Lucknowi: *Zinda hoon is tarah ke gham-e-zindagi naheen* (Mukesh/ *Aag*, 1948), and *Mere liye wo gham-e-intezaar*

chhod gaye (tandem songs by Lata and Meena Kapoor/ *Anokha Pyaar*, 1948)

➤ Bharat Vyas: *Chaand hai wohi* (Geeta/ *Parineeta*, 1953), and *Dil ka khilona haaye toot gaya* (Lata/ *Goonj Uthi Shehnai*, 1959)

➤ DN Madhok: *Shikwa tera main gaoon* (Talat and Lata/ *Anmol Ratan*, 1950), and *Haaye koi kehde papiha se jaake* (Lata/ *Baraati*, 1954)

➤ GS Rawal: *Jinhen hum bhoolna chaahen wo aksar yaad aate hain* (Mukesh/ *Aabroo*, 1968), and *Ye dil naheen hai ke jiske sahaare jeete hain* (Rafi/ *Aabroo*, 1968)

➤ Gulshan Bawra: *Tumhen yaad hoga kabhi hum mile the* (Hemant and Lata/ *Satta Bazaar*, 1959), and *Mil ke bhi hum mil na sake* (Talat and Lata/ *Sunehri Nagin*, 1963)

➤ Gulzar: *Ik tha bachpan* (Lata/ *Ashirwad*, 1968), and *Aaj bichhde hain* (Bhupinder/ *Thodi Si Bewafai*, 1980)

➤ Hasrat Jaipuri: *Koi naheen mera is duniya mein* (Talat/ *Daag*, 1952), and *O jaane waale mud ke zara dekhte jaana* (Lata/ *Shri 420*, 1955)

➤ Indeewar: *Waqt karta jo wafa aap hamaare hote* (Mukesh/ *Dil Ne Pukaara*, 1967), and *Hum the jinke sahaare* (Lata/ *Safar*, 1970)

➤ Jan Nissar Akhtar: *Hawa pichhle peher jab shehnai bajaati hai* (Kishore/ *Naya Andaz*, 1956), and *Bekasi had se jab guzar jaaye* (Asha/ *Kalpana*, 1960)

Bekasi had se jab guzar jaaye

- Javed Akhtar: *Ye safar bahut hai katthin magar* (Shivaji Chattopadhyaya/ *1942—A Love Story*, 1995), and *Saare sapne kaheen kho gaye* (Alka/ *Tum Yaad Aaye*, 1998)

- Kaif Irfani: *Dil tujhe diya tha rakhne ko* (Mukesh/ *Malhar*, 1951), and *Ek main hoon ek meri bekasi ki shaam hai* (Talat/ *Tarana*, 1951)

- Kaifi Azmi: *Waqt ne kiya kya haseen sitam* (Geeta/ *Kaagaz Ke Phool*, 1959), and *Jaane kya dhoondti rehti hain ye aankhen mujh mein* (Rafi/ *Shola Aur Shabnam*, 1961)

- Khumar Barabankvi: *Aaj mere naseeb ne mujhko rula rula diya* (Lata/ *Hulchal*, 1951), and *Pyaar ki duniya lutegi humen maaloom na tha* (Lata/ *Mehndi*, 1958)

- Kidar Sharma: *Piya bin naahin aawat naheen aawat chain* (Saigal/ *Devdas*, 1935), and *Kabhi tanhaiyon mein yoon* (Mubarak/ *Hamari Yaad Ayegi*, 1961)

- Majrooh: *Chaand phir nikla* (Lata/ *Paying Guest*, 1957), and *Bekas ki tabaahi ke saamaan hazaaron hain* (Asha/ *Sone Ki Chidiya*, 1958)

- Nakhshab: *Itni badi duniya mein naheen koi hamaara* (Lata/ *Aaiye*, 1949), and *Ghabra ke jo hum sar ko takraayen to achha ho* (Rajkumari/ *Mahal*, 1949)

- Naqsh Lyallpuri: *Phir teri yaad naye deep jalaane aayi* (Bhupinder/ *Aayi Teri Yaad*, 1980), and *Maana teri nazar mein* (Sulakshana/ *Ahista Ahista*, 1981)

- Narendra Sharma: *Saanjh ki bela panthi akela* (Arun Kumar/ *Jwar Bhata*, 1944), and *Nainan mein barsaat* (Lata/ *Nand Kishore*, 1951)

- Neeraj: *Caarvaan guzar gaya* (Rafi/ *Nayi Umar Ki Nayi Fasal*, 1965), and *Umariya bin khevat ki naiyya* (Hemant/ *Majhli Didi*, 1967)

- Noor Lucknowi: *Kat-te hain dukh mein ye din* (Lata/ *Parchhaiyan*, 1952), and *Apni naakaami se mujhko kaam hai* (Talat/ *Subah Ka Tara*, 1954)

- Nyaya Sharma: *Kis-kis ko deepak pyaar kare* (Lata/ *Anjali*, 1957), and *Jab gham-e-ishq sataata hai* (Mukesh/ *Kinare Kinare*, 1963)

- Pervez Shamsi: *Matlab ki ye duniya hai* (Lata/ *Nausherwan-e-Adil*, 1957), and *Ye Hasrat thi ke is duniya mein bas do kaam kar jaate* (Rafi/ *Nausherwan-e-Adil*, 1957)

- PL Santoshi: *Maar kataari mar jaana* (Amirbai/ *Shehnai*, 1947), and *Mehfil mein jal utthi shama* (Lata/ *Nirala*, 1950)

- Pradeep: *Papiha re mere piya se kahiyo ja* (Parul Ghosh/ *Kismet*, 1943), and *Pinjre ke panchhi re* (Pradeep/ *Naag Mani*, 1957)

- Prem Dhawan: *Kachhu samajh naheen aaye mohe* (CH Atma/ *Aasmaan*, 1952), and *Sab-kuchh luta ke hosh mein aaye to kya kiya* (Tandem solos by Talat or Lata/ *Ek Saal*, 1957)

- Qamar Jalalabadi: *Jab raat naheen kat-ti, ek raat naheen kat-ti* (Lata/ *Changez Khan*, 1957), and *Mere toote hue dil se koi to aaj ye poochhe* (Mukesh/ *Chhalia*, 1960)

- Raja Mehdi Ali Khan: *Ujda umeedon ka chaman* (Surinder Kaur/ *Shaheed*, 1948), and *Chaah karni thi chaah kar baitthe* (Asha and Mubarak/ *Punar Milan*, 1964)

- Rajinder Krishan: *Chhup gaya koi re* (Lata/ *Champakali*, 1957), and *Aansoo samajh ke kyoon mujhe* (Talat/ *Chhaya*, 1961)

- Sahir: *Lo apna jahaan duniya waalo* (Asa Singh Mastana/ *Dooj Ka Chand*, 1964), and *Jab bhi ji chaahe nai duniya* (Lata/ *Daag*, 1973)

- SH Bihari: *Jab tum naheen to chaand-sitaare main kya karoon* (Geeta/ *Kitna Badal Gaya Insaan*, 1957), and *Chain se hum ko kabhi* (Asha/ *Pran Jaaye Par Vachan Na Jaaye*, 1973)

- Shahryar: *Seene mein jalan aankhon mein toofaan sa kyoon hai* (Suresh Wadkar/ *Gaman*, 1979), and *Justju jis ki thi usko to na paaya humne* (Asha/ *Umrao Jaan*, 1981)

- Shailendra: *Mitti se khelte ho baar-baar kis liye* (Lata/ *Patita*, 1953), and *Yaad na jaaye* (Rafi/ *Dil Ek Mandir*, 1963)

- Shakeel: *Meri kahaani bhoolne waale* (Rafi/ *Deedar*, 1951), and *Dil laga kar hum ye samjhe* (Mahendra/ *Zindagi Aur Maut*, 1965)

- Shamim Jaipuri: *Mujhko is raat ki tanhai mein awaaz na do* (tandem solos by Mukesh and Suman/ *Dil Bhi Tera Hum Bhi Tere*, 1960), and *Akele hain chale aao jahaan ho* (Rafi/ *Raaz*, 1967)

Meri kahaani bhoolne waale

- Tanvir Naqvi: *Yahaan badla wafa ka bewafaayi ke siva kya hai* (Noor Jahan and Rafi/ *Jugnu*, 1947), and *Guzra hua zamaana aata naheen dubaara* (Lata/ *Shirin Farhad*, 1956)
- Yogesh: *Piya maine kya kiya* (Manna/ *Us Paar*, 1974), and *Badi sooni sooni hai zindagi ye zindagi* (Kishore/ *Mili*, 1975)
- Zia Sarhadi: *Jeevan sapna toot gaya* (tandem solos by Mukesh and Lata/*Anokha Pyaar*, 1948), and *Ek jhoothi si tassalli wo mujhe de ke chale* (Mukesh/ *Sheesham*, 1952)

"Our sweetest songs are those that tell of the saddest thought," wrote the poet Shelley in his Ode to a Skylark. Talat expressed it in Hindustani, rendering Shailendra's song from *Patita* (1953) in his ethereal voice: *Hain sab se madhur wo geet jinhen hum dard ke sur mein gaate hain.*

Shelley the poet reminds me of a hotel located within a hundred meters of where I live in Colaba, Mumbai. It's called Shelley's Hotel. One day I ran into the owner's son, an upwardly mobile young man. "So how come the name Shelley's Hotel? Was someone in your family inspired by or connected to the poet Shelley?" I asked him. "I don't know. I should have asked my dad. *Lekin aap batao woh kaun thi ji? Yahaan Bombay ki thi?"* was his reply. I wished he had at least said *Woh Kaun The.* So much for the rise in literary standards.

Resigned, within a few minutes I escaped to my home and the welcoming lyrics of *Naina barse rimjhim rimjhim* from *Woh Kaun Thi*

(1964), written sadly for Madan Mohan and Lata by Raja Mehdi Ali Khan. And another Lata beauty from the same film, *Jo humne dastaan apni sunaayi, aap kyoon roye?* In a world that sometimes seems strange, thank God there are songs. Sad ones too.

~~~~

The above article was published in DNA Jaipur on 11 August 2013. It has since been updated and enhanced.

♪♫♩♪
~~~~

75

Once Bitten, Twice Shy

First a special note

The term E & OE, commonly used on Invoices, Receipts, and Cash Memos, is a disclaimer that stands for Errors and Omissions Excepted. This means that if the information or figures are insufficient or there's a mistake, the document issuer is protected against legal action. The following essay could also do with such a disclaimer, because some of the people mentioned below, as also the films they worked in, are lost in antiquity. Even the people generally in the know do not know or remember everything correctly. For instance, it is generally believed that a certain poet with the unusual name Veer Mohammad Puri wrote just one song in cinema, that being *Tu humko dekh aur hamaari nazar se dekh* (Lata/ *Zindagi Aur Hum*, 1962). It turns out that the gentleman wrote many songs in V Shantaram's *Amrit Manthan* in 1934, that is, nearly 30 years earlier!

Adequate care has been taken while writing this essay, and experts have been consulted. Even so, there may be an odd error somewhere. For which we say, E & OE!

~ ~ ~

The Cambridge Dictionary defines the idiom 'Once Bitten, Twice Shy' as a condition in which you are frightened to do something again because you had an unpleasant experience in doing it the first time. This may be any kind of experience, like falling off a horse on your maiden outing, getting an upset tummy after eating eels for the first time, facing a financial loss after starting your own business, and so on.

Hindi cinema is a big universe with a long and huge history. Lots of people have succeeded in it, but many have failed too, some in their maiden outing. Let's peep into the bioscope of Hindi films and look at several people who were credited just once in a specific role. For the recall of the film, we are adding just one, usually randomly chosen song from it.

First, attempts as a director:

- ➤ **Abrar Alvi** is famous for directing *Sahib Bibi Aur Ghulam* (1962). He used to be a dialogue writer for many films made by Guru Dutt. Class song: *Saaqiya aaj mujhe neend naheen ayegi* (Asha).

- ➤ **Akhtar Mirza**, the father of filmmakers Saeed and Aziz Mirza, was a famous screenwriter who once romanced with direction. The result was *Mohabbat Isko Kehte Hain* (1965). The call-and-response song *Theheriye hosh mein aa loon to chale jaiyega* (Rafi, Suman) was in the film.

- ➤ Film actress Madhubala's father, **Ataullah Khan,** once opted to direct a film, *Pathan* (1962), which has the unique distinction of having more music composers than songs. There were 9 composers for the film's 7 songs. Song chosen: *Chaand mera baadalon mein kho gaya* (Talat).

- ➤ **Awtar Kaul.** *27 Down* (1973) was his only film. It is about two people who meet on the train numbered 27 Down (i.e. the Bombay Varanasi Express) and fall in love. These are MK Raina and Rakhee. On the evening of 27th July 1974, Awtar went to Juhu beach along with his friend. She went too deep into the water than was good for her. He jumped in to rescue her. Both were found dead the next morning. Ironically, that very morning the papers announced that his film had won 2 National Awards, for Best Black and White Photography, and Best Film. *Chhuk chhuk chhuk chhuk chalti rail* was the film's song by Ravi Kichlu.

- **Bal Chhabda** directed *Do Raha* (1952). The film was a commercial failure. He switched to painting, at which he became hugely successful. Identified song: *Muhabbat tark ki main* (Talat).

- The famous **Balraj Sahni** once co-directed (with Krishan Chopra) a film called *Lal Batti* (1957). *Bus*, he was done with being behind the camera. Fun song: *Yaari hui kaisi* (Manna, Shamshad).

- The famous lyricist **Bharat Vyas** thought of directing a film, so he did just that. The film was *Rangila Rajasthan* (1949). *Jal bin machhli piya bin sajni* sang Rajkumari in this film.

- **Biswajit** the actor was once persuaded to wield the megaphone. He did, in the feature *Kehte Hain Mujhko Raja* (1975), which had *Aiyo re main gaya kaam se* (Kishore, Asha).

- **Leela Chitnis** was a famous actress who matured from lead roles to character roles. She directed the film *Aaj Ki Baat* (1955) to launch her son Ajit Chitnis as a hero opposite Chitra. Song: *Muhabbat bane hain wo din suhaane* (Talat).

- Singer and character actor **Manmohan Krishna** also directed a film: *Noorie* (1979). It featured the Nitin Mukesh-Lata duet *Aaja re aaja o mere dilbar aaja*.

- **Pradeep Kumar**, the famous actor, also went in direction. His solo film was *Do Dilon Ki Dastaan* (1966). The Asha Bhosle song *Ye machalta sama* was in it.

- **Prithviraj Kapoor** was an accomplished stage and film actor. He directed *Paisa* (1957), which had *Paisa hi rang roop hai* (Rafi).

- **Radhu Karmakar** was a cinematographer who filmed most of Raj Kapoor's films, beginning with *Awara* (1951). He directed *Jis Desh Mein Ganga Behti Hai* (1960). Highlighted track: *Mera naam Raju gharana anaam* (Mukesh).

- **Rajneesh Behl** was the husband of the actress Nutan. He directed *Surat aur Seerat* (1962), which featured *Bahut diya dene waale ne tujhko* (Mukesh).

- **Romo Deb Mukherji** directed *Tuhi Meri Zindagi* (1965). Recall track: *Jidhar bhi main dekhoon udhar tu hi tu hai* (Asha, Rafi).
- **S Sukhdev** made *My Love* (1970). Memorable song: *Zikr hota hai jab qayaamat ka tere jalwon ki baat hoti hai* (Mukesh)
- The music maestro **Salil Chowdhury** once directed a film: *Pinjre Ke Panchhi* (1966). *Ye duniya kaisa Gorakh dhanda Jai Jai Ram Sita Ram* (Manna Dey) was in that film.
- The brothers **Shambhu** and **Amit Mitra** directed *Jagte Raho* (1956). The film was directed remarkably. Especially the last shots, featuring the song *Jaago Mohan pyaare* (Lata, chorus) which remain the high water mark in our films.
- Famous filmmaker from the South, **SMS Naidu** directed just *Azaad* (1955). The melody recalled most is *Kitna haseen hai mausam* (Lata, Chitalkar).
- **Trilok Jetley** directed the Munshi Premchand-written *Godaan* (1963). *Hiya jarat rehet din rain ho Rama* (Mukesh) stands out as a good track.
- **Zul Vellani** directed many documentaries, but when it came to feature films, he is credited with just one: *Dak Ghar* (1966). *Ye bhor jahaan se aati hai* was a short song rendered by Bhupinder Singh

Now in other aspects of filmmaking:

- The famous-in-Telugu cinema, **A Nageswara Rao** showed up only in *Swaran Sundari* (1958), and lip-synched this song with heroine Anjali: *Kuhu kuhu bole koyaliya* (Rafi, Lata).
- Prolific songwriter **Anand Bakshi** dressed up as a faqir and faced the camera for just once. The film was *Picnic* (1966), and the song was *Bijli giri kahaan se* (Rafi). Interestingly, it wasn't he who wrote this song. It was Majrooh.
- **Anwar Hashmi**, the father of actor Emraan Hashmi, acted in just one film. He was paired with Farida Jalal in *Baharon Ki Manzil* (1968). Song for recall: *Nigaahen kyoon bhatakti hain* (Lata).

- Punjab's famous folk singer, **Asa Singh Mastana** recorded just one song in a Hindi film: *Lo apna jahaan duniya waalo* (*Dooj Ka Chand*, 1964).

- An actor named **Balraj** (not the famous Balraj Sahni) was featured as the hero opposite Geeta Bali in the film *Vachan* (1955). He even appeared with his heroine singing the song *Jab liya haath mein haath* (Rafi, Asha).

Jab liya haath mein haath

- The Pahwa brothers, consisting of Bikram, Chaman, and Basant gave a directorial break to Shakti Samanta in *Bahu* (1955). **Basant** also acted as the second lead in the film, with Karan Dewan as the main lead. Song from the film: *Thandi hawaon mein taaron ki chhaon mein aaj balam mera dole jiya* (Geeta, Talat).

- **Biswajit** was known for his acting and singing in Bengali films. But he also sang a Hindi song, *Aye dil meri jaan teri manzil hai kahaan* in *Do Shikari* (1979).

- The film *Vachan* (1955) credited not just Ravi for its music, but a certain **Chandra**, for whom this was his only film. *Chanda mama door ke,* went Asha Bhosle in the film.

- **Dilip Kumar** went into production just once, for the film *Gunga Jumna* (1960). His banner was called Citizens Films. Song recalled: *Na maanoon na maanoon na maanoon re* (Lata).

- An American lady married to an Indian mimed her lips to the song *Aage bhi jaane na tu* in *Waqt* (1965). Her name was **Erica Lal.**

- **Gayatri Joshi** acted just in *Swades* (2004). Earlier, she was Femina Miss India in 2000. Song shortlisted: *Ye jo des hai tera* (AR Rehman).

- **Hansa Maker** made a great impression as the leading lady opposite Mahendra Sandhu in *Sweekar* (1973). Then she disappeared. Song chosen: *Kaheen pyaar ho na jaaye* (Asha).

- A man named **Haroun** has only one entry in Hindi films, as the lyricist for the song *Jumme ki raat ho ya din jummeraat ka* (*Dulha Dulhan*, 1964).

- **Iqbal Singh** rocked by singing *Bombshell Baby of Bombay* for *Ek Phool Chaar Kaante* (1960).

- **Kishori Amonkar**, the classical singer, composed music for just one film, *Drishti* (1990). Five of the film's six songs were her solos. Song chosen: *Megha jhar jhar barsat re* (Kishori Amonkar).

- Southern belle **KR Vijaya** couldn't manage her Hindustani well, so all she got by way of a role in Hindi films was in *Oonche Log* (1965). She performed to *Aa ja re mere pyaar ke raahi* (Lata, Mahendra) with Feroz Khan acting opposite her.

- Composer **Manohar Arora** remains a one film wonder, for his tunes in *Raees* (1948). In it, Meena Kapoor sang the ghazal *Gham sehna hai lab seena hai*.

- Filmmaker Vasant Joglekar launched his daughter **Meera Joglekar** as the heroine in his film *Ek Kali Muskaayi* (1968). She sank like the Titanic on its maiden voyage. High recall melody: *Na tum bewafa ho, na hum bewafa hain* (Lata).

- Bharat Ratna **MS Subbulakshmi** acted and sang in many Tamil films, but her Hindi appearance was in just one: *Meera* (1947). It was replete with Meera Bhajans and she sang all of them. Random selection: *Chaakar raakho ji* (MS Subbulakshmi).

- **Nirupa Roy** acted in hundreds of films, but she wrote a song once: *Mujhe dekh chaand sharmaaye* (*Samrat Chandragupta*, 1958). She played a Greek Queen in the film. This song was however filmed on supporting actress Kammo.

- **Parvez Shamsi,** lyricist, wrote all the nine songs in *Nausherwan-e-Adil* (1957). After that, he went into the ether. Highlighted song: *Bhool jaayen saare gham* (Lata, Rafi).

- Nothing is known about the actors of a 1950s film called *Siskiyan* because it was never released. We don't even know about the unfortunate composing duo, **Ragi-Rajan** who made some tunes for this film. Thankfully the film's music was released and can be heard on YouTube. Spotlighted song: *Dhake malmal ki saadi manga de manga de balma garmi laage* (Roshanara Begum).

- Songwriter **Shailendra** also showed up on the screen a few times, but he even produced a film once, *Teesri Kasam* (1966). He burnt his fingers doing so. *Sajan re jhootth mat bolo* (Mukesh) was in the film.

- **Shakeel Badayuni** wrote lyrics for dozens of films, and significant poetry outside films. But once he also recited, musically, his own ghazal: *Hungaama-e-gham se tang aa kar* in *Pak Daman* (1957).

- **Snehal Bhatkar** earned his fame for composing beautiful songs in many films, but he faced the camera once, in the song *Muhabbat ke maaron ka haal ye duniya mein hota hai* (Asha, Rafi) in *Bawre Nain* (1950).

Snehal Bhatkar

> **Sudha Malhotra** composed only one song, *Tum mujhe bhool bhi jao to ye haq hai tumko* (Sudha, Mukesh) in *Didi* (1959), but you wonder why she didn't compose more music for films.
> **Urvashi Dutta** was noticed as a vamp in *Shagird* (1967). Then she left films. Showcased for recall: *Kaanha Kaanha aan padi main tere dwaar* (Lata).
> **Vivian Lobo** crooned the multilingual *Ich libe deech, I love you* in *Sangam* (1964).

God knows how many more names are there of people who were logged in a film just once. But again, E & OE!

Endnotes

1   The Times of India, 21 September 2013
2   https://www.indiatoday.in/magazine/indiascope/story/19840515-drinking-habit-costs-ramrao-adik-maharashtra-deputy-cm-post-803601-1984-05-14
3   https://timesofindia.indiatimes.com/blogs/The-underage-optimist/the-power-of-rumour-modis-degree-controversy-obamas-birth-and-the-paranoid-style-in-politics/
4   https://timesofindia.indiatimes.com/blogs/thesiegewithin/a-paean-to-india-s/
5   Pavan K Varma: Ghalib—The Man, The Times
6   https://pudding.cool/2017/03/film-dialogue/
7   Filmindia, February 1955
8   Naqsh Lyallpuri passed away in Mumbai on 22nd January 2017
9   Why Should Women Not Go Out With Loose hair?" https://www.hindujagruti.org/hinduism/loose-hair

www.ingramcontent.com/pod-product-compliance
Lightning Source LLC
Chambersburg PA
CBHW051209130726
47988CB00001B/28